PRODUCTION PIPELINE FUNDAMENTALS FOR FILM AND GAMES

PRODUCTION PIPELINE FUNDAMENTALS FOR FILM AND GAME

Edited by Renee Dunlop

Routledge
Taylor & Francis Group
New York London

First published 2014 by Focal Press

711 Third Avenue, New York, NY 10017, USA
2 Park Square, Milton Park, Abingdon, Oxon OX14 4RN

Routledge is an imprint of the Taylor & Francis Group, an informa business

First issued in hardback 2017

Library of Congress Cataloging in Publication Data
Dunlop, Renee.
Production pipeline fundamentals for film and game / Renee Dunlop.
pages cm
ISBN 978-0-415-81229-0 (pbk.)—ISBN 978-1-315-85827-2 (ebook) 1. Computer
games—Programming. 2. Video recordings—Production and direction.
3. Motion pictures—Production and direction. 4. Project management. I. Title.
QA76.76.C672D863 2014
794.8'1526—dc23   2013032579

ISBN: 978-0-415-81229-0 (pbk)
ISBN: 978-1-138-42844-7 (hbk)

Typeset in Utopic Std
By MPS Limited, Chennai, India
www.adi-mps.com

CONTENTS

Acknowledgments

Section Acknowledgments 1: Special Thanks, Core Team

Renee Dunlop

I want to thank the entire book team for their amazing work and perseverance. In particular I want to thank Tim Green who went far above and beyond any expectations, Hannes Ricklefs for being there since day one, and Matt, Mark and Steve for their wisdom. For his friendship and hard work I'd like to thank Jim Thacker who could spin any content into poetry. Also Ben Carter and Rob Blau for their knowledge, insights, gracious encouragement, and for filling in the gaps. And Lauren Mattos who helped make this all possible.

In a class of his own I'd like to thank Meats Meier for his riveting cover art, and John Lindemuth for never failing to come through at lightning speed and for being such a great friend. Robert Fischer, for his brilliant support and friendship. And for their support, suggestions, talent, connections, and encouragement, I'd like to thank Bob Bennett, Flavia Wallman, Jessica Sterling, Dave Stephens, Rick Grandy, Michele Bousquet, Daniel Docou, Sam Richards, Ryan Laney, and Joe Straczynski.

Tim Green

I'd like to thank Ian Shaw for giving me my first job in the industry and to Matt Birch, Oliver Castle, Martin Griffiths, Leon O'Reilly, and Kris Beaumont for showing me the ropes.

I'd like to thank Pete Samuels, Harvey Wheaton, and Jonathon Amor for giving me a Supermassive opportunity.

And I'd like to thank my wife, Lisa, and kids, James, Harley, Marshall, and Takara for keeping me sane.

Matt Hoesterey

I want to give a special thanks to Camille Chu for being a bouncing board about all things animation while also not killing me for ignoring her on all the late nights spent writing.

Thanks to Alex Lifschitz who provided me with a plethora of knowledge regarding all the costs and considerations that go into making solid animation production choices.

Furthermore thanks to all the colleges I've worked with throughout the years who grew me as a person and helped me gain the knowledge I have.

Lastly thanks to my family and friends for supporting me when my schedule sometimes makes my time scarce.

Hannes Ricklefs

Since this is the closest I will ever get to an acceptance speech I would like to take this opportunity to thank everyone at MPC, specifically Nick Cannon, Clwyd Edwards, and Christian Roberton for their continuous trust and support.

Furthermore, I would like to thank my immediate colleagues: Ben Cole, Damien Fagnou, Rob Pieke, and Michael Stein for their ongoing drive to push the boundaries of our software.

Thanks also to the most outstanding team in the world, the global MPC software department! In particular my leads: Lorenzo Angeli, William Hall, David Stinson, and Olivier Thibaut who truly made all of this happen.

Finally and most importantly I would like to thank my friends and family, wife and daughter for their love and support; hab euch alle lieb, euer Hannes.

Mark Streatfield

Thank you to all my colleagues over the years who have so generously shared their time, knowledge, and passion with me. It has been an inspiration and privilege to work with so many talented people practicing their craft.

I'd also like to thank my friends and family for their unconditional support in allowing me to follow my dreams.

Steve Theodore

First and foremost, I'd like to thank my family for putting up with all the late nights and weekends I've devoted to the project. I literally couldn't have done it without your forbearance.

I'd also like to thank my colleagues at Undead Labs, for being the unwitting beta-testers of many ideas contained herein. Also responsible (or implicated) are Pat Corwin, Jens Hauch, Jeff Hanna, Seth Gibson, Jason Parks, and Paul Vosper—all of whom have spent many years meditating on the Tao of technical art.

Finally, while pondering the Tao, a shout-out to Rob Galinakis and the whole community at Tech-Artists.Org where practical wisdom is given away for free every day.

Section Acknowledgements 2: Special Thanks, Tech Editors

Rob Blau

First and foremost, thank you to my wife and kids, Holly, Sasha, and Emma. Love you.

Thanks too to all the amazing people I've gotten to work with through the years, especially Andy, Jim, Darin, and Don, who (whether they realize it or not) have been amazing mentors to me.

Ben Carter

My thanks to all my colleagues, past and present, who have been inspirational, educational and endlessly patient in putting up with me; to my friends, without whom I would have descended into utter madness long ago; and to my family, wife, son, and cats, for their love and support.

Jim Thacker

Thanks to all the authors for being so willing to respond to my requests for more information during the editing process, to Lauren Mattos at Focal Press for being so accommodating with the schedule, and above all, to Renee Dunlop for initiating and organizing the entire project.

Fran Zandonella

Thank you to my parents for their unconditional support and encouragement, and to David Benjamin for his support during this project. Finally, thank you to all of my colleagues throughout the years, and especially the pipeline community at large for their inspiration.

Section Acknowledgements 3: Special Thanks, Artists

John Lindemuth

Thanks to this great team for the opportunity and feedback.

Thanks to Renee specifically for the open door as well as your patience with my creative spelling.

Thank you to my wife Kelly, my son Shane and daughter Casie for the inspiration, feedback and patience.

Thanks to my mom and brother who have never doubted, and have always supported me.

Thank you to my many friends and relatives who have helped me along my wandering path.

Meats Meier

Thanks to Misaki, Mindy, and Mochi.

Section Acknowledgements 4: Baby List

Rhys Cooper Grandy
Emma Blau
Drake Sagan Pearl
Baby Streatfield

Biographies

Section Bio 1: Core Team Contributor Biographies

Renee Dunlop: Writer, Artist

Renee Dunlop has 20 years' experience in the entertainment industry. Starting with a degree in Art and Computer Animation in 1993, she cut her teeth on the 3D software packages Crystal Topaz, TIPS, and PowerAnimator V3. At the same time, she leveraged her traditional art skills, working as a Costume Designer at Collegeville/Imagineering, the second-largest Halloween costume company in the world. Her interest in both traditional and digital art has led to her work being featured in several gallery shows, including the James A. Michener Art Museum in Bucks County, Pennsylvania, where she also acted as Postproduction Coordinator and Supervising Editor for the Bucks County Animation Arts Festival.

Her work can be seen at the Please Touch Museum in Philadelphia, in the Wright Brothers HD documentary *The Race For Flight* for the National Park Service, and as Lighting Lead in the award-winning short film *Major Damage*, the first CG short created using staff working worldwide via the internet. She has presented at the SIGGRAPH computer graphics forum, and lectured annually at Cabrillo College in Santa Cruz and for CAEF (Creative Arts Entertainment Forum) for California's college instructors in the field of arts and entertainment.

Renee has worked at Sierra On-Line, Explorati and xRez Studio as a 3D Generalist, Roto Artist, Lighter, Art Lead, Art Director, and Production Manager; at Alias|Wavefront, SGI, Fox and Sony in administrative positions and PR; and at VFXWorld, Below the Line, Death Fall, CGSociety, 3D World, 3D Artist, Image Metrics, Craft Animations, the Visual Effects Society (published in *Variety*) and the Gnomon School of Visual Effects as a freelance technology journalist, writing roughly 200 feature and cover articles on film, games, and events. She is an Active Member of the Visual Effects Society.

Tim Green: Senior Programmer of Game Systems and Tools, Supermassive Games

Since he joined the gaming industry in 1999 Tim has worked on titles for PS2, GameCube, Xbox, PS3, Xbox 360, Wii, PC and PS4. Building on his previous expertise of design and program game systems, efficient data builds, user friendly interfaces, pipeline analysis, and debugging systems, he now focuses on runtime architectures

and R&D of efficient approaches in video game development. His EA game portfolio includes *F1 2000, F1 2001, Shox, Quake3, Harry Potter Quidditch World Cup, Prisoner of Azkaban, Goblet of Fire, Order of the Phoenix*, and *Half Blood Prince*. Since joining Supermassive, he has added *Start the Party, Tumble*, and *Until Dawn*.

Matt Hoesterey: Design Lead, Microsoft

Matt started as a Production Artist/FX Lead at Turbine, before moving to Tencent Boston as a System Designer. While at Tencent he simultaneously started his own company, Tribetoy, where he developed and released *Chu's Dynasty* on XBLIG. *Chu's* caught the attention of Microsoft who hired Matt to spearhead development for unannounced platforms, create new conventions, and temporarily join developers to assist in wrapping projects. He is currently leading his own project. His skills range from design to integration, programming, creation of art assets, outlining rules for sorting assets into source control, and creating tools for efficient asset creation.

Hannes Ricklefs: Global Head of Pipeline, MPC, Film Division

Since joining MPC in 2005, Hannes has led the development of core R&D projects including MPC's lighting pipeline and asset management software. He currently oversees MPC's custom production scheduling and resource management software, the development of MPC's next generation asset management system, aspects of the multisite setup covering MPC's offices in London, Vancouver, Los Angeles, New York, and Bangalore, as well as inter/intra departmental workflows. His film work includes: *Prometheus, Watchmen, X-Men 3, The Chronicles of Narnia: Prince Caspian, Clash of the Titans* and *Harry Potter and the Order of the Phoenix*.

Mark Streatfield: Production Technology Supervisor, Animal Logic

Mark has spent 8 years in the film industry honing his skills in asset management, production tracking, and software development/core infrastructure components, focusing on large projects across multiple sites. He has worked at MPC as a software developer in asset management, production tracking and infrastructure, Dr. D. Studios as Software Developer and Supervisor, and at Fuel VFX, now part of Animal Logic, as Head of the R&D department. He has also presented at the Australian Python Conference. Some of Mark's films include *10,000 BC, Harry Potter and the Order of the Phoenix, Slumdog Millionnaire* and *Happy Feet Two*.

Steve Theodore: Technical Art Director, Undead Labs

Steve started animating in the early Ninetie-s, doing titles for commercial and television projects. His first game job was building mechs and environments for *MechCommander* in 1995. He modeled and animated on *Half-Life, Team Fortress Classic, Team Fortress 2* and *Counter-Strike.* For the last dozen years he's been a technical artist and pipeline specialist. He's been Technical Art Director at Zipper Interactive (*SOCOM 3* and *M.A.G.*), Bungie (*Halo 3, Halo ODST*), and most recently Undead Labs (*State of Decay*). Steve was the Art Editor for *Game Developer Magazine* from 2002 to 2013, and is on the board of the Game Developers Conference.

Section Bio 2: Technical Editors

Rob Blau: Head of Pipeline Engineering, Shotgun Software

Ben Carter: Author, Game Developer, Heavy Spectrum Entertainment Labs

Richard Shackleton: Head of Corporate and Industry Intelligence, The Foundry

Dave Stephens: FX Supervisor

Jim Thacker: Freelance Writer and Editor

Fran Zandonella, International Senior Pipeline TD, Rhythm & Hues

Section Bio 3: Artists

John Lindemuth: Director of Art, Turbine Inc.

Meats Meier: Independent Artist and Animator, 3dArtspace.com

INTRODUCTION

Tim Green; Matt Hoesterey; Hannes Ricklefs; Mark Streatfield; Steve Theodore; Laurent M. Abecassis: *Di-O-Matic;* **Ben Carter:** *Game Developer and Author, Heavy Spectrum Entertainment Labs;* **Ben Cole:** *Head of Software, MPC Vancouver;* **Dave Stephens:** *FX Supervisor*

Section 1.1 Production Pipeline Fundamentals for Film and Games

There's no question that modern computer graphics (CG) are an art form, but an art form far removed from the traditional image of the solitary artist hunkered in an attic. In today's film and games industry, art production is a communal enterprise. Every CG element that the audience sees (or doesn't realize that they see) in a theater, and every character or environment that a player meets in a video game, is the result of the collective effort of many artists and technicians.

Pipeline developers are the dark matter that holds that constellation of artists and technicians together. Without them, even non-technical staff would be forced to take on coding tasks, files would proliferate unmanageably, and production schedules spiral out of control. In short, pipeline developers are the unsung heroes of the digital entertainment industry: while they shoulder some of the most difficult tasks, they are rarely noticed until something breaks.

This book is an attempt to shine some light on that dark matter. An introduction to the complex series of technical operations and human relationships that make modern graphics production possible, it brings together the knowledge of experts with just short of a cumulative 700 years of experience in the film, animation and games industries.

In it, we will attempt to provide information that will appeal to a wide range of readers, from students to artists, technical directors, developers, production coordinators and directors. In addition to providing a better understanding of the role pipeline management plays in production, we aim to outline the key challenges faced by today's pipeline developers, and help you to identify the questions you should address before building a pipeline of your own.

Section 1.2 How This Book Will Help You

For a student, understanding how production pipelines work increases your chances of employment. One of the most common failings of interviewees is a lack of understanding of the production process. Regardless of how good you may be at your particular craft, a prospective employer needs to be certain that you will be able to integrate your talents with those of the other staff working on a project—which may run to many hundreds of people, at studios all around the world. This doesn't mean becoming an expert in all those different disciplines, but it does mean becoming aware of them. While a programmer doesn't need to know how to rig a model, they do need to understand the impact a code change that necessitates rerigging all the models used on a project will have on its production schedule.

Established artists looking to transfer from film to games also need to understand how production pipelines differ between the two industries. Although game cinematics are similar to film, in-game models have strict polygon and texture budgets, while the complexity of in-game animations and effects is limited by the need to render every frame in fractions of a second. Conversely, those moving from games to film should understand the need to create highly detailed assets for a medium that often requires photo-realistic output. This book should help to highlight the differences between two industries that share parallel pipelines up to a point, but then suddenly and radically diverge to meet their different goals.

Those working at smaller or newer studios will discover tricks, techniques and insights into how to optimize their existing production pipelines. The book also provides an overview of fields that may be new to you, from audio work to LIDAR (Light Detection and Ranging) scans of environments. Understanding the needs of your coworkers in other disciplines not only helps you to support them better, but to communicate your own needs more effectively, ensuring that the work you create can be integrated more successfully.

Directors also benefit tremendously from understanding the production pipelines they work within, and the impact their decisions have on other departments. It is vital to know why one particular script or scene change will be easy to implement, while another will completely derail a production. Understanding how a pipeline works should help you to make decisions at the appropriate time, avoiding the budgetary or time crises that occur far too often in production.

Finally, a better understanding of game pipelines enables department directors to eliminate dependencies on other teams that slow down production or restrict their artists' ability to see their assets in-game. Doing so should reduce the integration bottlenecks that plague many games productions.

Section 1.3 What is a Pipeline?

The pipeline is the glue that holds together the work of each artist involved in a production. In this, a pipeline is much the same as an assembly line, in which each worker performs their task before handing off their completed work to the next. The main difference between creating art and creating factory goods is that the creative process incorporates review cycles through which the final product can be refined—and, if necessary, the pipeline itself modified.

It has been said that working on pipelines feels like standing next to a dam and trying to predict where the water will break through. Anticipating problems before they arise is a key responsibility. In that spirit, a pipeline can be defined by the questions it answers. How many shots are there? How many tasks does that break down into, and how many artists are needed to tackle them? Who is working on what? Where is their work being stored? Answering such questions will help you to determine what resources, both virtual and physical, should be allocated to a job: virtual, in the sense that files need server space; and physical, in the sense that artists need desks.

A pipeline has no reason to exist unless it has users. All pipelines have users feeding in data at the start and users consuming data at the end. But a closer look reveals that the flow of data is not linear. Most pipelines are made up of a network of smaller pipelines, forking and reconnecting. At each join, someone (or some process) is consuming data from one pipe and feeding it into the next.

Visualizing a pipeline as a flowchart enables us view patterns of data flow. This is handy for identifying trouble spots: if the flowchart looks like a plate of spaghetti, the underlying production process may be set up awkwardly. Analyzing the flow of work also helps to identify production bottlenecks. A typical example would be for an animation department to have too much work going to a single person for approval, preventing them from completing their own work and causing delays downstream.

As we noted earlier, graphics production is not only a technical process but a creative one. As such, the pipeline does not just enable data to move efficiently "downstream" from concept to execution: it also enables the team to see work in a form that can be evaluated and, if necessary, tweaked for better results. Where possible, time-consuming processes should not be placed in the middle of such creative loops. Instead, the focus should be on the cyclic nature of the pipeline, on iterative processes that are cheaply and reliably repeatable—and on the process that breaks the cycle: creative approval.

Constant iteration is a great way to achieve a high standard of quality, but requires a great deal of reworking. To reduce wasted effort, most pipelines make use of placeholder assets. These are low-quality assets that stand in for the finished versions during these iterative processes. In this way, artists can defer more time-consuming tasks, such as building high-quality assets, until later in production when we can be more confident that major changes are no longer required.

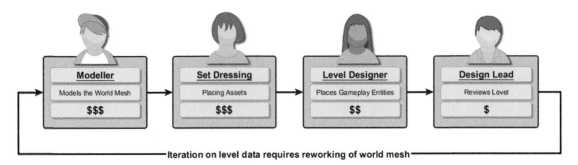

Figure 1.1 An evaluation loop from a game development pipeline. Creative feedback from staff downstream feeds back to those upstream, generating iterative refinements.

As data is modified, either within creative iterations or as it passes downstream, a further problem arises: how can upstream changes be communicated through the dependency chain without losing or invalidating the modifications already made by other departments? For this reason, successful pipelines must be bidirectional: there must be some mechanism by which updates made at earlier stages of production can propagate to tasks that have already passed beyond them, and to alert the production team to potential problems.

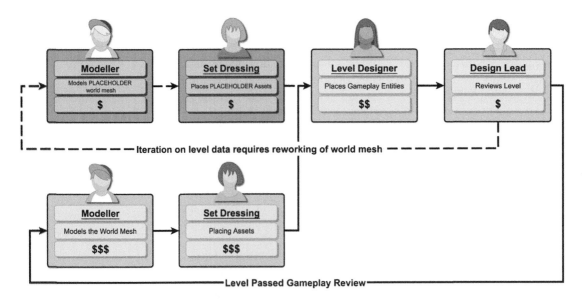

Figure 1.2 A more complex evaluation loop. Having to wait for finished models would delay the processes downstream that rely on them, such as level design. In order to gather feedback more quickly, placeholder versions are used early in production, then replaced by the real assets later.

The ideal pipeline is one that enables revisions to take place at any stage of production. No one ever got an effects shot or a level of a game right the first time. Instead, the pipeline must be flexible enough to enable assets to be tweaked over and over again. The faster each user can make changes, the more changes that can be made when the situation demands it.

Of course, realizing these high-level goals—avoiding bottlenecks, supporting iteration and maximizing efficiency—is a complex undertaking. The aim of this book is to provide both strategic guidance on these high-level problems and practical tips on how to implement solutions in your own productions.

Section 1.4 Differences and Similarities Between Film and Game Pipelines

Films, whether live action with visual effects (VFX) or full CG animation, rely on similar technologies to games. Both require models, textures, animation, lighting, particle effects, post-processing and audio. However, the way in which their production pipelines are structured are often quite different.

Film and video present the viewer with a fait accompli: a complete, polished package that presents the vision of the creative team. Unlike a game, the viewer has no say in how the content of a film unfolds: the action, camera angles and pacing are decided entirely by the director and production team. The end result is a linear sequence of images and audio. Short of making popcorn, there is no user interaction.

The biggest challenge in such a pipeline is managing the sheer volume of information that is required to produce photo-realistic imagery. It is not uncommon for a single creature in a VFX movie to comprise hundreds, if not thousands, of individual assets that must be assembled to generate a working render. Over the course of a production, it is often necessary to assemble terabytes of data and pass it through to the renderer or compositor.

Films are also produced under intense time pressure. Whereas games productions tend to run for between 1 and 4 years, a typical film runs from 6 months to a year. On a VFX blockbuster, this may require tens of thousands of person-days of work, which must be divided among hundreds of artists. As timescales and profit margins shrink, production processes must become more agile to enable artists to work in parallel across multiple time zones and adapt to ever-changing schedules.

During a film production, change is the norm: new directors come on board, problems on the shoot result in delays to the handover of assets to visual effect vendors, and there may be unscheduled deliveries for trailers or preview screenings. This makes it imperative that a

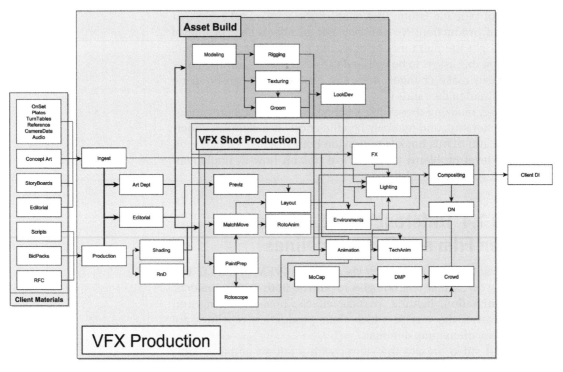

Figure 1.3 A representative film production pipeline. Note the number of different processes required to create photo-realistic imagery, and their complex interdependencies.

film pipeline can not only cope with vast quantities of data, but can also do so flexibly.

In contrast, in video games, while the production team makes the underlying decisions about the story, visual and audio style, it is the end user who decides how that content plays out. The player controls what angle they view the action from, the order in which they see it, and often even what content they see. Taking this control out of the hands of the creative team presents a daunting challenge.

First, a game requires input data. This data comes from controllers, touch screens, webcams (some with depth information), microphones and a multitude of other input devices. Unlike a film, a game must process all of these streams of information to generate the appropriate output.

Furthermore, processing must be done in real time. All of the elements that make up a game—2D and 3D assets, lighting and physics simulations, AI and audio—must be stitched together by the game code in such a way as to create a seamless, interactive user experience.

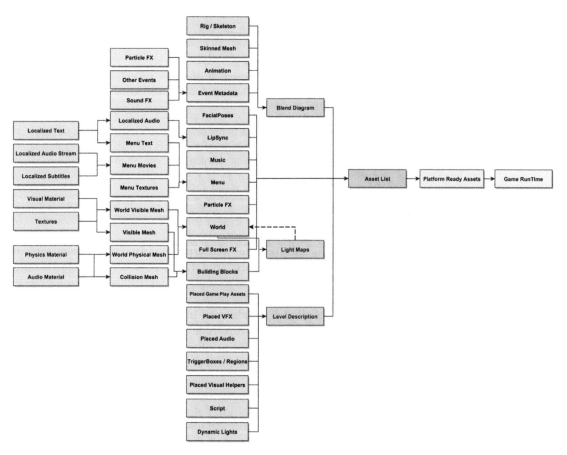

Figure 1.4 The many types of asset that make up a modern video game. Unlike in visual effects work, the final images are assembled in real time, at run-time.

As a result, games technology is often proprietary, and constantly changing in substantial and dramatic ways. While games artists often use similar asset-creation tools to their counterparts in film, those tools must integrate with the engine the game runs on, where assets may look and behave quite differently.

The output of the component pipelines may also be quite different to those for film, often resulting in more, smaller chunks of data. Whereas a film animator will typically create long sequences of movements, a game animator will create hundreds of smaller animations—step forward, left foot down, right foot down, walk forward, walk forward with a 45° turn left, and so on—that may be triggered in response to a player's commands. A blend tree controls how these animations are combined at run-time. Authoring such animations is not just about making them look good, but doing so in such a way that they may work alongside other data.

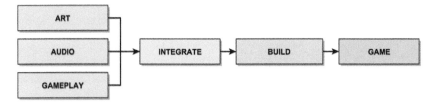

Figure 1.5 A simplified overview of the game-development process. Integration is the stage at which the individual assets are first assembled into a playable build of the game, and is the point at which problems often occur during production.

In the film industry, the "platform" that the end product runs on is fixed—since every film is ultimately a stream of linear video and audio data, there is no need to reinvent MPEG compression or write new DVD player software for each job. Games, on the other hand, do not have a standard output format. In addition to images and audio, it may be necessary to output rumble or force-feedback data to a controller, output network data to other computers—and, in rarer circumstances, output to some form of custom peripheral built specially for that game.

Therefore, a large part of the game development process is building the very platform the component pipelines are targeting. In film, it's unlikely that you will discover that, say, displaying color at the correct frame rate has proven too hard, and consequently all your assets will now appear in monochrome. But in games, the run-time engineering team may well suddenly declare that the particle system everyone is using won't work and needs replacing, or that the lighting model is being overhauled and all the scenes need to be relit.

Finally, pipelines vary according to the style of game being created. If a studio switches from a real-time strategy game (RTS) to a first-person role playing game (RPG), the existing pipeline may need to be thrown out or reworked to accommodate the new requirements. A pipeline that worked for the hundreds of equipment assets (for example, swords and shields) needed in an RTS may not work for the tens of thousands needed in an RPG. Likewise, a game with customizable characters will need its character models built, named, and organized differently from a game with predefined characters.

So how do these differences affect the actual production process? The best way to explain that is to take you through the production of a VFX film and compare it to that of a game, in both cases using fictitious—but hopefully representative—projects.

Section 1.5 An Overview of a Film Production

Ben Cole, Head of Software, MPC Vancouver.

On the surface, a visual effects pipeline looks simple. Think of it as a production line. Raw materials, such as plates from the live-action footage, come in and move through a series of repeatable processes that transform them into finished products. The final output of this production line is a collection of 2D image sequences, not too different to those you started with—at least, if you consider footage of a stunt double strapped into a harness and falling onto a mattress to be reasonably similar to a shot of, let's say Tom Cruise, free jumping from an airplane and crashing into an avalanche.

The reality, however, is quite different. Visual effects pipelines are complex. The reason that this is so comes down to a mixture of technical and philosophical considerations.

On the technical side, it turns out that the raw materials are actually a lot more varied than they first appear. The plates are, in fact, just the start of the avalanche. Let's dissect our hypothetical Tom Cruise shot to see why this is so.

The action in this fictitious film's shot (as outlined in our imaginary script with rough storyboards and detailed pre-visualization) is as follows: Tom Cruise is standing in the cargo bay of a moving airplane, the doors of which are open, his hair and clothing billowing wildly. The camera frames him in a medium close-up, but as he starts to run forward, we pull back and away, revealing both the rapidly receding plane and his plunging body, framed against a backdrop of wispy blue sky. We fall with him for a moment, tilting downward and drifting above him to reveal the snow-covered mountain range that is approaching vertiginously. At the last moment, the camera swivels round, catching Tom as he hits the ground and starts to roll, caught in an explosion of powdery white. Perhaps this should have been two shots, not one, but our imaginary inner director, brought up on a diet of first-person shooters and theme-park rides, likes impossible camera moves and continuous action.

Our clients have actually delivered us several elements. We have a shot of Tom Cruise, standing in the cargo bay of an airplane, his hair and clothes being blown by a couple of large fans, which at the start of the shot are out of frame, but which come into view as we pull back, revealing the plane itself to be a set piece in the middle of a sound stage. A rough green screen has been set up so that we can separate Tom from the background by "keying" out the green parts of the frame later—but it's more a suggestion of green than an actual key-able backdrop. We have also been given the aforementioned element of the stunt double, and a third element of Tom rolling on the ground. The plates with Tom were shot in anamorphic format on

35 mm film, but the stunt double was shot by the second unit, using a different camera: something digital with a different aspect ratio. This may seem like an unnecessary detail, but it will have an impact on how we undertake the work—and like many other aspects of the shoot, was not under the control of our VFX company.

We have also collected other materials that will help us to assemble the shot. On set, we negotiated to shoot chrome balls and HDRIs (High Dynamic Range Images) to help us capture the lighting of the environment. We also have a LIDAR scan of the inside of the aircraft, along with a bunch of reference photography. There is no real plane, so we have sourced images of this type of aircraft: a Boeing C-17 Globemaster III. We have hundreds of photos taken in neutral lighting conditions, which will be used both for model and texture reference. We also have a high-res digital scan of Tom Cruise and photographic reference of him in a variety of poses, not all of which are flattering and none of which will ever be seen by anyone who hasn't signed a non-disclosure agreement. There are also data sheets with camera lens information, frame counts, and the like. And reference photography for avalanches. This is not an exhaustive list.

We haven't even started working on this shot yet, but we have already collected a staggering volume of data, in a range of different formats.

By visual effects standards, the shot isn't too complicated: perhaps of medium complexity. We are going to start with the Tom Cruise airplane plate, which we are going to re-project onto a 3D model of the airplane's interior. We are then going to transition to a CG digital double of Tom falling through the sky and stay with this digital double all the way to the end of the shot, matching the pose and reprojecting Tom Cruise's face from the second element at the end. (Of course, we don't know this when we start work, so we will spend a little time trying to make use of the stunt-double plate and a face replacement.) The sky is going to be a matte painting: a digital backdrop assembled from photos and hand-painted elements. The mountains will be a combination of matte painting and projections onto geometry, with 3D geometry for foreground trees. The avalanche is going to be created from a combination of digital simulations mimicking the behavior of fluids, particles and rigid bodies, and stock footage from a library.

Each of our live-action cameras needs to be tracked and the two instances of Tom Cruise and the stunt double need to be rotoscoped so that the movement of a digital character can be matched to that of the live actor. This work is being done in a different facility, in central Asia, operating in a different time zone. Locally, the layout department will take iterations of this data and construct a single camera track and a rough animation track, conform this material to a logical world-space location and make sure it fits the continuity of the sequence. (This shot does not stand alone. It is part of a sequence of shots which must all flow together in the cut.) The rough animation

will be given to the animation department, who will finesse it until it looks perfect.

The digital models that the rotoscoping, layout and animation departments are using were put together by an asset team, which is actually distributed between several geographic locations. The assets were built to be used in several different sequences in the movie, so many variations have been made. (Although Tom Cruise *is* jumping out of the airplane in his tuxedo, this tuxedo is ripped, not the pristine one he has on when jumping out of the window of the hotel earlier in the movie.) Additionally, the asset department has created a number of different LOD (Level of Detail) models, including high-resolution models specifically for cloth simulation, and lower-resolution models for use in the physics simulations. Any changes required will need to be kept consistent between all of these variants. We also must "groom" the digital Tom Cruise's hair, which has to match not just the look but also the motion of the real Tom Cruise.

Thankfully, none of the work on this sequence is being shared with other visual effects facilities. However, we have been asked to export the Tom Cruise models, rigs and textures to another company which is using them elsewhere in the movie. This company runs a different pipeline to ours, so exchange formats need to be negotiated. (Another show we are working on concurrently has not been so lucky, requiring us to negotiate the transfer of a 1,000-foot-high stone tower in exchange for the fifteen marauding demons who are climbing it, over a series of thirty shots.)

Timescales are short, so many separate aspects of the shot are started in parallel. The lighting department begins setting up before animation has even started, making use of centralized look-development work that is only 70 percent complete for the character and the plane. The FX department, responsible for those digital simulations, also gets started pretty early, trying to block something out while they wait for updated animation.

We have agreed with our client that we will show them work in progress at regular intervals, and they have told us that they won't sign off on any animation until they have seen it with at least basic cloth and hair simulation, lit with motion blur and shadows. This means pushing incomplete iterations along the pipeline, keeping track of the different versions of assets used by different departments, and making sure that only approved assets are actually being used further downstream. It also creates some pretty large and circuitous feedback loops.

In addition, each iteration creates more data. With FX elements, the data-sets can be massive, occupying many terabytes of storage space. Although smaller, the textures, animation data and matte paintings also occupy a significant amount of space, as do the plates themselves. Sometimes, we will need to revert to older versions, or work with several alternatives in parallel. This makes archiving the data a complex process, as there isn't nearly enough space on the

facility's servers for it all, but you can't always know when you won't need a particular file any more.

Generating the data also leads to complexity. On this shot, each new avalanche simulation takes half a day to run, and this is just for one of several sub-simulations, or "simulation layers". (This shot is not particularly complicated. The next shot in the sequence, where the avalanche really kicks off, takes 72 hours to complete—that is, when it doesn't crash halfway through.) All of these simulations are being executed on the facility's server farm, along with all the rendering work—turning the 3D data into 2D images—and a lot of other, more mundane tasks. Scheduling all this computation is tough.

When it comes to the rendering itself, we aim for each frame to take no longer than one or two hours per render pass. Our current shot has five or six FX layers, plus renders of the airplane interior and exterior and the environments, meaning that each frame takes around ten hours in total to calculate. Being around eight seconds long, the shot itself is made up of 197 frames, so each complete iteration takes 2,000 hours of render time. (There are also one or two "trouble frames" that are taking fifteen to twenty hours each, and that need to be pushed through manually outside the farm.)

Iteration creates other problems, too, because some of the tasks we are performing are "destructive" in nature. Let's look at the difference between destructive and non-destructive processes.

As we discussed earlier, there are several variants of the digital model of Tom Cruise. There is the clean version of Tom in his tuxedo, which is being used in an earlier sequence, and there is the Tom who jumps out of the plane. This Tom has five days' worth of beard growth, along with bruises, scratches and rips in his clothing. However, he is otherwise basically the same. It makes sense that the textures for the clean variation get painted first, and the changes are applied on top of these. A destructive way of working would be to take the original image and paint a beard directly on top of it, eliminating the original pixels. A non-destructive way of working would be to paint the beard in a separate layer. In the first case, if the clean artwork changes, you will have to completely redo the other version, even if the beard itself doesn't change. In the second case, you simply reapply the layer with the beard—at most, you will need to touch it up a little. Clearly, this non-destructive way of working is more efficient, particularly since combining the two layers can be automated easily.

On our shot, the "tracked" animation of Tom jumping out of the plane generated during the rotoscoping phase has to be blended with the animation of the stunt double, with plenty of animation by hand in between. If the tracked animation is updated, the hand animation must be as well. However, in our pipeline, this doesn't happen automatically and the process of blending the animation is destructive.

This is where philosophy comes into play. Perhaps this process could be redesigned to make it non-destructive? Perhaps all VFX

processes should be designed this way? It seems obvious that this should be the case, but practical considerations stand in our way. The most immediate of these is that we don't have total control over how the pipeline works. For the most part, we are working with third-party tools, which have been designed by software vendors to perform a specific function and which offer varying levels of customizability. It may be difficult to modify these tools to work in a new way. In addition, the artists performing the job may not be comfortable with adopting a non-standard workflow within a tool they have been using for a large part of their career. The question of whether to "change it" or "work with it" is an important and deeply consequential one in VFX.

To make matters worse, there are many such third-party software tools—even a brief list might include Maya, Mari, Photoshop, Katana, RenderMan, Houdini and Nuke—and each department uses a different combination of them. The pipeline has to weave its way around this disparate set of tools, many of which weren't designed to play nicely with one another. This raises another philosophical question: which file formats should we use to transfer data between them all? When should we write out native data, and when should we switch to something application-agnostic? There are many trade-offs inherent in these decisions, and these, too, can have far-reaching consequences.

Meanwhile, back in shot production, the FX department, in a bid to increase its efficiency, has put together its own tool for switching between different variants of the boulders included in the avalanche. This has created a little avalanche of its own, as the way this tool manages files does not allow them to be transferred easily to the lighting department. We rectify this by helping FX make use of the asset-management system, which makes things a little more complex for the artists concerned, but smoothes things out overall.

At the other end of the pipeline, the compositing department, responsible for blending all of the live-action and digital elements into seamless final images, has realized that it will need to make use of a specific piece of camera information which is not currently being written out. This requires the pipeline team to make changes to the asset-management system and deploy an updated version of the camera export/import code—but only for this particular show.

This teaches us three things. First, that VFX pipelines need to be flexible, since they will undergo constant change. Second, that the capacity to make such changes varies greatly between departments. And third, that people are often happy to make changes that, while great for them, have a significant impact downstream.

To reach completion, our Tom Cruise shot will pass through more than a dozen departments. In total, we will work on 300 such shots on the show, fifty or sixty of them in parallel. We are also working on three other movies, each of a similar size and complexity. Some of these shots will be in production for many months, others only for a few days, yet all of them must attain a consistent look and level of quality. The shot where

Tom dodges the bullet in the cargo bay (we add a muzzle flash and sparks) needs to match the one where he finally breaks free of the handcuffs (sky replacement), and they both need to match the avalanche, even though the work on each one may be done many months apart, by different artists using different parts of the pipeline. All of this needs to be tracked and scheduled.

When looking at this particular shot, if we include the asset build for the digital double, we have easily 200 person-days of work to do. This needs to be completed in less than two months, because this shot is one of five in the teaser trailer that our client is broadcasting during the Super Bowl. The movie itself isn't due in cinemas for over a year yet, but there are a few early-stage deliveries like this one.

Our work on this film is bid at around 15,000 person-days in total, and we have a final delivery deadline in 9 months, to give the studio time to "dimensionalize" the movie so that it can be displayed in stereoscopic format. Assuming that there are 21 working days in a month, this means an average team size of eighty people. However, it is highly unlikely that there will be work for eighty people throughout the entire process. In general, the team size required to work on a show is more of a bell curve, increasing slowly at the start of production, then rising and falling away rapidly. This means that we are likely to peak at around 250 people during production—all of whom require somewhere to sit, licenses for third-party software and the other infrastructure needed do their work.

During development, these shots will be delivered to our clients ten or twenty times apiece, and reviewed internally hundreds of times. Our clients will also be receiving updates from the half-dozen other studios working on their movie, so they will have their own specifications for the format in which they want the data supplied, which will often change several times over the course of the production. Not only does our pipeline need to be flexible enough to cope with what is happening inside the studio but also with what is happening outside it.

So a visual effects pipeline is not exactly a production line. It is more like the world's longest Scalextric track. You race along it, switching lanes and doing loop-the-loops. Every so often you realize that you need to change the layout of the tracks, but you are rarely allowed to stop the cars. You can imagine Tom Cruise in one of those cars. But that's a different movie.

Section 1.6 An Overview of a Game Production

Ben Carter, Game Developer and Author, Heavy Spectrum Entertainment Labs.

At Fictitious Studios Inc, we are nearly a year into development on our new AAA action/adventure game *Final Violent Outburst XII: Unvengeance* (or just "Outburst" as the team refers to it). The

prototyping and planning phases are done, and it is full steam ahead with production.

Outburst is a pretty standard third-person character action game. The player runs through corridors, shoots people a lot and watches cut-scenes featuring cackling madmen with unsightly facial scars. Sometimes they are called upon to solve simple puzzles, although in common with most titles in this genre, few of these would tax the intelligence of the average trained hamster. The game is pretty much linear, which makes our lives easier because we can produce each level separately and not have to worry about what happens if the player decides to wander off.

We have just started work on Level 5, which used to be Level 6 until Level 4 got cut from the design because there wasn't enough time to build it. (Prior to that, it was Level 3, but when the designers started planning the flow of the game, they decided there were too many set-pieces in a row and moved it. Since we all know that next week it will probably be Level 8, everyone just calls it "the skyscraper level" and gets on with their lives.)

Not surprisingly, it's called the skyscraper level because it's set in a skyscraper. That came about because the story needed a stage set in a generic research lab—sorry, a *genetic* research lab. Originally, we talked about making it an undersea complex with all sorts of experiments in tanks, but it turned out that the team making *Death by Polygons* (our previous game, which was canceled before release) had already modeled a skyscraper, and since the schedule was looking tight, management made the decision to reuse what we could. And so a penthouse genetics lab with east-facing windows and outdoor swimming pool was born.

First, we retrieve the data for the old models from our project archive. We do this by walking around the office saying, "Does anyone have a copy of the skyscraper from DBP?" loudly until someone who worked on the project gets sufficiently annoyed by the noise to fish it off their hard disk.

Of course, what we find isn't a pretty sight. We don't have all the textures for some of the files (later, we will realize that this is because the artist who created them left the company after the game was canned, and IT wiped and reallocated his machine before anyone could check if there was anything on it that he had forgotten to copy to the network)—and everything is the wrong size because somewhere along the line, we changed from using meters to centimeters as our base units. This is nothing a bit of fiddling won't fix, but it all adds up, and before we know it, half the art team has spent the better part of two weeks just resizing, retexturing and reexporting assets.

While all this is going on, the designers are building rough "whitebox" layouts for the level, and the programming team is experimenting with AI (Artificial Intelligence) for the new enemies (the fearsome Cyber-Apes—"half ape, half robot, all cliché"). Cut-scene storyboards

(in the form of digital photos of Post-it notes with stick-men on them moving around on a whiteboard) also start to turn up on the project's network drive as the writing and art teams go into overdrive.

After this, things are quiet for a while: the team forms up into a bunch of little work units, each looking at a different problem. Some of the artists begin creating concept art and rough models for the additional scenery and props we need, a couple of artist-designer-programmer groups form to prototype gameplay and character AI, and in general, everyone is happy in their own little world. (Almost literally so in the case of the audio team, which works in a sound-proof office.) The only disruption is when marketing swoops in to let us know that next year's release in the competing *Duty of Battlefield* series is going to have fifteen unique weapons, and since we only have fourteen, we had better find another one somewhere or risk losing the Bullet-Point War.

A few hasty meetings later, we have a plan that seems workable: an exploding top hat that the player could steal from the heads of the Cyber-Apes and throw at them, causing massive damage. This ticks the box for marketing, while keeping the art requirements to a minimum (one extra model, no animation), requiring little new programming (the hat is mostly just a grenade with a really big blast radius as far as the code is concerned) and not unbalancing the whole game (as you can only get the hats on this level, there are no knock-on effects for the work already completed).

With this decided, we march merrily onwards, churning out first-pass art, test code and level-design prototypes. And so we arrive at integration.

In theory, integration is the keystone of the great gaming arch—the part where all the hard work comes together into a glorious, functioning whole. In practice, it does precisely what you'd expect of any large, heavy rock when placed atop a wobbly span made from half-constructed bits of game. The trick to integration, therefore, is not being underneath when it happens.

When we start integrating, it immediately becomes clear that there are a few things we've overlooked. The white-box level layouts the designers have built work well from a player navigation perspective, but they don't remotely resemble the models the art team has created. And neither of them takes into account the fact that at some point (no one is quite sure when, but it seems likely that a production request to "make the monsters more scary" was the culprit), the Cyber-Apes have doubled in size, which means that they don't actually fit through any of the doorways in the level. On top of that, the cut-scene storyboards have been redrafted and now include an encounter with the evil scientist midway through the stage (in a control room that doesn't exist outside of a sketch on a Post-it note), and it turns out that the exploding hat *does* need new animation work because when the player throws

one using the standard overarm "throw grenade" animation, he looks really, *really* stupid.

Resolving all this takes several frantic weeks of work—par for the course, to be honest, but more time than we have allowed in the schedule, putting more pressure on the remaining phases. Despite this, with the first-pass assets all integrated, we can finally see the light at the end of the tunnel, and get a feel for which areas are going to need the most work to bring them up to the quality required.

With the integrated build in hand, a production review is conducted, resulting in a fairly long list of things to change: everything from making corridors shorter (less boring "just walking from A to B" for the player) to making the Cyber-Apes shout before attacking (to give players a chance to react to attacks from outside their field of view). While it's annoying to have to make so many alterations now, just after we've rushed to get everything integrated, it's far better to do this sooner than later, when assets are closer to completion.

Making these changes happens in parallel with the process of refining the assets to bring them up to something resembling shippable quality. The build is now in a state where it is possible to play through the level—albeit with lots of rooms built out of nothing but cubes, cutscenes consisting of a single frame with "I AM CUT-SCENE 6" written on it by a programmer using MS Paint, and enemies whose attack cries sound suspiciously like one of the audio designers saying the word "roar" in a deeply uninterested voice.

This means that as assets are altered or added, we can conduct reviews of them in the environment in which they would actually occur, which makes fine-tuning a lot easier (although also slower, as the process of compiling game-ready data, running the game and then navigating to the right point in the level is surprisingly time-consuming, even with debug functionality and cheats). Weekly review meetings are kicked off to play the level and examine the overall progress being made, which provides both useful feedback and a strong incentive not to be the person who broke the game by adding faulty code just before the meeting is due to start.

With each passing day, a wider range of people are giving feedback: production, marketing, the test department, and random people we found loitering outside the front doors (otherwise known as "focus groups"). Some is processed into change requests or bug reports, which are filed in the appropriate databases in our bug-tracking system; some is handled more informally—either because to resolve it requires a discussion between different teams, or because, while it's very nice that the VP's daughter likes dinosaurs, we are quietly going to ignore his instruction that we put some in the game.

Unfortunately, we can't ignore the (equally upsetting, but slightly less frivolous) feedback we are getting from the executive producer, who has played *War of Dogs*, which one of our competitors has just released,

and decided that we should be aiming for a more gritty visual style. To address this, we produce a number of mock-ups, using screenshots or game footage with filters and hand-drawn effects applied and present them to him. This enables us to move beyond his vague initial feedback and home in on the key features of the style he wants. Since rebuilding environments or characters at this point would push the project beyond merely late (as in "over schedule") into really late (as in "dead"), we steer these discussions towards features we feel we can implement in a reasonable time frame: more camera shake when the player fires or takes damage, a motion blur filter that generates light trails from bright objects, and relighting the level to increase the contrast.

Fortunately, we are able to achieve a look that everyone is happy with, and so the level creeps on towards completion. (Of course, even now, it isn't all smooth running, since we have to relengthen the corridors after we discover that the streaming system can't keep up if the player runs too quickly between rooms, causing them to emerge into a featureless void where the walls pop slowly into existence as they load.)

Another hiccup occurs when one of the publisher's other action titles is delayed, putting it dangerously close to our release date and meaning that another 2 months disappear from the schedule as our own release is brought forward to avoid the clash. Fortunately, we are able to resolve the issue by removing one of the levels we had designed but not yet built and adding it to the DLC: the downloadable expansion pack that will follow after the game has been released.

As the game as a whole reaches the start of the alpha-beta-final process, the levels are content-locked one by one. This prompts a mad rush to supply any missing assets. In theory, after content-lock, nothing can be added except to fix a bug, but as always, we end up throwing in some placeholder assets in case the publisher (or more likely, the test department, which uses content-lock to finalize its own checklists for the remaining intensive testing phase) complains about new things appearing later. With this done, we are able to focus on the final rounds of polishing and bug-fixing.

It's traditional that at this stage something huge and, in hindsight, stupidly obvious crops up to derail things. In our case, it's the rooftop swimming pool. Since, in the remaining levels, the player can swim, they can swim in the pool. They can even fire their gun while swimming, if they're on the surface.

However, the Cyber-Apes can't swim. This is partly because their heavy robotic components would cause them to sink, but mostly because no one thought of creating the AI or animations they would need in order to do so. Also, they don't have any ranged weapons.

Given these facts, it shouldn't really come as much of a surprise when the bug report arrives from the test team that reads: "Observed behavior: if the player runs into a room, alerts the enemies, then runs back to the swimming pool and jumps in, all the enemies will follow and line up at the edge of the pool looking gormless as the player

shoots them to death at their leisure. Expected behavior: the enemies should not look gormless, but jump in the pool and tear the player limb from limb."

However, it's still a bit of a problem (or, as production people who don't like the word "problem" are prone to say, an "issue"). On one hand, this could be regarded as a legitimate tactic for the player. On the other, being able to clear the entire level of enemies without taking a single hit is hardly a sign of a great game. Videos of your game going viral on the internet are a generally good thing, but not when they're mocking your fearsome genetic cyborgs' inability to cope with a luxury water feature.

So we look at our options. The obvious answer is to give the Cyber-Apes the ability to swim. However, this would mean a whole new set of animations and AI code (and they would have to be able to get out of, as well as into, the pool—otherwise, we'd be risking an even more embarrassing "how many Cyber-Apes can you get in a swimming pool?" video). This would be prohibitively expensive at this point in development, so it's out. We could remove the pool, but that would mean art changes and a strangely pointless patio area appearing in its place. Or we could give the Cyber-Apes a ranged attack, but that would involve more asset work and rebalancing the rest of the level.

In the end, we settle on a cheap hack as both the simplest and safest resolution: the programmers add a special case to the AI code so that when the player goes near the swimming pool, all of the enemies stop chasing them and return to their original positions. This makes the pool a slightly incongruous "safe zone" for the player, but at least it can't be exploited to kill enemies.

In the weeks that follow, the number of bugs in the database slowly dwindles, and the number of people left on the team follows suit as artists move onto other projects or go on holiday. Eventually, only a handful are left—largely programmers fixing the final bugs reported by First-Party Quality Assurance at the hardware manufacturer, and producers trying to massage a range of DLC schedules to match various first-week sales projections. Then, one day, when almost everyone has forgotten that the project is still alive, an email arrives from the producer:

Subject: FW: Outburst [NA/EU/Asia]—FPQA submission PASS

And with that, we're done. Until the DLC, at least.

Section 1.7 Remember: Each Production is Unique

In the following chapters, we will explore the structure of a typical production process. However, it is important to note that there is no such thing as a "typical" production. There are dozens of options for

each of the component steps, with each decision you make leading to dozens more. This book is intended to help you think through the issues involved in structuring a pipeline for yourself—not to provide a formula for the One True Way of doing things. If a situation it describes doesn't match your circumstances, exercise your own judgment about whether to accept the advice offered in that section of the text.

THE STAGES OF PRODUCTION

Tim Green; Matt Hoesterey; Hannes Ricklefs; Mark Streatfield; Steve Theodore; Laurent M. Abecassis: *Di-O-Matic;* **Holly Newman:** *CEO, Liquid Entertainment;* **Marty Shindler:** *CEO, The Shindler Perspective, Inc.;* **Dave Stephens:** *FX Supervisor*

Section 2.1 What You Will Learn From This Chapter

In the previous chapter, we briefly addressed an important question: "What is a pipeline?" In this chapter, we will attempt to give a more detailed answer, providing an overview of the principal stages a game or film project will go through, and discussing how each one places different demands upon the pipeline and the pipeline team. Again, we will look at the similarities and differences between film and games, attempting to highlight the unique requirements of each.

In film, much of the challenge lies in organizing the massive quantity of data generated both within the animation or visual effects studio itself and by the wide range of vendors that provide content throughout the production. In games, the challenge is often managing the game engine. We will examine why the engine is the basis of many creative decisions and limitations, and how a game engine's data requirements result in a pipeline vastly different to that of film.

We will also explore how a production evolves over time. The adage of "failing to plan is planning to fail" couldn't hold truer than for films or games. Visual effects projects requiring hundreds of artists—or even thousands, split between facilities—and games requiring hundreds of artists and developers cannot be run successfully by luck alone. Contingency planning avoids the problems that will otherwise inevitably derail the project and even throw a company into bankruptcy.

But before describing the stages of production, let's take a look at the economics of production, and examine the demands that these financial pressures place upon a pipeline.

Section 2.2 The Economics of Film Production

Marty Shindler, CEO, The Shindler Perspective, Inc.

Movies are at times a very lucrative, but more often, a very risky business. For a major studio, making a movie is an expensive process: one that typically costs from $50 to $250 million before marketing and distribution, which can add a further $100 million or more to the total investment.

Some movies are certainly made at or through major studios for less. But in recent years, the big studios have tended to produce more blockbuster or "tentpole" movies and have left the low end of the market to their specialty divisions, and to the many independents that make movies at a lower cost, through organizations with lower overheads.

Thanks to this blockbuster mentality, the profits from a successful movie can be very large. Yet the losses from a $250 million film can be large as well. On average, some 65–75 percent of the movies made will lose money for their investors. Approximately 15–20 percent will break even; only 5–10 percent will be profitable.

To control costs effectively, studios make a concerted effort to produce their movies in states or countries that offer favorable tax conditions, many of which actively offer tax incentives to movie productions as a way of stimulating their economies.

As a direct result, many visual effects facilities have set up operations in the same locales. As well as tax incentives, these often offer lower labor rates. In many such locales, the combination has enabled an industry to grow where one was not previously present.

The risky nature of the business also prompts studios and producers to pressure the vendors providing services for their movies to reduce their rates. The mantra at most studios is to get the best quality possible for the lowest price.

This applies to visual effects facilities as much as, if not more than, other vendors. The industry's use of digital technology means that work can be done anywhere in the world, providing that the requisite equipment and qualified workers are available.

This result is outsourcing and offshoring. Visual effects work is currently being performed on a global basis, with an emphasis on locales offering tax incentives. Today, visual effects facilities in the West compete not only with local rivals but companies in Asia.

Furthermore, making movies is not only a costly business but a time-consuming one. The process of developing a movie property—beginning with the basics of story and characters, through scriptwriting, pre-production and pre-visualization, budgeting, shooting, post-production and visual effects, and on to distribution—can take 36 months or more.

Yet the commercial value of all those months of work hinges on just 2 critical days: the movie's opening weekend. The release patterns of major movies from major studios are dictated largely by the need to maximize the return on marketing investment for this opening weekend, particularly where the studio does not have confidence in a movie's ability to perform over a period of time—or in the language of the industry, to "have legs".

Major unscheduled events, whether resulting from national or international politics, or simply the weather, will play havoc with the opening weekend. While some movies can survive an occurrence of this sort, many do not and most never quite make up the box office lost.

The opening weekend cannot simply be put back: release dates are set far in advance, primarily due to the need to gain a competitive advantage on certain weekends, such as holiday periods and school vacations. Production is geared toward meeting those ironclad targets, starting at a point when there is, in theory, sufficient time to complete the movie—but not too far ahead of the release date, so the studio can manage its cash flow better. Since the date is set so far ahead, there is no "we'll finish the work tomorrow". Organizations that do not meet their delivery dates often do not get a second chance on future movies.

VFX is typically the last major department to complete its work on a movie, and thus the pressure to perform efficiently is enormous. For those facilities carrying out dimensionalization work—the conversion of a film from 2D to stereoscopic 3D, a process that often overlaps with, and extends beyond, the creation of the visual effects—deadlines are even shorter, and the pressure to complete work on schedule even greater.

In order to reliably produce work on schedule, while keeping rates as competitive as possible, there are a number of measures a VFX facility must take. These include, but are not limited to:

- Developing a robust pipeline, organized according to the many tasks that are required in order to complete the work as efficiently as possible
- Making sure that the overall workflow is communicated to all who need to know, from internal personnel to those at the studio, so that there are no unwanted surprises
- Communicating with the various other vendors from whom elements of the work are to be received, so as to be able to plan accordingly
- Using a DAM (Digital Asset Management) system that enables management and project producers to see at all times the status of the various shots being produced
- Making artists aware of the estimates that have been made for the time required to complete each shot
- Communicating the status of the shot to the studio when required
- Maintaining all equipment in the best possible fashion

- Developing benchmarks for the types of shots being produced (this enables the facility to estimate the time—and, if applicable, materials—required to produce a shot, and the resulting cost, for use in future bids)
- Tracking the cost to complete selected shots against the bid so as to refine the bidding process, enabling the facility to bid competitively for future work

Section 2.3 The Economics of Game Production

Holly Newman, CEO, Liquid Entertainment.

Video games have evolved a great deal since the days when they were played largely by teenage boys. According to the Entertainment Software Association, today's average gamer is 30 years old and has been playing games for 12 years. There are also now more adult women playing games than boys aged 17 or younger. This represents a diverse and sizable market. Transparency Market Research predicts growth from a roughly $70 billion industry in 2012 to $119.9 billion in 2015, with the Asia-Pacific region showing the fastest growth.

However, video games are not only a lucrative market but a volatile one. In 1972, Atari released *Pong*, the first mainstream video game, from which an entire industry was born. At the time of writing, Atari is in bankruptcy. Former top ten US game publisher THQ has completed its own bankruptcy proceedings, and has ceased to exist entirely, while both the president of Square Enix and the CEO of Electronic Arts have stepped down from their roles due to poor financial results.

Until recently, much of the game industry's revenue came from sales of so-called "AAA" titles for high-end personal computers and home console systems such as the Sony PlayStation 3 and Microsoft's Xbox 360. It is not unusual for the development of these games to cost $30 million or more. The most expensive game budgets rival those of the $100 million-plus budgets of Hollywood blockbusters and can take three years or more to develop. The cost of marketing must also be considered, which can frequently match, or in some cases eclipse, that of development.

These costs continue to rise with each successive generation of consoles. Development costs are expected to double with the next generation of consoles, and this may be a conservative estimate: Tim Sweeney of Epic Games, creator of the Unreal Engine, has been quoted as saying that costs could increase five-fold without the proper tools to support development.

Since a small minority of games make up the majority of the revenue, it becomes clear that the risk profile for AAA games is very high. For an elite few, profits can be substantial: according to its publisher, Activision Blizzard, the *Call of Duty* franchise has

generated over a billion dollars in revenue. But such success is the exception, not the rule.

In response, many game developers and publishers have attempted to reduce risk by capitalizing on existing brands. This "rinse and repeat" model has led to an AAA market dominated by sequels and a dearth of innovation in game design. These factors may be, at least in part, responsible for the financial problems of many of the "old guard" of game publishers.

In contrast, the lower end of the market is thriving. The rapid adoption of Internet-enabled tablets and smartphones like the Apple iPad and the Samsung Galaxy, coupled with new mobile and online distribution channels such as Apple's App Store, Google Play, Amazon.com and Valve Software's Steam platform, have effectively removed the barrier of "shelf space", creating many opportunities for smaller studios. Innovative, entrepreneurial companies have eschewed the consoles and their inflated development costs, and looked to mobile, social, and browser games to find new audiences. These markets now represent an increasing portion of overall sales.

In this new environment, companies like Rovio Entertainment, creator of *Angry Birds*, have been able to reap significant returns on products made at a fraction of the cost of AAA console titles, boasting over 1.7 billion downloads and 263 million active users as of December 2012. Mojang, maker of *Minecraft*, began as a team of one and has grown to a full-scale publisher (the company's website lists twenty-three staff members) with gross revenues of over $250 million in 2012.

In such a diverse market, it's difficult to generalize about the demands that economic factors place upon the development pipeline. Like films, AAA games require developers to manage large data sets, track complex production jobs, and control costs tightly. In contrast, indie titles require lightweight, agile pipelines that permit developers to innovate rapidly; while emerging sectors, like free-to-play online games, create new demands of their own, such as the need to track user behavior in order to fine-tune the in-game payments from which revenue is derived.

While it may be impossible to predict what comes next for video games, their potential is staggering. The rapid adoption of mobile devices is creating new types of games, new business models, and new marketing techniques. With several generations now having grown up with games, one thing is certain: video games are here to stay—and no matter who you are, at some point you are likely to play one.

Section 2.4 The Stages of Production

The task of discussing the production process is complicated by the fact that the terminology used in visual effects movies (live action with CG enhancements), CG animated features (CG only) and games

(CG only) has evolved along different paths, occasionally resulting in identical terms defining different processes. Clients who aren't familiar with such nuances tend to blanket everything under the term "post-production", further exacerbating the confusion. Therefore, when communicating with the client, it's best to confirm which stage they are truly referring to.

In film, the main stages are:

- Pre-production
- Production
- Post-production

In games, the main stages are:

- Pre-production
- Production
- Finalling

We will look at what each stage involves shortly. Post-production or finalling is where the two industries diverge the most, with film striving to conform to a predefined storyline by outputting a linear series of visual effects shots, while games provide a dynamic and interactive experience, with the engine generating the visuals in response to the player's actions.

Section 2.5 Other Language Barriers

It isn't just artists working in different industries who use technical terms differently. Despite their need to collaborate effectively throughout production, artists, developers and management may use language in quite different ways. An artist concerned with the esthetics of an image may describe the process by which it is created quite differently to a programmer concerned with the mathematics of simulating light. As a pipeline developer, you need to understand both ways of communicating.

In order to decide what language style to use when talking to an artist—or what type of interface to implement when building pipeline tools—consider what we will playfully call the "fluffy spectrum".

The fluffy spectrum is a scale with cold, technical logic at one end and warm, fluffy creativity at the other. Computers live at the cold, logical end of the spectrum while humans occupy the warmer, fluffier end. At the logical end, everything is true or false, right or wrong, black or white. At the fluffy end, we can describe things in terms of emotions, or aesthetics.

When people communicate, they do so with a degree of "fluffiness" appropriate to the task in hand. A programmer who has created a stunning fractal image might describe the code that created it in one way, and the artistic decisions they made in another. The fluffiness of the language we use depends on what we are talking about, and who we are talking to.

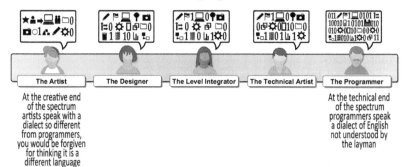

Figure 2.1 The "fluffy spectrum" in operation. At one end, artists communicate more in emotional and aesthetic terms; at the other, programmers communicate more in technical concepts.

Of course, the fluffy scale is just a bit of fun. But it's also, hopefully, a memorable way to think about communication. The way in which you talk with your peers becomes so habitual that, when you are called upon to communicate with other groups, it's often easy to forget that they may not share your assumptions about terminology.

A production team comprises many different groups of individuals, from concept artists to programmers, and each one uses language in a way appropriate to the work they do. The next time you build an interface, compile a manual, or write an email explaining how a new tool works, consider its intended audience. The pipeline should bridge the divide between members of staff who communicate in very different ways.

Section 2.6 Pre-Production: An Overview

Pre-production, also referred to as "pre-pro" or "pre-prod", is the planning phase of a project, and forms the basis for everything to come. Pre-production is where the full scope of the work is defined, and possible points of failure identified. Poorly executed pre-production tends to set the tone for everything that follows, making the next months or years of work a nightmare.

The goal of the art department during pre-production is to identify the visual style that will suit the film or game best. This may include creating concept artwork, building test assets, or shooting footage out in the lot and applying different visual treatments to it. It might also include pre-visualization: the process of creating animations or still images that help define the way in which a movie will be shot, and the other visual elements it will require. (For a longer discussion of this subject, see the Interlude "Previs and Related Data".)

Much of this exploratory work is done on paper or using digital painting software, in the shape of storyboards and concept sketches. Much of the rest can be done with off-the-shelf 3D software. Often, however, some tasks will require support from the pipeline team.

For example, a group of artists working on blocking out a shot—planning the camera angles from which it will be filmed, and the way in which the footage will be edited together—might request a tool to help them produce preview renders that can be handed off to an editor or compositor more quickly.

Ad hoc tools present the pipeline team with an interesting dilemma. If these tools are too clunky or too under-powered, they hinder the artists they are meant to help—but if they are built to the same exacting standards as conventional production tools, they monopolize the time of the few programmers available. It also becomes difficult to make any necessary changes fast enough to keep up with the hectic pace of pre-production.

For this reason, many studios find that TAs (Technical Artists, the term commonly used in games) or TDs (Technical Directors, the term more commonly used in film work)—staff who have the artistic sensibility required for production work but are also capable of doing their own scripting—are invaluable resources during pre-production.

On the technical side, pre-production is also the time for risk-minimization: the time to test and validate the ideas coming from the creative team to make sure that they can be achieved without bankrupting the studio or keeping everyone else chained to their desks, working graveyard shifts.

In many ways, pre-production is the most stressful part of the project for the pipeline team. New ideas are constantly bubbling up, and validating them typically demands a quick-and-dirty mini-pipeline that can translate them into concrete visuals. Ideas which look great as concept sketches or verbal descriptions often turn out to be technically impossible or artistically boring. Tools that promise cutting-edge new ways of working may prove to be incompatible with the rest of your pipeline. The only way to avoid wasting irreplaceable time and money on an unworkable idea is to start validating it early—which means that prototype pipelines must be assembled on the fly.

Prototyping often resembles a miniature production all of its own, including a jury-rigged pipeline to create test content. If the game is supposed to involve, say, a new method of fluid simulation as a gameplay element, that idea can only be validated with a prototype fluid-simulation engine and a pipeline to create data for the tests.

This is a fast-moving process. Requirements are hazy, plans change constantly, and new tools have to be cobbled together daily. Pipeline staff need to improvise solutions to new problems quickly, which often means trying things that common sense and good coding practice would frown upon. As prototyping wraps up, the pipeline staff will begin rebuilding this rickety code to more exacting standards. Since prototype code is notoriously unreliable, most companies aim to reimplement their prototype tools completely, rather than simply building upon them—but in practice, "temporary" solutions often become permanent due to a lack of time or resources.

At the same time, the foundations of the "real" pipeline—the one that will be used by tens or hundreds of artists once the project moves out of pre-production—must be laid down. When the modelers and animators arrive, they're going to need tools, documentation and training. If the resources they need to do their jobs aren't waiting for them, you haven't done yours.

There is one more thing that must be stressed about pre-production: always plan for change. However well thought out your pipelines are at this stage, they are going to change in production, as technology evolves, as the director changes their mind, or as the designer comes up with a better idea for gameplay. Structure your pipelines so that you can accommodate these changes without invalidating the work you have already done, or requiring content to be reworked unnecessarily. In this industry, there is one simple rule to live by: "The only thing that is constant is change."

Section 2.7 Pre-Production in the Film Pipeline

In visual effects, the term "pre-production" applies to all the preparation involved before the camera starts rolling. Storyboarding, previsualization and gathering lighting information all fall under this heading, along with such non-graphics-related tasks as budgeting, hiring actors, set building and costume design.

For artists, what happens during pre-production depends on the nature of the project. Common tasks include visual research, concept design of characters and environments, and defining the color palettes to be used throughout the film.

This is followed by determining the general feel of the film, including the pace of the edit and the composition of key shots: for example, where the camera will be placed in relation to the characters and how it will move to capture the action. This is handled either during layout (the term used in CG animations) or pre-visualization (the term used in live action).

In some cases, the result of this work may be a complete 3D animation, using low-resolution models as placeholders for the final assets, edited together with rough dialog and sound effects. In others, it may be an animatic: a series of still images, such as storyboard frames, cut together with the correct timings for the final shots.

Pre-production is also the point at which you define the assets you will need to create during production. For a full CG shot, this will include everything visible in the scene, including the camera, camera animation and digital environment. For a live-action shot, it will include a shot plate or green-screen element, which may need further paint-prep work (paint and preparation: for example, painting out wires or camera rigs visible in the shot), rotoscoping or match-moving.

It may also be necessary to construct a "digital extension" to the set. In addition, some types of assets—for example, digital characters, other foreground models and physics simulations—are common to both types of work.

For developers, pre-production is where you identify any major gaps in your pipeline and fix anything likely to bring the production to a halt later on. Perhaps a film is going to be heavy on character work and you know your rigging or animation pipelines are weak. Or perhaps you will need to implement a new technology: for example, to receive files in the Alembic data-interchange format in order to collaborate on a film with another studio. This is the time to put in as much preparation work as possible to make sure that your pipeline will handle the load later.

Section 2.8 Pre-Production in the Games Pipeline

In games development, the first task is often to define the "concept" of the game. This takes place before pre-production begins formally, and continues throughout this stage. The concept and genre of the game will play a factor in deciding what engine and pipeline choices are best for the task.

For example, not all games have stories as they would be understood in films—many games often only have a "progression structure". If story is important to the game, it will be necessary to create a script, storyboard and sets of rules governing things like characters' abilities and inventories. All of these will need to be supported by the pipeline.

It may also be necessary to evaluate new technologies. Though most web and mobile games are produced more quickly, it's not uncommon for AAA titles to go through a three-to-four-year development cycle, with the early stages involving an intense round of technology evaluations. For example, perhaps a new graphics technique developed by the academic community can now be attempted in real time, helping to shape the look of the game. Or perhaps other games have found ways to squeeze extra performance out of old hardware, requiring you to author content in a new way.

Meanwhile, the game design team will be busy on new gameplay elements. These elements need to be prototyped so they can be evaluated properly. Without a concrete implementation, it's often impossible to decide if a new feature will unbalance a game, or even if it can be realized at all.

Game pre-production often results in two different kinds of output, known as the "vertical slice" and the "horizontal slice". Each of these is intended to lay the foundation for a different aspect of the production work.

The horizontal slice consists of a broad set of gameplay features in a prototype environment known as a "white-box level". White-box

levels may include untextured assets, missing animations and very rough sound: their function is simply to get a feel for how gameplay will flow, or how long a game will take to complete. The result is a level that is playable from start to finish, blocked out with placeholder artwork or placeholder gameplay elements like puzzles. Since gameplay drives art, the more horizontal slices that can be created during pre-production, the less reworking of art content will be necessary later in production.

By contrast, a vertical slice consists of a small section of the game, often a single level or part of a level, authored as close to shippable quality as is possible. Its goal is to provide confidence in the development process itself, serving as a stress test for the pipeline and a benchmark for the quality of art assets.

The vertical slice is the gateway to production, pacifying producers and loosening their grips on their check books. The end-of-pre-production milestone is one of the major go/no-go decision points on the project, and there is every probability that a game with a lackluster demo will get canned rather than moving forward, or at least sent back into another round of pre-production.

Figure 2.2 A "vertical slice" is a small section of a game, authored as close to shippable quality as possible to convince management of the project's viability. By contrast, a "horizontal slice" is a larger section of the game, bulked out with placeholder assets, and is used to test gameplay.

A common goal at the end of pre-production is to produce a playable demo that can be released publicly to raise the profile of the game. This can only be achieved through the union of a horizontal slice (final-quality gameplay) with a vertical slice (final-quality assets).

In theory, until all the component pipelines are in place, not all of this data can be authored. In practice, some are less important than others. A prime example is what is referred to as "localization data": the information required to create a version of the game tailored to a particular language, including translations of on-screen text, new voice recordings, and even language-specific models or textures. However, although localization tends to be completed late in development, it's critically important to plan for it during pre-production so that all of the necessary assets can be collected later.

Section 2.9 Production: An Overview

During the production phase, the focus of the work shifts from planning to building. In both CG animation and games, where everything seen on screen is computer-generated, this means creating all the digital assets: the models, the textures, the control rigs the animators manipulate, and the animation data itself. (In contrast, in the world of visual effects, the term "production" typically refers only to the live shoot and the collection of on-set data: the digital assets themselves are created during post-production. We will explore this distinction later.)

Production is where team sizes ramp up. Whereas pre-production typically requires tens of artists, production may require hundreds. Production also typically generates a lot of data: usually orders of magnitude more than the relatively lightweight pre-production process. Pre-production is about broad strokes; production is about detail.

For this reason, while the early phases of production—building and storing assets—are similar for both games and CG animation, the later phases differ greatly. The divide occurs at the point at which individual assets are assembled into larger groups: in the case of an animation, when it enters shot production; in the case of a game, when level creation begins.

Here, hardware restrictions come into play. Even a modern-day console like the PlayStation 3 or the Xbox 360 is very limited in terms of memory and system resources compared to a PC. One of the many considerations involved in level design is how to cram all of the data the game requires into the storage space available. Go over budget, and the game simply will not work. In contrast, a scene from a feature animation is essentially unlimited in size: given enough computers—and enough time—it will be possible to render it.

A good pipeline has two key traits that help manage the chaos of full production: transparency and compartmentalization.

Transparency in a pipeline is analogous to Find and Replace functionality in a word processor: it enables the pipeline team to find problematic content automatically and update or fix it with minimal expenditure of precious artist time. In productions that encompass

hundreds of thousands of assets, it's critical that large-scale changes can be made without requiring individual assets to be rewritten manually.

For example, a change to the engine (in games) or the renderer (in film work) that occurs midway through production may change the way that assets look. This obliges the team to adjust those assets they have already created so that they are consistent with new content. Doing this manually is a production disaster—the entire art staff must drop their current tasks and start opening and reexporting files by the thousands. A transparent pipeline, on the other hand, will include tools or scripts to find and update content automatically.

Another key to success is compartmentalization. Rather than creating a giant, monolithic set of tools and processes all inextricably linked to one other, teams aim for a constellation of self-sustaining units that each do one thing well. Suppose—as happens quite often—that a change in the pipeline demands that animations need to be stored in a different format. Even with good transparency, reexporting all of the existing animations is a serious undertaking, requiring a considerable amount of time. However, if the pipeline has been compartmentalized well, the time taken can at least be minimized. Imagine that the same change required *every* asset—whether animated or not—to be reexported. It would bring the production to a standstill.

Section 2.10 Production in the Film Pipeline

In feature animation, production has multiple phases. Once the brief and story are finalized, the production of high-resolution assets begins. This includes the models, textures, environments, rigs and animation. Once these have been created, the next step is usually to assemble these assets into shots and building sequences, ready to render and composite. We will look at these individual processes in more detail in the next chapter.

During the production stage, the three most common tasks for pipeline developers are fixing bugs, adding new workflow features and optimizing existing ones. The new features may be details that were missed during the original development work, nice-to-have additions that you finally have time to work on, or subtle changes prompted by the way the tools are being used in the context of a real production.

Optimization is also important, particularly if a tool is slower than expected or needs to be used on more shots than anticipated. If a particular computational process is very slow, one common solution is to run it on the render farm rather than the artist's workstation. This frees up the workstation for more useful tasks, and means that the job can be distributed across many machines, reducing calculation times.

Once you identify a task that is being performed routinely in production, it makes sense to automate it via software. For example, it

is common practice for animators to export geometry caches—data files showing the position of each point on the model in each frame of the animation—for the lighting department to work on. Export is often done manually, and ties up the animator's workstation until it is complete. Automating the task so that it takes only a single click—and perhaps even executing the whole process on the render farm—frees up the animator to do more creative work.

Automation is also often necessary if it turns out that the assumptions you made during pre-production are wrong. For example, if the script calls for only two characters, it would be reasonable to assume that the animators will have time to export caches manually. If this is changed to two hundred during production, it's far better to automate the process.

Note that optimization and automation help push assets through the pipeline as efficiently as possible: they don't change its structure. Once the production stage begins, it's important to avoid making major changes that could bring work to a halt. While production is normally the busiest time for a facility, it is also the one in which you are least likely to be able to talk to key stakeholders to discuss pipeline changes. The focus at this point is on getting the film done.

Section 2.11 Production in the Games Pipeline

The production stage of a game is primarily about producing content: art assets, audio, gameplay elements, level designs, and so on. (Again, we will look at these processes in more detail in a later chapter.) The game team will expand as content creators are moved onto the project to churn through the vast quantity of assets required, and self-contained tasks such as creating cinematics—pre-rendered cutscenes, also sometimes released as trailers for the game—may be outsourced.

In theory, system programming and pipeline development should be completed during pre-production, content creation and assembly during production, and the remaining bugs fixed during finalling. In practice, this rarely happens. A pipeline may change quite significantly if the process of ramping up to full production reveals any weaknesses. It is also likely that the game's run-time will still be in development.

However, once you are in production, it is important to focus your attention on only the most important changes: generally, fixing the tools that generate the most complaints. Before building new tools or modifying existing ones, you should evaluate the relative cost of doing so: it may actually be better to use brute force and throw more artists at a task than to hold up production while you optimize a sub-optimal pipeline.

Section 2.12 Post-Production or Finalling: An Overview

Up until post-production (often simply called "post") or finalling, film and game pipelines are fairly similar. During this stage, they diverge radically. On an animated feature, the film will be nearly complete: the final images will have been rendered out and will be heading into the last stages of work before they are handed over to the client. (The same is not true of visual effects, as we shall discuss later.) But in games, some of the most technical work is yet to come, as bugs are fixed and art or gameplay problems resolved during finalling.

What post-production and finalling have in common is that they represent the last chance to improve a product. When the audience views your work, no one will care that you could have done better if you'd had more time. This stage is your final opportunity to make those tweaks that can rescue a failing movie, or turn a good game into a great one.

Even once a project is finally complete, there is no rest for the weary. This is the time for a postmortem of the show, evaluating what went well and what didn't, and to apply those lessons to the next project. It is also the time to do "blue-sky" work, such as evaluating new graphics technologies; and to make changes too fundamental to implement during production, such as switching to a new database system. This is when pipeline developers should be busiest—not on the project in post-production, but on the one about to enter the building.

Section 2.13 Post-Production in the Film Pipeline

Strictly, post-production refers only to those tasks that are carried out once the final images have been created. Under this definition, the only true post-production tasks are those like editing, dimensionalization (DM), digitizing footage to create a digital intermediate (DI), color correction or "grading", mastering, and film-out: printing the digital images to film for distribution to cinemas. This is the sense in which the term is commonly used in feature animation.

However, in live-action film-making, the term is commonly used differently. Most visual effects professionals use the term "production" to refer only to the live shoot and the collection of any data recorded on set, and "post-production" to refer to anything that comes after that—including the bulk of the visual effects work.

Under this definition, most of the art team's work happens during post-production. The same asset-creation processes—modeling, texture painting, rigging, animation, and so on—that take place during

the production of an animated feature also take place on live-action films, but during the post-production stage, as part of the visual effects. Again, we will look at these individual processes in more detail in the next chapter.

But no matter whether you consider asset creation to be part of production or post-production, post is the last chance you have to refine the images you have created. Many facilities never use the term "final" to describe a shot until it has been handed over to the client: they consider that, if time allows, they may be able to carry on tweaking it right up until the delivery deadline, and that, instead, it should be considered as "CBB" (Could Be Better).

There are three constraints on whether these tweaks can actually be made: budget, time and continuity. Continuity is important since a shot is not approved in isolation, but in the context of the entire film, so changes made to one shot may necessitate further changes in others.

For this reason, it is generally more productive to move as many shots as possible towards completion than it is to focus on polishing a single one. It's better to get an entire sequence "75 percent complete" and review all of the shots in context than to get a single shot "99 percent complete" but risk running out of time to bring the rest up to the same standard of quality.

Whether you have time to make a change may depend on how many steps of the visual effects process are involved in the feedback loop. It's easier to change the lighting of a shot than it is to change its layout, since the former only requires you to render and composite it again, whereas the latter may also require you to change the lighting and effects simulations.

As a result, a film tends to go out of production department by department: for example, the layout pipeline will usually settle down earlier than lighting and compositing. On large productions, where work is being split between multiple facilities, each with its own specialty, the same thing may happen with the facilities themselves: a company that specializes in fluid simulation will finish earlier than one that specializes in dimensionalization, for example.

Section 2.14 Finalling in the Games Pipeline

The process of finalling a game mirrors that of software development, where a nearly finished product is turned over to the QA (Quality Assurance) department for "bulletproofing". As well as the developer's own in-house quality checks, console titles must pass a formal QA process run by the console manufacturer to prevent low-quality games from reflecting badly on the hardware. But unlike bulletproofing, finalling is driven by artistic as well as technical concerns: as well as the quality of the code, the QA team must consider the quality of the data that ships alongside it.

As early as possible in the process, the game should be packaged and tested on its final media. Mastering—the process of laying out the assets on a DVD or Blu-ray—can throw up a number of problems that weren't obvious earlier: not least, that the files may simply be too large to fit. It may also be necessary to burn a separate disc for every territory in which the game is to be distributed, each containing a different set of localization data. These should be tested individually, since it is easy for bugs only to manifest under certain conditions.

Although the restrictions on file size may not be absolute, the same applies to games that are to be distributed digitally. Poor digital distribution can destroy the profitability of a product: if it takes the user more than a few hours to download a game, many simply will not bother. To get around this issue, some companies use live streaming solutions that enable users to begin playing before the entire game has downloaded. This kind of distribution model should be built into the pipeline from day one, since implementing a streaming system once a game is complete is incredibly error-prone and may require assets to be reworked extensively.

At the start of finalling, the game will be complete, but have many bugs. Some of these will reflect problems with the code, resulting in crashes or poor frame rates. Others will reflect problems with the art assets: for example, holes in a physics mesh that allow a character to fall through the world, or individual polygons that have flipped inside out, causing graphical glitches. All of these problems must be identified and fixed.

This is usually done in a series of formal steps, often known as "milestones". While the exact definitions vary from developer to developer, the following milestones are generally recognized:

Alpha: Alpha means the game is formally complete and can theoretically be played all the way through. Much of the artwork will be placeholders, performance will usually be well below predicted frame rates, and there will be plenty of bugs, but the game still exists in skeleton form. Alphas are typically internal milestones, negotiated between a studio and the game's publisher.

Content complete: Content complete generally means that placeholders have been replaced by, in the loosest sense of the term, shippable—though not polished or bug-free—versions of the final assets. Realistic constraints on memory and run-time performance are now being respected, and early assets have often been trimmed back dramatically in the interests of efficiency. Story arcs and the basic flow of the game are now regarded as locked; graphic tweaks are still going on but (in theory, at least) no new cinematics, characters, or gameplay areas will be added. Once a project hits its content-complete milestone, it's common for some of the production staff to begin moving on to other projects. Some of the artists remain for bug fixes or polishing, but the focus is on perfecting existing assets, not creating new ones.

Beta: By beta, all of the gameplay content is complete, and the game is in a shippable form, both in terms of resource use and the quality of the assets. There are still issues to resolve, but the game is now basically a buggy version of the final release, rather than a suggestion of it. Beta is also the time when play-tests and public demonstrations of the project are at their height. Professional testers, either in-house or provided by the publisher, will be working the game continuously, probing for flaws and inconsistencies. Some games also have "open beta" programs, where a select group of customers is allowed to play the game: partly in order to generate positive word-of-mouth, partly to get last-minute feedback that can help tweak the design, and partly to spot bugs that have slipped by the professional testers.

For the content team, the beta period is a mixture of optimization, polishing and bug fixing. Optimizing assets to make them more efficient at run-time can be painful, since fitting an asset into a smaller amount of memory often involves a loss of visual quality. Therefore, the pipeline should provide analysis and tracking tools to help identify the "low-hanging fruit": assets that can be cut completely because they are under-utilized, or those whose memory footprint is out of proportion to their real importance.

Although by beta no placeholder assets remain, there is typically scope to give the game some graphical polish. Assets that were built hastily, or without a proper context, can now be tweaked to match the overall feel of the game. Since by now the limitations of the engine should be well understood, it is often possible to create better-looking assets with the same run-time cost.

Of course, dealing with bugs remains the highest priority during beta. Because of the deluge of feedback, this is the point at which good communication is most essential, in order to direct the (slowly shrinking) production team towards the right problems. The pipeline's bug-tracking, task-assignment, and error-checking features are tested to their limits during beta.

Final: The finalling phase is often emotionally anticlimatic. As the game heads towards final certification from the publisher—and thence to manufacturing or online release—it is common to lock down the content: no new assets may be added to the game, while changes are only permissible to fix reported bugs. This is partly so that assets can be signed off (especially important with licensed titles, where it may be necessary to go through several rounds of approval), and partly because *any* change, no matter how innocuous, carries a very real risk of generating knock-on bugs. (An extra byte of memory used by a model can literally be the difference between a game working flawlessly and crashing constantly.)

As time goes on, fewer and fewer developers are allowed to touch the game at all. Well before the game is certified final, most of the artists have moved on to other projects—or to spend long-overdue time

with their families—and the team is reduced to a skeleton of senior people who have the authority to make last-minute changes. The message that the game has "gone gold" and is now ready for duplication and distribution often arrives at an office that is nearly deserted.

Of course, there are entire genres of games that are never "final" in the traditional sense. Persistent online games, from titanic productions like *World of Warcraft* to modest educational titles, are perpetually being updated and expanded. As a persistent-world project approaches a major release—which could be an engine change, a special in-game event, or the opening of a new gameplay area—it goes through the same QA process as a traditional boxed product.

With their very long lifespans, and constant trickle of minor updates, pipelines themselves resemble online games. Some developers take comfort in the knowledge that today's misstep can be corrected by next week's update, but smarter companies realize that legacy issues can be a burden for a very long time, and test accordingly. Pipeline developers, who face the same problem on a smaller scale, would do well to learn from their example.

2A

INTERLUDE: PREVIS AND RELATED DATA

Ron Frankel
Founder & Creative Director, Proof, Inc.

Previs entered the film production world through visual effects in the early Nineties. The idea was to leverage the same high-end computer graphics hardware and software that was being used to create ground-breaking visual effects in post-production, but to harness that power in the early stages of pre-production as a design and planning tool. Looking at low resolution models and simple animation, the film-makers could engage in an iterative design process, testing ideas, seeing what worked and what didn't, all long before the painstaking work of visual effects had even begun.

Previs follows the exact same process today, but the advances in computer hardware and software have allowed previs artists to apply their skills to even larger portions of the film-making process. What started off as one or two previs artists working on a few shots is now a highly specialized team comprising a dozen or more artists working for months to create incredibly complex animatics that replicate the action, look, mood and tone of the film. On a typical VFX-driven tentpole, the previs team might visualize an hour or more of the film, all in a fast, iterative environment that allows the film-makers to easily make changes and experiment with new ideas.

Whether it's a blockbuster studio picture or a more moderately budgeted film, previs follows the same basic steps:
- Create accurate, but low-resolution, 3D models of the necessary assets such as characters, creatures, sets, props, vehicles, etc.
- Animate the action
- Add cameras to cover the action
- Output the cameras, using either hardware or software rendering
- Edit the coverage to create an animatic
- Add sound effects, if desired
- Review, revise and repeat!

This work is frequently done in the film production offices. Proximity to the creative decision makers is essential, so a previs company like Proof will embed a team of artists to work alongside the

film-makers. If the production travels, then the previs team travels with them. That might mean going to a different city, but it could also require the artists to travel to a different state or country. Therefore it is important that the previs team maintains a small footprint so they can remain agile and move easily.

A typical setup includes a workstation for each artist, a shared server, a back-up drive and networking hardware. The workstations are loaded with all the software the artists might need plus a library of useful 3D models and animation. Most feature film previs is created with Maya, but other modeling and animation packages can be used as well. The workstations will also have Photoshop, Illustrator and video editing software. Larger previs teams will frequently keep a few extra workstations on hand that can function as a render farm or editorial workstation. The whole setup can be taken down and set back up in a matter of hours.

Previs occupies a unique position within a film production. It exists on the boundaries, between a variety of departments. To be effective, the previs team needs to accurately represent and reflect the specific circumstances that the production will encounter when they begin filming. For example, the previs camera that the artists use must match the specs of the actual film camera, including aperture size, aspect ratio and lenses. Sets need to match those being designed by the art department and locations need to be built as they exist in the real world.

To accomplish this, the previs team needs to go to the various film production departments and gather as much information as is available. Not every production has everything on this list, and some of this data is only available after the start of principal photography, so the information gathering is an on-going process that incorporates data as it becomes available. Below is a breakdown of what the previs team gathers, and whom it comes from.

- Production (Director and Producer)
  - Script pages (PDF; approx. 10 MB)
  - Storyboards in physical and/or digital form (JPG, PDF; approx. 250 MB)
  - Audio files for temp score or sound effects
- Art Department
  - Concept Art (JPG; approx. 100 MB)
  - Reference Images (JPG; approx. 100 MB)
  - Location photos (JPG; approx. 100 MB)
  - Dimensions for sound stages (DWG, PDF; approx. 10 MB)
  - 2D set designs in physical and/or digital form (DWG, PDF; approx. 50 MB)
  - 3D models of environments, props, vehicles, etc. (various 3D formats including SKP, OBJ, 3DM, MA; approx. 500 MB)
- Camera Department
  - Camera specs for shooting (e.g. frame rate, aspect ratio, resolution)

- Camera aperture (film) or sensor size (digital) and a complete list of lenses
- Details for any specific camera equipment to be used such as cranes, jib arms, cable cams, motion control rigs, etc.
- Visual Effects
  - LIDAR data (OBJ or MA; approx. 1 GB)
  - 3D models of characters, creatures, environments, props, vehicles, etc. from VFX vendors (MA, OBJ; approx. 10 GB)
  - Matte paintings from VFX vendors (PSD, TIF; approx. 500 MB)
- Stunts
  - Rehearsal footage (MOV; approx. 100 MB)
- Editorial
  - Rough edits (MOV; approx. 50 GB)
  - Principal photography plates (MOV; approx. 100 GB)

Additionally, during the initial data dump there are conversations about specific difficulties or issues the production foresees. Those concerns inform what shots or sequences the previs team will approach first. Armed with all of the available information, the team starts the process of modeling, animating, rendering and editing. Although it varies wildly depending on the complexity of the shots, it isn't uncommon for a team of four artists to produce 1-2 minutes of animation per week. Over the course of an entire production that translates into thousands of individual shots and hundreds of edited sequences requiring terabytes of storage.

Over the course of a single project the basic output of a previs team is:

- Scene Files (MA; approx. 500 GB)
- Movies (MOV; approx. 250 GB)
- Diagrams (PDF; approx. 100 MB)
- KeyFrames (JPG, PDF; approx. 100 MB)
- 3D models (MA; approx. 10 GB)

Scene files: The action described in the script or storyboards is divided into sections ranging from a few seconds to a few minutes. Each section is animated and saved as a Maya scene file. Within that scene file will be all the characters, creatures, props, vehicles and environments that comprise the essence of the action being described. The scene file will also contain numerous cameras to cover the action. In some cases there might be only one or two cameras per scene file, while in others there might be dozens.

Movies: Each camera in a Maya scene file is output as a Quicktime movie. These movies, also called shots, range in duration from a few frames to a minute or more. The shots are edited together to create sequences that last from a few seconds to over twenty minutes. Sound effects and temp scores are often added to the edit to help convey mood, tone and emotion. The film-makers review the sequences, and the previs team makes revisions, until the work is approved and distributed to the relevant department heads.

Figure 2.1 Interlude Previs helps resolve practical problems during live shoots. For *The Adjustment Bureau*, Proof, Inc. designed a practical camera move that followed the actors as they descended from the upper to the lower rooftop. The move used a SuperTechno crane and a small set piece designed by Kevin Thompson's Art Department. A critical part of the setup was determining the ideal height of the camera platform so the camera could reach the highest and lowest points of the move. © 2011 Universal.

Copies might be sent to the studio executives or to the VFX vendors responsible for the final work.

Diagrams: In certain instances the shots are represented as diagrams, created in a 2D program such as Photoshop or Illustrator. Diagrams are essentially blueprints describing the location of the camera and its path of travel. The diagrams might also document distances, speeds, positions of actors or vehicles and any other relevant production data. Shot diagrams are useful because even in the age of smartphones and iPads it is still far easier to distribute, review and annotate a piece of paper than it is a Quicktime file.

Keyframes: The edited sequences are frequently reduced to a series of still frames, because PDF files are easier to distribute, share and print. The keyframes are often seen on-set and are sometimes posted on large boards that are used as a guide for the day's shoot schedule.

3D Models: As the project winds down the previs team will package individual assets as well as complete scene files to be delivered to the various VFX vendors. In some instances, the visual effects will be awarded to a vendor before the project starts and the previs team can work with the vendor to ensure that scene

scale and orientation are consistent between the previs and vendor's pipeline. That's rarely the case, so the previs team goes to great lengths to ensure that the scene files are clean and well-organized so that whoever inherits the work will have an easier time working with it.

Within the film production environment there is very little in the way of DAM (Digital Asset Management), both in terms of people overseeing the data sharing process and in terms of software to track versions and changes. As digital tools become more powerful and as artists become more sophisticated there will be even more opportunities for data sharing. 3D models already move with ease and frequency between previs and the art department. Visual effects vendors occasionally hand assets over to previs as a way to test designs and to ensure that the previs conforms to their pipeline specifications. As this kind of inter-departmental cooperation and collaboration continues to develop, digital asset managers and DAM software will become an indispensable part of the film production process.

ASSET CREATION FOR FILM

Tim Green; Matt Hoesterey; Hannes Ricklefs; Mark Streatfield; Steve Theodore; Laurent M. Abecassis; Di-O- Matic; Huseyin Caner: *Head of Film and Entertainment Team, Plowman Craven Ltd.;* **Dr. Ken Museth:** *Supervisor and Principle Engineer of R&D in FX, DreamWorks Animation;* **Katherine Roberts:** *CG Supervisor, Double Negative*

Section 3.1 What You Will Learn From This Chapter

In the previous chapter, we examined the different stages of production. In this chapter, we will focus on the process of creating assets: the digital elements that make up a film or game. While the way in which assets are created is similar in both industries, there are also crucial differences. For that reason, we will only look at film work here. In the next chapter, we will explore how games pipelines differ.

Asset development for films is split across all three stages of production. Concept art, maquettes (physical sculptures of characters or creatures, used as a concept tool, or for 3D scanning), storyboards and previs are all created during pre-production. What happens next depends on whether the film is an animated feature or live action with visual effects.

On a visual effects movie, the only assets created during production are those captured on set. These may include LIDAR scans of the environment, lighting data and reference photography. On a feature animation, production is where the bulk of the digital assets, such as models, textures, rigs, FX and animation data, are created. Visual effects projects require a similar set of assets but—as we discussed in the previous chapter—this work is usually held to take place during post-production. In addition, VFX projects require types of assets that feature animations do not, such as camera-tracking data and prepared background plates.

In this chapter, we will look briefly at how each of these types of asset is created. Rather than providing a detailed guide to each process, the aim is to provide a high-level overview from the perspective of pipeline design, and to introduce technical concepts that you may encounter later in the book.

We will also be listing some of the key tools used for these tasks. Although many large facilities rely on their own proprietary software,

others use commercial tools, often augmented by custom plug-ins and scripts. This chapter is not intended as a complete list of the products currently available: only a brief guide to those most commonly used for feature animation and VFX.

Many facilities use an application with a wide range of capabilities as their principal 3D package, employing it for several of the tasks involved in asset creation. Such "all-round" packages include those developed by Autodesk—Maya, 3 ds Max and Softimage, which hold the majority share in this market—and those from smaller developers, such as Houdini, LightWave, EIAS and Cinema 4D. However, it is increasingly common for facilities to operate "heterogeneous" pipelines, which bring together a number of more specialist tools tailored to individual tasks.

Before we begin, it may be helpful to list the tasks we will be looking at here:

Carried out on set:

- Data capture (LIDAR, lighting data, reference photography)

Carried out in the facility:

- Processing the live footage (plate preparation, rotoscoping, camera tracking)
- Modeling
- Texture and shader creation
- Layout
- Rigging
- Animation
- FX
- Lighting
- Compositing

This is a simplified version of a real production pipeline: for a more detailed version, refer to the flowchart in Chapter 1. While the tasks are listed in roughly chronological order, it is important to note that many overlap; and that rather than being a linear process, asset development is cyclical, consisting of a series of iterative loops. One of the most important of these loops is "look development" or "look dev", in which the visual style of characters, creatures and props—including their geometry, textures, hair and fur, and sometimes the range of motion that their character rig is capable of generating—is refined prior to passing the asset through to shot layout.

Now let's look at each task in more detail. We will begin with the one that takes place earliest during production: collecting data on set.

Section 3.2 LIDAR and On-Set Survey Data

Huseyin Caner, Head of Film and Entertainment, Plowman Craven Ltd
Katherine Roberts, CG supervisor, Double Negative

Measuring tools like "total stations" (an instrument used in surveying for measuring angles and distances) and GPS (Global Positioning

Systems) have been used in the film industry for several decades. However with the introduction of LIDAR scanners in the late 1990s, geospatial data can now be used more effectively in the production of visual effects shots.

LIDAR scanning involves using a laser source to measure the distance from a fixed location to points on surrounding rigid surfaces (for example, buildings). This data is stored as a "point cloud"—a series of disconnected points in 3D space—which may be converted into a three-dimensional model of the set, and can be used to create accurate digital backgrounds for visual effects shots, set extensions or to improve the accuracy of camera tracking.

Figure 3.1 Used widely in visual effects work since the late 1990s, LIDAR scanners (left) enable productions to record sets and reconstruct them as digital 3D geometry, ready for effects work. The image on the right shows a scan of London's Houses of Parliament, used in the opening ceremony for the 2012 Olympic Games. Images courtesy of Plowman Craven Ltd.

However, LIDAR data is not the only data captured on set. The lighting department may require chrome or gray ball data (images of reflective and matte spheres photographed on set, used as reference by artists trying to recreate the same lighting conditions digitally) and HDRIs (High Dynamic Range Images). Digital photography can also be used to capture images that will later be used to create texture maps—or simply used as additional reference data.

When performing a LIDAR scan, it is important to capture any relevant metadata. Much of this auxiliary data, such as which "take" the scan represents, is collected on set using pen and paper or a digital hand-held device, on appropriate data-entry sheets. At the end of each day, this data must be sorted and entered into an on-set database.

Other raw reference material must be sorted and transferred in a similar way. It is imperative that the cameras used to collect reference material are calibrated correctly, so that time stamps match, ideally with synchronized time code. This ensures that the data synchronizes properly with other reference sources, such as "witness cameras" used to record the set from other angles. Since cameras can also record the position from which a picture was taken, this locates

the reference material in time and 3D space, making it possible to perform queries such as: "Show me all images taken three days ago within a 100 m radius of this point."

It is often useful to include a reference object of known dimensions to give an idea of the scale of the set being scanned. However, LIDAR scanners are survey-grade instruments, so this is sometimes taken care of automatically during setup: Leica Geosystems hardware has a very robust calibration procedure, so as long as the processing software is set to a known unit of measurement like feet or meters, the scale will be correct. It is also important to have a reference object in the final digital data as a final "sense check", in case the processing software and the vendor's art software are set to different units. Knowing the coordinate system of the art software is also useful: Maya, for example, likes to work in the Y-up coordinate system (in which the Y-axis in the software represents vertical height), so data is translated to the Y-up coordinate space.

You should also prioritize the areas to be scanned in order of their probable importance in the visual effects work. If time is limited, you may need to consider a "selective resolution approach" where important areas are captured at high resolution; others at lower resolution. However, always try to capture the entire scene at high resolution where possible. It is easy to reduce the resolution of data later, but the reverse is impossible!

After scanning is complete, the next step is to make backup copies of the scans. Always keep a copy of the raw data, sending it straight to archive without any processing. However, LIDAR technicians should be aware that their scanners are capable of recording billions of points, resulting in gigabytes of data. For this reason, it is helpful to deliver the data to the visual effects facility at multiple resolutions. This can be achieved through "decimation" algorithms that reduce the number of triangles that make up the 3D surface generated from the point-cloud data, while still preserving its overall form. The biggest challenge is correctly aligning the individual scans. Most LIDAR manufacturers provide software of some sort for this kind of work, although at present there are no fully automated solutions. Your ultimate goal is to provide the data in a form that will enable visual effects artists to do their jobs as quickly and efficiently as possible. Consider delivering three versions: 10 percent decimated, 50 percent decimated, and the original high-resolution scan data for reference.

Because human memories fade quickly, organizing and managing all of this data is a very important part of the data-acquisition process. Given the amount of information generated by a typical survey, without strict guidelines as to how data is entered into the on-set database, it would be almost impossible to find the relevant information. The most important thing is to define a file-naming convention to avoid any confusion as the project progresses. This is usually relatively straightforward when it comes to scans of the set itself, but

becomes a challenge when it comes to props or actors, which may also be scanned on set.

Once delivered to the VFX facility, all of this data must be resorted so that it appears in the facility's asset-management system in a form that is easy for staff to navigate. This involves remapping the data from the on-set database (which is date-ordered) to the facility's database, which is usually structured by shot or asset type. We will explore the issue of data structures in more detail in a later chapter.

For a more detailed discussion of on-set capture, see the Interlude "LIDAR asset capture on set".

Section 3.3 Match-Moving, Rotoscoping and Plate Preparation

Match-moving, rotoscoping and plate preparation happen early in the pipeline, preparing the plates for use by 3D artists and compositors. Although carried out early on during the asset-creation process, they can impact greatly on the success of the finished shot.

Match-moving is the process of creating a digital camera for use within the 3D art software that matches the movements (the translation and rotation) of the real camera. The digital assets the studio creates may then be rendered through this digital camera, ensuring that they match the live footage seamlessly. This process is automated using image-processing techniques, usually with some manual tweaking of the automatic "solve"; but very complex shots may require that the camera position is matched manually frame by frame. Tools commonly used for match-moving include those built into a facility's 3D or compositing software, and specialist applications like 3DEqualizer, boujou and SynthEyes.

Rotoscoping (or "roto-animation") requires an artist to draw or trace mattes (flat masks) around key elements (such as characters, props or scenery) in a live-action plate. These elements are usually divided up into layers representing objects at different distances from the camera, making it easy to composite rendered 3D elements into the plate. For example, to insert a rendered layer between the background scenery and a foreground character, a matte is rotoscoped around the character, isolating it from the background. This allows the character to be composited over the rendered layer. Tools commonly used for rotoscoping include those built into compositing software such as Nuke and Fusion, and specialist applications like Silhouette and mocha.

Plate preparation (or simply "prep") is the process of preparing the live-action plate for compositing, and comprises a mixture of tasks. The most common are rig and wire removal (painting out on-set structures visible in shot, particularly parts of the stunt and camera rigs), removing noise, dust and film grain, and removing lens distortion ("flattening" the plate by removing the circular distortion introduced by the camera lens,

most evident at the corners of the image). These tasks make the plates easier for the compositors to work with. However, some of these elements (particularly noise, film grain and lens distortion) must be reintroduced during the final composite to avoid the unnaturally perfect look of CG images, ensuring that shots with visual effects match those without. Facilities commonly use the same tools for plate preparation as they do for compositing work. We will discuss compositing later.

Section 3.4 Modeling

Modeling is the process of creating the digital 3D geometry used in animation and visual effects work, referred to as "models" or "meshes". Typically, a modeler is responsible only for recreating the overall three-dimensional form of an object: its surface properties, including its local color and small irregularities such as bumps and scratches, are represented by texture maps and shaders—something we shall discuss later in this chapter.

In addition to recreating the form of an object accurately, the modeler is responsible for ensuring that its topology is correct. This includes making sure that the polygons from which the mesh is constructed follow the underlying "flow" of the geometry, and are of an appropriate size and shape. Modeling practices vary slightly from facility to facility, but in general, modelers try to ensure that the "density" of polygons is roughly even across the surface of the mesh, and that the model is constructed largely or entirely of four-sided polygons, or "quads". Meshes that contain unevenly sized polygons, or large numbers of polygons with more than four sides, may cause surface textures to distort, or may deform oddly when animated.

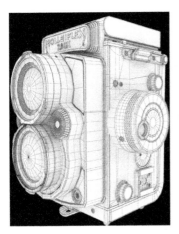 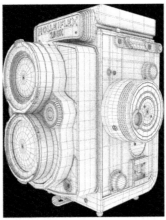 

Figure 3.2 A model with poor topology (left) and the same model with the topology corrected (center). Note how much more evenly the polygons are distributed. Models with poor topology may render correctly in still images (right), but often deform oddly when animated. Images courtesy of Anton Perlov, artist "Stubborn3D" at TurboSquid.

It may also be necessary to ensure that a model stays below a maximum polygon count, to make it quicker to manipulate and render. This issue is more significant in games than film work, so we will examine it in detail in the next chapter.

Models may be created semi-automatically by scanning real objects, or by reconstructing the geometry from reference photographs: a process known as "photogrammetry". Again, we will discuss this in more detail in the next chapter.

However, the majority of models used in animation and visual effects work are created by hand—or at least modified by hand. The tools used for this work vary according to whether the asset is a "hard-surface" model, such as a building or vehicle, or an organic model, such as a character or creature. To create hard-surface models, facilities tend to use the tools built into their principal 3D art package, or specialist CAD (Computer Aided Design) software. Organic models tend to be created using specialist applications that provide a workflow more like traditional sculpting, including ZBrush and Mudbox.

Section 3.5 Shaders and Textures

To reproduce the look of an object, 3D software relies on shaders: sets of computational instructions that determine how that object should be rendered to generate the final image. Shaders mimic the way in which materials react to light, creating mathematical representations of properties such as surface color and surface reflectivity. They range in scale from the very simple to the dauntingly complex, and may accurately reproduce the behavior of light or create effects driven entirely by artistry and imagination.

Since to describe the way in which material properties vary across an object's surface solely by writing code would be incredibly time-consuming, 3D software enables artists to create "texture maps". These are 2D images representing the value of a material property at each point on the surface of a model, and may be created by manipulating digital photographs, by painting them by hand, as the result of a computational calculation in a shader, or a combination of the three.

The set of maps created for an art asset varies from pipeline to pipeline. However, common map types include diffuse (the surface color of the model), bump (used to mimic fine surface details, such as bumps and wrinkles) and specular (used to control the form of the highlights on the object's surface). Other types of map are generated by the 3D software itself. These include the normal map (a special form of bump map, often used to give a low-resolution version of a model the appearance of a higher-resolution version) and the ambient occlusion map (used to represent the extent to which surrounding geometry blocks bounced light from striking each point on a surface).

The process of determining how the 2D texture map is displayed across the surface of a 3D model is known as "UV mapping". This may involve simply "projecting" a texture map onto the model as though it were a geometric object such as a plane, cylinder or sphere; or—as is more common for complex organic objects—"unwrapping" the surface to break it down into flat "shells" to which textures may be applied. This arrangement of shells is known as the "UV layout". The 3D paint package Mari, widely used in modern production work, further subdivides the layout into square tiles: a system known as "UDIM".

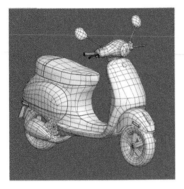 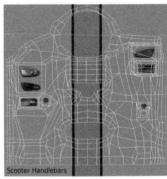 

Figure 3.3 The process of texturing a model. Left: the untextured geometry. Center: the geometry "unwrapped" to form a UV layout, used as a guide for creating texture maps, such as those for the scooter's headlights. Right: a render of the model showing the completed textures. Images courtesy of Michele Bousquet, TurboSquid.

UV mapping is dependent on both the form and the topology of a 3D model, and textures are in turn dependent on the UV layout. This can be a headache for the pipeline team, since changes to the model can invalidate some or all of the UV mapping, and hence any textures that follow those UV layouts. Some teams try to avoid this problem by mandating that texturing can't begin until the model has been carefully vetted, although this often makes it difficult to iterate on the look of an asset. Others create tools which can transfer the textures from one version of the model to another with different UVs—a process which rarely produces perfect results but can at least ease the pain of redoing work. Still others turn to texture-mapping systems that do not require UV assignment, such as the "Ptex" system, in which a separate texture is assigned to every face of a mesh. However, this is not currently supported in as wide a range of commercial 3D tools as UV mapping.

Tools commonly used for texture work include Photoshop, which is used in conjunction with UV mapping tools; and 3D painting packages such as Mari and BodyPaint, which enable the artist to paint directly onto the surface of the model, reducing the need to deal with UV mapping.

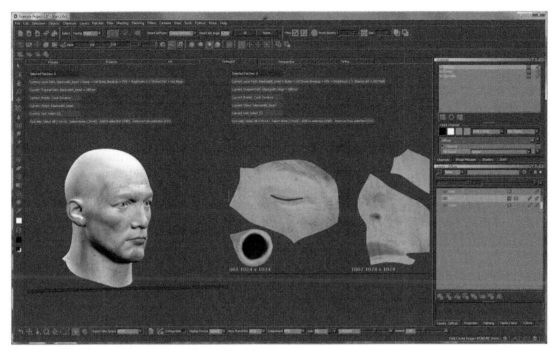

Figure 3.4 3D paint tools like Mari enable artists to create textures by painting directly onto the surface of the model, reducing the need to deal with UV mapping. Image © 2013 by The Foundry.

While texture maps are usually created by non-technical artists, shaders are usually authored by technical artists or programmers. These are an elite caste of specialists who combine high-end mathematical skills with artistic ability: they need to be able to program complex simulations, but also to make artistically inspired compromises when hardware constraints demand them.

For pipeline developers, it is important to note that real-time shaders (used to display an asset on screen within the art software itself) are quite different in implementation from offline shaders (used to render the final images), even if the underlying graphics algorithms are identical. Real-time shaders are limited by the capabilities of the hardware on which the software is run (particularly those of the GPU, or Graphics Processing Unit); offline shaders can be arbitrarily complex. We will explore this distinction in more detail in the next chapter.

In many ways, the relationship between shaders and art assets is one of the most critical dependencies in any production. Changes to shader code can easily change the look of rendered assets, while changes to the geometry or texture maps may also change the output of the shader.

Section 3.6 Shot Layout

The individual assets that make up a shot must be combined into a single 3D scene, ready for rendering. This is known as "shot layout" or "shot assembly". During this process, a layout artist will ensure that the digital characters, props and environments are positioned correctly in virtual space; and that the digital cameras are positioned to display the action correctly when the scene is rendered. In visual effects work, the 3D scene may be combined with the plates or with reference images captured on set to ensure that the digital elements match the live footage.

Layout enables a facility to visualize and adjust a digital set, planning camera locations and movements, and eliminating geometry that will never be seen by these cameras in order to make the scene faster to manipulate and render. It also ensures continuity between sequences: for example, so that a character who jumped from a castle wall in an earlier shot isn't seen back on top of the battlements, or that the horse he rode in on doesn't change color from shot to shot.

Since layout begins before all of the final assets for a shot have been developed, artists rely on low-resolution placeholder models that will be replaced with the high-resolution geometry later, and basic "blocking" animations in place of the final versions. This workflow creates dependencies between the two versions of each asset that must be managed by the pipeline team.

Furthermore, layout determines the file names for almost all the 3D assets. Being able to talk about the same file all the way from layout to compositing avoids a lot of confusion.

Section 3.7 Rigging

The "rig" is the core of the animator's toolkit—or at least, the character animator's toolkit. While simple objects, such as lights and cameras, can be animated by manipulating them directly within the facility's art software, it would be far too time-consuming to animate more complex models by moving every point on the mesh individually. Instead, artists create a simpler underlying structure, or "skeleton", and a set of controls to manipulate it. When the skeleton moves, the parts of the model to which it is bound move with it, making it easier to get the character into the pose required. Together, the skeleton and its controls comprise the character rig.

Rigs aren't just for organic models: they can also be created to control complex hard-surface models such as vehicles or machinery. However, the rigs for creatures and characters will usually be the most complex a facility creates.

A typical character rig used in visual effects work has three components. First, there is the skeleton itself. This is made up of rigid elements that, by analogy to real anatomy, are usually known as "bones". It is the

rigging artist's job to determine how these bones are linked together. Two technical terms commonly encountered here are Forward Kinematics (FK) and Inverse Kinematics (IK). In FK animation, a chain of bones, such as those controlling an arm, is posed by rotating each bone individually (in the case of the arm, this might be the upper arm, forearm and hand); in IK animation, an animator manipulates the end of the chain and the other bones follow along automatically (in the case of the arm, this would mean that when the animator moves the character's hand, the forearm and upper arm are dragged along with it). The rigger also sets up "constraints": a form of control that enables bones to be manipulated directly regardless of their relationships to other bones. For example, rotating the arm will normally cause the hand to rotate in turn, but it is possible to "constrain" the hand so that it keeps its original orientation regardless of what the rest of the arm does. Constraints enable animators to operate in a frame of reference that makes sense for a particular job—for example, to keep a character's head looking at a target even as its body moves.

Second, there is the "puppet rig". Although it is quicker to pose a character by moving bones than it is to move every point on the model's surface, this can still be a fiddly and time-consuming process. For this reason, facilities usually create a set of external controls around the character that an animator can manipulate more easily. These external controls direct the movement of the bones which, in turn, direct the movement of the mesh surface. This is a complex chain of computation, so the challenge when designing a puppet rig is to make it sophisticated enough to give the animators all the controls they need, but simple enough that they can continue to work in real time.

Third, there are the parts of the rig that determine how the skeleton affects the mesh surface. The rigger controls which points on the mesh surface are affected by an individual bone, and to what extent: a process known as "skinning" or setting up "skin weights". However, to simulate more complex secondary movements, such as the way muscles bulge and slide over one another, the rig may contain separate muscle set-ups, or may trigger "blend shapes"—complex deformations to the mesh surface, usually created by editing the model inside a digital sculpting package.

As well as providing controls for the animator, a rig may generate data used by other departments, such as FX or lighting. For this reason, the task of creating rigs is usually handled by dedicated specialists. Good rigging artists have a strong understanding of anatomy combined with programming and scripting skills: although rigging may be performed within the facility's principal 3D software, it is usually necessary to create custom tools.

Rigging presents a special challenge for the pipeline team because it is a field in which the problem of dependency management becomes particularly acute. A character rig is typically used in a variety of different animations. If the skeleton is simply copied from existing files into new ones over the course of the project, it is likely that different shots

will go out of sync. To make sure that skeletons stay consistent, many studios use "referencing"—a common function in 3D software that creates a live link between two files so that changes to one file are automatically propagated to the second. However, this means that changes to the master skeleton file can ripple out across the entire production, often with unforseeable consequences.

Like skeletons, rig control setups can be distributed by copying or by referencing—with similar pitfalls. Furthermore, rig controls are usually created by augmenting the tools provided in the facility's principal 3D software with custom scripts. Like anything created by writing custom codes, this means that they are often buggy and will require updating over the course of a production. It is important that the pipeline team manage this process in a way that allows for iterative improvements to the rigs without endangering the production schedule.

The pipeline can also make life easier for riggers and animators by providing good metadata and dependency-tracking services. For example, a team that relies on referencing to distribute rigs is well advised to track the flow of references using a database so that riggers can efficiently check the results of any changes they make—and if necessary, reprocess any downstream files that have been invalidated. It is also useful for animators to be informed if they are about to work on a file with a rig that is out of date.

Section 3.8 Animation

Once a model has been rigged, it is ready for animation. There are a number of different ways in which animation data can be generated. We will look at some of these below, exploring the key features of each one as it relates to a production pipeline.

Hand-Keyed

Hand-keyed animation is animation created manually by an animator. This is done by setting "keyframes" (poses that define a character's movement), between which the 3D software can interpolate automatically to give the illusion of movement.

Advantages:
- Setup costs tend to be lower for small productions
- Works well with models that have strange or non-realistic proportions
- Good for stylized movement and movement that does not follow the laws of physics
- Allows the use of techniques from traditional animation such as "squash and stretch" (deformations that preserve the total volume of a character but not its relative proportions, used in cartoon animation to exaggerate the visual impact of motion)

Disadvantages:

- High-quality results require a talented animator
- Highly realistic results tend to take longer to create than with other solutions
- The amount of work required varies according the length and complexity of the result

Hand-keyed animation is usually created in a facility's principal 3D art software, sometimes assisted by custom tools. However, for projects that require large quantities of animation data, particularly if they represent realistic human motion, facilities often turn to techniques that involve recording the movements of live actors—usually humans, but sometimes animals—and processing the data into a format that can be imported into the 3D software. These include full-body motion-capture, facial motion-capture and performance capture.

Motion Capture

The term "motion capture" tends to be used to refer to the process of recording an actor's whole-body movements. A number of different methodologies are used. Some of the most common are optical motion capture (in which an array of cameras is used to record the actor's movements, often by tracking markers attached to their skin or clothing) and inertial or mechanical capture (in which sensors attached to the actor's body record the relative motion of their body parts).

Advantages:

- Relatively high-quality results can be achieved with less experienced animators
- More animation data can be produced within a given time
- Creating complex or lengthy performances tends to be less costly, allowing actors to perform many different takes
- Easier to create realistic physical interactions, such as one character pushing another to the ground

Disadvantages:

- Initial setup costs can be prohibitive for smaller productions
- Turnaround time can be longer for projects using an external capture studio
- Iteration may be cost- or time-prohibitive if it requires a new motion-capture shoot
- Movements are limited to those the live actor can actually perform
- Cannot capture stylized movement, or movement that does not follow the laws of physics
- Can be difficult to "retarget" the captured data to models with bodily proportions different to those of the actor
- Captured data still requires manual cleanup
- Traditional animation techniques such as squash and stretch must be added later by hand

Figure 3.5 Motion capture is a good way to generate large quantities of detailed animation data quickly. This OptiTrack camera system tracks the motion of the markers attached to the actors' bodies. The data is then processed into a format that 3D software can interpret. Image © 2013 by NaturalPoint, Inc.

Facial Motion Capture

Facial motion capture refers specifically to the process of recording the movements of an actor's face. This is usually done using optical capture techniques. As with full-body capture, these may require markers to be glued to an actor's skin, or may rely on "markerless" techniques, such as using image processing to reconstruct the surface geometry of the actor's face. Compared to hand-keyed animation, facial capture shares many of the same advantages and disadvantages as full-body motion capture. However, in addition to movement, some facial-capture techniques are capable of recording other useful data, such as the detailed geometry of an actor's face or texture information from their skin.

Performance Capture

For purposes of this discussion, we will use the term "performance capture" to refer to a motion-capture solution that records an actor's facial and bodily performances simultaneously, along with the position and orientation of the camera, and other parameters such as lens calibration. The advantages and disadvantages of performance capture reflect the combined advantages and disadvantages of full-body and

facial motion capture, though because it captures both face and body at the same time, the resulting performance tends to be more unified.

Facial animation may also be created automatically without recording the movements of a live actor. This is more common in feature animation and games work than it is in visual effects, and is usually done to enable a digital character to lip-sync to a recording of a live actor.

Automated Lip-Sync

There are a number of commercial software tools that process recorded speech into its constituent "phonemes": the units of sound from which spoken words are made up. Once an artist has sculpted a series of variant models showing the character's mouth in a position corresponding to each one, the software triggers the appropriate face shape every time it detects a new phoneme in the audio stream, creating the illusion that the character is speaking.

Advantages:
- Potentially the cheapest and most efficient solution for large quantities of lip-sync
- Good for productions that can't lock down the script early
- (Games only) Dynamic generation of speech at run-time reduces storage space required for animation files
- (Games only) Audio files can be reused more easily, as longer dialogs can be generated by piecing together lots of shorter speech files

Disadvantages:
- Low quality compared to facial motion capture and hand-keyed animation
- (Games only) Requires more setup within the game engine

Facilities sometimes distinguish between "character animation"—the performance of the character itself, which is usually created through one of the techniques above—and "technical animation" or "tech anim", which includes the movement of its hair and clothing. Since these are usually generated semi-automatically by means of a physics simulation, some facilities refer to the work as "character FX" instead. The simulations may be created using the tools built into the facility's principal 3D package, specialist software such as Shave and a Haircut (for hair) or SyFlex (for cloth), or by means of custom code. The simulation data usually needs to be refined by hand to fix intersections with the character's body and to suit the character's performance.

Simulations are also used to control the movement of characters within a crowd, either by using AI systems to assign animated behaviors to individual "actors", or driving their movements via particle simulations. This is usually the responsibility of a separate department. Again, this may be achieved through commercial software—the best-known of these tools is Massive, which is AI-based—or proprietary code. We will look at simulations in more detail in the next section.

Shot Animation

Character animation is split into several phases. Working from the previs or layout data, animators first "block out" the action, setting the key poses necessary for the characters to deliver the action. At this stage, the focus is on overall timing, not fine details.

The next step is to refine the blocking pass. At this point the process ceases to be linear, since many departments, including FX and lighting, are working on the shot concurrently. Distributing a shot to multiple departments helps everyone to see their work in context, making flaws apparent earlier, and helps to push the work through production faster.

Many facilities handle animation on a per-sequence basis. Instead of working on making just one shot final, they work towards getting a complete sequence moving through the pipeline. It is common for animators to block a shot, get approval, then move on to the next shot instead of refining the blocking pass. This enables the director to review an entire sequence in one go, editing out or adding shots as needed.

Once keyframe animation is completed, a default muscle setup may be used to add secondary movement to the characters, followed by a technical animation pass that deals with geometry intersections, and adds cloth and hair simulations.

The animators will continue to refine the results until the shots are either approved or marked as CBB (Could Be Better) for tweaking later, if time allows. It is typical for facilities to specify a maximum number of iterations that can take place on the animation after blocking, called the "animation budget". It is also standard to agree with the client the various stages of refinement the animation will pass through—some companies use the terms "blocking", "primary" and "secondary", while others use the terms "primary" and "final". It is also important to define at what level of visual quality the animation is presented to the client: for example, blocking with "Playblasts" (animation recorded directly from within the 3D software, often without final textures and lighting); primary with standard lighting; or ready for final approval, complete with final hair and cloth simulations.

In film work, the output of the animation process usually consists of a mesh cache—a data file showing the position of each point on the model's surface—rather than a scene file in which the animation is still directly editable. Since the rig often consists of simulated parts, such as muscle setups, their effect on the mesh surface must be calculated before the data can be passed on to lighting and rendering.

Section 3.9 Effects and Simulations

Dr. Ken Museth, Supervisor and Principal Engineer in R & D FX, DreamWorks Animation

Effects (commonly abbreviated as "FX") is a generic term used to describe the dynamic elements in a shot calculated through mathematical procedures rather than animated by hand. Common examples include fire, smoke, water, hair, cloth, fracturing and destruction effects—and in fantasy films, effects intended to represent magic spells. Some facilities use the term "CFX" (Character Effects) to distinguish FX associated with characters, like hair and cloth simulations, from other types of FX.

Whereas conventional animation requires artist input or motion-capture data to drive character rigs or hero props, FX employs mathematical procedures to generate simulations (often known simply as "sims"). Unlike the physically accurate simulations used in scientific research or engineering, sims typically make significant approximations to reduce computational complexity, such as the use of simplified proxy geometry, LOD (Level of Detail) techniques, one-way coupling of complex multi-body interactions, or instancing prebaked simulations. An accurate simulation of water pouring into a glass might take weeks to calculate, whereas an FX artist can achieve the same approximate effect in minutes.

Another characteristic of sims is the fact that they are often based on reformulations of the physical equations of motions to provide some degree of artistic control. In contrast, accurate physical simulations are monolithic "turnkey" solvers that do not allow for artistic intervention once the simulation is initiated.

A favorite technique of FX artists is "proceduralism". One example would be the particle simulations used to mimic fire, smoke or dust. The inputs controlling the simulation—forces, constraints, the life-span of individual particles, and so on—are determined by procedures or rules that balance physical accuracy against artistic control.

Typically, proceduralism offers more directability, and is less computationally intensive, than physically accurate simulation. However, both approaches have their strengths and weaknesses, which leads many FX artists to adopt a hybrid approach. One example could be a rigid-body dynamics simulation of a collapsing building in which the fragments respond accurately to gravity and other forces, but the way in which they respond to collisions is defined by non-physically accurate procedures to ensure that the overall effect has the timing the director wants.

FX tools present significant challenges to pipeline developers. Some generate huge amounts of data; others generate data that requires challenging conversions before it can be consumed by other tools downstream. Examples of the former include fluid or liquid sims, which tend to produce large data sets (density, velocity, temperature, and so on) with significant memory and storage footprints. Examples of the latter include the implicit iso-surfaces commonly used in fluid and rigid-body simulations, which require conversion to explicit representations like polygonal models before they can be rendered. Additionally, the shot-by-shot nature of FX work often results in one-off tools with unique requirements, implemented in micro-pipelines.

To better illustrate all these issues, let's focus on a single aspect of FX work: volumetric data. However, bear in mind that most of this discussion is applicable to many other types of data encountered in modern FX pipelines.

Figure 3.6 Complex physical phenomena are usually created through mathematical simulations rather than animated by hand. To create this CG explosion, a fluid simulation is required to define the motion of the smoke and fire over time. Image © 2013 by Side Effects Software, Inc.

Volumetric data is essential to many "bread and butter" effects in movie productions, including clouds, dust, water, fire, and gaseous fluids. Typically, volumetric data is encoded in spatially uniform grids with values that represent discrete samples in index space at integer coordinate positions. These discrete sample points in index space are often referred to as "voxels".

This data is challenging for pipeline developers because of its large footprint, and because it often requires conversion to other formats before it can be used by other tools. Let's discuss these two issues separately and use the OpenVDB data structure to illustrate concrete solutions.

Traditionally FX tools both produce and consume volumetric data represented by a dense "box" of voxels in index space. This is a simple data representation that requires virtually no knowledge of the underlying data structure, and since simplicity is a virtue in most pipelines, it has prevailed for many years.

However, as the desire to create volumetric effects at higher resolution has grown, this simple approach has increasingly caused problems for FX pipelines, primarily due to the huge footprints of these dense grids. The solution is to employ more compact sparse volumetric data structures that use advanced techniques to only allocate voxels where they are needed: for example, where the velocity of a liquid is non-zero.

One example is the OpenVDB volume data structure that is setting a new industry standard for memory-compact volumes.[1] In concept, OpenVDB models an infinitely large 3D index space using a novel hierarchical data structure that shares several characteristics with modern CPUs, file systems and relational databases. OpenVDB can reduce memory consumption by orders of magnitude and is used in many studio pipelines and in commercial software packages like Houdini, RenderMan and Arnold.

[1] Ken Museth, "VDB: High-resolution sparse volumes with dynamic topology," *ACM Transactions on Graphics* 32, no. 3 (2013): 23.

Figure 3.7 This CG cloud uses OpenVDB volumes to define its overall shape. This effect was achieved by sculpting the volumes and does not require any simulation. Image © 2013 by Side Effects Software, Inc.

Another issue that plagues many FX pipelines is the fact that data often has to be converted before it can be passed between tools in the pipeline. Again, volumetric data is an excellent example of this. Conversion may be necessary because different tools use different representations of volumes (for example, dense versus sparse data structures) or more commonly, because many tools simply cannot operate on (or "consume") volumetric data.

To better understand why, it's important to recall that geometry (that is, solid surfaces), can actually be represented both explicitly and implicitly. Explicit surface representations are by far the most common in FX pipelines and often take the form of polygonal or parametric surfaces. However, implicit surface representations—those in which the surface is defined as an iso-surface of a 3D volume—are increasingly popular, since they allow for complex surface deformations, are compact, and integrate easily with many simulation tools. Therefore, to link a fluid simulator that generates level sets to a renderer that only supports triangles, a conversion or "polygonization" step is required. Depending on the nature of the effects involved, such conversions can be trivial, challenging, or even impossible, which can have a fundamental impact on which tools can be combined in an FX pipeline.

Section 3.10 Lighting

Lighting is often where a shot comes together. As well as being required simply to illuminate the action, lighting defines the mood of a shot, sets the time of day and the weather conditions, determines the color palette, and helps to lead the viewer's eye around the scene.

If the CG elements of a shot are to be integrated with live action, the digital lighting needs to match that of the plate as closely as possible, using on-set references such as HDRI images. If the shot is

entirely CG, the goal is to match the previs and concept art. Often the cartoony style of pure CG encourages outrageous lighting conditions rarely found in the real world.

In production, collections of individual lights or "lighting rigs" are created for each key location. It is common to work on key shots then, once these are approved, duplicate the lighting setup to other shots before making shot-specific adjustments.

Lighting work was traditionally carried out inside a facility's principal 3D art package. However, there are a growing number of specialist tools that enable artists to iterate lighting (or "relight" a shot) more quickly. The best-known of these is Katana, originally developed by Sony Pictures Imageworks, and now available as a commercial product.

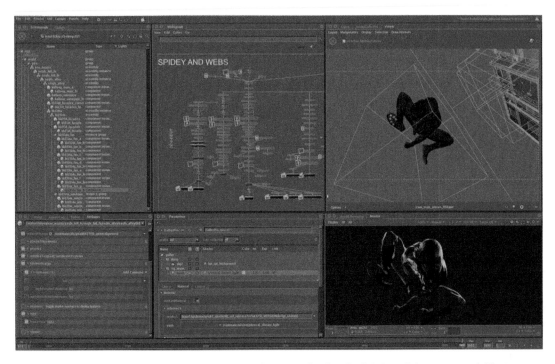

Figure 3.8 Specialist tools like Katana enable artists to iterate and refine the lighting of shots more quickly. Spider-Man image © 2012 by Columbia Pictures.

Section 3.11 Rendering

Rendering is the process of taking the data in the 3D scene and converting it into a series of 2D images seen from the digital camera's POV (Point of View). In film work, these calculations are done offline, typically taking anywhere from an hour to days to process an individual frame.

In films, it is common to render out a scene in a series of layers or "passes", each showing only a subset of the assets in the scene (for example, only the background, or only the foreground characters); a subset of the lighting data (for example, the reflections, shadows or ambient occlusion); or other information useful when compositing the shot, for example, a Z-depth pass (a gray-scale image representing the distance of each point in the scene from the camera) or other AOVs (Arbitrary Output Variables). Rendering a scene in passes makes it easier to combine CG elements with live-action footage. It is also quicker to iterate the look of a shot by combining passes in a compositing package than it is to rerender it entirely.

While some large facilities use their own in-house software, particularly for specific tasks such as rendering FX, commercial renderers are also widely used. For years, the film market was dominated by RenderMan and other tools based on its "Reyes" architecture, which is intended to strike a balance between realism and rendering speed. However, renderers that make greater use of "ray tracing" techniques— traditionally slower than Reyes algorithms, but capable of generating more realistic output—are becoming increasingly popular. These include Arnold, V-Ray and mental ray.

Section 3.12 Compositing

Compositing is the process of blending all of the rendered and live-action elements that make up a shot into a series of finished images. As well as the rendered elements and prepared plates, compositors rely on camera-tracking data to integrate the two seamlessly; LUT data (Look-Up Tables, used to represent the color space of the medium in which the images will be displayed) to ensure that the composited shot has the correct color balance; and lens distortion, noise and grain information, to match the look of the original footage.

Generally speaking, it is easier to make adjustments to the look of a shot during compositing than it is in 3D. For example, say that you want the entire image to be slightly redder in color. It is much easier to do this in the compositing package, in which it may simply involve moving a single slider, than it is to adjust the tints of a hundred separate lights within the 3D software. Similarly, a key part of the compositor's toolkit is a library containing clips of "practical elements"—live-action footage of things like flames, smoke, dust and water splashes—that can be integrated into the image rather than requiring the FX department to run extra simulations.

However, be wary of leaving issues earlier in the pipeline unresolved on the grounds that "they can fix it in comp". Just as the phrase "they can fix that in post" is sometimes used as an excuse for sloppy work on set—leaving equipment in shot that needs painting out later, for example—the role of the compositor is to make artistic adjustments

to the image, not solve other people's problems. The pipeline should minimize the number of issues that need to be fixed in comp, not add to them.

The number and nature of the render passes required for compositing depends on the subject matter of a shot, and the visual style required. Optimizing the set of passes is a key task for the pipeline team: you don't want to generate a pass only to discover that it is not actually required, or to render a character at high resolution only to discover that it will only be visible in the background of a shot.

Although 2D compositing packages such as After Effects are widely used in broadcast work, the visual effects industry is dominated by 3D solutions such as Nuke and Fusion. These can create internal three-dimensional representations of a scene, making it possible to make more complex adjustments to the final image.

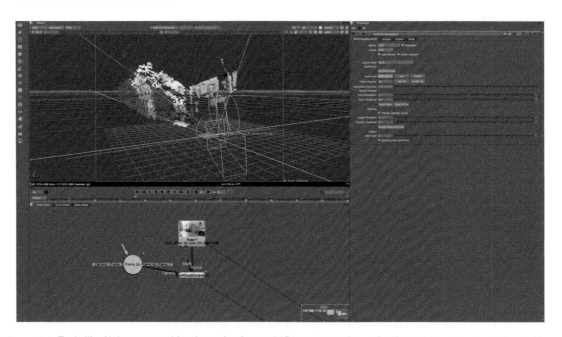

Figure 3.9 Tools like Nuke are capable of creating internal 3D representations of a shot, and are more widely used in visual effects work than 2D compositing software. Image © 2013 by The Foundry.

That concludes our exploration of the process of creating assets for film work. In the next chapter, we will look at how the process of asset creation differs for games.

INTERLUDE: LIDAR: ASSET CAPTURE ON SET

Steve Chapman
VP of Technology, Gentle Giant Studios

Cataloging sets for VFX, games or toys is a large part of our computer graphics atelier here at Gentle Giant. Having done this work since the mid-Nineties for big projects like *Star Wars*, *Harry Potter*, *Lord of the Rings* and *Star Trek*, we've had to develop and utilize digital asset management techniques for the very large collections of reference data gathered during a film's production. I can't overemphasize how important this is to the entertainment industry. At first glance you might think we've scanned the Millennium Falcon for just a single complex VFX shot, but such things aren't fleeting images—they eventually become toys, games, and with enough momentum, a cherished part of popular culture. The information you collect on a film set might be valued and utilized decades later, and is why companies like Lucasfilm have come to consider Gentle Giant as a sort of Memory Alpha for storing this data. Consequently we take DAM very seriously. DAM, for us, starts when we first get word of a new project, and the first step on any mission is forming an Away Team.

Remember *Mission Impossible*, that grainy 1970s UHF TV show (featuring the cast of *Space: 1999*, for some reason)? Before every mission our hero would be given a self-destructing dossier outlining the objectives, the key players involved, the location, expectations, and goals of the mission. Going on set is a lot like that, without the explosion at the end. (The person at the "Impossible Mission Foundation" who put together those dossiers never received enough thanks and appreciation in my opinion.) Putting together a comprehensive plan is a critical element that will make collecting data while mingling with Tom Cruise an enjoyable experience as opposed to the panic that awaits the unprepared.

Identify the key players and be sure to prepare your team with a comprehensive outline of the relationships and notable achievements of the persons involved. You may have a direct relationship with a VFX coordinator or producer, but as you will likely be given on-set direction from the VFX Supervisor it helps to know what projects he or she has been a part of and any notable process developments they've

pioneered. A healthy library of *Cinefex, American Cinematographer, Game Developer,* and *3D* magazines is a useful reference, as well as web searches targeting the films or games they've been involved with.

The production's VFX coordinator may have been promoted from acting as data wrangler or assistant on the Supe's last film, and may not understand all that you have to offer, so never assume that they know exactly what the VFX vendors who use your data downstream will want or need. For example, in the case of LIDAR, we may be commissioned to scan a pristine automobile for a crash scene, so we'll suggest that it is prudent to also scan the vehicle after practical effects and stunt work has "changed the geometry" of the vehicle. This is because one never knows what will be needed downstream months later when a director reviews shots in progress at the VFX vendor's facility and perhaps decides to "plus" a shot. It is far easier to capture and potentially discard data that doesn't end up being utilized versus limiting the artistic possibilities of a scene because the set was struck and the stunt vehicles discarded.

The film's actors may need to be scanned for use in rendered scenes. Diagnose your recipient vendor's pipeline to tailor the assets for their typical workflow, which will vary among companies. One vendor may be looking for an actor's squash and stretch muscle movement extremes through "range of motion studies", while another may want specific natural expression acted out, such as "anger" or "fear". Once the actor arrives and becomes involved, they may have more specific knowledge of how they have played or will play a scene that might involve a transition from live to digital double in the course of a shot. Although telling an Oscar winning actor how to look happy may invoke the opposite expression, it can be helpful to have source images handily placed that reference the works of such experts as Paul Ekman, George Brant Bridgman, Gary Faigen. Better yet, involve the VFX Supe ahead of time and ask for their input as to source reference material. They may respond "Ekman, Bridgman, Faigen, etc." but at least it will seem to them that you are listening. Of course these are people busy making a movie, so don't pester them or imply that obtaining this information is a prerequisite to doing the job. The work in the future will tend to flow towards the vendor that does the job well and is easiest to work with, so plan to be that vendor.

We've even had commissioned Neville Page 3D printouts of an actor frozen in example expressions. Such items, or perhaps something like Andrew Cawrse's anatomy tools, are helpful to have on hand for reference as well as providing a semiotic level of assurance to your VFX teams that you have an appreciation for the art and magic that is being created on set.

The amount of time available to complete a set LIDAR scan affects the amount of information that can be captured. If one is given control of a set for the duration of the crew's lunch break, the scanner resolution must be set in order to maximize coverage and still capture what is

needed before the crew returns. (They *always* come back earlier than anticipated.) Ideally, a set will be handed over for scanning and texture photography after the crew has wrapped for the day, meaning an all-nighter for you. However, with the busy production schedules laid out with limited consideration for the work that VFX needs to accomplish, there is often a crew standing by, watching over your shoulder, with the intention of striking the set and beginning construction of a new set the moment you announce you've finished. Keeping these folks informed and involved with the data collection process can mean they offer to help, rather than hinder, your progress.

Because one viewpoint precludes vision from all angles, your cameras and scanners must be moved to multiple locations to gather complete coverage of the set and all the larger items the set entails. (Smaller props will be covered later.) Being skilled in 3D modeling will allow you to judge objects to determine how much coverage is needed. For example, a cylindrical or symmetrical hard-surface set piece might be easier to reproduce through less scan data because it's easier to create by mirroring or revolving the proper cross-section needed to recreate it. Part of asset management involves avoiding creating more work than is needed, but it is a fine balance, because if you do not capture sufficient coverage it will be impossible to go back and capture weeks later. In fact, because this realization might even occur downstream at another VFX vendor without your being there to defend your work, it might simply be chalked-up to your incompetence. This could negatively influence your reputation, even though you were prevented from doing thorough work by the film's conflicting on-set conditions. (Perhaps a metadata scheme can be developed that includes notes such as "Thunderstorm approaching from the north while we are scanning from 80 feet above the set in a metal scissor lift.")

Always optimize your time. Borrow or bring your own radio so that you can be on top of what pieces are available or become unavailable by listening in on the walkie-talkie communications that are the lifeline of any Hollywood production. Always try to maximize opportunities and minimize interruptions that might affect the quality of the data assets. If you receive word that a set will be available soon, it helps to be nearby even before you are told by the VFX coordinator to move there, instead of rushing from the lunch tent a half mile away.

Because of the amount of time needed to wrangle the scanner, using a tethered laptop, though ideal, may be out of the question as priority must be placed on capturing the maximum amount of information in the time allotted. In terms of asset management, the camera or scanner now contains the vital set details; because the scanner usually provides vague filenames, once a set is captured, immediate priority must be placed on safe backup of the scans as well as properly identifying the data.

Figure 3.1 Interlude An example of common working conditions. Here, a metal scissor lift elevated eight stories during a sandstorm while thunderheads gather in the distance is preparing to scan the area. Because the set will be "blown up real good" within hours, there is no second chance to capture the set data.

The camera cards or scan systems have a finite internal storage limit, and each collection pass often results in several gigabytes of data, so the scanner may need to be "wiped", often ASAP, so that scanning of another set might commence. The first step is to download that data to portable field storage. However, it can be a tragic mistake to think that this is now "backed up" because if the scanner's storage is erased now you are once again in a situation where there is only one copy and a backup does not yet exist. The data is usually copied to two separate field drives, ideally using solid-state technology because spinning hard disks are more prone to failure. A third copy remains on the computer used to offload the data until it has been safely returned to the office for processing. If the set has been destroyed or even is simply no longer accessible because other crews are using it, then this will have been your only opportunity to capture it—and a sure way not to be invited back for the next film will be by breaking the news to the VFX Supervisor that you have lost data.

Because the first *Harry Potter* was in production shortly after the 9/11 terrorist attacks, concerned executives demanded to know how we were going to prevent their data from being lost in the event of another attack as it was being flown back to the studios. Although our

initial reaction was that we'd be dead and wouldn't really care, we were able to truthfully assure them that copies would be transported from London to LA on two separate flights. This may be an extreme example, though one should work to build a reputation for reliably archiving data that might not be accessed again until months later in post-production.

Texture and documentary photography is a separate step from scanning, because although some scanners offer a means of capturing color information it has never been the quality useful for realistic VFX rendering purposes. Texture photography also takes place in the same time slot allotted for scanning, which adds a layer of difficulty in coordinating the work because any persons or equipment in the scan but not a part of the set become extraneous data that must be removed in post-processing. This might sound trivial, but keep in mind that the scan is not instantaneous, so a crew member can not only corrupt a large area of scan data as they move, the same person might also appear in several different locations in the data as they walk about while the 3D scan progresses. It is sometimes helpful to remind the production's VFX coordinators that removing this "noise" from the model can add days to the downstream processing work.

Figure 3.2 Interlude This image shows a Faro life scanner along with the moving people and changing weather that the LIDAR crew must deal with, not to mention the angry park rangers demanding to see permits.

A good method for determining the locations for photography comes from experience using 3D software to map textures onto a model. By knowing what will be needed by the VFX artists months later, you'll be in a good position to judge the needs on set. HDR bracketing is preferred to allow maximum flexibility in processing the images downstream. If an object needs to be rendered with virtual lighting that contradicts the on-set shadow conditions, then HDRi will allow the texture artist to process out the shadows, revealing the underlying colors needed to re-render the objects with different lighting angles.

Texture photography is meant to replicate the set pieces as they appeared during filming, so it is good practice to request the same lights used during the shoot be left on for the duration of photography. This can be expensive, since the crew must be asked to work overtime if the scan takes place after the main unit has wrapped for the day. Nodal panorama shots are taken from as close to the position that a LIDAR scanner was used, so often a situation of "trading places" occurs as the scanner is used in the same place a 360 panorama was taken, and vice-versa. In addition, "straight on" shots that minimize distortion and maximize an object-to-image capture are taken. Sometimes this must occur from heights in order to look down on a set, potentially adding another expense for a lift operator if you cannot convince the VFX Supervisor that you have years of experience operating set rigging equipment. It is reassuring to arrive with your own safety harnesses to hammer home the point, as well as keeping safe; even inside a sound-stage, film sets can be five stories tall with a hard concrete floor you don't want to land on. On that note, never assume that anything on a film set is real or safe. Although the production will do everything they can to give you a safe working environment, you still need to be aware that the building ledge you are leaning over may be in reality a thin veneer of plaster over Styrofoam, or the steel column you are leaning against may really be cardboard sonotube. I recall on one film set my "Spidey" senses were tingling when I noticed a rope extending from the ceiling to the floor was jiggling slightly. I stared curiously but felt no reason for concern. After a few seconds some of the rope danced about like a snake, then fell to the ground. The incredible thud and blast of air was followed by a sudden realization that a seven-story length of rope probably weighs a hundred pounds. It's best to forget any expectations you have and, prior to every action you take, consider "Is it safe?"

So you've ended the work day with three duplicate sets of 3D data to manage, as well as "36 megapixel 11 shots per-viewpoint bracketed photographs" that must also undergo a triple backup process before leaving the set. Because human memories can fail quickly with that amount of data (and after the mandatory crew meetup at the Keg), we use Apple Aperture to quickly organize and label the images as well as the 3D scan data into one keyword indexed folder and project subsets. Convincing Aperture to ingest and archive 3D data involves simply adding the extension ".mov" to the file no matter what the true internal

format. Ignoring Aperture's protest that it cannot preview the file, an additional screen capture from the 3D scanning software tidily covers the needs for this "field archive". When the data is needed later, the file is simply exported and the ".mov" addition removed so that it is ready to be processed back at home base. This also allows any notes taken on set to be directly associated with the data and additional Aperture capabilities such as cloud-based backup can be performed, assuming the location provides connectivity. As a side note, there are always a dozen or so wireless hot-spots on any film set, of varying reliability. Although it might be possible to check email on a laptop using a hot spot named "Costume Gang," it will be unlikely and probably rude to attempt to transfer large data sets with such connections. It is better to ask the VFX coordinator what proper protocol and password is needed to log on to the studio's official connection, or use a hard wired connection that might be available in the VFX trailer or the primary production office. Risking that future readers will laugh at this notion: cellular based hot spots never offer the speed or data limits sufficient to transfer gigabytes of data. Ideally, all of the information you need concerning internet access, phone numbers, email addresses etc. will be provided before you arrive, in the form of an exploding dossier.

Figure 3.3 Interlude Often LIDAR requires creative problem solving. This image is of a scanner which Gentle Giant used on *Star Wars 2*. At that time, specialized scanning equipment was hard to come by, so they purchased a set/vehicle scanner from the French nuclear power industry (the purple canister) and fabricated their own body scanner (the aluminum towers).

4

ASSET CREATION FOR GAMES

Tim Green; Matt Hoesterey; Hannes Ricklefs; Mark Streatfield; Steve Theodore; Laurent M. Abecassis; Di-O- Matic; Ben Carter: *Game Developer and Author, Heavy Spectrum Entertainment Labs;* **Jeff Isselee:** *Technical Lead, Skull Theater*

Section 4.1 What You Will Learn From This Chapter

In the previous chapter, we looked at the steps involved in creating assets for films. Some of these are unique to visual effects: obviously, games have no direct equivalent for tasks such as plate prep or rotoscoping. Others, such as modeling, texture work, animation, FX, and rendering share commonalities with game development. However, there are also crucial differences.

In this chapter, we will look briefly at some of the more important of these differences, and explore the implications they have for pipeline developers. Again, we will run through the steps involved in asset creation in roughly chronological order. (For a definition of each step, and what it entails, refer to the previous chapter.) But first, we will examine one of the most fundamental differences between creating assets for film and games: the format in which data is exported.

Section 4.2 Data Import and Export

Unlike in film work, in games, assets cannot always be used in the format in which the software used to create them would normally save them. Readying them for use is a two-stage process in which data is "exported" out of the art package and "imported" into the game. Export removes data which is of use to the artist working on the asset but of no interest to the game: for example, the construction history of the model, or the visibility groups used to keep the file manageable. The export process usually produces a separate file known as an "intermediate" or "bridge" file. Import converts the exported data into an optimized format designed around the needs of the game engine.

Some game developers combine both operations into a single piece of software, which avoids the need to manage large numbers of

intermediate files. However, most prefer a two-step process. Keeping export separate from import enables the engineering team to reformat the assets when needed (for example, when a change to the engine necessitates a change in file format) without requiring artists to reexport them manually. Although exporting a single file is fairly painless, exporting thousands—or tens of thousands—of assets is a huge time sink and saps the morale of the artists assigned to the task. A two-step process means that assets need only be exported once manually from the software that created them. It is then possible to write tools to batch-convert the resulting intermediate files, greatly increasing the speed of the process.

Splitting up import and export also makes it possible to reformat assets for use on multiple different platforms without undue effort on the part of the art staff. These changes can be as simple as making file names case-sensitive, or as complex as changing the way values are padded out in memory or reversing bit order (the direction in which bits are written in a byte of memory). Asking the art staff to choose the right combination of options for each of several output platforms and for every one of tens of thousands of assets is asking for trouble. It's much easier for engineers to handle the conversion process in a way that is invisible to the artists.

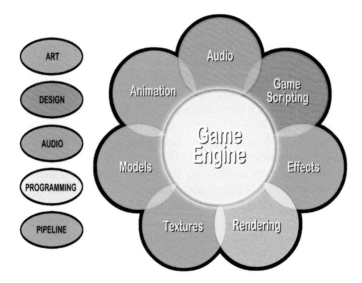

Figure 4.1 The range of assets required to create a modern game, and the departments that create them. The game engine forms the point of integration for all these different types of data, while the pipeline team is responsible for getting data into the engine efficiently.

The two key components of the asset-conversion pipeline are the exporter and the importer themselves. We will look at each one in turn:

Exporter

The exporter is usually—and ought to be—fairly simple, since its job is primarily to filter out unwanted data. Exporters are typically plug-ins that work inside DCC (Digital Content Creation) tools like Maya, Softimage or 3 ds Max. They may be written using the C++ API of the host package, or implemented via a scripting language. The latter option has become increasingly popular as computers have become faster: while Python and embedded scripting languages such as MEL or MAXScript handle data much more slowly than C++, they are also easier to maintain and update as the project evolves. A good exporter is nearly invisible and should not burden artists with a host of settings and options. In many cases, it shouldn't even present the user with a file dialog—it is far more efficient to derive the name of the exported file directly from the name of the work file, or from a database, so that the dependency relationship between the Maya or 3 ds Max scene file and the final in-game asset is unambiguous.

Importer

The importer is usually a far more complex piece of software than the exporter, since it evolves in step with the game engine and is subject to the often very exacting demands of the game and its target platforms. Given that the exporter typically runs inside the artist's DCC software, the importer should be responsible for as much of the "heavy lifting" work as possible. Generating collision geometry or lighting data for a scene can take hours, so it's better to offload this work to a build farm than tying up an artist's workstation for the duration.

While exporters are often designed by technical art staff, importers are usually the province of hardcore engineers. One of the unfortunate side effects of this division of labor is that the import process becomes fraught with misunderstandings. Many artists are bewildered by the cryptic warnings generated every time they process an asset. If the tool provides too much information, they tend to tune it out (the common artist slang for the feedback from importers is "the spew"). On the other hand, if the importer offers no guidance when an artist has done something wrong—for example, if it silently stops processing geometry with more than a certain number of polygons instead of providing a clear warning like, "This asset has too many polygons!"—confusion is sure to result. For this reason, it's important for the tech art team to act as a bridge between the engineers who manage the importer and the artists using the exporter. Tech artists need to lobby hard to ensure that the warnings generated by the importer are written clearly and include actionable information. Contrast this classically cryptic error message:

0x7000: Unable to generate orthonormal tangent frame at location 0xA8C

with this one:

Triangle #2700 in mesh 'example_object' has no UVs. Apply mapping and re-export.

Both represent exactly the same problem in the art file—but only one of them is likely to be fixed right away. Ideally, error messages should include wiki or http:// links to documentation which explains the problem in greater detail. They should also be tracked in a log file or database: this helps the engineers identify parts of the process that are error-prone and should be redesigned.

Section 4.3 Levels of Detail

For a model to survive scrutiny when seen in close-up, it needs to be detailed. Character models may require fine details such as individually modeled eyelashes or teeth, while environmental assets may require individually modeled nuts and bolts. This makes the model "heavy": large in file size, and slow to create and manipulate.

In film work, the polygon count of such models can stretch into the tens of millions. In games, models have traditionally been of lower resolution, with the detail added by clever texturing and shading effects. But as the power of games hardware increases, polygon counts are climbing.

Although both films and games try to alleviate some of the drawbacks of heavy data by using LOD (Level of Detail) techniques, these techniques are more critical in games. In simple terms, an LOD system swaps out the high-resolution model for a lower-resolution version (or series of versions) as an object moves further away from the camera. This improves performance and saves memory, but it also complicates the process of asset creation, since the LOD models need to be tied to the original so that any changes made to one can be propagated to the others. This is a classic example of dependency management in action: a solid production pipeline has to provide artists with the tools they need to figure out when changes should be propagated to LOD models.

LODs are not just used for meshes: a character rig may contain fewer bones when that character is viewed from a distance, or the character may use fewer, lower-fidelity animations. Textures and shaders may also need to be modified to create different levels of detail. Mipmaps (single files containing multiple versions of the same texture map of progressively decreasing dimensions) offer a way to create levels of detail for textures, and help to minimize the visual artifacts seen in some textures when they are scaled.

Since LOD creation is a thankless task, it's often a candidate for automation. Techniques for generating LODs automatically have

been around for some time, and some are quite sophisticated. However, there is no one-size-fits-all technology that handles all types of content equally well.

Progressive mesh reduction, for example, reduces the density of a mesh by removing vertices one at a time, using an algorithm to select the vertex that produces the least visually obvious change. The technique works quite well on dense models with complex, organic forms, particularly high-resolution character models. However, it rarely does a good job on mechanical or architectural models. On the other hand, environmental models can often be reduced to "billboards" or "cards"—simple planes bearing 2D images of the object they represent. This is a common technique for displaying, say, distant trees in a forest, but doesn't work well for characters or animated objects. A big modern production will typically have several different parallel tool chains for creating different types of LOD content, requiring a mix of automation and manual labor.

Whereas automated LOD systems typically start with a high-resolution asset and progressively reduce it in complexity, a related technique does the same thing in reverse. Tessellation harnesses the power of modern GPUs to subdivide a mesh, and is particularly good for smoothing out unsightly angularities when a pseudo-curved polygonal surface is in silhouette. This is akin to generating a very high LOD mesh from a lower LOD mesh, but only in the places that matter.

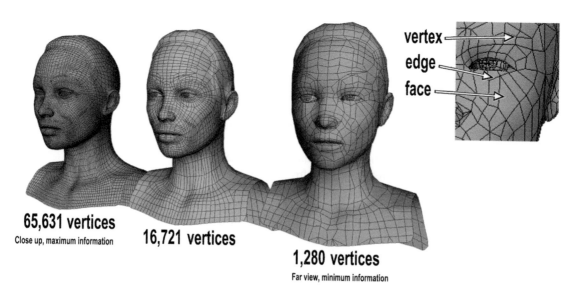

65,631 vertices
Close up, maximum information

16,721 vertices

1,280 vertices
Far view, minimum information

vertex
edge
face

Figure 4.2 Tessellation harnesses the power of modern GPUs to subdivide a mesh automatically when a model is seen close up, helping to create the illusion of smooth curves on organic objects like characters.

Automated Asset Creation: Capturing the Real World

Jeff Isselee
Technical Lead, Skull Theater

For a small independent videogame company like Skull Theatre, one of the greatest challenges is the creation of high-quality digital art. 3D art is typically very labor-intensive to produce, and can require a unique and varied set of skills. Larger developers rely on budgets that accommodate diverse teams, an expensive suite of tools, and a long development cycle. Indie studios typically have none of these resources, and as a result must either simplify their project goals, or find a creative solution to the problem of a costly art production pipeline.

One solution can be found in a technique called "photogrammetry", which uses a set of 2D photographic images taken of a physical object to generate a 3D representation of the object: typically, a textured 3D mesh. Photogrammetry tools enable artists to bypass the digital mesh- and texture-creation process and to fall back on classical skills, working in a medium where realism is a natural by-product rather than a conscious effort.

Photogrammetry isn't a new concept, and has been used in film production for quite some time. Recently, however, these tools have become much more accessible to the general public. As a small company, Skull Theatre has chosen to take advantage of these powerful tools to produce virtually all of the art assets used in our 3D world.

The major advantage of using photogrammetry for art asset creation is that it can produce compelling results without all of the fuss of digital authoring. However, it does require a unique production pipeline that can handle both

Figure 4.3 Indie game developer Skull Theatre uses a pipeline based on photogrammetry to create assets more quickly. Top: physical props ready for photography. Middle: the same props reconstructed from those photographs as textured 3D geometry. Below: assets in use in-game.

the physical and digital elements of the process. The pipeline that we've created at Skull Theatre can be conceptually divided into three stages: art asset capture, digital asset post-processing, and digital asset mapping. At each stage, our goal is always to preserve the quality of the original physical object while minimizing overheads for our limited staff.

Art Asset Capture

The point of entry into our art production pipeline is the photo studio. At a minimum, a photogrammetric "3D capture" studio should consist of a neutrally lit space with a central mount for the target object and enough clearance for a camera to photograph it from all sides, since photogrammetry can only reconstruct those parts of an object shown in the photographs. We have built an adjustable custom rig to house the camera so that it can pivot around a central table, rolling along on wheels. This speeds up photography, which otherwise can be a cumbersome process, and gives us consistent results.

The photo studio must solve two opposing problems. The 3D capture process benefits from having as many visual cues as possible to help the software determine the spatial position of each photograph. Here, things like multicolored backgrounds and strong contrasts in lighting all help to create better results. However, these photographs are also used to produce an "albedo texture" (a texture map that specifies surface color and reflectivity), and for this, strong lighting contrast and environmental interference should be avoided—otherwise, the lighting information baked into the albedo texture may conflict with that generated dynamically by the game engine.

In our photo studio, we've opted to keep the lighting as diffuse as possible with even coverage around the target object. We shoot with a white background, but with the addition of a lot of high-frequency noise. Brightly colored marks and doodles across background surfaces and around the base of the target object all help to create a frame of reference between photographs while keeping lighting neutral.

Digital Asset Post-Processing

After a set of photographs have been taken, they are handed off to the photogrammetry tool, which provides us with a textured mesh. The results look good, but aren't yet ready for production. For our purposes, we've found the resulting mesh to be way too heavy for a videogame asset and lacking the LODs necessary to render the object efficiently when it is in the distance. The texture can also be quite fragmented, making poor use of UV space and being ill-suited for mipmapping. Unfortunately, fixing these problems manually can be quite labor-intensive. In order to minimize overheads, we've opted to automate this portion of the pipeline. LODs are auto-generated using a mesh-simplification technique called "quadric edge collapse". Textures are optimized by constructing an extremely high-resolution interpolated version of the mesh and transferring color data from the texture to the mesh. The mesh is then unfolded to create a new UV mapping, which is used to rebuild the color texture from vertex data. Additionally, the high-resolution mesh can be used to generate normal and height map textures for high-quality run-time dynamic lighting.

Under ideal conditions, this process is completely automated. However, production environments are far from ideal. Mesh LODs can fail to generate and UV auto-unwrapping can occasionally produce substandard results. To handle this, our pipeline enables us to halt the process at each stage and switch over to a manual implementation if better results are needed.

Digital Asset Mapping

Once the art resources have been processed, they are associated with a parent object and imported into the engine. At this point, they're ready to be used in a production environment. However, as a small company,

we still face a problem of scale. If we have to take the time to create each object in our game world manually, our limited art team won't be able to build a compelling environment. To solve this, we componentize our game assets. When creating complex objects like buildings, we don't create the entire object as a single asset. Instead, we create portions of it. Doors, windows, extensions, roofs, foundations, and base pieces can all be constructed independently and assembled in our world editor environment. This has a number of advantages. It allows for object reuse with a high level of variation, which is key for any small team. It also lets artists work on whatever scale is most comfortable for them when creating each component. And finally, it allows for the assembly of objects that are much more complex than would otherwise be possible to digitize due to the limitations of modern photogrammetry tools.

Since our art pipeline relies on componentization, our engine has been written specifically to take advantage of these componentized objects and to streamline the process of assembling them. Each object is assigned a specific "topology" that controls how sub-objects can attach to and traverse its surface. A topology can be thought of as the combination of a geometric primitive shape with a height map. The artist selects the shape that best matches the object's mesh and a height map is generated to represent the difference between this shape and the actual mesh. This gives our artists the ability to construct complex static objects with little effort.

This is an exciting time for indie developers, as increasingly powerful tools become accessible to companies on a budget. Photogrammetry is one such tool. When used in a production pipeline that focuses on quality preservation and automation, a company of any size can build high-quality 3D game art, with artists spending their time at the workbench rather than the keyboard.

Section 4.4 Optimizing Assets

Memory and processing power are precious, finite resources, so making good use of them is vital. It's not an accident that games artists often talk about assets as if they were part of a national fiscal debate, worrying about how "expensive" assets are and whether or not they hit their "budgets".

Since games must be fitted into fixed budgets, optimization is a perennial issue for developers. The numbers may increase as hardware evolves, but the conflict between artistic ambitions and technical realities will never be resolved. Even in well-run, carefully planned projects, teams don't really know the limitations of their run-time environment until fairly late in the project. Often, the original estimates turn out to be too optimistic, meaning that the budgets for geometry, animations and textures have to be revised downwards. Less often, a bit of programming genius frees up unexpected memory and enables the team to add more detail to their assets. In either case, assets must be revised late in their lifespan to reflect the realities of the run-time environment. Assuming that a "perfect" budget can be worked out before production begins is as dangerous as assuming that it is possible to plan a "perfect" development schedule.

Two opposing forces influence the run-time cost of assets. As hardware becomes more powerful, assets tend to become more memory-intensive as developers make use of the increased capacity. In the 1990s, a typical in-game character model might have 500 triangles, 256 kb of texture memory, and a few hundred frames of animation. Today, a similar character might have 20,000 triangles, 8 MB of texture memory, and thousands of frames of animation.

At the same time, compression technology is improving, and new optimizations can make previously expensive data structures less expensive. For example, when normal maps—texture maps that store surface information from high-res models, making the low-res assets to which they are applied look more detailed at render time—first appeared in games, they could not be compressed. Now, however, there are a variety of compression techniques for normal maps that provide different trade-offs between visual quality and memory usage. One of the key research tasks at the start of any project is trying to incorporate new compression and optimization technologies into the pipeline, particularly those that "just work" and don't require manual input from artists.

However, the problem is not ultimately technological. Optimization is about artistic choices, so it is important for the artists involved to understand the ways in which their assets will be used in-game.

It's pointless to worry about the fine details of a distant mountain, but vital to preserve the facial details of a character who will deliver a critical line of dialogue in close-up. Some assets may not require detailed models, but will require detailed textures. Ultimately, these are aesthetic rather than technological decisions: a computer can't tell if the constant repetition of a few cheap assets will bore players, or if the blocky silhouette of a model is too crude for the visual style of the game.

For this reason, no technological solution will entirely eliminate human input from the optimization process. However, the pipeline team can help the process enormously by providing good, readily accessible data. It's vital for the artists who have to manage the game's run-time budget to be able to see total asset cost and patterns of asset usage in real time. By comparing assets to others in the same class, it becomes fairly easy to spot those in need of optimization: if most of the trees in a game weigh in at around 1,000 triangles, but one uses 10,000 it's a good sign that it is in need of work. Good information about usage also makes it easier to replace rarely used assets with more common ones: if that 10,000-triangle tree only shows up once in the game, it may be easier to cut it out altogether than to optimize it. Data mining can provide insights into why some sections of the game perform poorly, or suggest better trade-offs, such as swapping in more detailed geometry that requires lower-resolution textures in an area where texture memory is constrained.

Section 4.5 Creating Run-Time Animation

The way in which an animation will be used determines the best pipeline to get it into a game. Animations created for use in an FMV (Full Motion Video: that is, a prerendered cut-scene) will follow a pipeline similar to that used for film, and may be outsourced to a company that specializes in film work. We looked at the workflow of creating character rigs and animation for film in the previous chapter, and much of that information is relevant here too.

Animations destined for cut-scenes created through the game engine—those using the engine to animate a skinned mesh and render it in real time—will follow a similar pipeline up to the point at which the animation data is exported. Often, these animations will require additional information to trigger particle effects, audio, or AI or gameplay events. It is not uncommon for the player to maintain some degree of control while sequences play. At one extreme, the sequence may simply be scene dressing with the player remaining in full control; at the other, the cut-scene may take control of the camera and everything in front of it.

In-game animations, however, are much more complex. While some of the raw data is created in the same way, the movements of the player character and NPCs (Non-Player Characters) are rarely simple strings of keyframes: instead, the game blends a variety of smaller animations together at run-time. This may be a fairly simple transition from one animation sequence to another as the character moves between states: for example, from standing to running to walking. Alternatively, it may

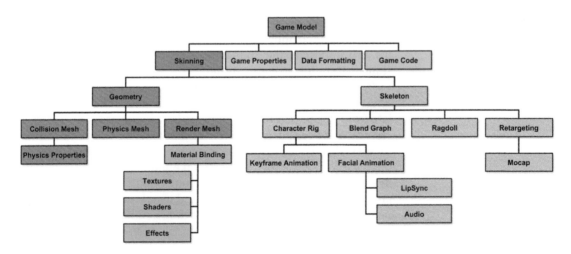

Figure 4.4 The dependency chain for art assets in a game pipeline. Note how differently the animation pipeline is structured to that for VFX work, with extra sources of animation data such as rag doll physics. In this chart, dark blue is geometry, light blue is texture and material, green is data, script and code, and gold is animation.

be a very complex mixture of animations overlaid upon one another, possibly augmented by procedural modifications such as the use of inverse kinematics to keep the character's feet from sliding, or switching to physically simulated "rag doll" animation in response to an event like the character being shot, or falling down stairs.

The way that these elements are combined in-game may be controlled using proprietary code or by using "middleware"—ready-made software tools that may be incorporated into the game—like Granny, Morpheme or Sage. Since the series of inputs used to create the final in-game animation is often displayed as a graph structure, run-time animation sets are often known as "blend graphs", "blend trees" or "blend diagrams". Because the blending is controlled at run-time by data generated from the player's input or from the game engine, these systems are also known as "parametric" animations. Blend graphs straddle the line between traditional art work and programming, and artists who know how to manipulate them are often highly skilled specialists.

Each node in the blend graph represents an individual animation or a blend between a set of animations. The blend nodes combine the animations using parametric inputs. A simple example would be a straight cross-fade between two animations controlled by a single variable, fading one animation out as the other fades in. A more complex example might combine several animations at once, playing one set of movements on the character's upper body and another on the legs while using inverse kinematics and changing the speed of playback to prevent foot slippage.

Achieving a naturalistic blend between different animations requires careful planning. It is important that the animations have similar dynamics—for example, you can't blend between a walk and a run without creating the appearance of a hop or a skating motion. It's also important the animations have similar frequencies, or the result will contain irritating stutters.

The complex web of relationships between the different sets of data used to create run-time animation makes it hard to extrapolate from the animation as it appears in Maya or MotionBuilder the result that will appear in-game. For this reason, many teams invest in specialized tools to allow animators to preview the results of their work in real time. This may take place in a dedicated editor or by using a special mode in the game engine. It's vital to provide animators with the ability to view and test their work in the form it will appear in the game. The faster they can iterate, the better the results will be.

Viewing assets in-game, an animator may discover a run-time problem with their animation. In such cases, it is useful to be able to track the assets involved back to the source. This requires

(a)

(b)

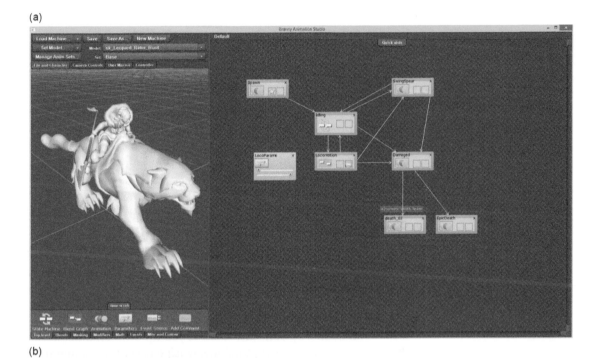

Figure 4.5 In-game animation is created by combining smaller animation sequences or procedurally generated content. These inputs may be displayed as a "blend graph", shown here in the middleware packages Granny (top) and morpheme (below). Granny image © 2013 by RAD Game Tools, Inc.

debug systems written into the run-time environment (these are usually excluded when the game is compiled for release), and for the pipeline to have tracked the relationship between the file exported from the art software and the asset used in-game. Since assets are usually built outside the game engine, as noted earlier, it is usual to record the course of the preparation process—and any errors it generates—in a log file. Again, it is critical that this reporting process is designed well. Useful information is often hidden in "logging spam"—reports that reflect trivial changes or that are simply unclear—and requires a great deal of skill and effort to extract.

Section 4.6 In-Game Facial Animation

Facial animations in games are usually much less sophisticated than those in films, due both to the constraints of run-time performance and the fact that games simply contain more content: whereas most films run for two hours or less, AAA games frequently take a player from twenty to fifty hours to complete. Producing hand-keyed facial animation—or even just hand-keyed lip-sync animation—for this amount of material is prohibitively expensive. It is common for games to rely heavily on procedural techniques to drive facial animations, particularly to match mouth positions to recorded dialog or the text of the script. Middleware solutions dedicated to this task like FaceFX and those developed by Annosoft are used extensively throughout the industry, and offer a level of quality adequate for the bulk of the dialog in most games. Facial capture techniques are more costly but produce better-quality results and are often used for close-ups.

Two main rigging techniques are used to control in-game facial animations: morph targets and bones. Morph targets are meshes depicting individual facial expressions or mouth shapes, created either by resculpting a character mesh by hand, or by capturing the facial expressions of a live actor. By blending between targets at run-time, it is possible to create the illusion of facial animation. Morph targets can create very good approximations of facial expressions, including fine details like wrinkles and the way that facial muscles bulge, but they are expensive to store, so it is not uncommon for a game to use bones to deform a skinned facial mesh, in the same way that bones might be used to control full-body animations.

It's also worth noting that in games, unlike in film work, it is virtually unheard of to calculate geometry caches from the animation: the storage requirements are simply too great, and it is too difficult to make changes to the results at run-time.

Choosing an Animation Creation Pipeline

Matt Hoesterey
Design Lead, Microsoft

One of the main choices to make when starting a new game project is what methodology to use for creating animation assets. There are a lot of different options at your disposal, from performance and motion-capture solutions to keyframe animation. All have their own strengths and weaknesses that need to be understood and related to your specific project.

One key question to ask is: "Will the interaction of the characters be static or dynamic?" A static interaction, such as in a prerendered cinematic, is one that cannot be influenced by the player or any other entity in the game. Let's consider two characters: Jim and Sue. A conversation between Jim and Sue would be static if the two were always shown in the same relative positions while it was being displayed, and could not be influenced until it was over. In this example, performance capture could work wonderfully: beyond cleaning up the data, very little work would be necessary before the animation recorded could be used in-game.

A dynamic interaction is one that can be influenced by the player or another entity in the game. For example, the conversation between Jim and Sue would be dynamic if Jim reacted to the player during the conversation, turning toward the player if they moved around him, or taking a step back if the player got too close. In this case, performance capture is unlikely to be the right solution, since Jim will probably require separate facial and body animations. A combination of motion and facial capture and/or hand-keyed animation would be a better fit.

Another thing to consider when choosing an animation solution is what type of game you are creating. If you are creating a game like *L.A. Noire*, in which the player is a detective who must interrogate suspects, high-quality facial motion-capture is a must, since the player needs to see every nuance of the characters' expressions. On the other hand, if you are creating a real-time strategy game in which the characters are never shown more than an inch tall on screen, facial capture would be a waste of valuable resources: instead, a simple hand-keyed looping "talk" animation should be perfectly adequate.

It's important to note that a single methodology may not be the right choice for creating all of the assets within a project. Understanding the way in which different classes of assets will be used in-game should help you to choose the right pipeline for each aspect of your project.

Section 4.7 Effects and FX

Unlike in film work, the terms "effects" and "FX" often have different meanings in games, particularly RPGs. If a character is hit by a fireball, the reduction in that character's health caused by the damage would be often be called the "effect", while the particles that create the on-screen explosion would be the "FX".

FX are animated art assets that represent things like explosions, smoke, or the effects of magic spells. While they may be created by hand, it is common to generate them procedurally, using similar

kinds of simulation techniques to those used in visual effects. Since FX are tightly integrated into the game engine, the problem of creating a toolkit for FX artists is similar to that of creating a tool for run-time animators. If the artists must continually reload the game and make characters throw grenades before they can view the explosion FX, they will have a hard time iterating the look of the FX efficiently.

Unfortunately, because the FX team is typically quite small, it is often last in line for pipeline support. While using middleware such as Fork Particle and Bishamon avoids the need to develop an FX-editing tool from scratch, even ready-made solutions will require additional work on the part of the pipeline team before the results can be viewed accurately in-game.

Section 4.8 System and Level Design

Where film assets are arranged into shots, game assets are typically arranged into levels. There are several important differences between this process and shot layout. However, before we look at these, we need to distinguish between system and level design.

System designers are technical designers who work closely with programmers to develop gameplay mechanics such as if and how the player jumps, the way a character interacts with objects, and the functionality of the equipment in a character's inventory. Level designers (LDs) determine the placement of art assets. The system designer is responsible for deciding how much health the player receives when picking up a health pack; the level designer is responsible for deciding whether that health pack is hidden or in plain view. The system designer is responsible for deciding how high the player can jump; the level designer for positioning the ledges for them to jump onto.

The first task of the level designer is to place the art assets into the scene. These range from background objects, like distant terrain or "skyboxes"—assets intended to make levels look bigger than they are by displaying the sky or unreachable areas—to platforms for the player to jump onto, enemy characters for them to fight, objects for them to pick up or destroy, lights to illuminate the scene, and triggers and other logic objects that determine gameplay.

However, placing these assets is only half of the level designer's job. Their role is also to determine the way in which the assets interact. This "level logic" could be as simple as making a door open when a lever is pulled, or as complicated as a multi-stage fight in which a player has to complete a series of tasks in order to maneuver an opponent into position, then drop a chandelier on their head. (Note that "level logic" is distinct from "game logic", which is the province

of the system designer. The level designer places the trigger that causes the chandelier to fall; the system designer determines how much damage the chandelier will inflict on the enemy when it falls on their head.)

Large companies creating open-world games may subdivide these tasks further, creating more specialist roles. Typically, "world builders" are responsible for creating the layout of world, while the level designers proper are responsible for creating the interactions within it. However, different companies have slightly different ways to split up the work.

The tools used by a system designer vary greatly from pipeline to pipeline. In some companies, system designers script directly in tools like Visual Studio; in others they use spreadsheet software like Excel to generate data that will later be imported into a database solution. The tools used for level design are linked to the game engine itself. There is no such thing as a "generic" level-design tool: if a developer has designed its own engine, it will have written its own tools; if it uses a commercial engine, the level designer will use the level editor that comes with that engine.

All level editors share some common functionality: they allow designers to create, decorate, and populate the game world. Because so much of the job involves placing assets created elsewhere, level editors typically have to provide some form of asset browser—ideally, one with metadata-based tagging and search facilities. The editor must also enable the designer to place game objects that are not tied to conventional art assets: for example, the marker that tells the game where the player enters the level. For a more detailed discussion of the subject, see "Types of level editor".

Types of Level Editor

Steve Theodore
Technical Art Director, Undead Labs

Terrain Editors

Games with expansive environments typically use "terrain editors". Users typically begin with a "height map": a gray-scale bitmap in which black areas represent points on the terrain of minimum elevation; white areas, those of maximum elevation; and gray tones, intermediate heights. This height map can be "sculpted" using tools that raise or lower terrain, or soften or sharpen its contours. Once the terrain is sculpted, roads, rivers and walls can be draped across its surface, and smaller objects such as rocks or trees placed by hand or scattered procedurally across the landscape.

Buildings and other large structures that players need to enter are typically created as separate assets, then placed onto the terrain. However, it is common for navigable areas to need extra data that controls the way players and AI characters move: this ranges from simplified meshes used to calculate collisions and physics interactions more efficiently to markers indicating features with which characters may interact, such as a climbable ladder, a breakable

window, or a locked door. The intimate connection between the visible geometry and the gameplay means that large structures will have a lot of these kinds of annotations.

Figure 4.6 Many modern game editors use the same rendering and lighting code as game engines, enabling artists to see exactly what their work will look like without having to boot up the game. In Crytek's CryENGINE 3 Sandbox editor it is even possible to fight—and die!—in a level under construction.

One of the unique challenges of managing this kind of pipeline is the scale of the level itself. Because it's such a large asset, containing so many other assets, the level may become a source of contention in the team: for example, the design staff may want to lay down paths for AI characters at the same time that the visual artists want to place props. If the editor is not designed to facilitate cooperation, the pipeline may be slowed down considerably as one artist after another waits to make their changes.

CSG Editors

In games in which most of the action takes place in confined spaces, and those in which the player can move vertically through a level by climbing, "constructive solid geometry editors" or "CSG editors" are more common. These trace their heritage to early 3D games like *Quake* and *Unreal*, and are really 3D modeling tools in their own right. As such, this type of editor tends to combine art creation with game design: many companies who use these tools maintain a distinct staff of "level designers" who are responsible for both visuals and gameplay.

Figure 4.7 CSG (Constructive Solid Geometry) editors like the Unreal engine's UnrealEd are effectively 3D art tools in their own right, enabling users to build and texture geometry or to place models created in other programs. Image © 2013 by Epic Games, Inc.

Although they are not suited to designing large, free-form open worlds, constructive solid geometry editors excel at creating complex 3D spaces quickly. Because they combine modeling and game-design tasks into a single application, they are also popular for games with a multiplayer component. Multiplayer environment teams need to iterate much more quickly than single-player projects, since online players are notoriously clever at finding and exploiting weaknesses in the design—and thus unbalancing the game. The speed of the CSG pipeline makes it attractive to teams who need to incorporate play-test feedback and respond quickly to bugs and exploits.

Tile-Based Editors

In some genres of game, it is desirable to build the world from a library of reusable pieces. "Tile-based editors" enable designers to snap prebuilt components together on a two- or three-dimensional grid. The grid structure enables designers to control variables such as the length of a player's jump or the timing of a moving obstacle accurately. This type of editor often isolates the visual development from the game design: the visual art staff produce assets as "puzzle pieces", but the assembly of the level is done by game designers. The specifications for the puzzle pieces are usually laid down very precisely during the concept design stage, since the gameplay is often related intimately to jump heights,

run speeds and ballistics. As a result, tile-based editors tend to be much simpler to build and use than terrain-based or constructive solid geometry editors.

The pipeline for a tile-based level editor is quite similar to a generic modeling pipeline: the art staff will create individual assets which are then exported into the game's model format. It's usually important to assist this with a good system for tagging the objects with searchable metadata, so that the level designers can find the pieces they need quickly.

Section 4.9 Rendering and Shader Management

The real-time renderer in a game engine differs substantially from those used in visual effects work. Whereas a single frame from a visual effects shot may take hours, or even days, to render, real-time graphics are constrained by the need to render the entire game world between thirty and sixty times per second. In order to make this possible, real-time graphics are rendered on specialized graphics processing chips (GPUs) which accelerate the mathematical operations used to create the images.

The key to GPU computing is parallelization. GPUs contain many individual processors, placed side by side on the chip, which process information simultaneously. This provides a lot of computing power, but only for tasks that can be carried out in parallel rather than in sequence. For example, many offline renders support ray tracing, a technique that simulates the way in which light bounces around a scene. Ray tracing generates accurate reflections and refractions, but it doesn't parallelize well: it is an essentially linear series of mathematical operations, each one dependent on the result of the one before. For this reason, GPUs have traditionally been ill-suited to ray tracing, and the technique is still rarely used in games for this reason.

Similarly, while the shaders used in offline render engines may be arbitrarily complex, those in game engines are constrained by the need to process them in real time. In games, there are two very distinct approaches to managing the relationship between art assets and shaders.

Some studios attempt to reproduce their run-time shaders directly inside the viewport of their 3D software. Tools like 3 ds Max, Maya and Softimage enable technical artists to write custom shaders using languages like HLSL or Cg. Recreating the run-time shaders in this way permits very rapid iteration of art assets, since there is no need to export data.

This approach was very common at the end of the sixth generation of games consoles (the PlayStation 2, the GameCube and the original Xbox), but has fallen out of favor in the last 5 years.

Firstly, it's extremely rare for the in-game shaders and the viewport versions to be precisely identical, since some features of the game engine—such as the use of precalculated light maps (2D image maps used to mimic the illumination of a surface without the need to run a full lighting calculation) and run-time tessellation—are difficult or impossible to reproduce inside the art software. Relying solely on viewport shaders often leads to unpleasant surprises when assets are seen in-game; but if it is necessary to export every asset to the game to view it accurately, the viewport shaders aren't speeding up the process of iteration. Secondly, maintaining parallel copies of the same shader is a serious complication for the pipeline. As well as the issues of data dependency it introduces, if viewport shaders aren't properly maintained, they may crash the art application itself, preventing the art staff from doing any more work until the problem is diagnosed and fixed.

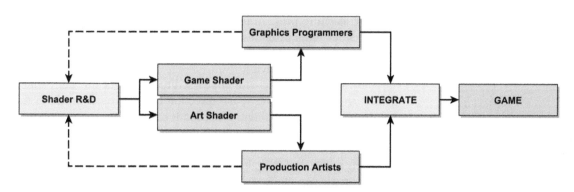

Figure 4.8 A dual-shader pipeline. Ideally, the art shaders used to display assets in the viewport of the production artists' 3D software should match those used in the game itself. In practice, ensuring an exact match often proves problematic.

For these reasons, most studios do not currently try to reproduce the behavior of their shaders directly inside their art tools. Instead, they focus on shortening the export pipeline so that artists can see their assets in the game—or in a dedicated editor that shares the same rendering engine—in very short order. The primary challenge in this kind of system is making sure that assets are tied to the right in-game shaders. The most common way to do this is simply to match in-game materials to proxy materials created in the 3D application by name. Under this system, an artist assigns one of their 3D software's built-in materials to an asset and gives it a distinctive name. Inside the game editor, a shader will be created for each named material present in the exported asset. These can then be edited in the game's renderer. This encourages the artists to iterate in the game environment and enables them to see the results of their changes in real time.

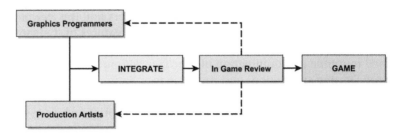

Figure 4.9 Because it's hard to reproduce the look of game shaders inside an art tool, it's common simply to ignore shader effects in the art package, treating the materials as mere placeholders for the game version. This simplifies the tool chain, but the final results can only be seen in-game.

Like blend graphs, shaders straddle the boundary between art and programming. Many modern commercial game engines, notably the Unreal Engine and Unity, enable artists to create their own shaders without learning programming by linking a set of prebuilt components. Other tools provide an editing environment reminiscent of a programmer's text editor, with auto-completion and syntax highlighting to improve productivity.

Allowing artists to create shaders directly offers the compelling advantage of keeping the visual direction of the project firmly in the hands of the art department. However, it can also cause performance problems: without engineering training, and lacking the tools necessary to accurately predict the real costs of their shader networks, artists are often accused of dragging down the game's frame rate by creating overly complex, inefficient shaders.

One common compromise is for artists to provide "first-pass" or "prototype" shaders, which establish the look of an asset but that are intended to be replaced by more efficient versions authored by a shader specialist before work wraps up. All too often, of course, these planned replacements fall off the schedule and the shipped shaders are messy and inefficient. To avoid this problem, many teams provide a single all-in-one shader that covers the entire range of permissible rendering techniques. These "ubershaders" usually enable artists to activate special features on a case-by-case basis, adding special effects like refraction or procedural noise by ticking a checkbox in the shader editor. Ubershaders provide a more predictable performance envelope (it's easy to design the editor UI to prevent artists from turning on all the expensive features at the same time, for example), and help to minimize the number of shaders necessary on a project. This is important, since switching shaders is one of the most computationally expensive operations on a GPU, and effects such as dynamic lighting can otherwise cause shader counts to balloon. However, ubershaders do tend to homogenize the look of the game.

In the last few years, many games have adopted a new rendering technology which further complicates the job of shader management.

Before 2007, most shader systems allowed each shader to write directly to the final rendered image: a methodology known as "forward" or "direct" rendering. Many modern systems try to improve performance and realism by breaking the rendering process into a series of discrete passes, in which different aspects of the image are rendered separately and combined on screen, in much the same way that images are rendered in passes and recombined in a compositor in visual effects work. This method, known as "deferred" rendering, allows complex lighting effects to be handled more efficiently. However, it ups the ante for shader authors. In a deferred renderer, shaders need to write out a series of "buffers" or image layers in a strictly defined sequence, and few production artists have the technical background to handle this. In many cases, teams with a deferred rendering system are obliged to go with the ubershader approach simply to manage the complexity of their graphics engine.

Building a Game Engine

As we have noted in this chapter, a game engine performs many tasks. These include those we have touched on here, including scene assembly, generating run-time animation, physics simulation, AI, and rendering—along with several we have not, including audio, memory management, processor threading, networking, streaming and localization support.

For this reason, writing your own engine from scratch is usually the preserve of big studios with large programming teams. Smaller developers typically choose either to license a commercially available engine (games industry website Develop recently published an overview of the main alternatives: http://bit.ly/YOSx9r), or to build one by linking together a set of ready-made middleware. A list of most of the main tools currently available can be found on the website GameMiddleware.org (www.gamemiddleware.org/middleware).

5

THE BASIC FUNCTIONALITY OF A PIPELINE

Tim Green; Matt Hoesterey; Hannes Ricklefs; Mark Streatfield; Steve Theodore; Laurent M. Abecassis: *Di-O-Matic;* **Rob Blau:** *Head of Pipeline Engineering, Shotgun Software;* **Ryan Mayeda:** *Product Producer, Shotgun Software;* **Manne Ohrstrom:** *Senior Software Engineer, Shotgun Software;* **John Pearl:** *Principal Artist, Crytek USA*

Section 5.1 What You Will Learn From This Chapter

In the previous chapters, we looked at the ways in which data is created during a production. In this chapter, we will look at how that data is managed. We will begin by exploring some general design criteria for pipelines, and the issues that affect them—such as the need for technical standards, data interchange formats and "micro pipelines"—then look at four key aspects of data management: directory structures, file-naming conventions, metadata and version control. Finally, we will look at how to exploit the production data you are tracking.

Section 5.2 What Pipelines Do

The goal of a production pipeline is to produce a product in an efficient and cost-effective way. To accomplish this goal, it must do two things. First, it must manage the flow of data from process to process. And second, it must direct the flow of work from task to task.

These two sub-goals are linked: to manage the flow of work, you must first understand the flow of data. Imagine building a house. In this analogy, the "product" is a finished building. The "data" is the material it is made up of—bricks, wood, plaster, wires, and so on—and the "work" is just that: the tasks the construction crew must accomplish to complete the building.

This list of tasks includes installing the wiring and plastering the walls. Since the wires go inside the walls, the electrician must install them before the plaster can finish work. If you don't understand

this relationship, the construction schedule will be wrong: either the plasterer will have to sit around doing nothing until the electrician is finished, or the electrician will have to destroy the plasterer's work to install the wires. The same thing is true of film and game production. If you don't understand that models and rigs must be completed before animation can begin, the animators will sit around with nothing to animate.

It's worth exploring the analogy between creating art and creating physical products a bit further. We use the term "pipeline" to wrap our processes in an aura of industrial competence. The image of a giant refinery humming along day and night, continuously converting the raw material of artistic inspiration into beautifully realized pixels is a very reassuring one. It suggests both great power and a comforting kind of predictability: ideas go in at one end, and products pop out the other. In between, a white-coated staff of technicians monitors the whole process, nodding sagely as they watch the dials that show things flowing along smoothly.

Unfortunately, in the real world, production pipelines more closely resemble those of a Dr. Seuss book than those of a factory, full of loopbacks, short circuits, and about-faces. All too often, a film or game pipeline is held together with contraptions that not even The Cat in the Hat would dare to rely on. So why is this? To answer that, let's take a look at why pipelines change.

Section 5.3 Why Pipelines Change

In part, pipelines change because technology does. New technology means new kinds of data, and methods for creating it must often be shoehorned into an existing pipeline in the middle of production. A new product for fluid simulation comes along, and now it's necessary to figure out how it works with your existing shader library. Or the company that developed the plug-in you've been relying on for rigid-body dynamics goes out of business, leaving you to decide whether to stick with a tool that is no longer being updated, or write your own version.

More importantly, pipelines change because they're used by people, not machines. A pipeline is really the technical expression of a complex web of human activities, encompassing everybody from the loftiest creative director to the humblest production assistant, and those people's tastes are as important as any technical constraint. Building a pipeline around software that meets all of your technical goals but which your artists can't stand is an exercise in futility. Pipeline development is ultimately a service business, not an engineering project.

As the nineteenth-century military strategist Field Marshal Helmuth von Moltke observed, no battle plan, however brilliant, survives contact with the enemy. In production, that might be rephrased

as "no pipeline survives contact with the client." The studio's latest change to the script demands a new and unanticipated effect. Or the multiplayer version of the game proves so important that you have to build fifty player characters where you had budgeted for five. Schedules change. Funding falls through. And creating a film or game isn't like building a car: there's always a little more work you can do before it's "complete".

Section 5.4 Defining Your Goals

To cope with change, you need to pick your own battles carefully. Your resources are limited, and you won't have the time to service every aspect of the production equally well. You need a solid strategic understanding of the project so you can prioritize your decisions, both during planning and when the inevitable crises arise during production. Let's run through the key questions you need to ask yourself.

What are the Project's Core Values?

Every project has a handful of defining features, and you need to articulate these in order to be able to support it well. A film about pirates needs a robust set of tools for creating fluid simulations; one set in a fantasy city needs tools for creating buildings. A game with tightly scripted linear gameplay can probably proceed down an equally linear production path; one with a strong multiplayer demands a quick turnaround in level design, for when beta testers discover game-breaking exploits.

How Big is the Project?

Projects vary widely in size and complexity, and the pipelines they require vary accordingly. It's usually more sensible to invest in custom technology on large projects with long schedules: there may be time to develop a new level editor for a game that takes two hundred artists three years to produce, but an indie title completed by two people in six months is probably going to have to use off-the-shelf software. However, there are exceptions: small teams have to think long-term too, and custom software can be a unique selling point for a boutique studio. Conversely, artists need to be trained how to use custom software, as a large studio may not want to disrupt a critical project to get everyone up to speed.

Can We Reuse the Tools We Develop?

Every piece of code you create should be designed with the idea of modularity in mind so that the pipeline for the next project doesn't have to be built from scratch. However, creating software that stands up

to the pressure of constant technological advances can be very hard, even for large facilities. The same goes for other forms of technology, including the machines you need to run the software packages and the file formats that transfer data between them. Sometimes, "building to throw away" may be the pragmatic choice.

Are There Any Other Technical Constraints?

Projects don't arise in a vacuum. In most cases, many important aspects of the production environment will be chosen for you before the project has even begun. For business reasons, your facility may already be committed to a particular piece of software or a particular outsourcing vendor, even if your particular project would be better served by something else. In games, your options may be limited by the choice of game engine or target platform. Last, but certainly not least, you will have to work within a budget that constrains your choice of tools and vendors.

Managing Legacy Systems

John Pearl
Principal Artist, Crytek USA

Over the years, I've been responsible for supervising the creation of a lot of different pipelines at a lot of different studios. The best pipelines are the ones that you never have to think about while you use them: they just work. While there's no magic path to creating one of those, one thing I've learned is to keep legacy systems in mind.

Legacy tools can be a huge bottleneck, especially in the game industry, where software changes every six months on average. Sometimes, just updating to the latest version will fix these headaches—and this is usually the cheapest way to do so. But if you're using the most up-to-date version of the software and it's still not doing the job you need it to do, look around on the net. There are a lot of start-up developers around, and they're creating interesting new ways to resolve common development bottlenecks all the time.

If neither option is available and you find that you need to stick with legacy software, account for it in your pipeline plan. Don't get discouraged: there are other ways to improve a pipeline.

The most difficult legacy issue to overcome is "legacy thinking". Whenever you create a new pipeline, you meet resistance—luckily, not usually of an aggressive sort, but a challenge nonetheless. Common objections include "it's worked for us so far" and "I'm comfortable with the way things are, so I don't want to change." Both are valid points of view, but they also stifle the potential of a project.

It's fairly easy to deal with "it's worked for us so far". If you know that in your proposed pipeline it will take someone 2 minutes to deal with an asset, whereas in the legacy pipeline it takes 10, those 8 minutes of waste per person per asset are a compelling reason to change.

This is obviously a black-and-white case, but similar examples crop up quite often. No one concerned with the productivity of a team can argue with hard numbers.

If the benefits of the changes are harder to quantify, or if you aren't in a position to make comparisons with the previous pipeline, it's better to look at the pipeline you are hoping to replace and ask: "Did it *really* work for us?"

At one company I worked at, we used a single 3ds Max shader for all of our 3D assets. This had been used for the previous three projects, and was added to as new technical needs were identified. However, since nothing was ever removed, over 6 years, the shader had accumulated over a hundred inputs and parameters, some completely redundant. These were laborious to navigate through, and most had cryptic names that had once meant something to someone no longer working at the company. Worse, a single misclick could break the asset in-game. The excuse of "it 'works', so why change it?" had trumped common sense.

The harder objection to deal with is "I'm comfortable with the way things are." Whereas the "worked so far" camp is usually made up of people who don't actually use the pipeline and have an outside view of the process, the "comfort" camp is made of people who use it day to day. Sometimes, they've been burned by pipeline changes in the past; sometimes it simply comes down to the fact that most people don't like change.

While you usually need to get the "worked so far" people to buy into your decisions, at the end of the day, you're making the pipeline for the "comfort" people. Understanding their needs—and their hang-ups with the current tool set—is critical here. The people who like change the least are often the ones most dissatisfied with their current tools: it's just that they've crafted their own work-arounds, and have developed a kind of Stockholm Syndrome in consequence.

In cases like this, it's hard to change minds with words: it's often better to show. Walk the hesitant developers through your proposed pipeline, step by step. Hear them out: people who use a pipeline day in and day out will have an insight you can't gain from observation alone. Then show them that you are making an effort to address their concerns in your revised plan. Making these individuals feel like they are crafting the pipeline alongside you helps them to feel invested in change, not that it is simply being thrust upon them.

Even then, you may still have detractors. At that point, you just have to move forward with your plans. Change is part of the job of a game developer: those that don't embrace it will eventually be left behind. I've seen this happen over the years—people refuse to grow and their skill set shrinks until eventually they make themselves obsolete. The best hope is that once the new pipeline is in place, they will appreciate its efficiency and embrace it with the rest of the team.

Legacy technology doesn't have to be a hurdle. In fact, dealing with it up front will make your pipeline stronger. Doing the research you need to prove your case may suggest other changes or additions you wouldn't otherwise have thought to make. At the end of the process, you will feel confident that you're making the best pipeline you can.

What Do The Artists Like?

Artists are notoriously picky about software, and they tend to be attached to the tools they know best. You might be able to save money by switching to a new art package, but you'll have to endure a lot of grumbling about its unfamiliar UI. It can be hard for pipeline developers, who frequently know and like aspects of many different tools, to sympathize with the tendency of artists to cling to their preferred software. However, it is a fact of life that needs to be included

in your planning. Attempting to force your chosen tool on an unwilling workforce can result in months of reduced productivity, if not outright mutiny. A clear rationale for the choice, coupled with good training, can take the sting out of the transition, but the process still demands tact and discretion. You need to consider your political capital with the end users as carefully as you would your budget. And remember that changes of software have a knock-on effect on recruitment. The new package may indeed be three times faster than the old one, but if none of the freelancers available know how to use it, you may waste more time than you save.

How Much Feedback Do The Artists Need?

How experienced the artists are will dictate important aspects of your pipeline design. Veteran staff may want very detailed technical feedback from your tools—feedback that more junior artists would find intimidating and confusing. Experts may be frustrated or even insulted by safeguards put in place to keep inexperienced users from endangering the workflow. Similarly, tools designed for outsourcers who will only work on the project for a few months will have to be simpler and more robust than those for permanent staff who may have had years to come to grips with their subtleties.

How Many Artists are There, and Where are They in the World?

Small teams can rely on email or instant messaging, but big groups—especially those distributed around the globe—will need a much more elaborate platform for collaboration. International collaboration can usually be done in English, but you still need to be aware of other localization issues: it's unwise to assume that all the artists at your outsourcing studio will have the latest versions of Windows or an always-on internet connection at their workstation, for example.

Are There Any Other Cultural Considerations?

Other aspects of organizational culture are harder to quantify, yet may have a profound impact on pipeline development. Some teams care passionately about the look of their tool chains; others are strict utilitarians who disdain fancy icons as a waste of time and money. Unfortunately, there is no one-size-fits-all methodology for uncovering these preferences—the literature of software development is full of discussions of the relative merits of user stories, executive summaries, functional specifications, UI wireframes, Q&A sessions, test cases, and the like—but the willingness to acknowledge them is key to successful pipeline development. It is remarkable how many

brilliant technical artists, prepared to spend days shaving milliseconds off a file-read time, fail to invest the same energy into getting the most out of other people.

What Constraints Do We Have to Live With?

All too often, the most important factor in determining what work can be done is simply how much time is available. When building a pipeline for the first time, focus on the "must-haves": a complete set of tools, automating any task that can't be achieved manually in a reasonable time frame—and above all, stability. Each tool you create should behave in a consistent, predictable way. This is particularly important when designing lower-level functionality upon which you will need to build later. Only when all of the basics are in place should you start to focus on the "nice-to-haves".

Getting the Right People Involved

It's important to consult with the right people before planning and building a pipeline. These include representatives of a number of different departments within the facility, and of a number of different levels of seniority:

- **Management**: to define how they expect the company's business to evolve, and what they see as the strategic aims of the pipeline.
- **Supervisors and producers**: people who will oversee projects logistically, and who can define how they want the pipeline to run from day to day.
- **Creatives**: key personnel from each creative department who can explain the needs of the artists working with the pipeline.
- **Technical staff**: to advise on anything infrastructure-related, including new technological advances and what is feasible in terms of development work.

It is crucial to strike the right balance of participants in the decision-making process. This includes balancing technical goals against achieving an artist-friendly workflow, and balancing the risk of having "too many cooks in the kitchen" against that of leaving key voices unheard.

It's important to note here that no two artists or programmers are alike. A few extra years' experience can make all the difference when it comes to planning a pipeline. If you get the right person with the right experience, a job can be done in a fraction of the time. This is particularly important when it comes to technical staff. Whereas it is common to recognize that modelers, animators, lighters and other art staff have distinct skill sets, programmers tend to be regarded—quite wrongly—as being interchangeable.

The people involved (particularly the main pipeline architects) need to have the long-term interests of the company in mind, balanced against the short-term needs of the projects in production. They should be permanent, full-time staff, not hired on a per-project basis. Continuity of personnel eliminates the time-consuming learning phase at the start of each cycle of pipeline development, and minimizes random "churn" in pipeline structure.

Everyone involved, but particularly supervisors, needs to buy into the aims of the pipeline, and understand best practices for working with it. Supervisors should push the people they oversee to work within the pipeline at all times.

Section 5.5 Defining Standards

Next, we will look at some of the technical considerations that arise when designing a pipeline. The first of these is the need to define technical standards. Such standards take several forms:

- Which software the facility is going to use for which task
- The file format in which data is shared between these applications
- Workflow standards that describe the steps by which an asset is created and the way in which it will be shared with the rest of the pipeline
- The attributes of these assets that will be stored as metadata
- Organizational standards, such as the way in which tasks are scheduled or asset reviews are conducted

These standards are unique to your facility, so it is important to ensure that they are understood fully by the staff and documented clearly. When you begin a new project, good documentation will reduce the time it takes new hires to get up to speed. Each standard should be self-contained, independent of other parts of the pipeline, and agnostic: its documentation should state the desired outcome without prescribing or constraining the solution chosen.

A concrete example might be the way in which new models are added to the asset-management system. The standard would define what constitutes a "valid" model in abstract terms (such as whether the geometry can contain n-gons or only quads, the maximum size of the file, and how the file is named). It should then be just as feasible for a developer to implement a system that exports valid models from the software automatically as it is for an individual artist to do so manually; the resulting models should be identical, as they conform to the same standard.

Section 5.6 File-Exchange Formats and Scripting Languages

One particularly important type of standard is the format in which data moves between tools. Graphics production often involves using a number of different third-party software packages, and it is the job of the pipeline developer to ensure they all work with one another. For example, getting a model ready for use in-game may involve getting the high-resolution sculpt out of ZBrush and into xNormal to create a normal map for use in Maya; while creating a shader may involve getting a specially packed texture map out of Photoshop and into FX Composer.

Unfortunately, these different packages don't share native file formats. And even though it is supposedly their raison d'être, interchange file formats like DXF, FBX and Collada are infamous for their inability to move data reliably: while it is *possible* to get

data from one package to another, the process is rarely smooth or predictable.

Alembic, an open-source development effort headed by Lucasfilm and Sony Pictures Imageworks, is designed to address this issue—at least as far as sharing geometry data for animation goes. The Alembic format is being adopted as an evolving standard by many third-party software vendors, and ultimately, looks likely to become adopted near-universally.

Muggins: MPC's Core Framework

Hannes Ricklefs
Global Head of Pipeline, MPC

Moving data reliably from one application to another is a major issue in production work. At MPC, we use a framework called "Muggins", a C++ library that provides:

- Our own representations of geometry, such as polygons and subdivision surfaces
- A range of common algorithms and geometry operations: from mathematical calculations to multithreading utilities
- A generic render context which abstracts the core aspects of any renderer, such as geometry, lights, cameras and shaders
- Integration with Maya, Nuke, Katana and our own OpenGL-based viewers
- An interface scriptable via the Lua and Python programming languages

Whenever possible, we try to export application-specific assets as Muggins data. This conversion enables us to bring a model, camera or animated geometry cache into any of the applications listed above, regardless of its original source. The conversion process happens automatically on asset release, for any asset type that has a Muggins representation. This enables us to share assets reliably between the different applications.

Another issue is that software packages don't share a common scripting language. Most major applications today include some kind of scripting, but there are a wide variety of languages in use—from general-purpose languages like Python to proprietary languages that exist only inside one application. The lack of a universal standard makes it hard for facilities that have to support tools written in several languages, often requiring an irritating amount of redundant work.

Throughout the industry, but particularly in visual effects, Python is widely used for pipeline integration. There are also specific open-source developments such as Cortex—a set of C++ libraries and Python modules tailored to VFX tool-development work—aimed at providing a common framework that can be embedded in any application.

Section 5.7 Micro Pipelines

Another technical issue that arises during production is the need to develop on a smaller scale. While the main concern of this book is the development of large, end-to-end, interdepartmental pipelines, it is important to recognize the impact of micro pipelines. In production, macro pipelines provide the rules; micro pipelines recognize the fact that rules are made to be broken.

Even though, at the macro level, a pipeline may suit a facility's needs, situations will inevitably arise for which it is unsuitable. In visual effects, these are typically individual shots whose creative requirements break the mold, requiring one-off solutions that live and die with the shot in question. While it is desirable to limit such exceptions, if only for the sake of the developers' sanity, commercial pressures and artistic freedom dictate that the pipeline should be able to support them where necessary. Fortunately, the impacts of these micro pipelines are only felt by the small number of artists working on the shot, and sometimes only a single person.

Alternatively, intradepartmental workflows may arise that are not discarded at the end of a production. These typically start out as ad hoc work-arounds designed to address new needs. These work-arounds form a micro pipeline that may later be unified with the pipeline at large.

In such cases, the micro pipeline may need to be "sanitized" before unification. In some cases, artists will simply have reconfigured their workflow within existing parameters—but more often, they will have developed custom scripts or plug-ins. In order to avoid a ripple effect requiring changes to surrounding pipelines, these tools may need to be rewritten so that their inputs and outputs match those currently required by the macro pipeline.

Section 5.8 Strategies for Managing Data: An Overview

The main technical issue that arises during production is the need to manage data. A large modern game or visual effects production generates an unimaginable amount of data: hundreds of thousands of files, occupying terabytes of storage space. Fortunately, this enormous cloud of files condenses into something more manageable if you focus on what your users care about.

When an artist gets tasked with fixing a jittery-looking run cycle or an undesirable-looking environment, the conversation always starts with a tangible problem: "the ogre's animation is a couple of frames too long" or "we need more trees to screen out the terrace in the temple level". The task of the pipeline developer is to ensure that artists can translate these tangible problems into the intangible world of

data, locating the animation file for the ogre's run cycle, or the level design for the temple.

In the remainder of this chapter, we shall explore four key strategies for managing data:

- Setting up an intuitive directory structure
- Adopting good file-naming conventions
- Using metadata to make files searchable
- Employing versioning or version control to ensure that files remain up to date

We shall introduce each topic briefly here, before returning to some of them in more detail in later chapters.

Section 5.9 Directory Structure

Every file in a production plays different roles for different people, but computer operating systems insist that everything fits into one—and only one—place. Segregating files into a hierarchy of folders certainly avoids the information overload that would result from viewing files as a single list, but the very thing that makes folders useful—the ability to filter information down to a manageable size—is actually a technology designed to hide rather than to locate data. Folders don't control what you can see: they control what you can't.

A modern pipeline will supplement this with tools that provide a more flexible view of the data—we will look at some of these later in this chapter—but it's still important to have a well-organized directory structure under the hood. No matter how fancy a database or asset browser you have, at some point you will find yourself manually clicking through folders looking for a particular file. So figure out a set of rubrics for filing data and stick to it. Better still, document it clearly, make sure your team understands the rationale, and back it up with tools that make it easier to save files in the right places. But whatever you do, don't leave things to chance.

The roots of a good hierarchy are functional, based around who is going to be looking at the data. If you can be reasonably certain that different sets of files will be viewed by entirely different sets of people, that's a good opportunity to separate them out into their own folders. For example, the source code for your pipeline tools should have its own branch in the hierarchy, separate from art files or production data. A game project will usually want to segregate the game code from the art assets, while a film might want to split data so that contractors can only see the part of the project they are working on. An international project might want to separate core components from those that are going to be local to one region.

Within the art assets themselves, some further subdivisions are obvious. For example, in film, visual effects data is usually organized on a project-sequence-shot basis, so it makes sense to have three corresponding levels in your directory structure.

Below that level, however, things begin to get contentious. Even on simple projects, there is no unique mental map that slots every asset into one-and-only-one place. Does a wrecked car model belong in the vehicles folder, or in the debris folder? Does a potted plant belong in the furniture directory, or a vegetation directory? Moreover, you don't just have to decide the categories: you also have to decide their pecking order. For example, most game projects will require that all of the character assets are placed in a single directory. But how are they to be grouped? There are several races, so the modelers would like each one to have its own folder. But then the animators point out that the characters share animations by gender, not by race, so they would prefer the top-level folders to be male and female rather than elf, dwarf, orc and hobbit. Meanwhile, the designers would like the hierarchy to be split between playable and non-playable characters, even though there are playable characters of every race and gender.

Such arguments are common, and inescapable. People don't think like computers; they use overlapping, fuzzy categories, not a rigid hierarchy of either/or choices. To make matters worse, the hierarchy is not simply a way of helping them to find data, but a way of marking out turf. And where there is turf, there are turf wars.

How users want data segregated often varies along departmental lines. For example, the motion-capture department might want to keep all of its captures and setup data in a hierarchy based around the date of a shoot. On the other hand, the animators who are going to use that data would prefer it to be organized around their own workflow: by character, or by scene. Modelers may want to group assets in a way that makes it easier to share textures and shaders, whereas environment artists may prefer them organized by function, making it easier to browse weapons, props, or other types of assets.

With so many conflicting perspectives, designing a hierarchy is always a contentious process. Where possible, try to do so on a need-to-know basis: is there a way to split up folders so that you only show some of them to certain members of the team? But eventually, you will run into conflicts that can't be reconciled. If you can't broker a compromise, you will need to pick one option and run with it. Document the rationale behind the decision so that users can use the system effectively, even if they don't agree with it; and plan for tools that reinforce your organizational structure: for example, by filing assets in the correct places automatically.

When building a hierarchy, it is also important to lay down clear rules for naming folders, particularly if you're using a mixture of operating systems. Windows is not case-sensitive, so on a Windows computer, there is no difference between the path c:/path/to/a/file and C:/Path/To/A/File. On a standard Unix, Linux, or Mac OS X machine, however, those two paths would point to completely different locations on disk. In order to avoid problems further down the line, you need to

pick a convention that works with your mix of systems and enforce it in your tools. We will look at naming conventions in more detail in the next section.

Section 5.10 File-Naming Conventions

As well as deciding on a directory structure, it is important to set up conventions for naming files and folders. A descriptive file system is crucial. If all else fails, if files are named intuitively, artists will be able to locate the assets they need through standard Open and Save dialogs.

Surprisingly for such a seemingly mundane topic, naming conventions are one of the most hotly debated issues in pipeline design. We will address this controversy in more detail in a later chapter. But for now, let's look at some of the key issues.

The primary concern of a naming convention is to give assets unique, global identifiers. For example, the shot-naming conventions commonly used in VFX work contain multiple identifiers. In a file name like "XX_TR_001", "XX" represents the project, "TR" represents the scene and "001" the shot.

A naming convention based solely on numbers or code letters would be impossible to navigate, so it is important to use identifiers that the human brain can comprehend intuitively. For example, all directories that contain content to build a character might use the prefix "char": "charBob", "charFoo", and so on. This same logic can be extended to "vhcl" (that is, vehicle), "prop", and so on. Using such labels makes it easy to find all the folders that contain your characters, even when using standard file-system-based searches and list operations.

Some facilities also use file names to store extra information about the status of those files—for example, in visual effects work, you might add "_render_" to a file name to signal that a scene is ready for offline rendering. Other facilities use suffixes to indicate whether a file is "WIP" (Work in Progress), "final" or "approved". It is also common to include the name or initials of the last person to work on a file, or a version number: an issue we will explore later in the chapter.

Adhering to a rigid naming convention enables automation to be built into the pipeline.

If file names are formed in a systematic way that the pipeline can decipher, assets placed in a particular folder can be integrated automatically into a shot or game level. This enables artists to add content to a production without having to run additional tools.

Of course, all the benefits of structured naming conventions can only be realized if the file names are correctly formed, so it is

common for studios that rely on this system to create tools within software applications to ensure compliance. These tools should provide a convenient way to fill out the information needed by the naming convention. Say that you want to ensure that the shot number is present: the Save dialog should have a field into which the artist must type the number before the save can be completed, rather than relying on them to add the information manually. Similarly, a game animator could be presented with a list of recognized actions when exporting to the game: for example, choosing "Walk" or "Jump" from a list that has been pre-populated with actions the game knows how to format correctly and save to an appropriate file path.

Figure 5.1 Building a structured "wizard-style" interface for creating new assets helps to enforce naming and file location conventions, and saves user time when setup operations are complicated.

However, automated naming systems are vulnerable to human error. Relying entirely on the clerical skills of 3D artists is risky: even the most careful of artists can transpose letters or misnumber items in a sequence. Moreover, the clerical errors can be very hard to track down: if a file fails to animate because someone has typed "junp" instead of "jump", it may take a good bit of staring at the folder listing to catch the problem. The importance you attach to naming conventions should correlate with your willingness to provide tools to enforce those conventions.

Coding naming conventions into tools also makes them harder to transfer to new projects. This can be mitigated by building the tools in such a way that non-programmers can change how the automation works: for example, by exposing all of the assumed variables such as folder paths and naming prefixes in a setup panel. However, even the best tools designers can't foresee every eventuality, so automation will inevitably add some degree of unpredictability into your pipeline.

Directory Scans and Conditional Files

Tim Green
Senior Programmer, Supermassive Games

When a tool needs to load data spread throughout many files, there are two common options. Given a root file, the tool may read file references out of that file, resolve those references to absolute paths, then load those files. Alternatively, it may be given a folder path and directory-scan all of the files within that folder.

The latter is easier to code and easier to maintain. Under the former system, if you want to add or remove a file, you need to edit the root file first; whereas directory scanning only requires the file to be saved into or deleted from the appropriate folder.

Yet I believe that directory scanning is evil. It tempts you with ease of use—then, when you least expect it, turns round and bites you. Let me explain.

Typically, files exist both on the user's local drive and as a master copy in a revision-control system such as Perforce. The user syncs the two during source control, updating the contents of the local folder. If you create a new file, it is created in that folder, tested, then checked into source control so that when others on your team sync, they receive a copy. This works fine as long as everything stays in sync. But here is the problem: rogue files often get into local folders. These are files that do not exist in source control and are only present on your machine. They are easy to miss among the thousands of other similarly named files in the folder.

In games, the result is that the artist with the rogue file will see the game behave differently on their machine to the rest of the team. This may result in the pipeline staff wasting time to resolve the problem—I have personally lost hundreds of hours hunting down rogue files on other people's machines—or worse, the artist checking in their content only to break the game for the rest of the team, since the rogue file is required to make it run correctly.

Conditional files are files where the pipeline changes its behavior based on the existence of a file and both existence and non-existence yield a valid result. They suffer the same problems as directory scans and should be avoided for the same reason.

As well as ensuring that files are named correctly, it may be necessary for the system to ensure that they are saved in the correct format. This is more difficult than it sounds. How often have you tried to open a file with a .jpg extension only to realize that it is actually a TIFF image? As a result, it may be necessary to rely on systems such as "magic numbers": a practice in which a file format is defined as beginning with a unique identifier. For example, files saved in the JPEG format always begin with the hexadecimal characters "ff d8 ff e0".

Again, pipeline developers may write tools to ensure that artists save assets in the correct format. For example, cameras created in Maya cannot be opened in Nuke if they are saved in Maya's native MA format. To ensure that data created earlier in the pipeline can be used during compositing, it may be necessary to write a tool within Maya

prompting the artist to save the camera in the FBX or Alembic interchange formats instead.

Section 5.11 Metadata

We've already discussed how hierarchies aren't really about *finding* information. Instead, they excel at *hiding* it. This isn't entirely a bad thing: if your project contains hundreds of thousands of files, you really don't want to see most of them most of the time, and you'd never be able to find anything if they were presented in a single flat list.

However, when you know what you want and you're trying to retrieve it quickly, a hierarchical folder setup can quickly get in your way. We've already pointed out that different departments—or even different personality types—will construct very different mental maps of a project. One person's efficient, logical layout is another person's chaotic nightmare.

Fortunately, folders are not the only way to find your assets. Most of us maintain music libraries with thousands, or even tens of thousands, of songs. But only the hardest of the hardcore design a folder tree to organize them. Instead, we let iTunes or Windows Media Player handle the problem of where the files are to be stored, using other types of information to browse them.

This information—genre, artist's name, date, and so on—is called "metadata". It seems mundane because we see it every day, but in fact, it is a sophisticated database system. It's sophisticated in the best sense: so good we take it for granted.

Metadata is a much more powerful way of viewing your files than simply hopping up and down a tree view. Unlike folders, it is inclusive, not exclusive. Organizing by metadata turns the stuffy, hidebound business of filing information into the much more efficient process of finding what you need by whatever route suits your needs at that moment. It doesn't force you to actually shuffle things around on disk if those needs change.

Since search-based navigation is considerably faster than navigating a directory hierarchy, it is replacing hierarchies in most areas of computing: just look at the way that modern search engines like Google have replaced the old-fashioned indexes popularized by Yahoo!, or the steady growth of Spotlight in Mac OS X. Since your users are certain to be familiar with the process of searching the web, or of searching their hard drive, it makes sense for your tools to work the same way.

In such systems, the way that files are "tagged" with metadata is very important. Unfortunately, tags aren't a standard OS feature, so it's up to individual applications to implement them. Tags may be stored in a number of ways: in a database, in file-system metadata, in dedicated metadata files on disk, or even directly inside other file types: for

example, Microsoft Office, Photoshop and MP3 files all contain inherent metadata for things like author names and copyrights.

But the real challenge with tagging isn't technological, but semantic: a computer won't know what a given asset is until you tell it. Luckily, you can get a lot of tagging done for free simply by leveraging the old-fashioned file hierarchy—many of your folder names are essentially tags already, so you can apply them automatically to the files they contain. For example, all of the files in the "characters" folder can be automatically tagged as characters. This approach is too generous—in this example, any props in the characters folder will be auto-tagged incorrectly—but usually that doesn't matter. It's uncommon to search for everything in a big category like "characters", so you can usually rely on the tags to filter the results down to a manageable size.

Again, it may be necessary to write tools—either standalone apps, or scripts that run inside art software—to ensure that artists generate good metadata. These tools usually provide a wizard-style interface that asks the user some basic questions about what they want to create, then names and tags the files on their behalf.

The scripting languages supported by heavyweight applications like Maya and Nuke make it easy to do this, but an asset browser—about which, more below—can still assist workflow for less sophisticated apps using drag-and-drop or native OS file launching. A hotkey that copies file paths to the clipboard is another great way to get the benefits of modern search techniques in even the clunkiest of old dialog boxes.

Section 5.12 Building an Asset Browser

One of the most valuable tools that you can add to any pipeline is an asset browser: an application dedicated to finding and managing files within your project. Like Windows Explorer or the OS X Finder, an asset browser is a tool for listing files, but unlike the standard OS finder, it is optimized for graphics production. A good asset browser has four key features:

Search

The most important function of the asset browser is to find files via a combination of keyword, metadata, or tag searches. The interface should be optimized for speed and immediacy, not database-like precision—users want to find their files quickly, not concoct SQL queries. A progressive search function that refines the search results as the user types—like the keyword auto-completion in Google's web interface, or the quick search in iTunes—provides the kind of fast feedback that gets users where they want to go.

Figure 5.2 Google's Picasa is an example of a search-based approach to managing files. Images can be located using a traditional folder hierarchy (top left) or via keywords, reducing a huge database of images to a small subset, even though the files are stored in different locations on disk.

Dependencies

An asset browser should understand how files relate to each other, enabling a user to locate all the relevant assets even when they are stored in different virtual locations. For example, it might allow a user to see all of the textures associated with a model, or all of the video clips associated with a particular composition.

Browsing

The "browsing" part of the asset browser is most useful for artists who aren't exactly sure what they need—for example, a set dresser looking to populate an environment with props from the studio library, or a compositor choosing video clips. With tag or keyword searches, such users can view thumbnails, text descriptions, or metadata to help decide which assets to import into their work.

Tagging

The essence of a search workflow is that assets are "tagged": that is, they are cataloged in all the ways in which they may be important

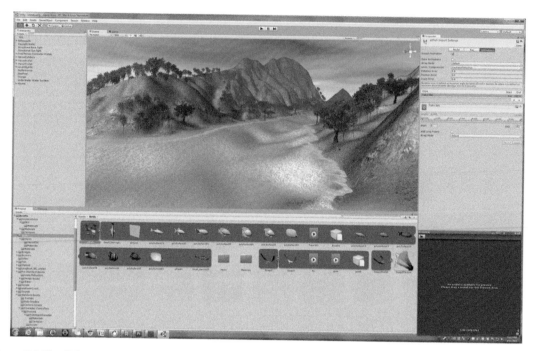

Figure 5.3 The Unity engine's asset browser enables users to find individual files using folders or keywords, but it also shows the relationships between assets, such as the different elements (meshes, skeletons, animations, and so on) that make up a game character.

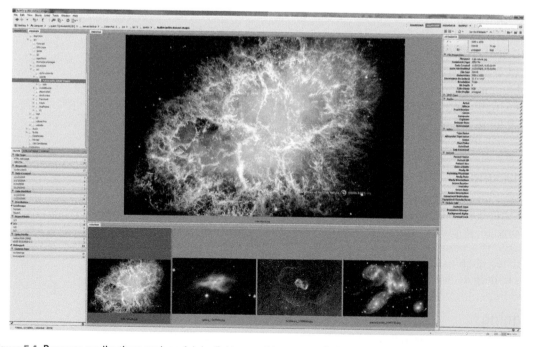

Figure 5.4 Browser applications such as Adobe Bridge enable users to find assets using keywords, tags or metadata such as creation times. A thumbnail view enables the user to locate appropriate assets even if they aren't certain exactly what file they are looking for.

to users. Tags tell the project, "This asset is a vehicle, but it's also drivable, military, and damaged," or, "That asset is a prop, but it's also animated, destructible, and Art Deco-themed." A search-based system without tags is really just an elaborate system for forcing users to memorize the name of every file they want, which is hardly a step forward. The asset browser needs to make it easy for users to tag assets—and to make sure that the whole team benefits from tagging.

Section 5.13 Versioning and Version Control

So far, we've looked at how pipeline developers can ensure that files are named correctly, placed in the correct directories, and made searchable. However, there are other important aspects of data management, including tracking the changes made to a file, and ensuring that only the correct version is presented to the users. This is where versioning and version control come in.

Almost every application allows the user to save their work into files. But some also provide incremental save options, which means that the program automatically adds a version number to the end of the file and increments it every time the user saves the file. This is known as "versioning", and is the simplest form of version management. It can be done even if your software doesn't support incremental saves, simply by adding a string to the file name representing the version number and updating it manually.

An alternative is to use dedicated "version-control" software (also sometimes known as "source-control" or "revision-control" software). In a version-control system, before an artist can access an asset, it must be "checked out". This creates a local copy of the master file on the user's machine. Once they have finished editing the local copy, it must be "checked in" to the system before the master copy is updated.

There are a number of commercial products that can do this, including general-purpose version-control software like Perforce, Subversion or Mercurial, and asset-management tools specifically aimed at graphics work, such as Shotgun and TACTIC. Facilities that use such tools, or that have their own proprietary asset-management systems, often overwrite the open and save dialogs in their art software with the check-in and check-out dialogs of the asset manager.

Both of these approaches have their strengths and weaknesses. The key strength of versioning is its simplicity. You don't need special tools in order to implement a versioning system, and you don't need to train artists to use it correctly.

But versioning systems, particularly manual ones, are prone to human error. Artists may not bother to increment a file name if they have only made minor changes to a file, or they may simply forget to do so. Even if the art software has an incremental save option built in, all of the incremental saves are available in the directory structure,

Choosing an Asset-Management System

Manne Ohrstrom
Senior Software Engineer, Shotgun Software

Ryan Mayeda
Product Producer, Shotgun Software

Rob Blau
Head of Pipeline Engineering, Shotgun Software

For something so critical to good production workflow as asset management, it's odd that the term itself is so poorly defined. Ask three different people what an "asset" is, and you're likely to get three different answers. In practice, it's easier to define the term circularly (an asset is anything the asset-management system manages), and focus on the role of the system itself.

One job of an asset-management system is to differentiate the working data for a task from the version that is meant to be handed off to the next task (the "delivery"). An asset-management system should be able to take a working set of files and extract clean deliverables from it, ready for use in downstream tasks. Another job is to help make sure that downstream tasks are using the right version of a delivery. To do this, the system needs to be able to track what assets should be used (the "breakdown") and check if any of them are out of date.

When choosing an asset-management system, consider what questions you need it to address. Here are a few of the most common, arranged in ascending order of complexity:

- What assets should a given task use?
- Are the assets for a given task up to date?
- What tasks are a given asset used in?
- What tasks are a specific version of an asset used in?
- What versions of which other assets were used to create a given asset?
- Do upstream changes need to be propagated automatically downstream?
- Do you need to be able to recreate a given delivery automatically?

Most asset-management systems can address the questions at the start of the list. By the time you get to the end (for example, being able to recreate an older render from the versions of assets that were current when it was created), you are talking about something far more complex. In general, it is easier to deliver traceability than it is to deliver reproducibility. Assets tend to remain traceable even where there are gaps in tracking data; but gaps in tracking will cause deliveries to be reproduced wrongly.

making it possible to move or delete the history of a file inadvertently. Two artists may begin working on the same file simultaneously, one save overwriting the other, whereas a version-control system could prevent this—or at least notify the second artist that the file had already been checked out. And the update history—who made what changes to which file and when—isn't stored centrally, making it difficult to troubleshoot when problems arise.

In contrast, version-control systems are more complex to use, and may carry a financial cost in terms of software licensing or staff

training, but provide more functionality. For example, it is possible to write tools that hook into version-control software to validate files before they are checked in or out of the system, making it easier to prevent common problems like non-manifold geometry (geometry that cannot be unfolded into a single flat sheet, causing certain modeling operations to fail) or polygons that have been flipped inside out.

Even without custom tools, a lot of relevant information is captured automatically in the history that is stored for each file. Each revision of the file will be associated with a particular date and user, and will carry a set of comments from that user explaining what was changed.

These records (typically known as "change lists" or "revisions") can be searched by date, user, or file name, which makes it fairly easy to home in on the source of a problem. Say, for example, a daily review shows that the latest version of a character has no head. A quick check of the file history shows that one of the artists has edited the character's skeleton to add bones for facial animation. Opening the character file from the change list reveals that the artist has accidentally disconnected the head during this update. Since the change list records the identity of the culprit, it's a simple matter to send the character back for head-reattachment surgery.

When Not To Use Asset-Management Software

Tim Green
Senior Programmer, Supermassive Games

The trend these days is to automate everything: where things were manual, stick in a computer. I'm not convinced that is always the best way. When teams get huge, or you have massive quantities of outsourced artwork, asset management becomes critical, but on smaller jobs, there is a point below which it is just not cost-effective to build or buy such systems.

At Supermassive Games, the only formal tracking we do is source control using Perforce, recording who has touched what file and when. Each department may (and in fact, should have) its own tracking system, but more often than not, this is just a spreadsheet.

If your department's work is only affected by a few thousand files—as would be typical with character animation, for example—a spreadsheet is ample. And don't neglect other traditional forms of organizational technology, either. A board with Post-it notes on is often a much better interface than a computer screen. It has a much larger display, is much easier to update, and comes with a sophisticated tactile input device called a pen. And it comes at a cost that would put a smile on any accountant's face—assuming that accountants are capable of smiling.

Of course, the problems that bedevil big modern productions are often much subtler and harder to debug. Most of the time, the assets we see on screen are not the products of a single file. In a film production, there may be many different versions of a given character, rigged differently to accommodate the needs of individual scenes or

shots. Moreover, each variant may include large numbers of elements that are shared with other characters: textures, props, hair or cloth simulations, reused animation or lighting rigs, and so on. Similarly, in a game, each character is really a complex network of models, shaders, animations, and even game code or AI scripts.

The relationships between these files are usually referred to as "dependencies", and present a number of serious challenges for the pipeline. Because dependent files don't always live together on the server, they can make it harder to design a logical, well-segmented file hierarchy. Artists get irritated when they open a file only to be confronted by error messages because of missing dependencies—or worse, get confused because the dependent files are out of date. It's also hard for artists to predict the ramifications of their changes, since a minor tweak may have major consequences elsewhere: for example, adjusting the proportions of a chair so that it looks better in one scene may break the animation in another, in which a character actually sits down in it.

For these reasons, a serious pipeline needs to provide users with good forensic tools for understanding and tracking dependencies between files. Unfortunately, these tools do not usually come as standard with version-control software, largely because there is such a bewildering array of possible relationships, so they must be coded by the pipeline team.

Section 5.14 Good Version-Control Policies

Version control has two faces. For the individual artist, it provides a safety net: no matter how badly you mess up a particular file, you can always get back to the last version. For the team, it's a way of keeping a project's resources up to date—you only need to sync up to the server to be certain that you have the latest version of everyone else's work.

But if misused, version control can turn on you very quickly. If team members aren't disciplined about making sure the assets they check in are functional, every morning becomes a nail-biting roller-coaster ride as you wait to find out what has been broken this time. And once shared assets turn ugly on a regular basis, more people will start avoiding the version-control system.

This keeps the staff working—but now they're working in little private universes disconnected from the flow of the production. They make esthetic decisions based on assets that have already changed, and technical decisions based on features that are no longer there. This leads to even more breakages when they submit their own work, and the whole production spirals down into a vicious cycle of mistrust and recrimination. The artists don't trust the pipeline, the tools team is sick of hunting down bugs caused by out-of-date files, and nobody is getting anything done.

Since this is a social problem, the solution is also social. Every team needs to create a culture in which people are serious about their responsibilities to their teammates, and take whatever steps are needed to make sure they aren't undermining the production out of haste or carelessness.

Test Games Assets, Or Else!

Tim Green
Senior Programmer, Supermassive Games

Before you check in any file, make sure you see it running in-game. Programmers tend to do this naturally, but it comes less automatically to artists, particularly when they are checking in assets that are still not finished, or checking in to a test level. The challenge is to enable these artists to see their content in-game as quickly as possible—but on their local machine where it won't affect anyone else. For this, like programmers, they need a sandbox environment to work in.

I'm fanatical about this, and have reached this point after long and bitter experience. I once worked on a project on which the audio pipeline was particularly bad. The team worked offline for about a month, producing lots of data. When we got close to a demo, the pressure would mount for them to release that data into the game, so they would open the flood gates—and the game would fall over.

This isn't surprising. Each bit of data has the potential to cause problems, so releasing a huge quantity of untested data into a game makes it almost certain that something will go wrong. But releasing a large number of files in one go makes it hard to diagnose which ones are the cause of the problem—and when the game falls over, it does so for everyone. Fifty or more people would sit around for days, unable to do any work, causing a huge loss in productivity.

When I realized what was going on, I blew my stack. I restructured the audio pipelines, and gave the team the power to test their changes in-game before they checked files in. Rather than opening the flood gates and letting loads of data rush into the game at once, now they could dribble in files gradually. And when things did fail, they failed only in local tests where they didn't cause problems for anyone else.

This is the important thing about rules and tools: the rules should be there to minimize lost work, and the tools you give people should only permit them to hurt themselves, not others.

For artists, these responsibilities are straightforward. Make sure that you have the latest version of other people's work, and are using the latest version of the tools. Visually verify that your work is good before checking it in, and make sure all your dependencies are added to the system.

For technical artists and programmers, being responsible is more complex. Good discipline is still key, but it's also important to have a solid build process that ensures that tools used by the rest of the team are reliable and always available. When you're supporting hundreds of artists, the costs of catching bugs late mount up quickly—and this is doubly true for tools like 3 ds Max and Maya plug-ins which can leave bad data inside art files long after the original issue is fixed.

Bugs are inevitable, but an aggressive testing program—complete with real, live testers, whether these are QA folks or volunteers from the art staff—goes a long way towards easing the pain. Formal build and test procedures do increase the time it takes to address feature requests and minor fixes, but the benefits in terms of tool quality and reliability—and therefore, in trust between the tools team and the content team—are more than enough to make up.

The further you get into a project—and in games, the closer you get to a demo or milestone—the more drastic the consequences of breaking the build become. In situations like this, programmers often use "code buddies" to review their work prior to check-in. Code buddies don't always literally check one another's work: often, the process of talking your buddy through the changes you've made is enough to make you realize you've done something wrong. Artists can do the same thing. It's not necessarily practical in the early days to grab somebody and review every little change you've made, but when you are finalling, peer reviews become critical.

Policing Your Pipeline

Matt Hoesterey
Design Lead, Microsoft

On some projects, it may not be enough to rely on artists to act responsibly: it may be necessary to enforce their good behavior. When I worked on MMOs (Massively Multiplayer Online games) whose tree—the hierarchy of folders and assets—needed to stay clean for upwards of ten years, one of our tech artists would act as our "pipeline police".

This was basically their full-time job, and involved them looking through every change list to ensure that all the files and folders were named correctly. Even at crunch times, when it wasn't possible for them to approve every file before check-in, they would check the change lists later, and if they found a problem, you would be required to check out the file and fix the problem before resubmitting it, no matter how massive an undertaking that was. If a problem with a change list was somehow missed, you were required to make the changes when it was eventually discovered, even months later.

Obviously, such a heavy hand isn't right for all projects—and in some circumstances, it may be counter-productive—but on MMOs, it is more or less a requirement to maintain the long-term health of the service.

While professional courtesy is the core of good version control, there are also ways in which the pipeline itself can help people to be good citizens. One common problem for teams with poor version-control discipline is overwrites: Artist A works on a local copy of a file for a long time but does not assert "ownership" of it by checking it out. In the meantime, Artist B checks out the file, makes a small change, and checks it back in. When Artist A finishes, he checks out the file, saves his local copy and checks it back in—destroying Artist

B's work. This problem can be minimized using a script in Max or Maya that automatically grabs the latest version of a file every time you open it, and warns you if there is a version mismatch. Similarly, the system can warn a user who wants to work on a file currently being used by someone else.

Another common problem is created by dependencies: artists frequently forget to check in all of the files needed to make a new asset work. Here, the version-control software can run a check every time a new file is submitted to see if it requires any files that aren't already in the system.

Finally, tools can be designed to auto-update themselves across the network—although this places a heavy burden on the development team: to ensure that all of the tools are working, all of the time.

Section 5.15 Asset Review and Approval

When artists update files, they aren't making changes at random. Instead, they are responding to requests for changes (often referred to as "notes") from the client, or from their supervisors. Another key data-management task is to ensure that these notes are communicated effectively, and that the status of each file is tracked as it moves towards being finalized. We will look at this process, first as it applies to film work, and then as it applies to games.

In film, assets are refined through a cyclic workflow: make changes, review the changes, then define the next set of changes needed. Reviews are carried out on a daily basis (sometimes weekly, if the project permits) so that no task can run off in the wrong direction for too long.

Reviews can happen in a number of ways, from a department head or lead looking over an artist's shoulder as they are sitting at their workstation, to a formal "dailies" session held in a dedicated theater or playback suite, sometimes in the presence of the client. These are generally more structured, with an entire sequence or entire department's work being reviewed at a time.

The first type of review is normally done inside the host application. In the theater or playback suite, it is more common to review a sequence of high-resolution images generated from the assets the artists have been working on, particularly for color-critical work.

In both cases, someone will be taking notes about the changes that have been requested. Some of these may not concern the department whose work is nominally under review. For example, in an animation review, the client may make comments on the lighting. This feedback must also be recorded and forwarded to the lighting department. For this reason, it is important that notes can be related to individual files, or groups of files, within the asset-management system, so that artists only receive feedback relating to tasks they are actually working on.

It is also important to ensure that notes use standard terminology. For example, when talking about a character, it is usual to use the terms "left" and "right" to refer to the character's left and right, not the left and right of the screen.

Where the feedback comes from the client, it isn't uncommon to have to "stage" the notes while they are sanitized for general consumption. Sometimes, the feedback isn't complimentary—so you may not wish to pass it on unedited to an artist who has been working sixteen hours a day, seven days a week. This staging process must be built into note-giving workflow and tools.

These tools vary considerably from project to project, and from facility to facility. In some cases, notes may be text-based; in others they may be written or drawn digitally on top of individual frames, using a virtual pen tool. However, in both cases, all of the information—what was reviewed, who reviewed it, what feedback was given, and whether the changes have been made—should be tracked in some kind of central spreadsheet or database.

When it reaches a certain state, the work will be approved. This state varies from department to department. Often, work doesn't have to be final-quality before approval: it may just be good enough to give to the next department so that the artists there can start working on it. For example, animation may be approved at the blocking stage so that the lighting department can start lighting the sequence while the animators continue to refine their work.

As we noted in an earlier chapter, in film, many facilities never describe assets as "final". They consider that, if time allows, they may still be able to tweak them further up until the point of delivery, and that instead, assets should always be regarded as CBB (Could Be Better).

In games, this problem of what constitutes "final" is even more acute. A modern game involves a bewildering number of assets, and almost no-one will know firsthand what they all are, what they look like, and whether they are ready to be seen by the general public. This problem is compounded by the fact that the artists who work on the assets and the managers responsible for tracking the production may use language in quite different ways.

For example, a manager may think something is "done" because it has been checked in on schedule, while the art staff may assume that it can be refined further as the project progresses. This creates problems for developers of asset-management systems, since it is difficult for computers to record such ambiguities accurately.

That said, it is usually better to handle such a big, data-intensive task directly, using a serious set of tools, than it is to try to manage it via email and Excel spreadsheets. If the production has a good tagging system, asset status is really just a slightly specialized form of metadata. However, more evolved tools can enable managers to communicate their wishes more effectively: for example, an asset browser could allow art leads or the art director to attach comments (again,

a form of metadata) to assets while viewing them. The next artist to work on the file will have these comments to hand and know who to contact if more feedback is needed.

Treating status as part of the metadata for an asset—rather than as a special category in a production list—also makes it easier to leverage dependency-analysis tools to stay on top of a production. Looking at an asset to see how many of its dependencies are regarded as "final" is an easy way of assessing relative risk. If time is tight late in production, it's better to cut assets that have few final dependencies than those where props and animations have already been refined.

However, there is a real danger that this kind of information leads to false confidence. A database can record the fact that the file "Dr_ Atomic.mb" has been tagged "final"—but it's unlikely to know that the art director has always hated that particular super-villain and is going to can him. No computer can rival a well-informed human being's understanding of the state of the project. Automated tracking is there to help producers and leads, not replace them.

In games, there is another type of status information that must be recorded: bugs. An asset can be "final" in the sense that its look and functionality have been nailed down, but it may still have technical problems: for example, bad texture mapping on part of a model. In an ideal world, the same tools that enable you to see the status of an asset while browsing should also enable you to see any bugs associated with it.

Section 5.16 Tracking Production Data

In the previous section, we touched on how production data can help producers and supervisors stay abreast of the progress of a production. To conclude this chapter, we will explore the concept of data tracking in more detail.

There are two kinds of production data worth tracking. The first is the kind that helps answer important production decisions. Artists are terrible at manual record-keeping—which is why half the check-in comments in a Perforce depot are things like "updated model" or "fixed bug"—so if collecting this data takes manual effort, you need to justify that effort to the staff members responsible. In general, you should know in advance the questions that the information will answer. These are usually things like:

- Who is working on this shot, and how much time do they have to finish their task?
- What is currently being reviewed, and what has changed since the last time?
- Have the notes from a previous review been addressed?
- How close to completion are the tasks handled by this department?

You should also know where those answers will be displayed. If the information is useful to artists, show it inside the applications they spend most of their time in. If the information is useful to crew who spend their time running around, make sure that it can be printed out, or made available on a tablet. Often, when you are capturing more data than can easily be displayed on a monitor, productions will dedicate a wall in a central location to pinning up information, such as shot cards, so that everybody can see the status of a project easily.

Make collecting information as easy as possible. If you want artists to provide notes on what has changed during an asset revision, don't make them switch applications in order to enter the information. Also, make sure those notes are visible to anyone who needs to see them. In other words: make it easy for artists to do the right thing—and make it obvious when they don't.

The second kind of data worth tracking is the kind that you can collect automatically. If you have the infrastructure to host a data warehouse, you should capture as much data from your pipeline as you can. How long a render takes or how many times a given script is run may seem inconsequential, but over time that information can be mined to answer questions you could never have anticipated. Log where a script is run, and on what versions of the software, and after an upgrade to a core application, you will be able to track down any machines you've missed. Log the total number of render hours taken on a project, and you will be able to decide whether you need to upgrade the render farm for the next one.

Often, you will find that you are already capturing relevant information: you just need to get it into a format that you can exploit. For example, you can find the size of every file in a production by trawling through Perforce. By cross-referencing this with your metadata, you can run queries to extract more useful information.

This can be useful when it comes to keeping track of what outsource studios are doing. For example, are they charging you to create detailed 3D assets when these will only be seen in the background of shots—perhaps in situations where a 2D texture would suffice? By keeping a running tab of models sorted by triangle count and by physical volume, you will be able to spot discrepancies quickly. Again, the key is making this information easy to collect. If you have to ask the artists to enter the data manually, it won't get done. But if you include a vendor-specific patch in your tools that tags the assets they create with a vendor ID, the information is captured for you automatically.

6

SYSTEMS INFRASTRUCTURE

Tim Green; Matt Hoesterey; Hannes Ricklefs; Mark Streatfield; Steve Theodore; Laurent M. Abecassis: *Di-O-Matic;* **Ben Carter:** *Game Developer and Author, Heavy Spectrum Entertainment Labs; The Motion Picture Association of America;* **Martin Weaver:** *Head of Core Systems, MPC;* **Fran Zandonella:** *International Senior Pipeline TD, Rhythm & Hues*

Section 6.1 What You Will Learn From This Chapter

A production pipeline is only as strong as the systems infrastructure (IT) on which it is built. In this chapter, we will explore how this hardware and software influences a pipeline's development and management. We will look first at the kinds of infrastructure required for film and games work, then examine key issues that relate to any pipeline, including the need to manage operating systems and utility software, and the need for pipeline security.

Section 6.2 IT for Film: Types of Hardware

Film productions have an enormous appetite for data. With its highly detailed models, complex animation rigs, simulation caches, and high-resolution renders, a single film can generate many terabytes of data, while a facility running multiple projects can easily find itself in the petabyte range. In this kind of extreme environment, a solid hardware infrastructure is vital.

Exactly what this hardware consists of depends on how the company is organized. A company may consist of a single facility, or—since it is becoming increasingly common to acquire former competitors or open satellite offices overseas—multiple facilities connected through a private network, or over the internet.

Any of these scenarios requires at least the following types of hardware:
- Workstations (desktop machines and laptops)
- Network (cables, switches, and Wi-Fi connections)
- Core servers (for email, user accounts, DNS, databases, and so on)

- Storage cluster (for data storage and backup)
- Render farm (for processing computationally intensive tasks)
- Telephony and communication hardware
- Backup power supply (not usually large enough to power the entire facility, particularly the render farm, but enough to keep core services alive or power down gracefully)

In any of these scenarios, the following types of hardware are optional, but near-universal:

- Extra monitors (for artists)
- Graphics tablets (for artists)
- Headphones (for animators doing lip-sync work)
- Stills cameras, video cameras and microphones (for recording reference material: these can usually be shared between several artists)

Scenarios with multiple facilities require the following additional types of infrastructure:

- Private network connections or dedicated routing setups (to guarantee an adequate bandwidth between sites)
- Some form of accelerated data transfer between each facility
- Video-conferencing equipment (ideally, with a remote screen-sharing system)

Two of the main cost centers are the storage cluster and render farm, particularly when it comes to "capex" (Capital Expenditure). We will look at each one in more detail.

Section 6.3 IT for Film: The Storage Cluster

The storage cluster is the cluster of file servers where all the production data is kept. To ensure that enough data is available, most studios break down their storage into multiple tiers:

- Tier 1: storage that is accessible for the production
- Tier 2, or "nearline" storage: disks that are not accessible from the production machines but can be used as a "parking ground" to get data off Tier 1 storage more quickly
- Tape-based storage: used for long-term archives of production data, most likely the final output delivered to the client

Although often overlooked, a facility's workstations and local render machines are also a source of storage space. The total space available on local machines is often greater than that available in managed storage, meaning that local caching strategies and proxy generation should be considered when planning storage requirements.

Tier 1 and 2 storage consists of NAS (Network-Attached Storage) devices from vendors like EMC Isilon or NetApp. Those used in Tier 1 storage are more expensive but faster, being optimized for read performance; those used in Tier 2 are cheaper but slower.

Figure 6.1 Fast Network-Attached Storage devices such as EMC Isilon's IQ 3000x are used to provide artists with direct and "nearline" access to production files.

When planning managed storage, it is important to consider a number of questions:

- How the render farm will interact with the storage
- How to track the amount of data produced and when the data was last accessed
- How the storage is presented to the artists: as multiple disks or a single mount point
- What data is essential to the production
- What data needs to be archived, and for how long
- How to monitor the storage

One of the biggest issues is the way the render farm interacts with the storage. Everyone working in VFX production will have come across a situation in which a single render has brought down the whole facility. In most cases this is due to a texture file stored on a single disk which thousands of machines are trying to access over the network. To avoid this, the render farm may be connected to an SSD caching system, such as those produced by Avere, or other specialized systems optimized for file I/O (Input/Output). However, such systems come at a huge price. Every CTO will have heard comments such as, "How come storage is so expensive? I just bought myself a 2TB external hard drive for $100!" when the equivalent 2TB high-performance system costs thousands of dollars.

Procurement of the cluster is normally incremental, with additional capacity added yearly or with each major production. In larger

facilities, this is handled by a dedicated data-operation department liaising with IT, R&D, and production. In smaller facilities, it is handled by IT.

The facility's backup and archive capabilities must also grow alongside the storage cluster. Here, the storage consists of LTO (Linear Tape-Open) half-inch magnetic tape cartridges. Tapes are bar-coded to associate them with particular projects, then archived in "libraries". These are usually automated systems, produced by vendors like HP and IBM, and include a robot to load tapes automatically into tape drives when required.

The backup process is controlled by software such as that produced by commercial vendors such as CommVault or open-source alternatives like Bacula. Backups occur incrementally as frequently as the studio can manage: normally at least daily, but never less than weekly.

Archiving is normally a one-off operation once a project has finished—or, for large projects, once a shot or sequence is complete—and can involve sending a copy of the data to the client. Normally two copies of a tape are kept, one on-site and one off-site. Both of these processes have a high "opex" cost (short for "Operational Expenditure" or "Operating Expense"). "Snapshots", read-only copies of data from that moment, will also be taken to aid data management.

Another step that is often overlooked is the restore process: be sure you understand the procedure thoroughly, and test it before you need to use it. Downtime due to mismanaging data recovery is not an option, so an untested backup system is not a backup system at all.

Once in place, the storage cluster will require ongoing monitoring to ensure that sufficient free disk space remains available for production. Common data-management policies include moving files from fast to slow storage after a certain period of time, or only keeping a certain number of previous versions of an asset online. Some studios have gone so far as to set up automatic data-culling procedures, either deleting files that have not been accessed in a given period of time, or according to file path (for example, Playblasts or temporary render data are easy to reproduce from other files and need not be stored online for long). Outside the reach of the asset-management system, the onus is put on artists and production staff to manage their own local data footprint, deleting files they don't require from their hard drives.

Another issue to consider is that 3D data tends to have a fairly short half-life. The developers of the major commercial tools release new versions of their software every twelve to eighteen months, and specialty tools and plug-ins come and go. It is by no means certain that a file four or five years old can be opened reliably using the most recent version of the software.

This poses a serious problem for studios that need to maintain the core assets for ongoing IP, such as movies likely to generate sequels. Even when old assets are no longer needed for production, they form an important source of reference for artists working on the latest movie.

Some studios make a point of archiving critical assets in stable file formats (such as OBJ or FBX) which are less tied to specific versions of third-party software. Others have been known to stash a working computer with its current OS, software, and content in a storage unit. This is, of course, an embarrassingly low-tech solution to a high-tech problem, but pragmatism is a key virtue for anyone involved in a production pipeline. Virtual machine images are another way to achieve the same result without having to keep potentially unreliable hardware around.

The pipeline team should record historical metrics for the storage facility. Knowing how much data each user, department, shot, or project has generated is useful information when it comes to planning how much storage will be needed on the next production. In a brute-force approach, a dedicated process will trawl the file system daily, interrogating each file for information such as the last time it was accessed, its owner, its size, and its location. This may be combined with data from the asset-management system (for example, which shot the file belongs to) and made available via a "dashboard" interface on a company web page, through which senior staff may perform custom analyses. A number of third-party software vendors specialize in such tasks: for example, Zenoss provides systems for monitoring storage usage.

There are several good reasons to do this:

Data Has a Cost

Calculating a dollar-per-gigabyte figure for storage, including the cost of buying, powering and maintaining the server, and paying a data wrangler to manage the process, enables a facility to budget more accurately for future jobs.

Data Takes Space

Calculating the average amount of storage required per shot, per asset, or per artist enables a facility to predict how much storage it will need for future projects.

Patterns of Data Use Change Over Time

As workflows evolve, the amount of data generated by a "typical" project changes. Sometimes, cause and effect may not be

obvious: for example, a new tool may cause disk usage to spike unexpectedly. Tracking such changes back to their sources enables pipeline staff to minimize problems and forecast future data use more accurately.

And remember: in visual effects work, there is no such thing as "too much storage". This is a field in which a single fluid simulation may generate terabytes of data.

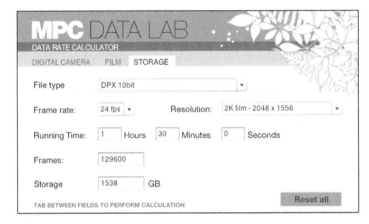

Figure 6.2 In production, data quickly mounts up. This online calculator developed by MPC enables users to work out how much storage space a single iteration of a movie will occupy, based on parameters such as file format, frame rate, and resolution.

Managing Filer I/O

Fran Zandonella
International Senior Pipeline TD, Rhythm & Hues

Problems with "filer I/O" (file system input/output) can be difficult to diagnose, and heavy I/O can bring a facility to a halt. Managing this risk is crucial, as periods of heavy I/O usually occur at the worst possible times, such as during the "crunch" period before a delivery deadline. The following strategies may help here:

Identify Departments That Have Heavy I/O Requirements and Sequester Them

For example, the FX department runs simulations that hit the network heavily, and may benefit from using its own dedicated fast disks. Alternatively, other departments (such as animation) may have work that must not be interrupted, and would benefit from a protected place to work.

Identify and Manage Peak Times of Disk Usage

Large numbers of artists starting or ending their working day at the same time can have a huge impact on filer I/O, while scheduled backup and restore times put hidden load on the storage system. At one studio I worked at, artists working late used to complain about how long it took to open and save files on the Unix file system. A casual conversation with one of the Mac guys revealed that the Macs got backed up at 7pm because the production staff had left for the day. Delaying the backups until the artists had also ended their day improved productivity greatly.

Assign Different Types of Data to Appropriate Types of Storage

Separate out data that will not need high I/O access (scripts, configuration info, Maya scene files, and so on) from the data that does need it (geometry, textures, rigs) and assign each type to an appropriate type of storage.

Develop a Strategy for Handling Frequently Used Files

Watch for types of files that every render reads multiple times (textures, simulation data, logs, and so on), and focus on ways to minimize their impact on I/O. It may be necessary to:

- Distribute the files to servers that have big memory caches.
- Distribute the data locally to all the render nodes, then reassemble the information later if needed. Pay attention to the disk speed of the local render nodes, as this could be a bottleneck if the data is larger than the cache.
- Use caching devices, especially if they can be identified procedurally. This can work well for data that can be segmented (for example, shared textures), especially when it is used by multiple shots. It won't work so well for per-frame data.
- Use dedicated filers with local SSD storage for particular types of files, and round-robin between the systems.

Follow Best Practices When Creating Scripts

When creating scripts, keep the following points in mind:

- Opening a file over NFS (the Network File System protocol) can be expensive when directories and files need to be checked for existence and read/write permissions. Manage what goes into a file and keep the number of files to a minimum.
- When compressing files or converting them to another format, processing the files on a local machine before sending them over the network saves filer I/O and network time.
- It is good practice to batch up frames and other fast-running tasks into larger chunks before they are run on the farm. This is particularly useful for minimizing the time taken by shared tasks like starting up an application or loading configuration files.

Make Use of Monitoring and Debugging Tools

Finally, get to know your monitoring and debugging tools before an emergency arises. Get into the habit of reading system logs and using strace (Linux's utility for monitoring the system calls a process makes) to identify problems before they become critical. And if the worst happens, and a simulation or render brings the filer to its knees, keep a sample that can be used to test new deployments in future.

Figure 6.3 A visual effects facility's storage cluster and render farm are dedicated sets of machines used for tasks that would be too demanding for artists' desktop workstations.

Section 6.4 IT for Film: The Render Farm

The "render farm" or "render wall" is used for tasks that require a lot of computing resources. Rather than tying up an artist's workstation while these are completed, it is more efficient to process them separately. Despite its name, the render farm handles more than just render jobs: it is a high-performance computing cluster to which all offline processing is sent, including simulations (for FX), caching (for animation), proxies (for compositing), and service-related tasks such as creating QuickTimes to deliver to clients. As a result, it is often best to divide up the farm based on criteria such as department or task type. This allows the farm scheduler to fairly allocate resources to all users, and execute each job on a machine that best meets its requirements.

The machines that make up a render farm are usually "headless"—that is, lacking a monitor and input devices—and historically, were CPU-based. However, it's difficult to buy anything without some kind of on-board graphics card, and recent years have seen an increase in the number of tasks that may be processed on the GPU, meaning that many modern farms also include a large number of machines with GPUs. For specialized tasks—for example, a server whose only task is processing motion-capture data—dedicated machines may be required, and will require specific configurations.

If artists' workstations are not in use, IT may also include them as "slaves" in the render farm, using processing power that would otherwise be sitting idle.

As with the storage cluster, procurement of the render farm is normally incremental, with additional capacity added yearly or with each major production. In larger facilities, this is handled by a dedicated render-operation department liaising with IT, R&D, and production. In smaller facilities, it is handled by IT.

At medium and large studios, the farm may run to hundreds or thousands of CPUs. This means that power and cooling are also major considerations. To illustrate why, let's look at what is required to run an 80-server farm: a modest size, by modern standards. Let's assume that two servers can be fitted into 1 U (one "rack unit": a standard unit of measurement corresponding to 1.75 inches in height in a standard server rack) and that each server contains two 8-core Intel Xeon CPUs, plus RAM, local system drives, and so on. This means the eighty servers will fit exactly into a 40 U rack (standard racks are 42 U to 44 U) and will contain 1,280 CPU cores (80 servers × 2 CPUs per server × 8 cores per CPU).

The servers are already pretty heavy, but add in power management, Ethernet cables, rack rails, nuts and bolts, and each 900 mm × 600 mm rack will probably weigh 600 kg, perhaps more: probably above the recommended weight limit for your office.

The total power draw of the two Xeon processors, RAM, hard drive, and other components of the server could easily be 250 W to 500 W, so the entire 40 U rack will draw 20 kW of power. Add 50 percent on top for air conditioning and air handling, and the total power draw will be 30 kW.

This often means that the main factor limiting render-farm performance is not, as is commonly assumed, processor power, but the need to provide electricity and cooling to keep the farm operational. To maintain operational performance, a farm must be maintained within narrow ranges of temperature and humidity. For this reason, the design of data centers is becoming an art form in its own right, touching all aspects of architecture, design, and structural, mechanical, and electrical engineering.

The render farm is normally managed by a single piece of software—a "scheduler" or "render manager"—which is responsible for distributing tasks. Those commonly used in production include Deadline, Tractor, and open-source tools like Arsenal.

The tasks the scheduler manages can be as simple as rendering a single high-resolution image, or as complex as a series of operations carried out in different software packages. The scheduler collects the tasks submitted by each artist and assigns them to particular servers according to an algorithm. This scheduling algorithm can use several different approaches, from simple "first come, first served" task assignment, through priority- or weight-based scheduling, to a purely

metrics-driven approach based on previous render times, current filer or network performance, and the production schedule. In order to do this, it must also track which servers are currently free, and which are busy or offline. The scheduler then reports the progress of the task back to the artist, and sends them error messages if the task runs into problems.

Executing Workflows on the Render Farm

Hannes Ricklefs
Global Head of Pipeline, MPC

At MPC, we have written a Python module containing classes representing different types of task that can be executed on our render farm. These range from general tasks such as executing other Python commands to application-specific ones such as Maya or Nuke. The module enables us to set up dependencies between individual tasks, creating complex task graphs.

The task definitions and graph descriptions are agnostic when it comes to render farm management software. To enable the graphs to be executed in a particular application, we write translators that convert them into the native format of the software: at the minute, we support Pixar's Alfred and Tractor. This enables technical artists to quickly script custom workflows and execute them on our render farm.

The render farm is managed by a render operation department to ensure that it is operating effectively. This generally means monitoring the progress of jobs on the farm and triaging errors: encouraging artists to fix mundane problems themselves and directing larger problems to tech support. Technicians (nicknamed "render wranglers") will also manage the priority of jobs to ensure that key tasks are completed on time. Shots or projects that are close to deadline will be prioritized above others, but it is also important that each artist and department has their fair share of the resources. Render wrangling, like data wrangling for the storage cluster, is seen as an entry-level position, and a pathway to a more senior technical role.

As with the storage cluster, keeping historical metrics for the render farm is important, and for similar reasons:

Rendering Has a Cost

Calculating out a dollar-per-hour figure for processing, including the cost of buying, powering, cooling, and maintaining the servers, and paying a render wrangler to manage the process, enables a facility to budget more accurately for future jobs.

The Render Farm is a Finite Resource

Calculating the average render time per shot, per asset or per artist enables a facility to predict how much farm capacity it will need for future projects.

Patterns of Processing Use Change Over Time

As workflows evolve, the way in which a "typical" project uses the render farm changes. Tracking such changes back to their sources enables pipeline staff to minimize problems and forecast future data use more accurately.

Section 6.5 IT for Film: Managing the Infrastructure

Managing a facility's infrastructure has two main aspects: configuring the infrastructure, and monitoring the state of that infrastructure.

When configuring the infrastructure, it is important to be able to deploy new computing resources quickly and easily. This means that it is best to define a standard setup for artists' workstations, and stick to it. There are various tools available to help system administrators to automate the process of building and configuring new machines: the best-known such Configuration Management (CM) tools include CFEngine, Chef, and Puppet. It's also important to have ready-made disk images that can create a fully specified workstation with a single install. Finally, have spare parts and drivers to hand at all times: in a large studio there is a constant dribble of hardware failures, and you need to prevent artists from being sidelined by bad hard drives, anemic power supplies or dead GPUs.

The Need for Repeatable System Setups

Fran Zandonella
International Senior Pipeline TD, Rhythm & Hues

Whether a facility has five machines or five thousand, having reliable baseline system images from which to build new systems makes it easier to roll out machines at the start of a project, or replace defective ones. Several separate disk images may be required—for example, for desktop machines and render servers, or separate setups for different departments—but for simplicity, try to keep the number to a minimum.

It may also be necessary to have several versions of the same software installed on different machines throughout the facility. For example, Side Effects Software sometimes releases two new versions of Houdini

in a single day, and usually releases several versions each week. Perhaps one department requires a particular bug fix, but others do not. Being able to version the application helps manage those needs. Consider localizing applications that change infrequently and providing a fallback to the network version if there is a problem with the local copy.

Before deployment, the baseline image(s) needs to be tested with the needs of each department in mind, as well as on a sample of current and planned rendering machines. Automated tests keep costs down and ensure consistency between deployments.

It is important to have a process for checking that individual machines conform to the baseline, particularly where a facility has staff working in separate offices. If artists halfway around the world receive an incorrect update, their work may fall a day behind schedule.

When building the infrastructure for a facility, one important thing to consider is the way in which software is installed on each machine. The two most common methods are to deploy software to the local disk of each machine, or to operate a shared software server to which every application gets installed.

A shared software server means that only basic operating system components need be installed on individual machines: other software will be made available via the server. It also means that once a new piece of software is installed, it becomes available to every machine immediately.

However, such a system requires proper infrastructure: it takes quite a hefty machine to serve users' software requests simultaneously, along with a solid network infrastructure—particularly during crunch periods when the network is under heavy load. It also creates a single point of failure: if the software server fails, the entire system will fail. The way to counter this is to build "redundancy" into the system (multiple servers able to satisfy the same need, so that if one fails, another can take over).

Installing all the software on each individual machine removes these demands on network infrastructure. However, installing and configuring the software can be time-consuming. Sometimes in the heat of a production, quick fixes need to be installed to get a render completed overnight. If your render farm contains thousands of machines, it may simply not be possible to complete the installations fast enough to get the job done on time.

Some studios use hybrid approach, in which software that doesn't change rapidly is deployed to each individual machine, whereas software that changes often is made available via a shared network server.

The second major aspect of managing a facility's infrastructure is monitoring the state of that infrastructure. This includes:

- Network bandwidth utilization
- Network traffic

- CPU load on individual machines
- Memory usage on individual machines
- Application-specific statistics such as memory footprint, CPU resources used, or how database performance varies with the number of queries being served

Monitoring solutions should be able to send out alerts once a certain critical threshold is reached: for example, if a disk reaches 75 percent capacity, or the load on the database server is above a certain threshold. Alerts notify system administrators of potential issues before they affect any of the users. Monitoring solutions should also work remotely: it is not always clear why a system is running slowly, so being able to inspect machines without having to log into each one is vital.

The Many Faces of "Slow"

At some point, everyone working within pipeline or system administration will get a call from a user saying that their machine is "running slowly". Since there are so many possible reasons why this could be so, to get to the root of the problem requires diligent—and patient—investigation.

Possible local causes include:

- The machine is slow due to heavy load as it is running multiple simulations.
- The machine is swapping memory because a single process such as a render is consuming all the available memory.

Or it could be that the cause lies outside the user's machine:

- The machine was added to the render farm overnight, and the render has not finished.
- The user is working on a file that is stored on a server that is under heavy load and can't retrieve it quickly enough.
- The user's application is asking for a piece of information from a database where a table is locked and the function call is blocking it.

One of the first questions to ask is whether the slowness affects only the user, or other people around them as well. In the first case, it is more than likely that the cause is the user's machine. Then it is important to find out if the slowness affects only a single application, or every application. In the second case, it is more than likely that the cause is something central. In such situations, it is important to get a quick overview of the state of the facility's system as a whole. There are various tools available to do this, including Cacti, Nagios, OpenNMS, and Zabbix.

Section 6.6 IT for Games: The Build Farm

The data needs of games are rarely as gargantuan as those for films, so they commonly demand a less impressive infrastructure. A game studio will typically have those resources you would expect in any other office environment: email, shared drives for non-critical data, a wiki or other centralized documentation, and so on.

However, it is not uncommon to find some sort of centralized "build framework" or "farm" that is used for all the tasks too slow to

carry out on developers' individual machines. Such tasks depend on the game engine, but often include rendering light maps or generating light probes. The farm is also often used for unit tests (testing individual units of game engine source code), continuous builds (merging those individual units into a single "main line" of the code), and smoke and soak tests (testing that critical features work when the build is first run, and that it does not fail under sustained load). No two game teams or facilities will perform exactly the same build farm tasks.

The build farm may be made up of high-end machines (with or without GPUs, depending on the tasks expected of them) or old workstations that are now too slow to be given to a developer, but which can be used to increase the "node count" of the farm.

The software that manages a farm is as unique as the hardware it comprises. There are a number of commercial solutions available—some listed earlier in this chapter—but it is not uncommon for a studio to develop its own management software. Even a simple approach to farming out tasks can achieve a lot in a short time, particularly if each machine in the farm is configured to specific tasks.

Small Tasks Soon Add Up

Tim Green
Senior Programmer, Supermassive Games

When managing game projects, don't just pay attention to the large tasks. When they are repeated over and over again, small tasks soon add up.

The game *Harry Potter and the Goblet of Fire* was developed using RenderWare Studio: a level-authoring tool enabling users to place objects and author event-centric game logic. In RenderWare, a level comprises tens of thousands of objects, each with a set of properties and links to other objects. Each object is saved to an XML file, resulting in tens of thousands of very small XML files per level.

When I was working on the title, a common complaint from the team was that levels were slow to load, often taking as long as 10 minutes. I was new to the team, so I synced the level XML files, but found that everything loaded in around thirty seconds on my machine.

After eliminating other causes I concluded that this was purely due to disk access time. I noticed that on the slow machines the hard drive was badly fragmented, so we defragmented those drives and retested them, expecting an immediate speed boost—but the result was the same. What was going on?

At this point I need to explain a little about NTFS, the file system used on the PCs. NTFS stores metadata about each file in a structure called the Master File Table (MFT). The metadata is stuff like the name of the file and its date of creation, and even stores part of the data in the file. This data has a fixed block size of 1 kb. This means that the data for

a file is normally somewhere on the hard drive, maybe split into fragments, and the metadata is in the MFT—but if the file is under 1 kb in size, it may exist in its entirety in the MFT.

Defragmenting moves fragments of files around on the machine's hard drive, joining them into continuous blocks to reduce seek times while loading a file, but it does not move anything in the MFT. The majority of our tens of thousands of XML files were under 1 kb in size, so they lived only in the MFT and were not affected. When loading a level, RenderWare Studio would load these XML files sequentially, requiring the file system to seek all over the MFT in order to do so.

If only the files had been written to the file system in one go, their metadata would have been written sequentially to the MFT, meaning that fewer block seeks and loads would be required.

The solution was to rename the folder containing the files, copy it back to the original name and delete the old folder. This meant that the metadata files were now close together in the MFT, increasing the likelihood that a cached block of MFT would contain all the data required.

One simple tool later, over a hundred people had better level load times, saving around thirty minutes per person per day, or around fifty hours per day in total.

Section 6.7 IT for Games: Version Control

Although games projects may not require as much storage as visual effects projects, there are other aspects of IT infrastructure that are critical to their success. Game developers have to cope with constant, and sometimes unpredictable, changes to their game designs and game engines. For this reason, they need to be able to track the evolution of game content over the course of a project with great exactitude: for example, they may need to roll assets back to earlier versions in order to analyze a particularly subtle bug, or to maintain parallel versions for different game consoles. For this reason, they are especially dependent on version-control software. We looked at how version-control software works in the previous chapter. Here, we will explore aspects that are particular to games—especially those that affect a studio's infrastructure—in more detail.

As files change, the data and metadata for those changes are stored in the file history—but the old versions of the file remain available as well. Maintaining a secure and "redundant" set of backups for this data is by far and away the IT department's most important job. If a change causes a bug, it is vital for the users to be able to revert to an earlier, unbroken version.

The historical information included in the version-control system is also vital for diagnosing and fixing more subtle problems. Since many people work on each asset, it's easy for lapses in communications or simple human error to cause problems which can then be maddeningly difficult to resolve.

Another import benefit of version-control software is its ability to create modified versions of the project while leaving the original code and data intact. "Branching" enables the system to maintain multiple concurrent versions of the same files (including their history and metadata). Branches are useful to enable different parts of the team to work safely in parallel. For example, a small group of animators and designers might want to prototype a new kind of movement animation for the game's player character. This will be a slow, iterative process generating plenty of temporary bugs. If the team is assigned its own branch, it can work without impacting the rest of the studio. Once the new feature is working reliably, the branch can be reintegrated into the main line of the code so that the whole team can share it.

Since version control is so critical for game teams, choosing the right version-control solution is one of the most important steps in creating a game pipeline. There are several version-control systems on the market, both commercial and open-source, but not all of these are equally well suited for games. For programmers, the current trend in version control is towards distributed systems such as Git, Subversion, or Mercurial. Unfortunately, these systems are optimized for text-based code files, and they tend to choke on the masses of large graphics files that make up a modern game. It's gradually becoming possible to configure distributed systems to work with graphics files, but this is still an expert-level task, and should be approached with caution. For this reason, centralized versioning systems like Perforce and Alienbrain remain more common in game production.

An important consideration when choosing a system is the size and complexity of your tool chain. If you have a significant investment in automation, you will need a system that offers good API access for your scripters and tools programmers, such as Perforce or Mercurial. On the other hand, if you're sticking with off-the-shelf software, you may opt for a system like Alienbrain that offers a more polished UI and ready-made plug-ins for art tools like Maya and Photoshop.

Another critical factor when choosing a versioning system is distribution. If your project involves collaboration between multiple locations, or working with off-site contractors and outsourcers, you will need to decide whether or not to allow these teams access to your version-control system. Some teams absolutely refuse off-site access to their data in the name of security; others insist on it so that they can use versioning features to track their partners' activity. If you plan on allowing outside access to your data store, you will need to find a system that permits remote access, either via a web-based client or via a VPN (Virtual Private Network) connection. Perforce, in particular, enables you to create proxy servers, which act as local caches for data from a master version of the project. These are useful if you want

to provide users at a satellite location with faster access to commonly used files.

It's also important to make sure that you have a clear strategy for controlling access to your data. Most version-control systems include some form of authentication to make sure that only authorized personnel can see the data. Administrators can also create user profiles which determine which portions of the version control are visible to which users: for example, to permit programmers to access finished game assets but not raw Maya or Photoshop files, or artists to access the latest version of the game engine but not all of the source code. Access control is absolutely critical if you plan to give outsourcers direct access to your version-control system.

Finally, you'll need to make sure that your versioning system has adequate hardware support. This should include plenty of disk space (the history on those big binary files adds up fast), and at least a competent processor. Regular backups and redundant architecture such as RAID drives are vital: if your version-control system goes down, your project is dead in the water. Nowadays some teams opt for cloud-based hosting for their version-control servers to take advantage of the high up-time and round-the-clock maintenance offered by big data centers—although many other teams shudder at the thought of allowing their precious project data to leave the building. The network itself must also be very robust to cope with the "morning sync": the daily ritual of getting the most recent version of the game's files that is as much a part of an artist or developer's day as the first cup of coffee—and in fact, usually happens at the same time.

Section 6.8 Managing Operating Systems

In both film and games, it is typical to use more than one operating system (OS) throughout a facility in order to accommodate different tasks or software packages. The most common operating systems are Windows, Mac OS X and Linux. Although many VFX facilities define themselves as "Linux houses", they usually have to support all three operating systems to some degree, as there are always some applications—for example, Photoshop and After Effects—that don't work on the primary OS.

It is becoming increasingly common to partition a single machine so that a number of OS instances run on it: a process known as "virtualization". Each instance, or "virtual machine", gets a share of the host's physical resources but is isolated completely from the others, so for most purposes, they can be treated as separate machines. (For example, rebooting a virtual server will not affect any others running on the same hardware.) Virtualization allows you to maximize use of a resource, enable "transparent failover" through "hot backups" (that is, back up data while users are accessing it), and scale horizontally.

This approach is suited to less resource-intensive tasks, such as running web or FTP servers, or license management. More intensive tasks, such as running file servers, may still require dedicated hardware and physical connections.

To simplify the process of managing operating systems, it is common to make every computer identical unless strictly necessary, and choose an OS based on its "hero application": for example, if a machine is to be used primarily to run Nuke, it would be appropriate to install Linux; for Photoshop, it would be necessary to install Mac OS X or Windows. Alternatively, it may be necessary to choose an operating system compatible with the machine's GPU, or with key peripherals such as graphics tablets.

When you have decided on an operating system for each machine, only change it (usually to upgrade to a new version) when you really have to!

Section 6.9 Managing Utility Software

Many kinds of utility tools are vital to keep a facility functioning. System software (such as the Java Runtime Environment and Microsoft's .NET Framework and Visual C++ redistributable packages) is used by many programs, so it's important to keep it up-to-date and available to all users, particularly if you're deploying home-grown tools that depend on these libraries.

Graphics and audio drivers are another source of potential problems, particularly for 3D artists. It's important to ensure that your users have the latest approved versions of these critical bits of infrastructure. If you have a large studio, it's wise to invest in tools for auditing software configurations remotely—manually checking the graphics control panel on a hundred workstations is not a good way to spend your evening!

Section 6.10 Production Security

Finally, we will look at production security. This is an aspect of IT infrastructure that is easily underestimated. Production contracts require strict confidentiality, so IT must have a proper setup in place to ensure that no security breaches are possible. This includes both authentication (is the person accessing the data who he or she claims?) and authorization (does that user actually have permission to access those files?)

In general, any production is confidential unless a contract is in place between the vendor and client that states otherwise, and details of the process remain off-limits until any embargo dates have cleared. Given the money at stake, this is hardly surprising: with costs and potential revenues running into the hundreds of millions—or even

billions—of dollars for large projects, it is necessary to ensure that content is kept as secure as possible prior to release.

This is particularly true in visual effects work. The VFX industry is subject to very strong security audits that test every aspect of production: how staff and visitors gain access to the building, how staff log onto machines, whether they can mount external storage devices or burn CDs and DVDs, how the network is partitioned, and how easy it is to upload data to the internet. But, by far, the biggest concern for the VFX industry is security in the cloud: the major motion picture studios contractually require vendors to ensure that data is hosted internally without the option to access the data from the outside. It is essential to take these factors into account while building a pipeline, since retrofitting security measures later can be very costly. It is not uncommon for these audits to happen several times a year, either instigated by the client or by the MPAA: the Motion Picture Association of America.

For more than three decades, the MPAA has managed site-security surveys on behalf of its member companies, the six major US motion-picture studios: Walt Disney Studios Motion Pictures, Paramount Pictures Corporation, Sony Pictures Entertainment Inc., Twentieth Century Fox Film Corporation, Universal City Studios LLC, and Warner Bros. Entertainment Inc.

These MPAA surveys cover a vast range of topics, including management systems such as incident response; physical security, such as how access points to the facility are secured, and the security of physical storage media and file transfer; and digital security, including authentication and authorization protocols, and aspects of the file-management system.

Such surveys identify risks to productions and controls that should be implemented to decrease these risks to an appropriate level. The International Organization for Standardization (ISO) defines risk as the "combination of the probability of an event and its consequence." In this case, the former would include the probability that content can be stolen from a facility's network; the latter would include the business consequences to the facility and the client should this occur (for example, breach of contract and/or loss of revenue for that release window).

In consultation with its client, a facility is responsible for determining which of that client's assets require a higher level of security. This is done through a four-step process:
- Identify and classify assets
- Monitor and evaluate effectiveness
- Determine minimum security control set
- Implement controls

Security controls are typically selected according to the classification of the asset, its value to the organization, and the risk of it being leaked or stolen. In order to mitigate identified risks, facilities should

implement controls commensurate with each specific risk. The effectiveness of such measures should be evaluated periodically based on the current threat environment.

Best practices are organized according to the MPAA Content Security Model, which provides a framework for assessing a facility's ability to protect a client's content. It comprises forty-nine security topics, and can be found in the MPAA's Content Security Best Practices document, available from the Best Practices section of its Fight Film Theft website www.fightfilmtheft.org).

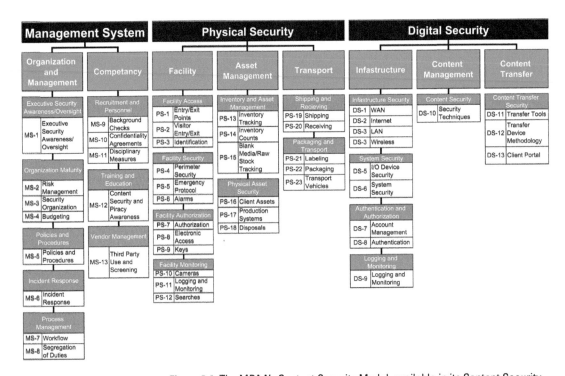

Figure 6.4 The MPAA's Content Security Model, available in its Content Security Best Practices guidelines, comprises forty-nine security topics, divided into three categories: management system, physical security, and digital security.

6A

INTERLUDE: MITIGATING RISK THROUGH REGULAR MAINTENANCE AND DISASTER PLANNING

Fran Zandonella
International Senior Pipeline TD, Rhythm & Hues

Studios often have the expectation that their projects will run smoothly with no interruption until the project delivers. Sadly, the real world has a habit of interfering: new hardware, software updates, hardware failures, server crashes, or natural disasters such as hurricanes and earthquakes are rarely taken into account by the production schedule, but can seriously delay work if a plan is not in place to address the unexpected. Planning and regular maintenance are the key to being in control and to minimizing impacts on the schedule.

Section 6 Interlude 1: Planned Downtimes

Facilities need downtime for maintenance, but projects want to run 24/7 no matter what. Regardless of production pressure, the downtime maintenance window needs to be protected as much as possible. The three types of planned downtime are:

- Regular maintenance windows are typically for larger tasks lasting 4–12 hours and are performed during non-working hours.
- Incremental maintenance windows are for tasks that can be easily broken into sub-tasks lasting 10 minutes to 1 hour, and are commonly performed during the week, ideally during off peak hours.
- Lighting maintenance windows are for quick server restarts lasting less than 10 minutes and are performed during the work day at any time needed.

The type of downtime planned will depend on the facility's needs and the work to be done. If the facility has offices in multiple time zones, this will require good communication between offices to ensure that the downtime does not negatively impact them. There

are consequences to not scheduling planned downtimes: failures will occur anyway, resulting in unpredictable downtimes with increased frequency and duration, and that happen at the worst possible time.

Section 6 Interlude 2: General Guidelines

Planning facilitates a smooth downtime that completes in the time allocated. These are some good general guidelines for all types of downtimes:

- Involve Production in the planning early, in case there are production issues that have not been exposed previously. All work should be done in less than the amount of time agreed to by Production.
- Create a communication plan that includes:
  - A list of people who need to be contacted about the downtime. This list can be integrated into a downtime notification system.
  - A hardcopy of the list somewhere handy in case the system that is down contains the list. Keeping this list next to the phone (office or mobile) is wise.
  - A list of other offices and vendors who need to be aware of outages which affect them. What if someone is sending files to a system that is down for maintenance and they expect it to be available? Who is your contact at your ISP or server vendor?
  - A way to inform people of the downtime if the usual way of notifying people is down for maintenance or due to emergency.
- Choose small, cohesive areas of maintenance to minimize testing and troubleshooting time if there are problems.
- Create a checklist of what tasks are planned and identify which tasks are critical vs. nice to have.
- Create a test plan or automated test suite to verify that the state of the system is ready for use by Production.
- Plan how to roll-back in case something unexpected happens. Leave a large chunk of the planned downtime unscheduled for surprises.
- Practice the work to be done during the downtime to uncover assumptions and reduce surprises.
- A good strategy is doing the work on the side and then swapping it in during the outage.
- When the work is complete, send out notification to the interested parties. This note should contain the details of the outage: what changed, duration of the outage, why the outage had to occur (if not obvious), what problems to look for in the future and who to contact if problems appear.
- Keeping statistics and "lessons learned" on the successes and failures of the downtimes will assist in the planning of future

downtimes. This information should be tracked as it is important for planning the amount of downtime per year, for budgeting, and for improving downtime processes.

Planning downtimes with a focus, time for testing and rollback leads to successful maintenance.

Section 6 Interlude 3: Regular Maintenance Window

Scheduling a regular block of time to perform maintenance is a good practice. Some maintenance tasks require a larger window (four or more hours) in order to complete work, particularly if it is complex or affects a lot of systems or requires a lot of coordination with multiple vendors or systems. Additionally, it is possible to schedule multiple needed tasks, and perform work that might affect the facility if the majority of people were in the office. In some studios, this work is performed on Sundays when most production and staff are paused. Examples of the type of work done might be installing a new home server, network maintenance, upgrading the database or other key software. Arranging a regular time with Production takes their needs into account, makes scheduling easier, and reduces unexpected downtimes.

Section 6 Interlude 4: Incremental Downtime

When it is difficult to get a larger chunk of time, plan instead small amounts of periodic downtime during the hours when the facility can most afford it. Incrementals can last anywhere from 10 minutes to 1.5 hours. In addition to the above guidelines, the following tips keep things simple:

- Choose a regular time to do this maintenance at a time of day when it will affect the least number of people. Make sure this time will not adversely affect other offices or anyone expecting deliveries.
- Choose a single area of maintenance to minimize testing and troubleshooting time if there are problems. The time for maintenance could be as short as 10 minutes.
- Be ready to execute the roll-back plan in case something unexpected happens. Leave half to one third of the planned downtime unscheduled for surprises.
- Practice the work to be done during the downtime so that the work progresses quickly.
- When the downtime is short, doing the work on the side and then swapping it in during the outage increases the likelihood of success.

Short, focused, incremental downtimes with time for testing and rollback lead to successful maintenance.

Section 6 Interlude 5: Roll-Overs

Roll-over downtimes are lightning downtimes, less than ten minutes, which focus on one maintenance task. This type of downtime is often performed in the early morning, during lunch, or other time when people are not rushing to publish or export their work. Common tasks include "rolling" the database (uploading new schemas, releasing very minor patches), adding more disk space, redistributing hardware or replacing redundant or backup hardware, or distributing emergency patches. The point is to disrupt the facility as little as possible by making the maintenance window extremely short, the type of maintenance extremely low risk (by sidelining, testing, and practicing), and the work easy to undo. Ideally, the downtime should go unnoticed by artists. The benefit of doing this type of maintenance during the day is that the IT staff are on hand to monitor the system status and make adjustments quickly when problems are uncovered. Even though roll-overs are short and small, notification to the interested parties should still be sent and a brief review of the events should be conducted and recorded for use in later analyses.

Unplanned/Emergency Downtimes

Unplanned or emergency downtimes will happen. Planning should still occur even though one does not know when an emergency will happen. The key techniques for managing this risk are:

- Have a communication strategy in place
- Have a plan of what to do in case of emergency
- Know who can help. What vendors are available? Who do you need to call?
- Have a defined escalation policy. When and how does this need to be kicked upstairs?
- Practice, practice, practice! This is just like a fire drill, and the purpose is to learn what is working about the plan and what needs to be improved before the emergency happens.
- Have alternate routes/processes in place so the facility can keep going if possible. For example:
  - Backups that reside in another city in case the facility loses the building
  - Backup staff in case someone is sick or quits or is on sabbatical/unreachable
  - Alternate network routing
  - Alternate disk drives
  - Alternate computers (could be left over from the last upgrade)

- After recovering from the emergency, make sure to do the following:
  - Inform interested parties that
    - The emergency is over so people know they can get back to work
    - What the emergency was and what caused it if you know
    - What lingering problems they may encounter
    - How and to whom they should report problems
  - Hold a retrospective or post-mortem so that
    - This type of problem can be avoided in the future if possible (via regular maintenance, improving hardware, or making physical improvements like strapping down equipment for earthquake safety)
    - The response time and procedures can be improved for next time, and
    - Costs can be measured and accounted for in the next budgeting cycle
  - Keep information about the "lessons learned" in a searchable location (wiki, Alfresco, database, etc.) and review it for the next year planning cycle

In conclusion, whether the downtime is for maintenance or an emergency, planning keeps the process manageable in terms of cost, schedule and stress.

7

SOFTWARE FOR A STUDIO ENVIRONMENT

Tim Green; Matt Hoesterey; Hannes Ricklefs; Mark Streatfield; Steve Theodore; Renee Dunlop; Allan Johns: *Senior Pipeline Engineer, Method Studios*

Section 7.1 What You Will Learn From This Chapter

In previous chapters, we looked at the types of software that a studio needs to complete a film or game project. In this chapter, we will look at where that software comes from.

Traditionally, there were two ways to get hold of new tools: to buy them in, or to build them in-house. However, with the rise of embedded scripting languages in art software and general-purpose scripting languages like Python, facilities are increasingly taking a third way: of writing smaller tools to extend or modify the functionality of existing applications.

We will look at all three options in this chapter. Having discussed the circumstances under which each strategy is most appropriate, we will set out the questions a studio should consider before buying in software; examine how scripting is opening up the world of tools development to artists without formal programming backgrounds; and explore some of the key issues involved in running an in-house R&D department. But first, let's look briefly at the history of computer graphics software development.

Section 7.2 Ours and Theirs: Approaches to Pipeline Software Development

Graphics production for film and games has always been deeply intertwined with software development. In the early days of computer graphics, studios that wanted to explore the new medium had to invent the tools that would be used to create new kinds of imagery. The most famous names in early computer graphics—like Jim Blinn, known for his work on the Blinn-Phong shading model; John Warnock, the founder of Adobe; Ken Perlin, the inventor of Perlin noise; and Ed Catmull, later

President of Pixar—were all PhDs in Computer Science. Even the names of the earliest CG studios, such as the Mathematical Applications Group, Incorporated (one of four companies responsible for the pioneering digital effects in 1982's *Tron*) and Pacific Data Images (now a part of DreamWorks Animation SKG) demonstrate clearly that the first generation of graphics studios were, at heart, software companies.

Those first-generation companies had to invent almost everything for themselves: not only rendering algorithms and pipeline tools but hardware; Pixar once tried to make money selling its own custom workstation, the Pixar Image Computer. Nowadays, of course, there is a large and well-developed market for off-the-shelf graphics software that runs on commodity hardware. It's no longer necessary to invent new technology for every film or game. Even so, most productions still demand a good deal of in-house software development, from simple scripting to the creation of full-blown applications.

The most common strategy is to use commercial software for core production tasks and create a library of lightweight tools and scripts to tie the commercial packages together into a coherent pipeline. However, many studios still develop complete applications from scratch. Some of these in-house tools become so sophisticated that they evolve into commercial products in their own right: RenderMan started life as Pixar's in-house rendering tool, while both the 3D sculpting program Mudbox and the crowd-simulation engine Massive were created at Weta Digital during its work on *The Lord of the Rings* trilogy. While most in-house applications don't rise to this level of sophistication, such programs illustrate how complex proprietary software can be.

For this reason, any successful production needs a clear methodology for creating and managing its software infrastructure. This goes beyond simply choosing good tools from reliable vendors: it is also important to understand the long-term goals of the pipeline and the culture of the production team.

Culture is often the most intractable problem when choosing production software. It's easy to imagine a world in which technical decisions are made by the experts in charge and the folks on the production line happily get with the program. However, that's not the world we actually work in. It may seem obvious to the leadership that Application X or Product Y is the way to go for a new project, but to artists who have invested many years in developing application-specific skills, it may be a lot less so. At best, switching may involve months of retraining and lowered productivity. In the new package, familiar hotkeys may not work, meaning highly evolved muscle memories need to be relearned, and habitual workflows may work differently. For an experienced, highly efficient artist, this can be supremely frustrating, especially if production deadlines are looming. At worst, an unpopular choice of tools can lead to passive resistance—or even mass defections—by artists who would rather quit than work in a way they find unnatural. Picking or changing software is more than just a technical choice.

How a studio's pipeline will change over time also determines its choice of software. Studios with high turnover—for example, facilities that expand rapidly to complete a big project, then shrink back down until the next contract—typically need to stick closer to the familiar interfaces and workflows of off-the-shelf applications. Their choices may be driven by the availability of contractors in their local area. In such cases, most custom work needs to be done behind the scenes, while any new tools that artists do come into contact with directly must be intuitive and easily taught. On the other hand, studios with longer strategic horizons, such as those working on IP likely to spawn many years' worth of sequels, have more leeway to introduce custom tools. It only makes sense to create tools with significant learning curves if you expect to recoup your investment in training in the long run.

Over many years of production, the amount of software built and bought by a studio quickly begins to add up. As new versions of commercial tools are released and one-off software is written for specific projects, the number of applications in use can quickly rise from tens to hundreds. This is especially true when you consider what counts as software in pipeline terms. Although to most artists, a "piece of software" is a large, easily identifiable, self-contained application like Maya or Shotgun, to an R&D department, it also includes everything from one-line scripts through to low-level graphics libraries.

In the rest of this chapter, we will look at some of the key questions that face a studio when deciding how to manage that unwieldy software infrastructure, beginning with the most obvious one: should it buy in new tools, or develop them itself?

Section 7.3 When to Build, When to Buy, and When to Tinker

There are many businesses in which technical, legal or financial considerations demand proprietary tools. Large manufacturing and service companies frequently hire outside consultants to create bespoke applications rather than relying on off-the-shelf software. At the opposite end of the spectrum, smaller or less specialized businesses often rely entirely on commercially available tools for tasks like word processing, image editing, or web publishing.

Film and game studios fall somewhere in between these extremes. Few studios want to rely entirely on proprietary tools: not only are the up-front costs significant but the ongoing costs of training and support are daunting. At the same time, most graphics productions have requirements that commercial products don't fulfill. Whether it is the need for a cutting-edge rendering technique, integration with a production-management system, or the need for a custom data format, there is often some important part of the pipeline that cannot be handled efficiently using the available off-the-shelf solutions.

Of course, most studios would rather concentrate on developing intellectual property than on developing software. Creating software from scratch is a significant investment. Even if the entire production team is certain that a custom tool is needed, there is sure to be somebody from accounting who wants to know what, exactly, necessitates all that time and money and risk. One good rule of thumb is simply not to build anything in-house unless you *must*. "Not invented here syndrome", the need to reinvent the wheel because existing solutions aren't designed in exactly the way you would have done so yourself, is a vice of software developers everywhere, and is one to be resisted strongly.

For this reason, every pipeline team needs to be diligent about keeping up with the tools market. Every SIGGRAPH or GDC throws up a new crop of production tools, and finding the right one is well worth the cost of a conference pass. It's especially important to keep up with the chaotic secondary market for plug-ins that extend commercial packages like Maya, Houdini, or Photoshop. Plug-ins are a cost-effective way to extend the functionality of your pipeline without confronting artists with unfamiliar new user interfaces. Some of them are highly sophisticated, and a few have eventually become industry standards. However, plug-in vendors are often small companies with uncertain futures and limited support capabilities, so it's important to vet them carefully when building their tools into your pipeline.

When it becomes clear that a need exists that can't be filled by existing commercial software, the team needs to come up with a cost-benefit analysis of the possible solutions. For example, a studio may find that it has trouble handling large simulations. Having artists sit idle while waiting for simulation results is clearly a problem—but how much time is actually being lost? Is the problem isolated to small number of individuals, or does it affect everybody? Wasting an hour a day of one artist's time is a shame; wasting ten minutes a day of everyone's time is blowing 2 percent of your art budget. Quantifying the problem in this way should help you find the most cost-effective solution.

The first step is usually to look for a "cheat": a readily available low-tech solution. In the example above, this might be to give the artists affected extra CPUs. Perhaps simulations can be handled by an existing server farm where they can run unattended, allowing the artists to work on other projects. Brute force can be an economically effective— if not an elegant—solution to many production problems.

Sometimes, though, brute force alone is not enough. Usually, the next step is to try to solve the problem using the scripting functionality that most major graphics applications provide. Scripted tools tend to be slower to run and less flexible than custom-built software, but they are quicker to develop and test. In the example above, the team might try to tackle long simulation times by creating a networked job-management system to queue up and run simulations on remote machines using Python or MAXScript.

However, there are cases where building a tool from scratch is the only answer. Implementing a radical new rendering or simulation

technique, for example, might only be achievable using custom code. Carefully written, highly optimized tools may also be the only way to meet performance requirements: in the case above, the real problem may not be that artists are sitting idle, but that the director needs to see simulation results more quickly to home in on the right look for a shot.

When a new tool must be built, it is important to be realistic about how long this will take, and how much it will cost. The development schedule must include adequate time for testing, while the budget must include the cost of maintenance and future development. Pipeline software is never "done".

It may be possible to recoup some of the costs of creating a tool by commercializing it. We looked at examples of in-house software that have been commercialized successfully earlier in the chapter: to that list, we could add Nuke, Mari, Katana, and the Unreal Engine, to name but a few. However, there is also a long list of products that were released commercially but failed because their parent companies were unable to focus effectively on important, but less glamorous, aspects of selling software like bug fixes, documentation, customer service, support, and long-term product development.

For game developers, the choice of whether to build or to buy carries especially great weight, since games are frequently built around licensed engines: either in full, or to handle key tasks. Licensed engines can enable a team to start working on the first day of pre-production, rather than requiring months or years of work just to get the project bootstrapped. Using a licensed engine also makes it easier to find experienced labor: it's fairly easy to find artists who have already used Unreal Engine's editor, for example, while the Source and Unity engines support large communities of hobbyists who are often just as skilled as professional artists—and who are eager to find jobs in the industry.

At the same time, using a licensed engine commits a team to using a pipeline that may not reflect the needs of their project—and sadly, the pipeline tools that accompany an engine are usually low on the engine developer's list of priorities. Understandably, teams are loath to tinker with a ready-to-run tool that can be used effectively from the first day of the project. However, as a game diverges from the licensed engine's template, it may become necessary to update the tools that come with it, or to improvise workarounds.

In some cases, trying to adapt an existing engine may become a bigger project than creating one from scratch. However, writing your own engine is a formidable task, and one that is often underestimated: teams often fail to plan for the amount of work involved in creating and maintaining the dozens of supporting technologies required, which range from custom data formats to level editors.

Many developers try to minimize the number of custom tools required by leveraging existing software: it's quite common for smaller teams to build game levels directly inside 3ds Max or Maya, for example. While this saves up-front costs, it also involves risks that may not be apparent until later: such packages are designed for modeling and

animation, not level design, and their user interfaces are not optimized for viewing spaces from a player's perspective or annotating a level interactively. A halfway house is to use new technologies designed to reduce the pain of developing custom applications. For example, Fabric Engine's Creation platform offers a collection of ready-made components that can be used to build high-performance 3D tools, while some teams even license the Unity game engine in order to build custom tools around Unity's extensible editor.

Section 7.4 Buying In Software: Points to Consider

Before deciding to buy in software rather than develop it in-house, there are several key questions a pipeline team should ask. We will run through some of the most important ones here.

Does the Software Do What You Need—and Only What You Need?

It's obvious that you should check whether a software package can do everything you expect of it. It's less obvious that you should also check whether it can do anything you don't. Companies often fall into the trap of buying software that does more than they need without factoring in the time it will take artists to master those extra features.

How Much Confidence Do You Have in the Software Vendor?

It's important to evaluate the vendor itself alongside the tools it produces. Studios and vendors have an interesting relationship, in that they are mutually dependent but have opposing needs. While vendors would prefer a world in which everyone upgraded their software on a regular basis, studios would prefer not to have to buy the same software again every year—but would still like quick responses to bug reports and support calls. It's important to be confident that your vendor will still be around in future to provide that support.

There are several points to consider here. First, are you dealing with a major corporation or a small business? As a crude generalization, larger businesses tend to be more stable and less prone to disappear completely. On the other hand, if a vendor has thousands of other clients, you should consider where you will rank in its priorities. Second, is the business currently having financial issues? A dip in recent stock prices may hint at future problems and warrant an additional pre-purchase investigation. Third, who are the vendor's current clients? Are those clients known or reputable? Contacting a past client can give you a lot of insight into the kind of support you can expect.

How Active is the User Community?

Even if you can't rely on the vendor for training or support, you may be able to rely on its user community. A strong community can help you master a tool, give you tips and tricks for improving your workflow, or help you fix technical problems. Always consider how active the other users of the software are on forums, mailing lists, and social media before committing to a purchase.

How Much Will the Software Cost to Maintain?

It's a common misconception that the cost of buying in software stops when the initial purchase is complete. In reality, the costs are ongoing. As well as how much it costs to buy a software package, factor in how much it will cost to integrate into your pipeline, how much it will cost to add features or fix bugs, and the price of support contracts or future upgrades.

Don't Skimp on Support Contracts!

Renee Dunlop

Back in 1991, I was lucky enough attend one of only three US colleges teaching computer animation. It had invested $200,000 in two SGI workstations and two seats of Alias's PowerAnimator, the precursor to Maya. These were tucked away in a special room where only elite students could hope to go.

Unfortunately, the college had forfeited spending a few thousand dollars on the support contract, which covered not only technical support but software upgrades. Even more unfortunately, it turned out that version 3 was one of the buggiest versions of PowerAnimator ever released: so much so that Alias released a patch almost immediately. However, since the college had bought the software before the patch was released, and hadn't paid for the support contract, it wasn't eligible to receive the upgrade.

For the next four or five years, students were forced to work with software that had more personality than the animations we created, and because the school delayed upgrading for several years in order to avoid further expense, it wound up faced with the decision whether to continue teaching archaic software, or purchasing anew. The results were, (within a matter of years) the room that housed the $200,000 investment that had made the school so cutting-edge had been converted into a storage closet.

How Often Will You Need to Upgrade?

To encourage existing users to spend more money, software developers tend to release upgrades every twelve to eighteen months. Deciding which ones you need to purchase is not simply a matter of whether you need the new features they contain. The complex interactions between tools in a pipeline mean that you should also consider

an application's "dependencies": the other tools it requires in which to function, and those that rely on it in turn. For example, if your company purchases a plug-in that only works with a particular version of its parent software, this will affect your ability to upgrade the parent application. Are you sufficiently committed to the plug-in that you will hold off upgrading until your plug-in vendor also releases a new version?

Such dependency relationships can affect many applications at once: if the new SDK for Package X requires a new version of Visual Studio or the GCC compiler, for example, this may affect a large number of ostensibly unrelated tools. "DLL Hell", the problems caused by conflicts between Windows libraries, is one of the reasons that many studios now rely more on scripting languages like Python: tools written in such languages are usually much less vulnerable to versioning problems.

Even if you decide that you need a particular update, it may not be possible to roll it out immediately. It's generally regarded as foolhardy to attempt an upgrade in the middle of a production, since this can cause a short-term hit in productivity as artists come to terms with the changes, and introduce bugs or workflow problems. For all of these reasons, it's not uncommon to find studios with a reputation for being on the cutting edge of technology running software that is three or four years out of date.

Rez: An Open-Source Tool for Managing VFX Software

Allan Johns
Senior Pipeline Engineer, Method Studios

Managing visual effects software comes with its own unique set of problems. There are often many different versions of each software package in use simultaneously at a facility: on different jobs, sequences, or even individual shots. Maintaining all of these configurations is a huge undertaking, since each software package may be dependent on several others, so making an update in one place can cause a series of conflicts elsewhere. Visual effects could even be said to take the old concept of "dependency hell" to a new level.

An inefficient dependency-management system will create bottlenecks where there should be none. On one hand, without robust dependency management, you may not be able to support different versions of dependent software at the same time, which limits your ability to support new applications without branching your code. And since a system that is unable to describe dependencies properly—or that relies on a lot of error-prone manual work in order to do so—often results in run-time bugs, your developers will spend a lot of time dealing with build and release issues that they could otherwise have spent on developing new tools. On the other hand, a system that is too rigid in its description of dependencies increases maintenance overheads, since releasing new versions of core libraries forces you to rerelease many dependent software packages. The road to robust and efficient software management is riddled with potholes like these.

An effective technique is to split the problem into two parts: dependency management and environment management. Dependency management is about answering the question, "If I require these versions of these software packages, what versions of the dependent software packages do I also require?" Resolving these dependencies must avoid version clashes, since it is problematic (if not downright impossible) to use two versions of the same software

within the same environment. Environment management is about answering the question, "How do I determine which versions of these software packages I want in this particular job, sequence, or shot?"

All too often, these two problems are combined into one. This results in a brittle development environment, where changes made by a developer can break existing production environments. It also puts the onus of managing job configurations onto the developer, when really they should be concerned only with the immediate dependencies of their own project. When developers are free to write software independently of such concerns, and when specifying project dependencies is easy, they can concentrate on correctly dividing software into modular components, and keeping them that way.

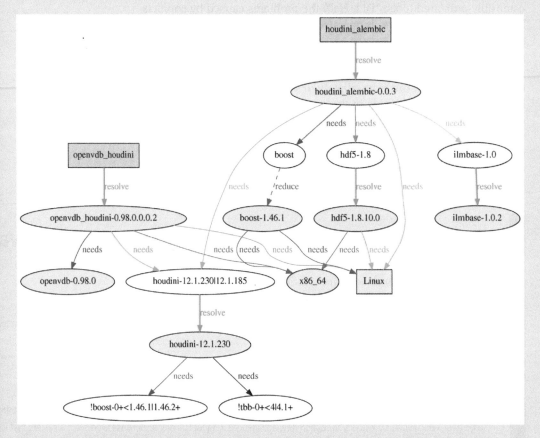

Figure 7.1 Rez is one of the few dedicated solutions available for managing software dependencies in visual effects work. Above, you can see a graph generated by Rez showing how dependencies within an environment were resolved.

Rez, an open-source project for building, managing, and deploying software, is one of very few solutions for dependency management tailored to visual effects work. It enables the developer to be concerned with managing only the direct dependencies of their own project, and has a dependency-resolving algorithm that ensures that no version conflicts occur within an environment. This is used both to configure the build environment for a software package and to configure production environments, guaranteeing that run-time version conflicts do not arise.

Rez software packages are self-contained, and describe in a single configuration file what other software they depend on, and how they affect the environment they are used in. Version requirements are flexible, and can be described as loosely or as strictly as required. Let's look at an example of such a configuration file:

name: my_maya_utility

version: 1.0.2

requires:

```
- maya-2012
- acme_util_lib-4.5 + <5
- foo-5.0.7
```

commands:

```
- export PYTHONPATH = $PYTHONPATH:!ROOT!/python
- export MAYA_PLUGIN_PATH = $MAYA_PLUGIN_PATH:!ROOT!/lib
```

Here, a Maya plugin requires any version of Maya 2012 (2012.0, 2012.1, and so on); any version of acme_util_lib equal to or greater than 4.5, but less than the 5; and a specific patch number of the foo software package. When resolved into an environment, the Python and Maya plug-in path variables are updated so that the software becomes visible to the relevant applications.

What Will You Do When the Software is Discontinued?

The last question to ask when considering whether to buy in software is what you will do once the vendor no longer supports it. Even a tool that has worked well for years may cause problems in future if a deep-rooted bug emerges, or your workflow changes. If that tool is integrated deeply into your pipeline, that lack of support could have a huge impact on your company.

Why Software Support Matters

Matt Hoesterey
Design Lead, Microsoft

The biggest impact that lack of vendor support had on my career was when I was working on a small indie game using an engine made by a well-known studio. At the time, it was the only XNA engine available, and having had good experiences with the studio's products in the past, we decided to build our game around it.

A little over a year into development, we began experiencing huge performance issues after the game had been running on the Xbox for over thirty minutes. Since I was the only member of our team of three who could program, I began to optimize my code looking for memory leaks. When I did so, I discovered that there were huge memory problems

in almost every part of the engine—but at that point, the company that made the engine announced that it would no longer support it.

Since other people had invested in the engine, the user community banded together. Months later, it had succeeded in finding and fixing most of the memory problems, but a larger one had been uncovered in the core systems of the engine. The community asked the vendor for help—but sadly, the vendor went bankrupt shortly afterward.

Though we never solved the problem, we brought on an expert programmer and community leader who helped us work around the unfixable engine problem so we could release our game problem-free. However, the problems caused by our engine choice literally doubled our development time.

Looking at experiences like ours, it becomes clear how an unsupported product can have drastic effects on a company. Not only was our product affected but after shipping we had to switch engines, meaning that we had to abandon our existing pipeline and much of the framework we had built. The loss of many custom tools, and the time we spent learning new tools and reworking our pipeline can both be attributed to a single bad software choice.

Section 7.5 Working with Open-Source Software

Production software can be extremely expensive, often running to several thousand dollars per user. In recent years, it has become common to work with free open-source software as an alternative to conventional commercial products.

The best-known example is an operating system: big studios with large render farms save large amounts of money using the free Linux OS instead of commercial alternatives from Microsoft and Apple. However, many other pipeline tools are available open-source. Popular scripting languages like Python, Lua and JavaScript are free and generally supported with a host of free, high-quality programming tools such as text editors. Database engines like MySQL and MongoDB, and web servers like Apache are also open-source projects.

There are also a number of open-source art tools, including the GIMP image editor; Blender, a complete 3D modeling, animation, and rendering suite that provides similar capabilities to 3ds Max and Maya; and even renderers that can process files intended for RenderMan.

The low cost of open-source software is an obvious attraction, but another important benefit of open-source tools is their extensibility: if the existing package does not meet your needs, it may be possible to extend or update it, since the source code is freely available. Even if you don't plan on changing the software, access to the source code can make it possible to track down bugs or understand why things are not working as expected. Big open-source projects also generally have a high reputation for quality. With large communities of contributors and many eyes on their problems, the core functionality of open-source projects is often as good as, or better than, competing paid products.

However, there are pitfalls in using open-source software. Not every open-source project has the same number of people working on it as Apache or MySQL, and smaller open-source initiatives often fall victim to a loss of community interest or feuding among their contributors. Updates can be spotty and may reflect the internal politics of the project developers more than the needs of the users. When considering an open-source solution, it is particularly important to vet not only the software itself, but the community that develops it. This is one of the reasons why many companies successfully sell "free" software: they provide a degree of predictability when it comes to upgrades that a loose community of enthusiasts can't or won't offer.

But for pipeline software, the main sticking point is often aesthetic or emotional rather than technical. Open-source projects historically excel at heavyweight computing tasks like compiling code or providing programming tools, since a large, passionate user community is very good at spotting bugs. However, user interface design is often a weak spot, since the subtleties of user interaction don't always lend themselves to an evolutionary, community-based approach. Artists tend to be very picky about the aesthetics and ergonomics of the tools they work with. These preferences can't be ignored, since they have a big impact on productivity, meaning that in the long run, it may be cheaper to opt for a commercial software package, even if it costs thousands of dollars per seat.

Using open-source software can also have important legal implications. There are a wide range of different open-source software licenses, and some can have a significant impact on a studio. The GNU General Public License (GPL) and other "copyleft" licenses stipulate that any software that includes copylefted components must itself be released under the same license, meaning that its creator can't sell or distribute it unless they are willing to provide the source code. Many companies (particularly game developers, who may want to distribute some of their tools to fans or engine licensees) positively ban the use of copyleft tools in order to avoid having to share their secrets with the world. For this reason, a legal review is a standard step in evaluating open-source software for studio use.

Section 7.6 Scripting and Tinkering

It's important to remember that the "buy versus build" dichotomy encompasses only part of the software used in production. Big applications with fancy GUIs, 3D views, and startling computational abilities are eye-catching, but in many studios the bulk of in-house development takes place in the realm of scripting, creating a variety of smaller productivity tools.

Eliminating error-prone clerical work, cutting down the number of mouse clicks needed to perform common tasks, and making sure

that vital files are always easy to find may not be the most glamorous of tasks, but in a big studio with hundreds of artists, the return on such investments can be enormous. If you already have a hundred artists, you get the equivalent of another staff member for free by saving each person a measly *5 minutes* per day.

It's also important to remember that no piece of the production pipeline stands on its own. A tool that doesn't work with the others in the studio is no more useful than a length of pipe whose ends are welded shut. Connectivity is the "killer app" for any pipeline, and the keys to connectivity are well-defined, open APIs and data-interchange formats—and scripting to customize interactions.

Most professional art applications include embedded scripting languages: either shared languages such as Python or Lua, or application-specific ones like MAXScript (MXS) in 3ds Max, MEL in Maya, or ZScript in ZBrush. The scripting capabilities of graphics applications began as simple macros before evolving into more fully featured scripting tools capable of automating complex but repetitive tasks, such as changing the render settings for a large number of scene files. However scripting has grown from simply speeding up boring grunt work to playing a critical (some might even say *the* critical) role in modern productions. Scripting languages are the glue that holds a graphics pipeline together.

Scripts are supremely versatile: they can handle tasks ranging from trivial clerical jobs like renaming files all the way up to creating complex tools like asset databases accessible from inside art software. Moreover, they're usually easier to create and distribute than full-blown traditional applications, being less dependent on specific shared libraries and processor architectures, and are often cross-platform: a script-based tool can be used on Mac OS X, Windows, and Linux machines with little or no extra work.

Scripts can run inside a host application for art-specific tasks, or on their own, and both sets of tools can share code to avoid duplicating effort.

The crowning virtue of scripting, however, is the speed with which scripts can be written. While advanced scripting languages offer the same sophisticated programming constructs as traditional languages like C or C++, scripts can also be improvised on the spot to handle the many minor emergencies that arise in every production. Creating a C++ application to change the extension of every file in a project from ".tiff" to ".tif" is building a rocket launcher to swat flies. Tackling the same task in script is as simple as typing four or five lines into a Lua interpreter or a Python shell.

The main practical distinction between a general-purpose scripting language and a conventional programming language is performance. For computing-intensive applications such as simulation or rendering, scripting languages can be several orders of magnitude slower. For this reason, math-heavy tasks tend to fall into the province of tools programmers using C or C++. For many ordinary productivity

applications, however, performance may not be the primary concern: while the difference between a render that takes 12 hours and one that takes 10 minutes is enormously important, the difference between a file operation that takes 4 milliseconds and one that takes 400 may not be significant for low-volume tasks.

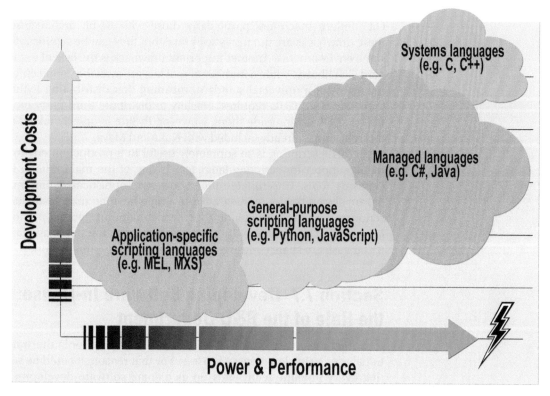

Figure 7.2 The relative development cost of some common types of programming languages relative to the performance of the tools they create. Traditional languages like C and C++ can create tools that run more efficiently, but the trade-off is a dramatic increase in development time.

Until fairly recently, scripting in DCC applications was dominated by application-specific languages like MEL or MAXScript. However, at the time of writing, there is a strong trend towards general-purpose languages such as Python that work in a wider variety of contexts.

Python is the most ubiquitous scripting language in modern pipelines. It is embedded in Maya, MotionBuilder, Softimage, Nuke, Houdini, LightWave, and Blender (and is available in other applications, such as 3 ds Max, via plug-ins). It's a "serious" programming language as well; it's often used to teach computer science classes and it has full support for sophisticated object-oriented programming techniques. Python's greatest strength, however, is its enormous library of built-in extension modules. Python devotees like to say that the

language "comes with batteries included", meaning that many general programming problems can be tackled with the tools included in the default installation, which cover everything from reading XML files to setting up a web server. This adds a lot of power and flexibility to any application that incorporates Python.

Python isn't perfect, however. It's fairly slow, even by the standards of scripting languages, and it demands a significant chunk of memory. On modern machines, particularly those with 64-bit architectures, these drawbacks are not necessarily fatal, but they can be significant in some environments. Another important drawback is the lack of a standard GUI library: while a number of tool kits are available, none enjoys the status of a universal standard, meaning that distributing Python tools that need GUIs requires a facility to distribute third-party modules and DLLs alongside them. However, PySide is quickly taking on this role, and is already included with Nuke and Maya.

Because scripting is so supremely useful in a production environment, support for scripting languages is one of the main criteria for choosing tools. Unscriptable tools, however sophisticated they may be, are always harder to integrate into a pipeline than those with good scripting support, particularly those which support general-purpose languages. If all of the tools in your pipeline speak the same language, it's far easier to share code and economize on development effort.

Section 7.7 Developing Software In-House: the Role of the R&D Department

Sometimes, there's no substitute for developing tools the traditional way, using languages like C++. For that reason, it could be said that every pipeline team ends up as a small software-development company. If that's the case, it's important to have a good understanding of the role that software development plays in production, even if you're hoping to keep in-house work to a minimum.

Every in-house development team needs to provide four main services:
- Developing completely new projects
- Enhancing existing projects
- Maintaining projects to stay up to date with OS and dependent library changes
- Bug fixes and support

How effort is split between these four services depends on many factors, but for all but the very largest studios, tasks lower down the list will occupy the majority of developers' time.

The size of the development team is normally relative to the size of the studio. In a visual effects or animation facility, a 20:1 ratio between artists and "technical" staff (including both the IT and R&D

departments) is not unreasonable. There is a trade-off between technical and budgetary concerns here: a larger R&D team increases the scope of the tools a facility can create, but may make it financially uncompetitive when bidding for new work.

Games, by comparison, have a much more significant engineering component, so the ratio is usually much smaller. Anything from 1:1 to 6:1 is "normal", although the figure may go higher if you count art staff involved in creating material not used directly in the game, like pre-rendered cut-scenes and marketing materials. Games companies rarely have an actual R&D department and if they do, it's usually for blue-sky research: development is done as part of the team, or by a central "tools group".

Section 7.8 Developing Software In-House: Who to Recruit

When hiring development staff, remember that programmers are not created alike. Like artists, they specialize in a number of different disciplines. A programmer who specializes in low-level run-time tasks for games will have a very different skill set to one who specializes in writing simulation tools for films, for example. While it is possible to find staff who can fill a number of different programming roles within a company, it is unlikely you will find a single person who can do everything.

But programmers aren't the only members of the team who can contribute to in-house software: designers and artists who can code can be some of the best tools developers. In many games companies, technical artists (TAs) have taken over part of the role traditionally occupied by tools programmers. First, a technical artist or designer typically uses the tools they create. Having the person who built the tool use it on a daily basis will ensure that it stays up to date and in touch with the changing needs of the project. Technical artists also excel at interaction design: they tend to have a good eye for intuitive, visually pleasing interfaces.

However, one of the main reasons to look for tools developers with art backgrounds is that graphics tools are so specialized, making it difficult for programmers with no art experience to resolve problems effectively. It can be harder to explain the problem to someone from outside the discipline than it is to write the solution for yourself. Smart teams empower non-programmers to help themselves.

In film, Technical Directors (TDs) play a similar role. They are often artists who began their careers in production but gradually assumed more technical duties, either following a passion for technology, or because they were frustrated by inadequate tools and felt compelled to take matters into their own hands. They specialize in tasks where

the line between content and coding is blurry: creating character rigs, building shaders, and setting up complex simulations, for example. They usually work in scripting languages rather than developing large-scale stand-alone applications, although many cross over into full-time programming later in their careers. Because they deal daily with the realities of producing both tools and content, they are well placed to help less technically inclined artists and hardcore engineers work together effectively. Moreover, TDs are well placed to create the tools that artists really want. Intimate knowledge of artists' needs and working environments enables TDs to buff the rough edges off workflows and provide quick shortcuts for common operations. A button that saves five or six mouse clicks is not worth the trouble of creating a complete C++ plug-in, but it can still be a huge boost to artists' productivity and morale.

However, the move from creating art to creating tools takes time. Tools written by artists need to be as reliable and easy to maintain as those written by programmers, meaning that TAs and TDs need to learn on the job many of the basic principles that traditionally trained programmers learned in school.

Finally, remember that artists don't need to be able to code, or even to script, in order to create simple tools. In games, Excel is a great example of a tool that can be used to build other tools. For example, designers may create Excel spreadsheets that automate tasks like creating progression curves (graphs that define how a parameter, such as monster toughness or weapon strength, changes as the player progresses through the game, thereby making later stages more challenging than earlier ones) before the data is copied into a database.

Section 7.9 Developing Software In-House: Development Policy

Internal R&D departments will normally try and follow some formal software development methodology to make sure they run efficiently. Commonly, this is a variation of "agile" programming, in which development proceeds iteratively, in brief cycles. (We will look at "agile" and "waterfall" methodologies in a later chapter.) The elements of such a formal development process may include:

- A methodology for defining the specifications of the software (for example, user stories: short sentences that describe what the users need the software to do)
- A schedule and budget that define when the software needs to be completed by and the resources that are available to build it
- A user interface standard (and possibly even a dedicated UI designer)
- A build/release/deployment system for building software
- A code review process

- A testing environment (perhaps tied in with the build process as "continuous integration": a concept we will explore later in the chapter)
- A QC and/or QA process (Quality Control involves checking software for defects; Quality Assurance involves creating systems to prevent defects from arising in the first place)
- A documentation process
- A system for tracking bug reports and feature requests

We will look at some of these elements in more detail in the remainder of this chapter. While a highly formalized process like this is often an ideal rather than a reality, particularly in games development, there are a few key points that should be agreed upon right at the start of any development project:

- Which version-control system to use for the source code
- Which languages will be used by the development team
- A standard for how to build the software
- A standard for how to install/deploy the software, complete with a versioning schema
- A standard for how to configure the software: this should define both application-specific configurations, and which versions of the software to run

Section 7.10 Developing Software In-House: Testing New Tools

At some point, a decision must be made whether an in-house tool is being built "to get the job done", or being built to last. Both approaches are valid, but have significant drawbacks—and an equally significant impact on how the tool is tested.

The former approach will almost certainly produce code that will not be extensible, will be hard to maintain, contain more bugs, and have little or no documentation. However, it will be quick to produce, and require much less formal testing. The latter will require a completely different approach to development, and a more formal testing methodology. This may significantly improve the quality of the code base, but may also significantly increase the development effort required.

The important thing is to make sure that both developers and "clients" have similar expectations about the probable quality and life span of the software. Artists often expect that in-house tools will look as polished as third-party tools, and will have been tested as extensively before deployment. The reality is that a lot of the time, the art staff act as the tool's test team: they just don't know it. For a tool that will be only used on a single project, to do more extensive preliminary testing would be a waste of money.

However, there will be cases where software originally only intended to get a particular shot out of the door is deemed worth

reusing. Such tools should be moved over to a more formal development methodology as soon as possible: the later this is done, the harder it will be to refactor the software.

Unit testing is a practice that emphasizes automated testing of code on a module-by-module basis (testing each "unit" in isolation rather than the program as a whole). In particular, "regression testing" using unit tests helps to maintain consistent behavior as code changes. Suppose, for example, that a particular module is designed to parse file names correctly. The tests for that module would feed in a list of known file names and check that the outputs are as expected. This can then be used to verify that the behavior does not change as the module evolves over time.

To support regression testing, tests are generally integrated into a framework that allows them to be run as a batch operation. To help, there are a variety of open-source tools that can be integrated into the version-control system to run these tests on all the code committed, and to present reports of the state of each project. This is often used in conjunction with the practice of "continuous integration", where developers merge their changes into the main version frequently so as to catch problems more quickly than if long periods are allowed to elapse between merges.

Unit testing and regression tests do not guarantee that software is bug-free, but at least they ensure that it is outwardly stable. By guaranteeing that each module of code in the project presents a stable public face with predictable inputs and outputs, they foster user confidence in in-house tools. It's a particularly important practice for programmers working in scripting languages: in C or C++, the compiler will prevent you from accidentally changing the return value of a function from, say, a string to a number. In Python or JavaScript, there's no way to prevent that, except by unit testing.

Test-driven development takes these principles a step further still, by making the test process the foundation of the engineering effort. In TDD, the first code to be written in any development project is the unit test; then the actual program code is written in such a way that it fulfills the test criteria. This process not only ensures that comprehensive tests exist for all codes but can help minimize unnecessary effort (as—at least in theory—only functionality necessary to satisfy the test conditions is actually implemented).

Testing is great for catching changes in behavior or the way that different pieces of software talk to one other. However, only human testers can tell you when a piece of software is technically functional but not actually doing the right job! Although it may not be possible to give in-house software the same level of quality assurance as a commercial product, it is still important to have testers check that a tool is doing the job it is designed for before it is deployed. This is one of the roles in which TAs and TDs excel, since they can often spot flaws in the way in which a tool works in practice that a pure programmer might miss.

Section 7.11 Developing Software In-House: Developing a Release Policy

Each software release has the potential to introduce bugs into a production. Once a new version of a tool has been tested and approved, it's important for it to be rolled out in a planned, predictable fashion to minimize disruptions to the schedule.

Where possible, make changes in small increments. Minor changes may happen almost daily, but the art team needs to be warned about any significant changes to work flow or data layouts in advance—and, if necessary, supplied with documentation and training.

It's particularly important to involve the art staff in release planning. The effectiveness of a new tool depends on the willingness of the production team to use it, and a botched release can saddle a new tool with a bad reputation that lasts long after the problems have been fixed. It's unfair to ask art staff to absorb new tools (presumably with a whole crop of minor flaws) right before an important milestone or in the middle of a big crunch. And, of course, pushing out tools that don't reflect user feedback is unlikely to generate a lot of enthusiasm. For all these reasons, it's important for the tools team to do internal marketing—and market research: finding out what the art team really needs the most—so that each new release is integrated into production smoothly.

Section 7.12 Developing Software In-House: Producing Documentation

Without the resources of a dedicated software-development company behind them, many studios develop tools that are well engineered but abysmally documented. Unrecorded, tribal knowledge is the bane of any pipeline. Teams that undertake serious in-house projects need to understand that creating accurate, readable documentation and training materials is as much a part of development as coding new features or fixing bugs. Your software stinks if no one in the building knows how to use it—no matter how many benchmarks it hits.

To create basic documentation, developers can use tools like the open-source document generator Doxygen. Doxygen can extract information from the annotations in source files, helping to build documentation semi-automatically. It was originally designed to work with C++ code, but supports a range of other programming languages, including Python.

For teams looking to bring their documentation up to a higher level, contract technical writers are a great resource. There's no better way to force developers to clarify their ideas than to make them explain them

to an intelligent, generally knowledgeable outsider: explaining things to a technical writer often reveals long-standing problems in the design or implementation of tools that previously went unremarked because they were just things that "everybody knows". The fact that a good technical writer produces literate and accurate documentation is often a bonus: their real value is forcing the development team to sense-check its work. As Einstein used to say: "You do not really understand something unless you can explain it to your grandmother."

Anyone writing software should also understand the concept of "technical debt"—the backlog of under-the-hood work that must be done on a development project before that project can be considered "complete". Any time a piece of software is released into production without documentation and testing, the technical debt of that software increases. Beyond a certain point, the debt will become unsustainable: no change can be made to the software without affecting production severely, since the impact of that change cannot be predicted accurately. It's very easy to underestimate just how long production software will be around for—or how much work it will take to maintain each new feature that you add.

Section 7.13 Developing Software In-House: Reporting Errors

The last big component of safe in-house development is robust maintenance. No tool should be released to the users without a system that immediately informs the tools team when problems occur. Error reporting might be as simple as a log file dumped to the user's hard drive or as complicated as a complete memory dump uploaded to a database after every crash.

The key to good error reporting is that errors should be reported automatically, with as much detailed contextual information as possible. Obviously, user feedback is still important, but since the artists using the tools are not trained QA testers, they rarely supply the information necessary to help the programmers figure out what went wrong.

Moreover, artists have their own jobs to do: reporting bugs takes time, and if deadlines are looming, they are more likely to work around problems than risk jeopardizing their own schedules to generate good debugging information. If a tool gets a bad reputation, it isn't uncommon for artists to stop using it entirely without ever passing word back to the programmers. Many tools programmers are stunned to find out that their "users" haven't actually been using a particular tool for weeks or even months because of a rocky release or a bug that was never reported. In addition to recording breakdowns and errors, many studios record the frequency with which tools are actually used, since this is a great help when planning how to allocate resources in future.

The most important benefit of good error reporting is that it generates good will. If errors are reported as they happen, in the form of emails or SMS messages, tools programmers, TDs or TAs can respond right away. Nothing enhances the standing of the tools team as much as a reputation for prompt responses to emergencies: if every crash is followed by the appearance of a helpful TA or programmer a few minutes later, the art staff embrace their symbiotic relationship with the pipeline team, and actively collaborate in making tools better.

If, on the other hand, complaints and bug reports vanish into the bureaucratic ether, it's easy for the production staff to see the tools team as aloof and uncaring. In this kind of environment, the art department develops superstitions and secret workarounds, and fights the tools rather than using them effectively. Service is the real calling of the pipeline team—and nothing says "good service" like prompt, well-informed responses to problems.

Systems for reporting bugs include open-source tools like Bugzilla, MantisBT, and Request Tracker, and commercially available systems such as JIRA and YouTrack. Such systems can also be used to track requests for new features. Some might argue that there should be different mechanisms for each, but for simplicity's sake, it is often beneficial to handle bug reports and feature requests together.

8

DIVING DEEPER INTO DATA MANAGEMENT

**Tim Green; Matt Hoesterey; Hannes Ricklefs;
Mark Streatfield; Steve Theodore; Rob Blau:** *Head of Pipeline Engineering, Shotgun Software;* **Ryan Mayeda:** *Product Producer, Shotgun Software;* **Manne Ohrstrom:** *Senior Software Engineer, Shotgun Software;* **Fran Zandonella:** *International Senior Pipeline TD, Rhythm & Hues*

Section 8.1 What You Will Learn From This Chapter

In the previous chapters, we looked at the hardware and software on which a pipeline is built. In this chapter, we will look at how pipelines are designed. In particular, we will explore four key topics:

- Directory structures
- File-naming conventions
- Version control
- Metadata and databases

Some of these concepts were introduced in Chapter 5. Here, we will explore them in more detail. But first, let's take a brief look at how a data-management workflow typically evolves.

Section 8.2 How Data-Management Workflow Evolves

As assets normally consist of files on disk, the file system forms the bedrock on which the pipeline and asset-management system are built. Therefore, the simplest approach to data management is to agree on a sensible directory structure and file-naming convention and maintain these manually.

While this approach is fine for small studios, it doesn't scale well to larger ones. What usually breaks the system is human error caused by users not adhering to the conventions that have been set up, with the integrity of the data suffering as a result. As a facility strives to improve data accessibility, security and level of quality, databases

and metadata become the obvious solutions. The metadata and/or database doesn't replace the file system: it simply provides a more convenient way of searching for files.

As a result, the development of the pipeline tends to go through the following stages:

1. Acquire an appropriate number of workstations.
2. Acquire centralized storage.
3. Define and implement directory structures.
4. Define other useful ways in which to classify assets, based on the ways that staff are making use of those directory structures.
5. Build a database to store this metadata, creating the foundation of an asset-management system.
6. Define the most efficient way to group assets and define dependencies.
7. Link assets and production-scheduling tasks.

We will discuss some of these processes over the course of this chapter. First, let's look at some of the issues determining directory structure.

Section 8.3 Directory Structures: Flat Versus Deep Structures

When starting a new project, it's important to plan your directory structure from the outset. There are a couple of fundamental decisions to make here. The first is what data you want to encode in the name of the directory. The second is how the directory structure will be arranged.

A directory structure can be either "deep" (with many levels of sub-directories within each directory, but few individual files in each) or "flat" (few levels of sub-directories, but more individual files in each). This choice can have a major impact on the speed at which both human users and automated systems can access files. Ultimately, you want a structure that is not so deep that you can easily become lost in it, but not so flat that you are drowned in files that you have no way to sort or filter. There is no scientific method of determining the correct solution here: instead, setting up an efficient directory system is more of an art form.

Before defining a directory structure, you must decide between using either the file system directly or an abstraction layer which enables users to choose how they wish to organize their view of the data. Abstraction layers such as FUSE (a kernel module for UNIX-like operating systems), allow users to specify arbitrary file system views on top of an abstract directory structure that may be incomprehensible to humans in its raw form, but require considerable development effort, and are not usually the solution of first choice.

Directory Structures and Version-Control Systems

Manne Ohrstrom
Senior Software Engineer, Shotgun Software

Ryan Mayeda
Product Producer, Shotgun Software

Rob Blau
Head of Pipeline Engineering, Shotgun Software

When it comes to designing a directory structure, there are a few basic decisions that will serve as a framework for all of the choices you make in future. One of these is how you will handle iterations of work. There are two main ways of representing versions in the file system: as versioned files or a check-in/check-out system. As we discussed in Chapter 5, the strength of versioned files lies in their simplicity. You don't need special tools to give a file a name that complies with the versioning strategy, or to pick the appropriate version of a file. However, this setup is a lot less structured that a check-in/check-out system. Since all the files you have online are available within the directory structure and can be accessed in arbitrary ways, it may be possible to move or delete the history of a file inadvertently, and tracking "dependencies"—the way in which one file relies on another—is more difficult. And since versioning changes the name of a file each time it is updated, all of the references to that file must be updated too: often a lengthy process, with important consequences if it is not done correctly.

A check-in/check-out setup is more complicated and requires more infrastructure to implement. Less technically minded artists can get lost in such a system, since details of which version of an asset they are working on may be hidden from them. However, it is easier to provide true data isolation for things like long-running renders. Dependency tracking is also easier, since usually only one version of a given file is available at a given time. And when an updated file is checked in, such systems can update all of the references to it automatically, saving a lot of manual effort.

Another basic decision to make when designing a directory structure is how updates to files flow to downstream tasks. The choice here is between a "push system" and a "pull system". In a push system, updates are picked up automatically; in a pull system, somebody needs to pull them in explicitly. This is not an all-or-nothing choice: some parts of your pipeline can pull and others can push. The more expensive a task is in terms of human or computational effort, the better a candidate it is for a pull-based workflow, since this makes it easier to achieve true data isolation. However, over a long period of time, such as the production schedule of an animated feature, the time spent trying to track down which version of an asset is used where can become significant. A push-based workflow will reduce the number of different versions of an asset in use and make it easier to ensure that all active tasks are using the latest versions of all of the files.

Even when using a mostly push-based workflow, it is likely that there will be times you want to lock down some tasks (for example, when a shot is close to final and the decision is made not to permit any further updates to its component assets), so it is good practice to make sure that a pipeline supports both modes of operation.

Both file versioning and check-in/check-out systems are compatible with either push or pull workflows. To achieve a push workflow, versioning systems usually use tricks like "symlinks" (symbolic links: files that contain a reference to another file or directory, like a Windows shortcut) to represent the latest version of a file, while check-in/check-out systems use strategies like shared workspaces or regular updates to sandbox environments.

With both of these basic decisions, there is no right or wrong answer. When it comes to directory structure, the saying "as simple as possible, but no simpler" is very apt.

Section 8.4 Directory Structures for Film

On a high level, the process of asset creation on a film is split into two parts. The first is building all the characters, creatures, props, buildings, vegetation, environments, vehicles, and so on required for the production, often referred to in production as "asset builds". The second is assembling those asset builds into scenes and shots.

Arguably, the most common model for organizing assets is to encode the project, scene and shot in the directory structure. Consequently, an initial structure might look something like:

/projects/<project>/<scene>/<shot>

The first thing to notice here is that there is no appropriate location for asset builds, since they are not typically based around scenes or shots—and, in the case of assets stored in a shared library, may not even belong to a single project. A workaround is to create a scene called "assets" that will store all of the asset builds, then file the asset builds as if they were individual shots. For example:

/projects/<project>/assets/<asset>

The directory structure is now functionally identical for anyone working on shots or asset builds—which is pretty much all of the artists on the production. The next decision is how much deeper the directory structure should be. While you could simply store everything in the shot folder, this folder would soon become cluttered with files with confusingly similar names. The alternative is to create a few more directory levels.

One obvious option would be to divide the next level of directories according to discipline:

/projects/<project>/<scene>/<shot>/2d
/projects/<project>/<scene>/<shot>/3d

Another option is to divide them by department:

/projects/<project>/<scene>/<shot>/anim
/projects/<project>/<scene>/<shot>/comp
/projects/<project>/<scene>/<shot>/model

Under that, you can add directories for each type of data:

/projects/<project>/<scene>/<shot>/anim/maya/cache
/projects/<project>/<scene>/<shot> /anim/maya/curves

For clarity, you might also include a further level of directories indicating the version number of the asset:

/projects/<project>/< scene>/<shot>/anim/maya/cache/v1
/projects/<project>/<scene>/<shot>/anim/maya/cache/v2
/projects/<project>/<scene>/<shot>/anim/maya/cache/v3

Directories used by the asset-management system rather than accessed manually follow a similar structure, often with a directory immediately below shot level to make their function explicit:

/projects/<project>/<scene>/<shot>/assetManagement/

<assetType >/<assetName>/<version>/

Or to use a concrete example:

/projects/bob/SB/SB_0001/assetManagement/AnimatedCharacter/ foo/v10

Naming conventions for the directories themselves vary from facility to facility. VFX projects tend to have multiple names, including the actual movie title, a code name, and an abbreviation of this code name. Any of these may be used for the project directory. Scenes and shots are denoted by strings of alphanumeric characters, usually with an additional level between the project and the scene—not reflected in the directory structure itself—to denote the sequence. For example, a scene might be called "XX_01", with "XX" representing the sequence and "_01" representing where that scene falls within the sequence. Shots tend to inherit the name of the scene, plus an additional alphanumeric suffix: for example, "XX_01_01a".

Another fundamental decision a facility has to make is whether the file-naming convention it uses for a project should match that of the client, or whether it should reflect its own internal workflow. Using an internal or "virtual" naming convention of this kind means that files must be renamed before passing to the client for review or delivery, but means that that the same structure can be used for multiple projects, and that the names of shots can be changed more easily if a client changes its own convention midway through a production.

Section 8.5 Directory Structures for Games

Directory structures for games differ from those for films in several important respects. Firstly, when developing a game, you are not just developing content: you are also developing a code base. This is reflected in the high-level directory structure:

/projects/<project>/code
/projects/<project>/tools
/projects/<project>/assets

As in film work, each asset consists of an important chunk of data required for the game: for example, a skeleton, an animation, a texture, or a script. However, unlike film work, assets are not simply divided up according to the software that created them.

As we have discussed in previous chapters, art tools such as Maya do not save content in a format that is appropriate for a game engine to use directly. Their native file format may contain information that is not required by the engine, making it slow to read; or it may lack information that the engine does require. It is typical for game engines to read content in a binary format that matches the target platform's "endianness" (the order in which binary data is encoded for storage) and "structure alignment" (the alignment of data structures to memory address boundaries).

This means that there is often an offline preparation process that transforms the assets created by the art software (the "work files") into platform-specific versions (the "game assets"). In some cases, this is done by plug-ins that export all or a selection of the data from a work file to create a game asset. This means creating separate directories for the two types of content: a division that usually happens close to the root of the file path:

/projects/<project>/assets/workFiles
/projects/<project>/assets/gameAssets

Most of the directories below this level are mirrored from work-Files to gameAssets. This means that an export process may auto-generate the correct export path simply by replacing "workFiles" with "gameAssets".

Alternatively, some pipelines convert the work file into a game asset on the engine side. In these cases, the artist simply saves their file into the gameAssets directory. The engine detects the file the next time it is run, and saves a converted game-appropriate version into a caching or data-management system. The game uses this converted file in the engine during the build process.

The benefit of such a system is that it avoids the need for duplicate workFiles directory trees and means that artists don't have to spend time converting files manually. The drawback is that artists must keep their files "clean" if they are to be converted properly. For example, if the import process brings in all the meshes from the Maya scene file, an animator working on a character's attack animation may have to remove any references to a sword before the animation will work properly in-game. File converters can usually be built to deal with references automatically, but the problem cannot be eliminated completely: an extra material, a ground plane, or an object the artist has added as a scale reference all have the potential to cause problems. Furthermore, there is no immediate feedback when errors occur—even if the conversion tool can detect the mistake, it cannot report it until it is run, which may be quite some time after the offending file was saved.

Below the level of the gameAssets and workFiles directories, assets must be subdivided further. Whereas films are broken down

into scenes and shots, games are usually split into levels, chapters, or tracks. For example:

projects/<project>/assets/workFiles/levels/<level>
projects/<project>/assets/gameAssets/levels/<level>

Each level is then broken down further into some logical high-level separation. For example:

.../levels/<level>/levelInfo
.../levels/<level>/scripts
.../levels/<level>/sequences

Games also often break large levels up into smaller sub-levels that are "streamed" (loaded into memory) individually:

.../levels/<level>/section

Games may further categorize files by purpose so that the correct assets can be loaded and unloaded at the proper times. Common sub-sections include collision, effects, gameplay, geometry, lighting, props, sequences, and sound (ambient, FX, and dialog). For example:

.../levels/<level>/section/collision
.../levels/<level>/section/sound/dialog

Not all assets live within a single level: many are shared across multiple levels. Therefore, in parallel with the levels directory, it is common to create other directories reflecting types of shared content. Common directory titles include AI, gameflow, systemAssets, animatedProps, characters, interactions, cinematics, controller, debug, effects, entities, icons, frontend, models, savegame, schemas, scoring, scripts, shaderLibrary, trophies, and vfx.

Most of these directories will be mirrored across gameAssets and workFiles:

projects/<project>/assets/gameAssets/AI
...
projects/<project>/assets/gameAssets/vfx
projects/<project>/assets/workFiles/AI
...
projects/<project>/assets/workFiles/vfx

However, where a particular type of content is authored using custom tools that export directly in a game-ready format, there is no need for a conversion process. The corresponding directories will exist solely in gameAssets and will not be mirrored in workFiles.

Choosing the Right Folder Structure for Your Game

The directory structure you choose will have important logistical consequences for your project. To illustrate this, let's look at a fictional example. Imagine that you're working on a games project in which the environment assets are structured as follows:

- The game comprises twenty different environments
- Each environment is made up of three different types of object: structural elements, interactive objects, and decorations
- Each object type comes in three sizes: small, medium, and large
- Each object consists of three file types: models, textures, and animations

Each environment and object type needs its own directory. Let's examine two ways in which this might be done. First, you could divide the assets into environments; then the environments into object types; the object types into sizes; and finally, into file types. This would result in the directory structure shown in Figure 8.1, for a total of 800 separate directories.

An alternative would be to divide the assets into object types first, then into sizes, and finally into environments. The lowest level of directories again consists of file types. The resulting directory tree can be seen in Figure 8.2, and consists of 732 separate directories.

The example above represents a very small subset of the assets that would be required for a real game, yet there is already an 8.5 percent difference in the number of folders that need to be created—and, more importantly, navigated hundreds of times throughout the life of the project. It's easy to see what difference in time and effort this could represent.

Section 8.6 Directory Structures: Designing for Ease of Navigation

As well as the total number of directories a directory structure generates, it's important to consider how easy it is to navigate. To do this, consider how its intended users will go from one object to the next.

An example from games that really highlights the importance of minimizing navigation time is the level designer's workflow. Level designers need to access large numbers of different types of art objects—tile sets, structures, decorations, FX, characters, and so on—in order to assemble a level, so it is critical that they can do so as quickly as possible.

Let's say that your level designers need to access two particular types of asset in order to decorate a room: chains that hang from the ceiling, and lanterns that hang from those chains. You might design a folder structure as shown in Figure 8.3.

This is perfect if the artists' workflow is:

1. Navigate to chain folder.
2. Place chain.
3. Place chain.

(Continued on page 184)

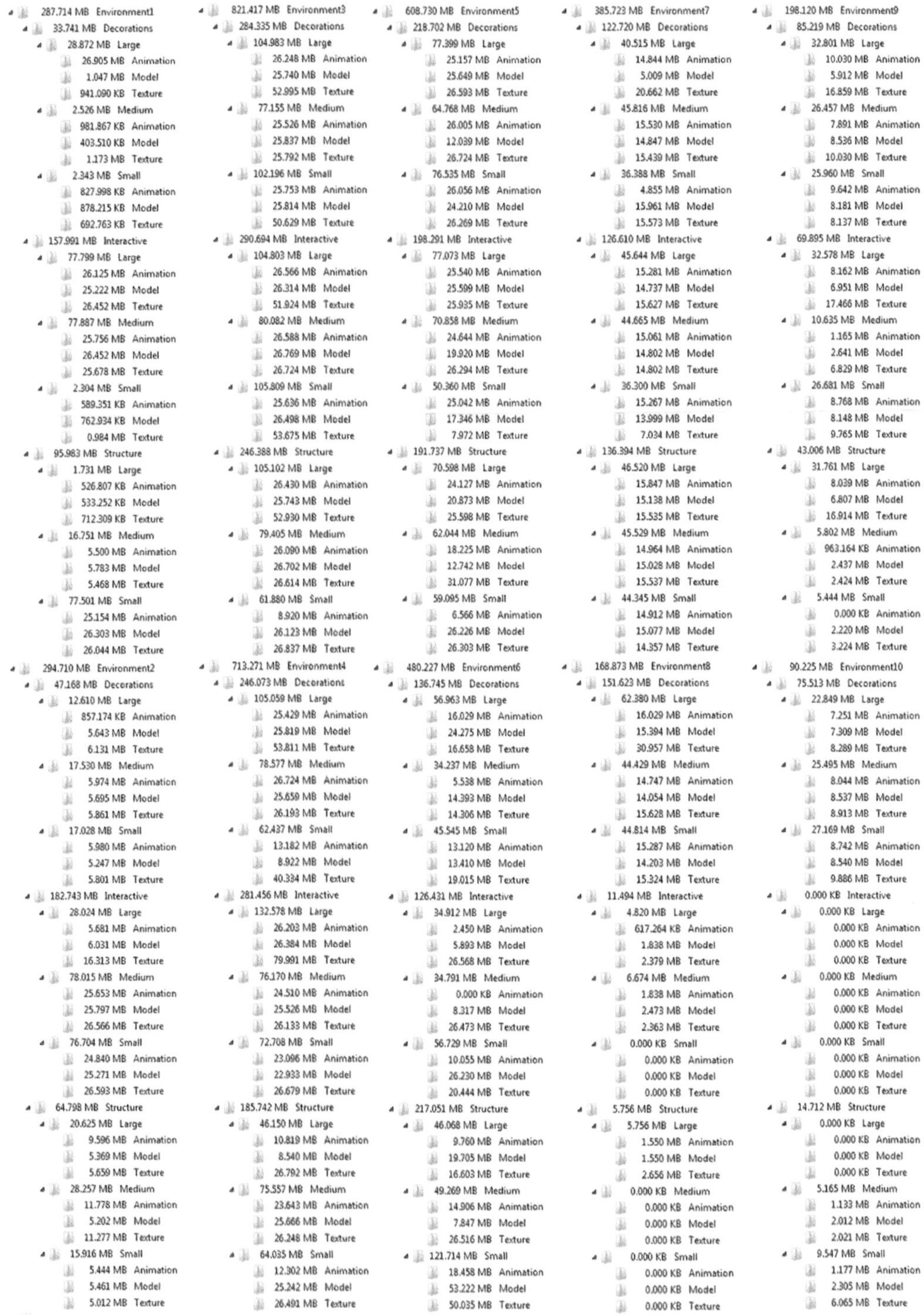

- 287.714 MB Environment1
  - 33.741 MB Decorations
    - 28.872 MB Large
      - 26.905 MB Animation
      - 1.047 MB Model
      - 941.090 KB Texture
    - 2.526 MB Medium
      - 981.867 KB Animation
      - 403.510 KB Model
      - 1.173 MB Texture
    - 2.343 MB Small
      - 827.998 KB Animation
      - 878.215 KB Model
      - 692.763 KB Texture
  - 157.991 MB Interactive
    - 77.799 MB Large
      - 26.125 MB Animation
      - 25.222 MB Model
      - 26.452 MB Texture
    - 77.887 MB Medium
      - 25.756 MB Animation
      - 26.452 MB Model
      - 25.678 MB Texture
    - 2.304 MB Small
      - 589.351 KB Animation
      - 762.934 KB Model
      - 0.984 MB Texture
  - 95.983 MB Structure
    - 1.731 MB Large
      - 526.807 KB Animation
      - 533.252 KB Model
      - 712.309 KB Texture
    - 16.751 MB Medium
      - 5.500 MB Animation
      - 5.783 MB Model
      - 5.468 MB Texture
    - 77.501 MB Small
      - 25.154 MB Animation
      - 26.303 MB Model
      - 26.044 MB Texture
- 294.710 MB Environment2
  - 47.168 MB Decorations
    - 12.610 MB Large
      - 857.174 KB Animation
      - 5.643 MB Model
      - 6.131 MB Texture
    - 17.530 MB Medium
      - 5.974 MB Animation
      - 5.695 MB Model
      - 5.861 MB Texture
    - 17.028 MB Small
      - 5.980 MB Animation
      - 5.247 MB Model
      - 5.801 MB Texture
  - 182.743 MB Interactive
    - 28.024 MB Large
      - 5.681 MB Animation
      - 6.031 MB Model
      - 16.313 MB Texture
    - 78.015 MB Medium
      - 25.653 MB Animation
      - 25.797 MB Model
      - 26.566 MB Texture
    - 76.704 MB Small
      - 24.840 MB Animation
      - 25.271 MB Model
      - 26.593 MB Texture
  - 64.798 MB Structure
    - 20.625 MB Large
      - 9.596 MB Animation
      - 5.369 MB Model
      - 5.659 MB Texture
    - 28.257 MB Medium
      - 11.778 MB Animation
      - 5.202 MB Model
      - 11.277 MB Texture
    - 15.916 MB Small
      - 5.444 MB Animation
      - 5.461 MB Model
      - 5.012 MB Texture

- 821.417 MB Environment3
  - 284.335 MB Decorations
    - 104.983 MB Large
      - 26.248 MB Animation
      - 25.740 MB Model
      - 52.995 MB Texture
    - 77.155 MB Medium
      - 25.526 MB Animation
      - 25.837 MB Model
      - 25.792 MB Texture
    - 102.196 MB Small
      - 25.753 MB Animation
      - 25.814 MB Model
      - 50.629 MB Texture
  - 290.694 MB Interactive
    - 104.803 MB Large
      - 26.566 MB Animation
      - 26.314 MB Model
      - 51.924 MB Texture
    - 80.082 MB Medium
      - 26.588 MB Animation
      - 26.769 MB Model
      - 26.724 MB Texture
    - 105.809 MB Small
      - 25.636 MB Animation
      - 26.498 MB Model
      - 53.675 MB Texture
  - 246.388 MB Structure
    - 105.102 MB Large
      - 26.430 MB Animation
      - 25.743 MB Model
      - 52.930 MB Texture
    - 79.405 MB Medium
      - 26.090 MB Animation
      - 26.702 MB Model
      - 26.614 MB Texture
    - 61.880 MB Small
      - 8.920 MB Animation
      - 26.123 MB Model
      - 26.837 MB Texture
- 713.271 MB Environment4
  - 246.073 MB Decorations
    - 105.059 MB Large
      - 25.429 MB Animation
      - 25.819 MB Model
      - 53.811 MB Texture
    - 78.577 MB Medium
      - 26.724 MB Animation
      - 25.650 MB Model
      - 26.193 MB Texture
    - 62.437 MB Small
      - 13.182 MB Animation
      - 8.922 MB Model
      - 40.334 MB Texture
  - 281.456 MB Interactive
    - 132.578 MB Large
      - 26.203 MB Animation
      - 26.384 MB Model
      - 79.991 MB Texture
    - 76.170 MB Medium
      - 24.510 MB Animation
      - 25.526 MB Model
      - 26.133 MB Texture
    - 72.708 MB Small
      - 23.096 MB Animation
      - 22.933 MB Model
      - 26.679 MB Texture
  - 185.742 MB Structure
    - 46.150 MB Large
      - 10.819 MB Animation
      - 8.540 MB Model
      - 26.792 MB Texture
    - 75.557 MB Medium
      - 23.643 MB Animation
      - 25.666 MB Model
      - 26.248 MB Texture
    - 64.035 MB Small
      - 12.302 MB Animation
      - 25.242 MB Model
      - 26.491 MB Texture

- 608.730 MB Environment5
  - 218.702 MB Decorations
    - 77.399 MB Large
      - 25.157 MB Animation
      - 25.649 MB Model
      - 26.593 MB Texture
    - 64.768 MB Medium
      - 26.005 MB Animation
      - 12.039 MB Model
      - 26.724 MB Texture
    - 76.535 MB Small
      - 26.056 MB Animation
      - 24.210 MB Model
      - 26.269 MB Texture
  - 198.291 MB Interactive
    - 77.073 MB Large
      - 25.540 MB Animation
      - 25.509 MB Model
      - 25.935 MB Texture
    - 70.858 MB Medium
      - 24.644 MB Animation
      - 19.920 MB Model
      - 26.294 MB Texture
    - 50.360 MB Small
      - 25.042 MB Animation
      - 17.346 MB Model
      - 7.972 MB Texture
  - 191.737 MB Structure
    - 70.598 MB Large
      - 24.127 MB Animation
      - 20.873 MB Model
      - 25.598 MB Texture
    - 62.044 MB Medium
      - 18.225 MB Animation
      - 12.742 MB Model
      - 31.077 MB Texture
    - 59.095 MB Small
      - 6.566 MB Animation
      - 26.226 MB Model
      - 26.303 MB Texture
- 480.227 MB Environment6
  - 136.745 MB Decorations
    - 56.963 MB Large
      - 16.029 MB Animation
      - 24.275 MB Model
      - 16.658 MB Texture
    - 34.237 MB Medium
      - 5.538 MB Animation
      - 14.393 MB Model
      - 14.306 MB Texture
    - 45.545 MB Small
      - 13.120 MB Animation
      - 13.410 MB Model
      - 19.015 MB Texture
  - 126.431 MB Interactive
    - 34.912 MB Large
      - 2.450 MB Animation
      - 5.893 MB Model
      - 26.568 MB Texture
    - 34.791 MB Medium
      - 0.000 KB Animation
      - 8.317 MB Model
      - 26.473 MB Texture
    - 56.729 MB Small
      - 10.055 MB Animation
      - 26.230 MB Model
      - 20.444 MB Texture
  - 217.051 MB Structure
    - 46.068 MB Large
      - 9.760 MB Animation
      - 19.705 MB Model
      - 16.603 MB Texture
    - 49.269 MB Medium
      - 14.906 MB Animation
      - 7.847 MB Model
      - 26.516 MB Texture
    - 121.714 MB Small
      - 18.458 MB Animation
      - 53.222 MB Model
      - 50.035 MB Texture

- 385.723 MB Environment7
  - 122.720 MB Decorations
    - 40.515 MB Large
      - 14.844 MB Animation
      - 5.009 MB Model
      - 20.662 MB Texture
    - 45.816 MB Medium
      - 15.530 MB Animation
      - 14.847 MB Model
      - 15.439 MB Texture
    - 36.388 MB Small
      - 4.855 MB Animation
      - 15.961 MB Model
      - 15.573 MB Texture
  - 126.610 MB Interactive
    - 45.644 MB Large
      - 15.281 MB Animation
      - 14.737 MB Model
      - 15.627 MB Texture
    - 44.665 MB Medium
      - 15.061 MB Animation
      - 14.802 MB Model
      - 14.802 MB Texture
    - 36.300 MB Small
      - 15.267 MB Animation
      - 13.999 MB Model
      - 7.034 MB Texture
  - 136.394 MB Structure
    - 46.520 MB Large
      - 15.847 MB Animation
      - 15.138 MB Model
      - 15.535 MB Texture
    - 45.529 MB Medium
      - 14.964 MB Animation
      - 15.028 MB Model
      - 15.537 MB Texture
    - 44.345 MB Small
      - 14.912 MB Animation
      - 15.077 MB Model
      - 14.357 MB Texture
- 168.873 MB Environment8
  - 151.623 MB Decorations
    - 62.380 MB Large
      - 16.029 MB Animation
      - 15.394 MB Model
      - 30.957 MB Texture
    - 44.429 MB Medium
      - 14.747 MB Animation
      - 14.054 MB Model
      - 15.628 MB Texture
    - 44.814 MB Small
      - 15.287 MB Animation
      - 14.203 MB Model
      - 15.324 MB Texture
  - 11.494 MB Interactive
    - 4.820 MB Large
      - 617.264 KB Animation
      - 1.838 MB Model
      - 2.379 MB Texture
    - 6.674 MB Medium
      - 1.838 MB Animation
      - 2.473 MB Model
      - 2.363 MB Texture
    - 0.000 KB Small
      - 0.000 KB Animation
      - 0.000 KB Model
      - 0.000 KB Texture
  - 5.756 MB Structure
    - 5.756 MB Large
      - 1.550 MB Animation
      - 1.550 MB Model
      - 2.656 MB Texture
    - 0.000 KB Medium
      - 0.000 KB Animation
      - 0.000 KB Model
      - 0.000 KB Texture
    - 0.000 KB Small
      - 0.000 KB Animation
      - 0.000 KB Model
      - 0.000 KB Texture

- 198.120 MB Environment9
  - 85.219 MB Decorations
    - 32.801 MB Large
      - 10.030 MB Animation
      - 5.912 MB Model
      - 16.859 MB Texture
    - 26.457 MB Medium
      - 7.891 MB Animation
      - 8.536 MB Model
      - 10.030 MB Texture
    - 25.960 MB Small
      - 9.642 MB Animation
      - 8.181 MB Model
      - 8.137 MB Texture
  - 69.895 MB Interactive
    - 32.578 MB Large
      - 8.162 MB Animation
      - 6.951 MB Model
      - 17.466 MB Texture
    - 10.635 MB Medium
      - 1.165 MB Animation
      - 2.641 MB Model
      - 6.829 MB Texture
    - 26.681 MB Small
      - 8.768 MB Animation
      - 8.148 MB Model
      - 9.765 MB Texture
  - 43.006 MB Structure
    - 31.761 MB Large
      - 8.039 MB Animation
      - 6.807 MB Model
      - 16.914 MB Texture
    - 5.802 MB Medium
      - 963.164 KB Animation
      - 2.437 MB Model
      - 2.424 MB Texture
    - 5.444 MB Small
      - 0.000 KB Animation
      - 2.220 MB Model
      - 3.224 MB Texture
- 90.225 MB Environment10
  - 75.513 MB Decorations
    - 22.849 MB Large
      - 7.251 MB Animation
      - 7.309 MB Model
      - 8.289 MB Texture
    - 25.495 MB Medium
      - 8.044 MB Animation
      - 8.537 MB Model
      - 8.913 MB Texture
    - 27.169 MB Small
      - 8.742 MB Animation
      - 8.540 MB Model
      - 9.886 MB Texture
  - 0.000 KB Interactive
    - 0.000 KB Large
      - 0.000 KB Animation
      - 0.000 KB Model
      - 0.000 KB Texture
    - 0.000 KB Medium
      - 0.000 KB Animation
      - 0.000 KB Model
      - 0.000 KB Texture
    - 0.000 KB Small
      - 0.000 KB Animation
      - 0.000 KB Model
      - 0.000 KB Texture
  - 14.712 MB Structure
    - 0.000 KB Large
      - 0.000 KB Animation
      - 0.000 KB Model
      - 0.000 KB Texture
    - 5.165 MB Medium
      - 1.133 MB Animation
      - 2.012 MB Model
      - 2.021 MB Texture
    - 9.547 MB Small
      - 1.177 MB Animation
      - 2.305 MB Model
      - 6.065 MB Texture

Figure 8.1 One way to organize assets for a games project. Dividing the assets by environment before object type and size results in 800 separate directories.

- 198.955 MB Environment11
  - 96.806 MB Decorations
    - 59.181 MB Large
      - 19.636 MB Animation
      - 9.454 MB Model
      - 30.090 MB Texture
    - 37.626 MB Medium
      - 9.784 MB Animation
      - 9.155 MB Model
      - 18.687 MB Texture
    - 0.000 KB Small
      - 0.000 KB Animation
      - 0.000 KB Model
      - 0.000 KB Texture
  - 80.233 MB Interactive
    - 21.308 MB Large
      - 3.277 MB Animation
      - 8.193 MB Model
      - 9.839 MB Texture
    - 31.664 MB Medium
      - 6.839 MB Animation
      - 6.476 MB Model
      - 18.349 MB Texture
    - 27.260 MB Small
      - 9.551 MB Animation
      - 8.012 MB Model
      - 9.697 MB Texture
  - 21.915 MB Structure
    - 21.915 MB Large
      - 7.473 MB Animation
      - 5.954 MB Model
      - 8.488 MB Texture
    - 0.000 KB Medium
      - 0.000 KB Animation
      - 0.000 KB Model
      - 0.000 KB Texture
    - 0.000 KB Small
      - 0.000 KB Animation
      - 0.000 KB Model
      - 0.000 KB Texture
- 219.207 MB Environment12
  - 48.434 MB Decorations
    - 48.434 MB Large
      - 20.060 MB Animation
      - 9.097 MB Model
      - 19.277 MB Texture
    - 0.000 KB Medium
      - 0.000 KB Animation
      - 0.000 KB Model
      - 0.000 KB Texture
    - 0.000 KB Small
      - 0.000 KB Animation
      - 0.000 KB Model
      - 0.000 KB Texture
  - 84.101 MB Interactive
    - 77.163 MB Large
      - 8.124 MB Animation
      - 30.090 MB Model
      - 38.949 MB Texture
    - 5.077 MB Medium
      - 0.000 KB Animation
      - 2.035 MB Model
      - 3.042 MB Texture
    - 1.861 MB Small
      - 0.000 KB Animation
      - 846.378 KB Model
      - 1.034 MB Texture
  - 86.672 MB Structure
    - 21.383 MB Large
      - 4.442 MB Animation
      - 7.967 MB Model
      - 8.975 MB Texture
    - 22.238 MB Medium
      - 7.570 MB Animation
      - 5.618 MB Model
      - 9.050 MB Texture
    - 43.051 MB Small
      - 18.633 MB Animation
      - 6.281 MB Model
      - 18.137 MB Texture

- 194.019 MB Environment13
  - 102.315 MB Decorations
    - 32.610 MB Large
      - 6.322 MB Animation
      - 7.985 MB Model
      - 18.303 MB Texture
    - 23.333 MB Medium
      - 6.186 MB Animation
      - 7.362 MB Model
      - 9.785 MB Texture
    - 46.372 MB Small
      - 8.497 MB Animation
      - 19.635 MB Model
      - 18.240 MB Texture
  - 91.704 MB Interactive
    - 25.206 MB Large
      - 8.816 MB Animation
      - 7.871 MB Model
      - 8.519 MB Texture
    - 32.299 MB Medium
      - 8.416 MB Animation
      - 5.599 MB Model
      - 18.284 MB Texture
    - 34.199 MB Small
      - 7.836 MB Animation
      - 8.371 MB Model
      - 17.992 MB Texture
  - 0.000 KB Structure
    - 0.000 KB Large
      - 0.000 KB Animation
      - 0.000 KB Model
      - 0.000 KB Texture
    - 0.000 KB Medium
      - 0.000 KB Animation
      - 0.000 KB Model
      - 0.000 KB Texture
    - 0.000 KB Small
      - 0.000 KB Animation
      - 0.000 KB Model
      - 0.000 KB Texture
- 215.467 MB Environment14
  - 111.025 MB Decorations
    - 44.250 MB Large
      - 17.352 MB Animation
      - 8.775 MB Model
      - 18.122 MB Texture
    - 43.494 MB Medium
      - 8.707 MB Animation
      - 7.841 MB Model
      - 26.946 MB Texture
    - 23.282 MB Small
      - 5.088 MB Animation
      - 9.242 MB Model
      - 8.951 MB Texture
  - 80.489 MB Interactive
    - 24.145 MB Large
      - 6.534 MB Animation
      - 7.937 MB Model
      - 9.674 MB Texture
    - 32.661 MB Medium
      - 8.016 MB Animation
      - 6.672 MB Model
      - 17.973 MB Texture
    - 23.682 MB Small
      - 7.133 MB Animation
      - 6.689 MB Model
      - 9.861 MB Texture
  - 23.953 MB Structure
    - 23.953 MB Large
      - 8.076 MB Animation
      - 6.856 MB Model
      - 9.021 MB Texture
    - 0.000 KB Medium
      - 0.000 KB Animation
      - 0.000 KB Model
      - 0.000 KB Texture
    - 0.000 KB Small
      - 0.000 KB Animation
      - 0.000 KB Model
      - 0.000 KB Texture

- 234.951 MB Environment15
  - 67.502 MB Decorations
    - 35.062 MB Large
      - 8.678 MB Animation
      - 8.501 MB Model
      - 17.883 MB Texture
    - 30.890 MB Medium
      - 7.347 MB Animation
      - 6.299 MB Model
      - 17.245 MB Texture
    - 1.550 MB Small
      - 0.000 KB Animation
      - 1.550 MB Model
      - 0.000 KB Texture
  - 81.027 MB Interactive
    - 24.564 MB Large
      - 6.961 MB Animation
      - 7.866 MB Model
      - 9.738 MB Texture
    - 32.053 MB Medium
      - 8.309 MB Animation
      - 6.630 MB Model
      - 17.114 MB Texture
    - 24.410 MB Small
      - 8.292 MB Animation
      - 6.565 MB Model
      - 9.554 MB Texture
  - 86.422 MB Structure
    - 33.600 MB Large
      - 8.108 MB Animation
      - 7.733 MB Model
      - 17.759 MB Texture
    - 34.421 MB Medium
      - 6.970 MB Animation
      - 9.553 MB Model
      - 17.898 MB Texture
    - 18.401 MB Small
      - 4.186 MB Animation
      - 2.409 MB Model
      - 11.806 MB Texture
- 257.358 MB Environment16
  - 62.868 MB Decorations
    - 15.634 MB Large
      - 7.211 MB Animation
      - 4.076 MB Model
      - 4.347 MB Texture
    - 19.193 MB Medium
      - 4.786 MB Animation
      - 3.403 MB Model
      - 11.003 MB Texture
    - 28.041 MB Small
      - 3.512 MB Animation
      - 6.333 MB Model
      - 18.195 MB Texture
  - 100.552 MB Interactive
    - 52.145 MB Large
      - 2.855 MB Animation
      - 20.060 MB Model
      - 29.230 MB Texture
    - 25.189 MB Medium
      - 6.034 MB Animation
      - 6.107 MB Model
      - 13.049 MB Texture
    - 23.218 MB Small
      - 7.076 MB Animation
      - 6.277 MB Model
      - 9.865 MB Texture
  - 93.937 MB Structure
    - 30.971 MB Large
      - 4.684 MB Animation
      - 8.329 MB Model
      - 17.958 MB Texture
    - 36.373 MB Medium
      - 17.329 MB Animation
      - 9.626 MB Model
      - 9.418 MB Texture
    - 26.593 MB Small
      - 6.159 MB Animation
      - 6.798 MB Model
      - 13.636 MB Texture

- 259.943 MB Environment17
  - 104.924 MB Decorations
    - 23.089 MB Large
      - 5.422 MB Animation
      - 9.914 MB Model
      - 7.753 MB Texture
    - 43.544 MB Medium
      - 16.821 MB Animation
      - 9.484 MB Model
      - 17.239 MB Texture
    - 38.291 MB Small
      - 14.980 MB Animation
      - 6.213 MB Model
      - 17.099 MB Texture
  - 101.099 MB Interactive
    - 33.940 MB Large
      - 9.258 MB Animation
      - 7.612 MB Model
      - 17.069 MB Texture
    - 33.672 MB Medium
      - 8.154 MB Animation
      - 6.932 MB Model
      - 18.586 MB Texture
    - 33.487 MB Small
      - 9.793 MB Animation
      - 7.086 MB Model
      - 16.608 MB Texture
  - 53.921 MB Structure
    - 27.012 MB Large
      - 9.192 MB Animation
      - 8.872 MB Model
      - 8.949 MB Texture
    - 26.908 MB Medium
      - 9.623 MB Animation
      - 8.016 MB Model
      - 9.269 MB Texture
    - 0.000 KB Small
      - 0.000 KB Animation
      - 0.000 KB Model
      - 0.000 KB Texture
- 218.064 MB Environment18
  - 33.728 MB Decorations
    - 33.728 MB Large
      - 8.927 MB Animation
      - 6.774 MB Model
      - 18.027 MB Texture
    - 0.000 KB Medium
      - 0.000 KB Animation
      - 0.000 KB Model
      - 0.000 KB Texture
    - 0.000 KB Small
      - 0.000 KB Animation
      - 0.000 KB Model
      - 0.000 KB Texture
  - 104.983 MB Interactive
    - 47.115 MB Large
      - 9.258 MB Animation
      - 7.767 MB Model
      - 30.090 MB Texture
    - 36.335 MB Medium
      - 9.334 MB Animation
      - 9.361 MB Model
      - 17.641 MB Texture
    - 21.532 MB Small
      - 6.587 MB Animation
      - 7.205 MB Model
      - 7.740 MB Texture
  - 79.354 MB Structure
    - 32.641 MB Large
      - 6.630 MB Animation
      - 7.511 MB Model
      - 18.500 MB Texture
    - 24.603 MB Medium
      - 8.154 MB Animation
      - 7.310 MB Model
      - 9.139 MB Texture
    - 22.110 MB Small
      - 6.015 MB Animation
      - 6.278 MB Model
      - 9.817 MB Texture

- 192.147 MB Environment19
  - 87.495 MB Decorations
    - 27.653 MB Large
      - 9.808 MB Animation
      - 8.390 MB Model
      - 9.454 MB Texture
    - 32.285 MB Medium
      - 6.447 MB Animation
      - 8.297 MB Model
      - 17.541 MB Texture
    - 27.557 MB Small
      - 7.375 MB Animation
      - 8.198 MB Model
      - 11.983 MB Texture
  - 50.357 MB Interactive
    - 24.634 MB Large
      - 6.404 MB Animation
      - 8.396 MB Model
      - 9.834 MB Texture
    - 25.722 MB Medium
      - 8.699 MB Animation
      - 7.114 MB Model
      - 9.909 MB Texture
    - 0.000 KB Small
      - 0.000 KB Animation
      - 0.000 KB Model
      - 0.000 KB Texture
  - 54.296 MB Structure
    - 27.450 MB Large
      - 9.287 MB Animation
      - 8.431 MB Model
      - 9.732 MB Texture
    - 25.561 MB Medium
      - 9.167 MB Animation
      - 7.038 MB Model
      - 9.356 MB Texture
    - 1.285 MB Small
      - 0.000 KB Animation
      - 1.285 MB Model
      - 0.000 KB Texture
- 90.182 MB Environment20
  - 65.270 MB Decorations
    - 56.052 MB Large
      - 3.743 MB Animation
      - 20.060 MB Model
      - 32.249 MB Texture
    - 3.784 MB Medium
      - 573.855 KB Animation
      - 1.203 MB Model
      - 2.021 MB Texture
    - 5.433 MB Small
      - 0.000 KB Animation
      - 2.659 MB Model
      - 2.774 MB Texture
  - 14.242 MB Interactive
    - 7.045 MB Large
      - 0.000 KB Animation
      - 2.859 MB Model
      - 4.187 MB Texture
    - 4.882 MB Medium
      - 0.000 KB Animation
      - 1.781 MB Model
      - 3.100 MB Texture
    - 2.315 MB Small
      - 0.000 KB Animation
      - 838.563 KB Model
      - 1.496 MB Texture
  - 10.670 MB Structure
    - 0.000 KB Large
      - 0.000 KB Animation
      - 0.000 KB Model
      - 0.000 KB Texture
    - 7.207 MB Medium
      - 1.298 MB Animation
      - 2.809 MB Model
      - 3.100 MB Texture
    - 3.463 MB Small
      - 717.899 KB Animation
      - 1.431 MB Model
      - 1.332 MB Texture

Figure 8.1 (Continued)

Figure 8.2 An alternative way to organize the same assets. Dividing the assets by object type and size before environment results in 732 separate directories—a saving of 8.5 percent!

- 586.072 MB Small
  - 2.304 MB Environment1
    - 589.351 KB Animation
    - 762.934 KB Model
    - 0.984 MB Texture
  - 76.704 MB Environment2
    - 24.840 MB Animation
    - 25.271 MB Model
    - 26.593 MB Texture
  - 105.809 MB Environment3
    - 25.636 MB Animation
    - 26.498 MB Model
    - 53.675 MB Texture
  - 72.708 MB Environment4
    - 23.096 MB Animation
    - 22.933 MB Model
    - 26.679 MB Texture
  - 50.360 MB Environment5
    - 25.042 MB Animation
    - 17.346 MB Model
    - 7.972 MB Texture
  - 56.729 MB Environment6
    - 10.055 MB Animation
    - 26.230 MB Model
    - 20.444 MB Texture
  - 36.300 MB Environment7
    - 15.267 MB Animation
    - 13.999 MB Model
    - 7.034 MB Texture
  - 0.000 KB Environment8
    - 0.000 KB Animation
    - 0.000 KB Model
    - 0.000 KB Texture
  - 26.681 MB Environment9
    - 8.768 MB Animation
    - 8.148 MB Model
    - 9.765 MB Texture
  - 0.000 KB Environment10
    - 0.000 KB Animation
    - 0.000 KB Model
    - 0.000 KB Texture
  - 27.260 MB Environment11
    - 9.551 MB Animation
    - 8.012 MB Model
    - 9.697 MB Texture
  - 1.861 MB Environment12
    - 0.000 KB Animation
    - 846.378 KB Model
    - 1.034 MB Texture
  - 34.199 MB Environment13
    - 7.836 MB Animation
    - 8.371 MB Model
    - 17.992 MB Texture
  - 23.682 MB Environment14
    - 7.133 MB Animation
    - 6.689 MB Model
    - 9.861 MB Texture
  - 24.410 MB Environment15
    - 8.292 MB Animation
    - 6.565 MB Model
    - 9.554 MB Texture
  - 23.218 MB Environment16
    - 7.076 MB Animation
    - 6.277 MB Model
    - 9.865 MB Texture
  - 0.000 KB Environment17
    - 0.000 KB Animation
    - 0.000 KB Model
    - 0.000 KB Texture
  - 21.532 MB Environment18
    - 6.587 MB Animation
    - 7.205 MB Model
    - 7.740 MB Texture
  - 0.000 KB Environment19
    - 0.000 KB Animation
    - 0.000 KB Model
    - 0.000 KB Texture
  - 2.315 MB Environment20
    - 0.000 KB Animation
    - 838.563 KB Model
    - 1.496 MB Texture

- 1.672 GB Structure
  - 593.237 MB Large
    - 1.731 MB Environment1
      - 526.807 KB Animation
      - 533.252 KB Model
      - 712.309 KB Texture
    - 20.625 MB Environment2
      - 9.596 MB Animation
      - 5.369 MB Model
      - 5.659 MB Texture
    - 105.102 MB Environment3
      - 26.430 MB Animation
      - 25.743 MB Model
      - 52.930 MB Texture
    - 46.150 MB Environment4
      - 10.819 MB Animation
      - 8.540 MB Model
      - 26.792 MB Texture
    - 70.598 MB Environment5
      - 24.127 MB Animation
      - 20.873 MB Model
      - 25.598 MB Texture
    - 46.068 MB Environment6
      - 9.760 MB Animation
      - 19.705 MB Model
      - 16.603 MB Texture
    - 46.520 MB Environment7
      - 15.847 MB Animation
      - 15.138 MB Model
      - 15.535 MB Texture
    - 5.756 MB Environment8
      - 1.550 MB Animation
      - 1.550 MB Model
      - 2.656 MB Texture
    - 31.761 MB Environment9
      - 8.039 MB Animation
      - 6.807 MB Model
      - 16.914 MB Texture
    - 0.000 KB Environment10
      - 0.000 KB Animation
      - 0.000 KB Model
      - 0.000 KB Texture
    - 21.915 MB Environment11
      - 7.473 MB Animation
      - 5.954 MB Model
      - 8.488 MB Texture
    - 21.383 MB Environment12
      - 4.442 MB Animation
      - 7.967 MB Model
      - 8.975 MB Texture
    - 0.000 KB Environment13
      - 0.000 KB Animation
      - 0.000 KB Model
      - 0.000 KB Texture
    - 23.953 MB Environment14
      - 8.076 MB Animation
      - 6.856 MB Model
      - 9.021 MB Texture
    - 33.600 MB Environment15
      - 8.108 MB Animation
      - 7.733 MB Model
      - 17.759 MB Texture
    - 30.971 MB Environment16
      - 4.684 MB Animation
      - 8.329 MB Model
      - 17.958 MB Texture
    - 27.012 MB Environment17
      - 9.192 MB Animation
      - 8.872 MB Model
      - 8.949 MB Texture
    - 32.641 MB Environment18
      - 6.630 MB Animation
      - 7.511 MB Model
      - 18.500 MB Texture
    - 27.450 MB Environment19
      - 9.287 MB Animation
      - 8.431 MB Model
      - 9.732 MB Texture
    - 0.000 KB Environment20
      - 0.000 KB Animation
      - 0.000 KB Model
      - 0.000 KB Texture

- 545.091 MB Medium
  - 16.751 MB Environment1
    - 5.500 MB Animation
    - 5.783 MB Model
    - 5.468 MB Texture
  - 28.257 MB Environment2
    - 11.778 MB Animation
    - 5.202 MB Model
    - 11.277 MB Texture
  - 79.405 MB Environment3
    - 26.090 MB Animation
    - 26.702 MB Model
    - 26.614 MB Texture
  - 75.557 MB Environment4
    - 23.643 MB Animation
    - 25.666 MB Model
    - 26.248 MB Texture
  - 62.044 MB Environment5
    - 18.225 MB Animation
    - 12.742 MB Model
    - 31.077 MB Texture
  - 49.269 MB Environment6
    - 14.906 MB Animation
    - 7.847 MB Model
    - 26.516 MB Texture
  - 45.529 MB Environment7
    - 14.964 MB Animation
    - 15.028 MB Model
    - 15.537 MB Texture
  - 0.000 KB Environment8
    - 0.000 KB Animation
    - 0.000 KB Model
    - 0.000 KB Texture
  - 5.802 MB Environment9
    - 963.164 KB Animation
    - 2.437 MB Model
    - 2.424 MB Texture
  - 5.165 MB Environment10
    - 1.133 MB Animation
    - 2.012 MB Model
    - 2.021 MB Texture
  - 0.000 KB Environment11
    - 0.000 KB Animation
    - 0.000 KB Model
    - 0.000 KB Texture
  - 22.238 MB Environment12
    - 7.570 MB Animation
    - 5.618 MB Model
    - 9.050 MB Texture
  - 0.000 KB Environment13
    - 0.000 KB Animation
    - 0.000 KB Model
    - 0.000 KB Texture
  - 0.000 KB Environment14
    - 0.000 KB Animation
    - 0.000 KB Model
    - 0.000 KB Texture
  - 34.421 MB Environment15
    - 6.970 MB Animation
    - 9.553 MB Model
    - 17.898 MB Texture
  - 36.373 MB Environment16
    - 17.329 MB Animation
    - 9.626 MB Model
    - 9.418 MB Texture
  - 26.908 MB Environment17
    - 9.623 MB Animation
    - 8.016 MB Model
    - 9.269 MB Texture
  - 24.603 MB Environment18
    - 8.154 MB Animation
    - 7.310 MB Model
    - 9.139 MB Texture
  - 25.561 MB Environment19
    - 9.167 MB Animation
    - 7.038 MB Model
    - 9.356 MB Texture
  - 7.207 MB Environment20
    - 1.298 MB Animation
    - 2.809 MB Model
    - 3.100 MB Texture

- 574.200 MB Small
  - 77.321 MB Environment1
    - 24.853 MB Animation
    - 26.398 MB Model
    - 26.070 MB Texture
  - 15.916 MB Environment2
    - 5.444 MB Animation
    - 5.461 MB Model
    - 5.012 MB Texture
  - 61.880 MB Environment3
    - 8.920 MB Animation
    - 26.123 MB Model
    - 26.837 MB Texture
  - 64.035 MB Environment4
    - 12.302 MB Animation
    - 25.242 MB Model
    - 26.491 MB Texture
  - 59.095 MB Environment5
    - 6.566 MB Animation
    - 26.226 MB Model
    - 26.303 MB Texture
  - 121.714 MB Environment6
    - 18.458 MB Animation
    - 53.222 MB Model
    - 50.035 MB Texture
  - 44.345 MB Environment7
    - 14.912 MB Animation
    - 15.077 MB Model
    - 14.357 MB Texture
  - 0.000 KB Environment8
    - 0.000 KB Animation
    - 0.000 KB Model
    - 0.000 KB Texture
  - 5.444 MB Environment9
    - 0.000 KB Animation
    - 2.220 MB Model
    - 3.224 MB Texture
  - 9.547 MB Environment10
    - 1.177 MB Animation
    - 2.305 MB Model
    - 6.065 MB Texture
  - 0.000 KB Environment11
    - 0.000 KB Animation
    - 0.000 KB Model
    - 0.000 KB Texture
  - 43.051 MB Environment12
    - 18.633 MB Animation
    - 6.281 MB Model
    - 18.137 MB Texture
  - 0.000 KB Environment13
    - 0.000 KB Animation
    - 0.000 KB Model
    - 0.000 KB Texture
  - 0.000 KB Environment14
    - 0.000 KB Animation
    - 0.000 KB Model
    - 0.000 KB Texture
  - 18.401 MB Environment15
    - 4.186 MB Animation
    - 2.409 MB Model
    - 11.806 MB Texture
  - 26.593 MB Environment16
    - 6.159 MB Animation
    - 6.798 MB Model
    - 13.636 MB Texture
  - 0.000 KB Environment17
    - 0.000 KB Animation
    - 0.000 KB Model
    - 0.000 KB Texture
  - 22.110 MB Environment18
    - 6.015 MB Animation
    - 6.278 MB Model
    - 9.817 MB Texture
  - 1.285 MB Environment19
    - 1.285 MB Animation
    - 0.000 KB Model
    - 0.000 KB Texture
  - 3.463 MB Environment20
    - 717.899 KB Animation
    - 1.431 MB Model
    - 1.332 MB Texture

Figure 8.2 (Continued)

3.463 MB   Decoration

1.912 MB   Chain

1.912 MB   CeilingChain

1.551 MB   LightSources

1.551 MB   Lanterns

Figure 8.3 Workflow determines optimal directory structure: this structure would be ideal if a designer likes to place all the ceiling chains in a level before they attach the hanging lanterns—but less so if they prefer to attach a lantern to each chain before moving on to the next.

(Continued from page 179)
4. Place chain.
5. Navigate to lantern folder.
6. Place lantern on chain.
7. Place lantern on chain.
8. Place lantern on chain.

On the other hand, it will be very cumbersome if the artists' workflow is:
1. Navigate to chain folder.
2. Place chain.
3. Navigate to lantern folder.
4. Place lantern on chain.
5. Navigate to chain folder.
6. Place chain (and so on).

In the latter case, you may want to work with the artists to explain how they could improve their workflow—or simply alter the directory structure to minimize wasted navigation time. The same principle applies to film work.

Section 8.7 Directory Structures: Planning Shared Asset Use

Another consideration when designing directory structures is how to handle assets that don't fit into any of your predetermined categories. This often occurs with shared textures.

For example, in games, a "floor" object may share the same texture as a "ramp" object or even a "wall" object. It's important to group the objects that share the texture in such a way that the performance cost of adding them to a level is quickly understood by your design team. One historically very common way to do this is to group objects into "environment sets".

For example, you could group your environment assets as follows:
• Cave: assets that use the cave textures
• Forest: assets that use the forest textures

- Mine: assets that use the mine textures
- Generic: objects meant to be used in multiple levels with their own smaller textures

Using this methodology, a level designer can keep track of how many textures they are using and how much memory they occupy simply by checking which environment sets they have loaded. You can also help to ensure that a level stays within its texture budget by restricting designers to using objects from a given number of environment sets: for example, the cave and the mine sets, or the cave and the forest sets, but not all three simultaneously.

Although films don't have the same kind of memory restrictions, your team can still plan to minimize the number of textures kept in memory, and reuse textures wherever possible. These textures may be pulled from a library, another shot in the same project, or even another project.

Section 8.8 Directory Structures: Building from Most to Least Generic

As a general rule, a project's directory structure should be built from most to least generic. Ignoring this rule makes it difficult to know where to begin looking for a particular asset if other search methods fail.

Let's imagine that you're working on a game in which the artists need to create three spiral staircases, two normal staircases, and one very special staircase called the "Stairs of Zenobia". Figure 8.4 shows a directory structure built according to the rule of Most to Least Generic.

Figure 8.5 shows a directory structure that breaks the rule. Imagine how confusing this would be to a designer who needs to add a staircase to a level, but doesn't know what types of stairs are available. It would be like trying to find an address by starting with the house number, not the name of the street.

Figure 8.4 Directories organized according to the rule of Most to Least Generic. The top-level directory is the most generic asset type (Stairs); the lower-level directories are specific types of staircase.

13.783 MB Normal

13.783 MB Stairs

11.162 MB Spiral

11.162 MB Stairs

11.438 MB Zenobia

11.438 MB Stairs

Figure 8.5 A directory structure that breaks the rule of Most to Least Generic. As well as creating more directories than is necessary, this structure is far more difficult for new users to navigate.

It's important to note that "most generic" may mean different things for different projects. To understand why, let's look at some concrete examples, first from film, and then from games.

Imagine a zombie movie in which the artists are creating FX for the characters' skin and hair. If the results are to be convincing, each zombie must have its own unique set of effects. This can be achieved in two very different ways.

In the first, "generic" is defined as character type. In this case, each character will receive custom effects, so the zombie FX for one character will not look like those for another. This will result in a directory structure like that shown in Figure 8.6.

This works well when there are only a few zombies. However, as the number of characters increases, creating individual FX for each one quickly becomes time-consuming. If there are many zombies, a different approach will be needed.

In this case, "generic" is defined as the FX type. A particular hair or skin effect will be identical for each character to which it is assigned. However, each character may still be made to look different by assigning it its own unique permutation of FX. This will result in a directory structure like that shown in Figure 8.7.

One thing to note is that the directory tree shown in Figure 8.7 only includes three variations of each FX. If you were managing large numbers of variations, it would be better to use the asset-management system to encapsulate the information, not the file system.

Next, let's look at an example from the world of games. Imagine that you are working on a turn-based RPG with six character types. The characters have magical abilities: healing, damage, buffing other party members, and so on. The FX for each needs to be visually

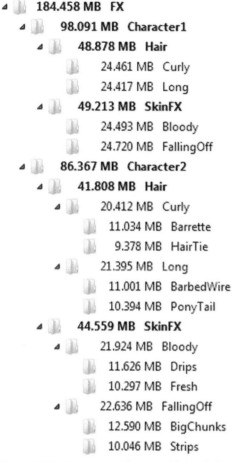

- 184.458 MB FX
  - 98.091 MB Character1
    - 48.878 MB Hair
      - 24.461 MB Curly
      - 24.417 MB Long
    - 49.213 MB SkinFX
      - 24.493 MB Bloody
      - 24.720 MB FallingOff
  - 86.367 MB Character2
    - 41.808 MB Hair
      - 20.412 MB Curly
        - 11.034 MB Barrette
        - 9.378 MB HairTie
      - 21.395 MB Long
        - 11.001 MB BarbedWire
        - 10.394 MB PonyTail
    - 44.559 MB SkinFX
      - 21.924 MB Bloody
        - 11.626 MB Drips
        - 10.297 MB Fresh
      - 22.636 MB FallingOff
        - 12.590 MB BigChunks
        - 10.046 MB Strips

Figure 8.6 A directory tree for a zombie movie in which each character has its own unique FX. In this case, individual FX are defined as being less generic than the characters to which they are assigned. This works well if there are only a few zombies.

distinct, but since the game is turn-based, the player does not need to be able to react to an ability when it is used.

When considering these goals, an FX artist might decide that each character will get unique FX for each of their abilities: a heal spell cast by one character will not look like that cast by another, for example. In this case, "generic" is defined as character type. This might result in a directory structure like that shown in Figure 8.8.

Now let's look at the equivalent directory structure for an action RPG. Again, there are six character types, but here, the player needs to be able to respond to abilities when they are used: by the time the FX have finished playing, they should be able to decide whether

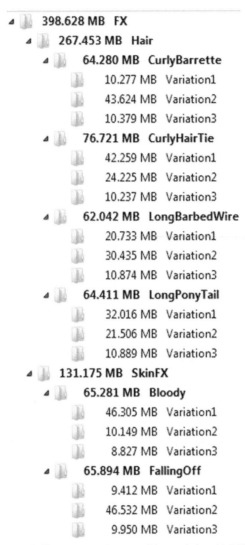

Figure 8.7 A directory tree for a zombie movie in which FX are identical for each character to which they are assigned. Here, characters are made to look unique by assigning unique permutations of FX. This works well when there are many zombies.

another character has cast a healing or damage spell. This means that the FX must not only be visually distinct but consistent and identifiable.

In this case, an artist might decide that characters will use shared FX for the various ability types. Although the FX for healing and damage will still be different, a heal spell cast by one character will look

Figure 8.8 A directory tree for a game in which each character has its own unique FX. Here, character type is defined as being more generic than FX type. This might be appropriate for a turn-based RPG.

exactly like a heal spell cast by another. Here, "generic" is defined as ability type. This might result in a directory structure like that shown in Figure 8.9.

As you can see, the term "generic" means something different for every project. Understanding the design of your film or game will help you create a folder structure that enables team members to find assets quickly and easily.

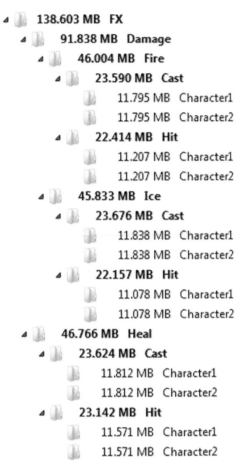

Figure 8.9 A directory tree for a game in which the FX for a given ability are identical for each character. Here, ability type is defined as being more generic than character type. This might be appropriate for an action RPG.

Section 8.9 Directory Structures: Incorporating Asset Templates

Creating "templates" from which art assets may be developed—for example, a generic human model, a standard smoke FX, or a library of stock motion-capture data—can save a lot of production time. While these templates are starting points for building individual assets, they are not necessarily used in the finished product. Therefore, they must be kept separate from the finished art assets. There are several ways of organizing a directory tree in order to do this, each with its own advantages and disadvantages.

The first is to create a directory tree for the templates that mirrors that of the finished art assets. This results in a structure like that shown in Figure 8.10.

34.040 MB   FinishedArt
   11.892 MB   Characters
      11.892 MB   Humans
   22.148 MB   FX
      11.454 MB   Damage
      10.694 MB   Heal
32.256 MB   Templates
   10.454 MB   Characters
      10.454 MB   Humans
   21.802 MB   FX
      11.010 MB   Damage
      10.792 MB   Heal

Figure 8.10 A setup in which the directory tree for the templates mirrors that of the finished art separates the two sets of assets clearly, but increases navigation time.

This setup has the advantage that it separates the two sets of assets clearly. In a film, this has the benefit of keeping the size of the project area small, helping to ensure that template assets are not moved to offline storage along with the other files once work is complete; in a game, it keeps build times down. However, over the course of a project, the time spent navigating back and forth between the template and finished art directories can be significant; and any changes to the directory tree for finished art assets must also be made to that for the templates.

The second option is to create a directory structure unique to the templates, as shown in Figure 8.11.

The advantages of this setup are the same as before: the two types of asset are kept separate, reducing the size of the project area or game build. Again, time spent in navigating directories can reduce the benefit of using templates in the first place, but now a change to the directory tree for the finished art assets need not automatically result in a change to that for the templates.

The third option is to integrate both templates and finished art assets into a single directory tree, as shown in Figure 8.12.

This setup has the advantage that navigation time is reduced and files are easier to manage, but increases the risk that templates will become mixed up with final art assets. On a film, they may be altered as a "one off", or simply forgotten when the files are archived; on a

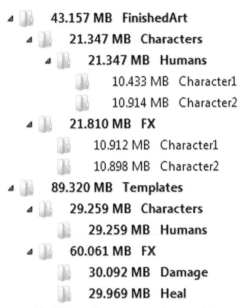

43.157 MB FinishedArt
   21.347 MB Characters
      21.347 MB Humans
         10.433 MB Character1
         10.914 MB Character2
   21.810 MB FX
      10.912 MB Character1
      10.898 MB Character2
89.320 MB Templates
   29.259 MB Characters
      29.259 MB Humans
   60.061 MB FX
      30.092 MB Damage
      29.969 MB Heal

Figure 8.11 A setup with different directory trees for templates and finished art assets. Again, the two types of asset are kept separate, but now changes made to the directory tree for finished art do not have to be made to that for the templates.

9.508 MB Characters
   9.508 MB Humans
      9.508 MB Template
22.334 MB FX
   11.155 MB Damage
      11.155 MB Template
   11.179 MB Heal
      11.179 MB Template

Figure 8.12 A setup with templates and finished art assets integrated into a single directory tree: quick to navigate, but running the risk of unwanted template assets being archived with the project files or incorporated into the game build.

game, without engineering support, they may become part of the build, increasing install size and build time.

Ideally, artists should create all the templates necessary at the start of a project. However, in practice, templates are created through the course of production—often becoming less and less generic as time goes on. These "templates that are not really templates" cause the directory tree to bloat, making it harder for artists to find the ones that

are actually useful. Before you create a new template, think about how many assets it can actually be used for. If in doubt, don't create it!

Section 8.10 File-Naming Conventions: Common Syntax

Next, we will discuss file-naming conventions. As we have already established, strong naming conventions are essential in order to maintain an efficient pipeline. Not only do they make it easier for artists to find assets, they make it possible for coders to write tools that locate or modify those assets automatically. We discussed the pros and cons of such automated systems in a previous chapter. Here, we will look at the syntax on which naming conventions are based.

Separating Name Elements

An important step in establishing a strong naming convention is determining how to separate the elements that make up the name of an asset. It might be tempting to use the file name to reflect the fact that a steel sword is particularly large, but calling the asset "sword-steellarge.extension" is a bit hard to parse.

Using spaces in filenames is generally frowned upon for the simple reason that, although spaces work correctly in 90 percent of applications, the remaining 10 percent (most often scripts) cause so much havoc that it simply isn't worth the hassle this "convenience" creates. Instead, there are two common ways to separate elements in a file name. One is to use underscores:

sword_steel_large.extension

Underscores are easy to parse, but they increase the length of the asset's name, which may cause problems with software that limits file names to a specific number of characters. The alternative is to use a mixture of capitals and lower-case letters, a system sometimes known as "camel case":

swordSteelLarge.extension

Camel case isn't quite as easy to parse as underscores, but gives shorter file names.

Capitals

Another thing to consider is how file names are to be capitalized. One of the most common causes of duplicate files and folders is inconsistent use of capitals. These are especially problematic when tied into a case-sensitive scripting system.

The easiest way to avoid such inconsistencies is to just not use capitals. If this isn't possible, establish a solid rule set that governs their use. These might include always capitalizing the first letter of an asset ('Sword' as opposed to 'sword'), or camel casing as shown above.

Plurals

Inconsistent pluralization causes the same problems as inconsistent capitalization. Again, the simplest way to avoid such problems is always to use plurals or never to use them.

Abbreviations

Abbreviations are often used in projects to shorten elements of a file name. This reduces the time it takes developers to type in each name. Without abbreviations, the file name of a tree model used in an environment might be:

environment_tree_maple_red_large.extension

With abbreviations, the same asset could be named as follows:

env_tree_maple_red_lrg.extension

This is a saving of ten characters—roughly 30 percent of the entire file name.

When designing abbreviation conventions, the first thing to determine is which part of the file's name will be abbreviated. The second is how each of the words it may comprise will be abbreviated: for example, is "environment" going to be abbreviated as "env" or "envi"?

There are some general rules to follow here:

- It's usually good to abbreviate the names of asset types, like "environments", "special effects" or "weapons".
- Specific asset names such as "maple" usually should not be abbreviated.
- Descriptors such as "red" or "large" should only be abbreviated if it is still completely clear what the descriptor is referring to.
- If a descriptor is abbreviated, for example when "large" becomes "lrg", this abbreviation should be used everywhere in the project!
- If a particular abbreviation is used on more than one project, try to make sure it has the same meaning on each one. This helps to avoid surprises if assets are shared later—which may not be until long after the original project has ended.

Once you have established the conventions you will be using throughout your project, document them! Everyone on the team must use the same abbreviations or much of their usefulness will be lost. Content creators can then read the document to learn, reference, or add to the convention structure that has been established.

Section 8.11 File-Naming Conventions: Mirroring the Folder Structure in the File Name

In film, a common and useful practice is to mirror the folder structure in the name of an asset. To do this, simply include the name or abbreviation of the name of each folder one would need to "travel" through to reach the asset.

This results in file names such as:

<shot>_<assetType>_<assetName>_<version>.extension

For example:
SB_0001_animationCurves_fooRun_v30.ma

In film work, many types of data—shadow maps, geometry caches for animations, simulations, and so on—are written out as sequences of images. This frame information is normally stored in the file name. Most facilities place it just in front of the file extension:

<shot>_<assetType>_<assetName>_<version>.####.extension

It is common practice to use four digits for frame numbers. At twenty-four frames per second, this is sufficient to cover just under seven minutes of footage, which far exceeds the average shot duration in a film. However, in later stages of the pipeline (such as during the creation of digital intermediates), where the film is being treated as a whole, not as individual shots, this convention becomes unsuitable, and six-digit padding is used.

Similar conventions are used in games. For example, consider a file located in the following directory:

/GameRoot/Assets/Models/Equipment/Weapon/Sword/Rare/

This could be named:

eq_wp_sword_rare_demonshard_a.mdl

or:

eqWpSwordRareDemonshardA.mdl

Notice that "GameRoot", "Assets", and "Model" are not included within the asset name. Since it's safe to assume that every asset will be stored in the GameRoot/Assets directory, including the directory names in the file name wouldn't provide any additional information. Including the word "Model" is also unnecessary since the .mdl suffix already defines the asset as a model. Keep names informative, but don't waste space with unnecessary clutter.

There are several major benefits of mirroring directory structure within the names of your assets. The first is that the location and type

of an asset can be determined from its file name alone, saving artists a lot of search time. Consider a file named:

fx_wpn_sword_glowy_a.extension

This must be an FX element for a sword, and reside somewhere in the following directory:

/FX/Weapon/Sword/

Mirroring directory structure in file names is also beneficial for programmers who can create tools that use the information to speed up workflow. For example, a tool could automatically save or export an asset within a specific folder based on name alone, reducing navigation time.

Finally, mirroring directory structure in asset names also helps ensure that no two assets have the same file name. This becomes incredibly important on large projects with multiple artists where it is far more likely that two separate artists will, for example, create assets named "stairs_evil" in two separate folders. Having two or more assets with the same name creates confusion for everyone concerned, makes it harder to identify and fix bugs, and can actually break things on projects with "flattened path" architectures, as they may need each asset to have a unique name in order to load files correctly.

Section 8.12 Version Control: Exclusive and Non-Exclusive File Access

We looked briefly at version-control systems and how they work in previous chapters. Next, we will discuss some key aspects of version control in more detail.

The first of these is the question of exclusive versus non-exclusive access to files. Since many people work on assets in parallel, conflicts may occur when two people want to modify the same file at the same time. When this happens there are two options: to grant one user exclusive permission to modify the file, or to permit both users to modify the file simultaneously, then merge their changes together later.

Granting exclusive use of a file is restrictive, and means that one user holds up the other. However, it is often the only option if the file is in a binary format or a text format that is not structured with merging in mind.

If the version-control system does permit two users to check out the same asset, the first user to check it back in does so as normal. The second should receive a warning that the asset has already been checked in, and three options: to overwrite the first user's work, to discard their own changes, or to merge the two sets of changes together. As most version-control systems don't understand the

meaning of a file's contents, merging tends to work on a line-by-line basis, and it is largely left to the user to ensure that the results are valid.

Section 8.13 Version Control: Treating Code and Art Assets Separately

Another consideration is whether code and art assets should be treated separately. In film, programmers tend to use standard version-control systems for keeping track of code changes, while the artists use a custom system designed specifically for keeping track of assets. Non-specialist version-control systems tend not to handle art assets well due to the sheer amount of data involved.

However, in games, content is no different to code when it comes to managing change conflicts. Changes to content may look wrong, play wrong, cause an "assert" (the game run-time displays an error message warning you there is an error in the data), or, worst of all, cause the run-time to crash. Therefore, pipeline developers should treat artists in the same way as programmers: they should be provided with a sandboxed environment in which to test content, and only submit changes once they have established that they will not affect other team members adversely, in the same way that a programmer would only submit tested code.

Section 8.14 Version Control: Handling Special Projects

When working on a project, it may be necessary to address special requests: for example, to create film trailers, or demos for executives or the marketing department. This means deciding where the assets used to create these requests will be stored, and how they will be tracked.

One way to handle these special versions is to "branch" a copy by taking a "snapshot" of the project: a copy of all of its assets at a specific point in time. This has the advantage that the snapshot exists in a separate location so that work can continue on the project itself without introducing any unexpected changes or bugs into the special version.

The disadvantage of branching appears when changes made in the main project need to be merged into the special version, or vice versa. These merges can be time-consuming and need to be handled carefully as errors can be introduced and/or data go missing.

In games, branching has a further disadvantage: bug fixes often need to be done twice. This problem can be mitigated through source control, but merging becomes complicated if a file was changed only

in one branch before a bug was discovered. As a result, it's often wise to have teams work in low-risk areas until the main branch has passed QA and is pushed to release.

Let's look at how branching works in more detail, first for film, then for games. In film, there are two main reasons for branching. One is to create something special: trailers, DVD extras, commercials, marketing materials, and so on. The second is to branch code that is used to generate assets: for example, to convert files from one format to another, or to process them for use in other media, such as games or print marketing.

When branching shots, it is often just a case of copying the directory structure from the original and tacking a special character onto the name. For example, take the following shot:

SB_0001_animationCurves_fooRun_v30.ma

By tagging an "A" onto the file name, the branched file becomes:

SBA_0001_animationCurves_fooRun_v30.ma.

Branching code for processing assets is done in a similar way as in games: the new code is tagged with the project name or designation in the source code repository and then checked out into the project.

In games, one common use of branching is to create a demo. Ideally, the demo should use the game build, perhaps by polishing up a level for public consumption. However, this is not always possible, especially during early phases of the project, or when making sweeping changes: the level you took the time to polish may become unplayable if a designer later decides to change, say, the jump height of a character.

The advantage of separating the demo into a separate branch is that it ensures that no bugs introduced into the full game affect it. The disadvantage is that any changes needed by the demo will have to be integrated into both builds, increasing the time it takes to complete the task.

Branching is a substantial concern for ongoing projects, particularly those that are updated long after release, such as MMOs (Massively Multiplayer Online games). With MMOs, it is common to branch the product monthly to a QA build before releasing an update. This practice allows the team to continue working on new content safely while the isolated update is being tested, thus protecting the update from any bugs the new content might inadvertently create.

Section 8.15 Metadata: Embedded Versus Extracted Data

As we discussed in a previous chapter, pipelines generate a lot of metadata: the "extra" data stored in a file alongside the information

that makes up the asset itself. This can come from a number of sources: user input (information a user generates by filling in a form in the UI of a piece of software), the file system (file size, access times, and so on), the files themselves (file types like EXR and DPX include information embedded in the header of the file, such as when the files were created), and other processes within the pipeline (for example, information generated at render time, such as maximum memory usage, CPU load and I/O).

There are two key points to consider here. First, you need to decide which of these pieces of information are useful to you. We looked at this question in a previous chapter. Second, you need to decide whether they are useful to you in their current format, or whether they need to be recorded somewhere else.

What defines the optimal place to store metadata depends on the workflow you need to support. In general, if metadata is required by more than one application or if a process requires quick access to a piece of information, it is better to extract the metadata from the asset file and store it separately.

For example, let's assume the number of objects in a Maya scene file is a useful piece of data for another process. To extract this data, the other process must read a Maya file (not a trivial task) and read it quickly (which is unlikely for large scenes). A better solution is to extract this piece of data when the asset is created and store it separately.

There are two principal methods for storing metadata outside assets: as separate files on the file system (usually plain-text files in formats such as XML, YAML or JSON), or in a database. It is important to note that the assets themselves are not normally stored in the database: only the metadata is. The database simply forms an extra layer on top of the existing directory structure and naming conventions, and includes "pointers" to the actual assets in the shape of their file paths.

These two methods should be seen as complementary: which one you adopt will depend on the use case in question. We will look at the pros and cons of each in the next section.

Section 8.16 Metadata: Flat Files Versus Databases

The simplest way of storing metadata is as flat files in the file system. However, this approach typically results in either many small files (one for each version of each asset, each of a few megabytes or less), or few very large files (one per asset, or per project, each running into many gigabytes). Neither result scales smoothly. Generally, file systems are poor at handling lots of small files and the decentralization of metadata makes it slow to run queries. Conversely, files

that contain information for many assets run a higher risk of corruption, as well as a higher risk of contention during concurrent edits.

A database solves the problems that managing metadata via files introduces. Databases are designed to store vast amounts of data and provide mechanisms to query this data quickly.

This means they process queries more efficiently than flat-file systems, particularly queries that encompass many assets.

Another advantage of databases is that they can be used to create validation rules for data that are impossible to violate. For example, you can restrict the values for a field like "Asset Type" to a known set of words like "Character" and "Effect". When done properly, this helps to preserve the integrity of the data in the asset-management system.

Setting up databases also enables a facility with multiple offices to share or replicate data between them more easily: file-based systems typically do not scale well to multi-site setups. In recent years, a lot of effort has gone into solutions for "hot" backups and updating without downtime: a significant requirement, as a database is typically in use continually.

Finally, databases make it easier for a company to crew up or crew down. These changes in the number of users can quickly change the way in which metadata is accessed. Databases are well placed to deal with this through techniques such as "clustering" (running the database software across a group of networked machines), "master-slave replication" (maintaining both a canonical "master" copy of the database and replicated "slave" copies on other machines that can take some of the load) and "sharding" (splitting the records in the database into a number of independent partitions that can then be queried separately).

All this sounds great. So why *wouldn't* you want to use a database? First, because a database is much more complicated than text files on disk, and that complexity comes with significant costs. For simple data that does not need to be aggregated, or for binary data, files will tend to be faster and easier to use than a database.

The second reason is that the database introduces another point of failure, alongside the file system itself. If the database goes down or becomes corrupted, you may lose access to some or all of your assets and their metadata, a potentially production-stopping event. With good infrastructure support, a database can be made incredibly reliable, but this infrastructure doesn't come cheaply, and maintenance and monitoring will be an ongoing cost. If your facility is global, you may also need to take long network transit times for database access into account.

Third, using a database effectively is a skill just like any other, and expertise is needed to structure database queries in a way that will return results quickly and efficiently. If generalists write significant portions of your asset-management system, you will need to make sure that there is at least one database specialist keeping an eye on things.

You will also need to provide an interface to get information into or out of the database in a suitable fashion—normally a UI for users and an API for developers. These interfaces must be provided by the pipeline team, but keep in mind while some commercial tools provide a generic view of your data, they lack the user-friendly features required by non-technical artists and management.

It is also important that the data in the database is accurate and up-to-date, and since databases are not omniscient, this is typically the pipeline team's responsibility. It's important to define at the outset just what the database is and is not expected to know, and how strongly other tools in the facility can rely on the data it stores. For example, in games, it is common to use the database to record the memory footprint of each individual asset. This value might be updated when the asset is exported from a DCC tool, when it is checked in to version control, or even via an explicit manual update process. In any of these cases, if the database is out of sync with the version-control system, the user may be working on a version of the asset that has a different memory footprint to that recorded in the database. In many situations, it doesn't matter if the database lags the version-control system by a few hours, or vice versa. In others, it will be necessary to design a more elaborate update mechanism.

Finally, there are certain circumstances in which individual metadata files provide a positive benefit. In visual effects, letting processes running on the render farm access the database is generally frowned upon, since serving requests from so many machines simultaneously can bring the database to a standstill. Providing external metadata avoids this issue.

Metadata files can also provide proxies for complex assets with many dependencies that do not constitute a single file: for example, a game level that consists of a collection of geometry, lighting data, scripts, and other information. Capturing all of these inputs in a single file that can be put through version control makes it much easier to track the progress of a project accurately.

Section 8.17 Databases: Relational and Non-Relational Databases

We will finish this chapter by looking at how to choose database structures for production work. Before we do so, let's run through some of the basic technical concepts. This is only a very brief overview of a much larger topic, so if you plan to work with databases, you should read around the subject for yourself.

There are two basic types of database. "Relational databases", created using languages such as SQL, use a highly structured set of information organized by strict rules. Other databases like MongoDB or CouchDB (sometimes grouped together as "NoSQL databases") use

less structured storage methods for greater flexibility. We'll come to exactly what these terms mean later. But first, let's look at how a relational database stores information.

Within such a database, data is grouped into "tables", analogous to worksheets in software like Excel. Like an Excel worksheet, a table is divided into "columns" and "rows". Each column (or "field") represents a particular piece of data that you want to capture. The column has two main properties, a name and a type of data (for example, integers, floating-point numbers, or alphanumeric strings) that may be stored in the column. Each row (or "record") represents a collection of data that you want to record. Each row places a value in each column, conforming to the data type specified for that column. As in a spreadsheet, rows may be inserted into or deleted from the table, and individual values within a row updated.

For example, we might have a table which consists of columns titled "Description" (a description of each task: an alphanumeric string), "Start" (the start date of the task: a date), "Artist" (the artist assigned to the task: another string), and "Artist ID" (a unique identifier: an integer). Each row in this table would represent a single task, and would provide data for each of the four fields we have defined. You can see how this works in Figure 8.13.

The "schema" of the database defines how the data is divided up into tables, the columns that comprise each table, and other aspects of data structure.

It would theoretically be possible for the schema to define a single table with lots of columns, one for each type of data you want to record. However, this would be a very inefficient structure, resulting in a lot of duplicated information. This can be reduced by "normalizing" the database: organizing it in such a way that redundancy is minimized. This usually involves dividing larger tables up into smaller ones, and defining the relationships between them.

For example, let's imagine we have another table, shown in Figure 8.14, storing information about art assets. The columns define the job, scene and shot in which it appears, what type of asset it is, the name of the asset, and which version it is.

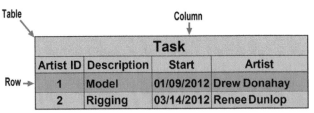

Task			
Artist ID	**Description**	**Start**	**Artist**
1	Model	01/09/2012	Drew Donahay
2	Rigging	03/14/2012	Renee Dunlop

Figure 8.13 A table from a database, storing information on the tasks that make up a project. It consists of four columns, each one storing different types of data about the tasks in question, and two rows, each one representing an individual task.

Asset					
Job	Scene	Shot	Asset Type	Asset Name	Version
Job1	Scene1	Shot1	Model	Joy	1
Job1	Scene1	Shot1	Model	Joy	2

Figure 8.14 Another table from the database, storing key information about each asset used in production, including its type and version number, and in which job, scene, and shot it appears.

An operation to rename an individual Job, Scene, or Shot would be fairly costly, as it would mean scanning the whole table to identify which rows need to be updated. If, however, jobs, scenes, and shots were stored in their own tables and this data referenced using a unique ID, such an update would only need to alter the appropriate row of the corresponding table, since the ID is an automatically generated number, and never changes, even if other details do.

It is this act of splitting data into multiple tables and defining relationships between them that gives us the term "relational database". In a simple case like this, the relationship can be defined simply using the unique ID number as a "key". The column within the table being referenced (in this case, the Job, Scene, or Shot table) that contains the unique identifier is known as the "primary key". The corresponding column in the other tables that reference it is known as the "foreign key". Records where the primary key and foreign key values match are said to be "related".

To see how this works, let's say that we want our Asset table to store information on the artist responsible for creating an asset. This information could be represented in a number of ways: first name, last name, email address, desk number, and so on.

However, our table of tasks also currently stores some of this information in its Artist column. We don't want to duplicate this information, since that would make the database harder to maintain. Instead, we store just the Artist ID value for the artist in question as a foreign key. In Figure 8.15, the Artist ID column has also been added to the table of assets, and both the Asset and Task tables now reference our (newly created) Artist table, which has "Artist ID" as a primary key and stores a single canonical copy of the artist's information alongside it.

SQL (Structured Query Language) is a programming language commonly used for managing data in a relational database system. Although, strictly speaking, SQL deviates from the relational model in a number of details, database systems that use it, including Oracle, DB2, MySQL, Postgres, and SQLite, are usually described as "relational".

There are also a number of alternatives to the relational model, including the "document", "object", and "graph" models. Databases that use such models are commonly referred to as "NoSQL" databases.

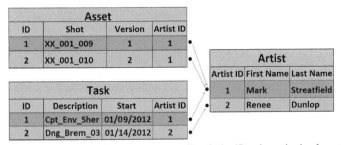

Figure 8.15 A relational database structure. The Artist ID column in the Asset and Task tables links them to a separate Artist table storing information about the artist responsible. This is more efficient than duplicating the information in both the Asset and Task tables.

Document databases use analogous terminology to relational databases: here, a table is a "collection", a row is a "document", and a column is a "field". However, they have a more open and flexible structure: unlike relational databases, not every document needs to contain the same set of fields. This is sometimes referred to as a "dynamic schema".

Both SQL and NoSQL database have their pros and cons. SQL databases provide strong tools for ensuring that the data stored in them is reliable and consistent: for example, every record for an artist can be made to have a field for their email address, or every record for a texture be made to have a file format field. The fact that the data is tightly structured also makes it easy to perform complex queries, such as: "Find all assets over 6 MB in size that are used in Shot 145 and have more than three textures." However, they are relatively complex to set up and maintain, and are inflexible: adding new types of information requires rebuilding the database to a new schema.

In contrast, NoSQL databases are much more flexible. They are also scalable: they can be "parallelized" onto large numbers of servers to increase response speed and storage capacity. However, the integrity of the data they store cannot be assured, so code using the database must always be able to deal with missing or malformed information.

Section 8.18 Databases: Choosing a Database Structure

Which type of database you choose depends on what task you need it for. For asset management, a document database might be a better fit, as its less structured approach means that a single set of assets can be described by a collection of documents containing different fields without some of the performance penalties you might get with a relational model.

If you do use a relational structure, a good guide is to have one table for each thing you need to track: for example, a scene, shot, task, user, or asset. Each table should then contain columns specifying each piece of information you need to record about that "thing". Mimicking the nature of your data in the schema of your database makes it more intuitive for developers (and potentially, your users) to construct queries to retrieve the information they need.

However, structuring a database is a bit like choosing a deep or flat directory structure, particularly when it comes to the question of how to record assets. Using too many separate tables may make the database hard to maintain. Instead, it would be possible to use only one table storing information on every asset. However, this would mean either storing only columns that apply to every asset or creating a wide table storing every column you want to use, but in which individual columns are sparsely populated (that is, not every row contains a value for every column).

In practice, the structure you choose will be a balance between best practices (the process of normalization: minimizing redundancy and dependency between tables), and what is practical for your purposes (denormalization: deliberately adding redundant data to improve read performance). Most database systems provide functionality to make striking this balance easier.

8A

INTERLUDE: METADATA

Dan McGraw
CEO/Principal Consultant, Seven Dials Media

Section 8 Interlude 1: What is Metadata?

Whenever a digital file is created, saved in a system, searched, converted, edited, used, or delivered, metadata plays a critical part. Metadata is a fundamental component for any production pipeline or delivery process whether it's for gaming, film, or visual effects. It is used to describe, control, structure, or understand the content to which it is ascribed. Metadata is essentially "data about the data". Without it, our productions would suffer in every conceivable way including extended production cycle times, compromised security, and even decreased creative expression.

Although it may not be obvious, we use metadata everyday without really thinking about it. To understand what metadata is, how it is different from the essence of the content, and its intrinsic value, consider a simple metaphor with a can of soup. When shopping at a grocery store, what is wanted is not the metal can or the label, but the soup itself. The soup (the content) is what we really want, but the label (the information about the soup) is used to help identify pertinent details about the soup such as the ingredients, the weight, the nutritional value, and its expiration date. These bits of information on the label are the equivalent of metadata for your content. If the label were to be removed and shoppers were only able to browse rows of silver cans hoping for the right type, the result would be mass confusion, eventually resulting in few cans sold. Quality metadata produces confidence in a process.

When considering the metadata for a digital asset such as a film clip, a background plate, an audio file, or graphic, creating and maintaining quality metadata is critical. Just as keeping labels for soup cans is critical to maintaining a quality standard, so is maintaining metadata for content files for optimizing their use and control.

Some metadata is carried by the asset itself and can be read by systems or applications. Examples of this type of metadata would be an asset's file size or creation date. Other metadata attributed to an asset, depending on the file type and the system used to manage it, can only be linked to the asset and stored in a database. A video may

have a director named John Smith, but the video file doesn't carry around this custom value. The value must be referenced by asset by using a metadata management system such as a DAM (Digital Asset Management), or an application that links the content file to its related customizable metadata fields and values.

One could argue that the director's name could be used in the naming convention of the digital asset to provide this information. However, this is a shortsighted workaround that users often adopt when handling files in shared folders without any true method of managing media with metadata.

Photography and most creative documents such as graphics, layouts, and print materials can use several embedded metadata schema models. The metadata within these types of files use standard schemas such as EXIF (Exchangeable Image File), IPTC (International Press Telecommunications Council), or XMP (Extensible Metadata Platform). These metadata values are either hard coded into the file or allow a user to create, edit, or remove the values that are carried. As long as a file is viewed or edited within a system or application that supports the schema, the metadata will be maintained and be used.

Video files have typically been more reliant on proprietary file types, applications, and wrappers (such as MXF, which stands for Material Exchange Format) to maintain some limited embedded metadata. Determining one's needed asset types and how metadata can be linked or embedded into a given type is a good place to begin designing a metadata schema.

A metadata schema, or model structure, is often provided to a user within an application to support the asset types or workflows it manages. Other systems allow for complete independent and customizable schemas. Others use a mixture of both application based and customizable schemas. In general, metadata schemas are grouped into five categories:

- Descriptive
- Technical
- Rights
- Archival
- Structural

Descriptive metadata is information that is used, as expected, to describe the asset. A video clip of a blonde woman riding a blue motorcycle on the 405 Highway would need a good description for it to be found via search: "A blonde woman rides her blue motorcycle on the 405 near Mulholland Drive." Other metadata of this type include keywords (motorcycle, woman, blonde, blue, highway, California, 405, mountains, Mulholland Drive). Other descriptive metadata would include fields such as Title, Subject, Project ID, etc. These fields are typically used in search and retrieval.

Technical metadata provides information about an asset that is typically not editable. These are embedded aspects about the asset

such as the bit-rate, file extension/mime type, resolution, aspect ratio, etc. These are useful when determining the proper format for a specific use in post or distribution.

Rights metadata deals with the control and use of an asset. Metadata such as the asset's owner, expiration date, and contract ID, are important fields to limit an asset.

Archival metadata is used for an asset's long-term preservation and maintenance. An asset will have an indefinite lifecycle that may be highly relevant and important to its stakeholders when it is created. Over time, this relevancy may wane but its importance may ebb and flow depending on circumstances. An asset may need to be saved in a particular format to preserve it on an archival medium. Over the years, it may need to be "re-preserved" onto another format at certain intervals. Archival metadata informs custodians of assets how to maintain the asset throughout its lifecycle.

Structural metadata is used to indicate an asset's placement within other, more complex objects such as a book, layout, or effect. An example is a graphic being placed behind another layer. The metadata in this case exists to orient one asset in relation to another.

Strategically, to reduce the number of silos of automation and disconnected information, organizations are encouraged to develop an overall metadata model to which all systems and users can subscribe. Subsets of this overall structure are then used within the various applications and platforms for consistent vocabularies and information data sources. When internal or external, metadata needs to be integrated and this common schema allows for simpler data mapping between systems. A common mistake is for each department to create its own schema of metadata. Over time, these silos develop into departmental "institutions" that are difficult and costly to integrate.

Often organizations will turn to metadata standards such as PRISM, Dublin Core, or, for standard image licensing, Plus Coalition. These standards are well suited for certain workflows and industries, but don't offer, nor are intended to offer a complete organizational metadata model. An organization can find these helpful for integration and to conform to industry standards, but they shouldn't be relied on as an entire model. Again, application vendors attempt to create open standards or frameworks such as MXF, Quicktime, AAF (Advanced Authoring Format), etc. to aid in integrating metadata and content files.

Even systems that accept the same content files and embedded metadata can require more advanced integration. With no standard schema that can satisfy every business operation or production pipeline, metadata will often require import-mapping procedures. Mapping is required when one system employing a variety of metadata fields and values must port or migrate those values with another system with similar or entirely different metadata fields. This can occur between departments or separate companies looking to share metadata.

For example, assume Company A calls a Production ID a "job" and Company B refers to it as a "project" yet each need to share the information. Both job and project mean the same thing to each. If Company A sends metadata records to Company B, the receiving company will fail to import the values into their system. The receiving company's system expects to find "projects", but received "jobs" instead.

To solve this problem, similar or even disparate systems supporting web services such as XML (Extensible Markup Language) or APIs (Application Programming Interfaces), can connect and share their metadata. XML is an open standard document that is used to transport and store data such as metadata, customer lists, or any other information. XML is readable by both machines and humans and provides a powerful means of metadata sharing. Users who desire to use XML as a metadata sharing process must adhere to strict rules on formatting, naming, case sensitivity, and import configuration rules within the receiving system.

In larger organizations where several platforms or data repositories are maintained, metadata management systems are deployed. Metadata management systems allow users to capture and manage the standard business terminology and structures including vocabularies, preferred terms, and object relationships across all disconnected repositories while maintaining a common platform. Users may then search and retrieve results from all metadata repositories for maximum visibility without customized integration through XML. This is particularly useful when searching media assets across completely different business units such as news archives, photo libraries, and marketing collateral.

Organizations are encouraged to avoid casually named metadata fields to reduce issues with integration projects. This is accomplished by standardizing on metadata conventions, where possible, out of business-oriented strategies. Once the business needs are clear, theses strategies generate technical *requirements* rather than technically *dictating* the business needs. Quality metadata (technical, rights, etc.) will be derived by thoroughly understanding the business needs for managing and controlling assets within a production process. Typically, stakeholders of a production process are the best sources for metadata fields and their relationship to the assets. Business managers, subject matter experts, and digital workflow specialists can work together to develop schemas out of primary workflows, digital asset types and asset lifecycles.

The quality of an asset is significantly impacted by how well it is cultivated and maintained throughout its lifecycle. It is not uncommon for departments or organizations to start entering metadata for an asset after it is completed or for it to be entered by users with no real understanding of the asset's value or relevancy. This will yield extremely limited and low value metadata. To improve the quality of

metadata, it's important to begin its entry as early in its lifecycle as possible. For example, camera manufacturers provide for geo-location coordinates and other information to be used later in other production phases. As specific authorized users of asset elements or various versions of a final asset are developed, small amounts of metadata can be inputted. Over the course of the production and its release, metadata is refined, cleaned, and updated resulting in a high degree of reliability. Low reliability in metadata will lower trust in systems.

Metadata ownership is also key to maintaining the quality of metadata. Organizations that maintain their metadata have implemented metadata ownership teams or joint cross-functional accountabilities. Without these in place, departments and organizations will lack confidence in the metadata and overall process. These teams also can serve as a governance entity to maintain and improve the metadata as the business needs or asset types evolve.

Business managers within organizations and departments should work closely with their technical managers to create platforms upon which metadata frameworks will be adopted, relied, and scaled. Without these fundamental principles of metadata, assets will be lost, uncontrolled and wreak havoc on already pressured production cycles.

9

ASSET MANAGEMENT

**Tim Green; Matt Hoesterey; Hannes Ricklefs;
Mark Streatfield; Steve Theodore Ben Carter:** *Game Developer
and Author, Heavy Spectrum Entertainment Labs;* **Nolan Murtha:**
Digital Effects Supervisor, Lightstorm Entertainment

Section 9.1 What You Will Learn From This Chapter

We touched on the importance of asset management in previous chapters. In this chapter, we will explore the nature of an asset-management system itself. We will outline the components of such a system, examine the goals a successful asset-management system should meet, then discuss key technical topics that relate to system design. Some, like version control and metadata, have already been discussed in previous chapters, and will only be covered briefly here. Others, like dependency tracking, are new, and will be discussed in detail.

Section 9.2 What is Asset Management?

Asset management is the backbone of any production—but not a term that is easy to define. It encompasses many tasks, including the classification of asset types, tracking digital and physical assets, version control, and processes for automating and controlling data flow.

We looked at some of these tasks, notably version control, in earlier chapters. It is important to note that asset management and version control are not identical: rather, asset management is often implemented on top of version control, offering a powerful combination of the search and analysis capabilities provided by metadata and the option to browse within the "vertical" slice of a project provided by a version-control system.

There are two key components to any asset management system:

The data model describes how the data governed by the asset-management system is structured. This must be provided through some form of API (Application Programming Interface) through which developers can create tools and define the custom data types

used by the facility. The data model is where asset types are defined and versioning and dependency tracking are implemented.

The repository is the infrastructure used to store the data: both hardware and software like database systems. It must enable users to access both the metadata contained in the data model and the assets themselves. The repository should be able to handle the peaks and troughs of production, scaling from projects with a handful of users and a handful of assets to hundreds of users and millions of assets while maintaining a consistent response time.

As this breakdown suggests, an asset-management system is something more than pure software. While commercial asset-management tools do exist, they are not one-size-fits-all solutions. At present, no single off-the-shelf product exists that can handle all of the tasks listed above.

Section 9.3 The Goals of Asset Management

Before we examine how data models are designed, let's review the goals the design must meet. To be successful, an asset-management system must meet a number of criteria. We will look at some of the most important here.

Scalability

As we have seen, films and games generate a huge amount of data. In the case of a visual effects project, individual disciplines can generate terabytes of data, while an entire show can run to petabytes. The asset-management system must be able to cope both with the total volume of data and the number of user requests generated at times of peak throughput.

In addition, films and games require an enormous amount of human input. A six-to-nine-month VFX project can represent ten or twenty thousand person-days of labor. Since facilities usually crew up or crew down to meet the peaks and troughs in production, the asset-management system must be able to cope with changes in the numbers of users accessing it. This task is made slightly simpler by the fact that most large facilities work on a per-project and per-department basis: artists are assigned to an individual project, and work on it in isolation; and work within a single department, using a consistent set of tools. However, it is still necessary to design the asset-management system in such a way that it can accommodate permanent, long-term growth.

The need for scalability also extends to the range of asset types the system will manage. It is necessary to consider whether new asset types will be added by configuration mechanisms built into the system, or by writing code. If the asset-management system is written in an object-oriented programming language—which tends to expand

a "base" asset that describes the core functionality of all the assets within the system—this typically results in one class per asset type. Defining each asset type in code also means that new functionality can be introduced more easily without affecting other assets within the system.

As well as being able to accommodate new asset types, the system should have the capacity to screen out assets that don't fit its existing categories, or to mark them up for special treatment.

Parallel Access

Production schedules are constantly shortening. In the past, major movies and games were typically allotted two- or three-year schedules. Today, some games franchises are updated yearly, while visual effects projects may need to be completed in a matter of months. For this reason, it's essential to get every department working as quickly as possible—and to do that, artists need to be able to access assets in parallel.

We explored some of these issues when we discussed the asset-creation process (for example, the need to pass rough proxy models to the lighting department so that work on a shot can begin before the assets are finalized). To prevent artists working in parallel from overwriting or invalidating one another's changes, facilities often use version-control systems. Again, we introduced the basic concepts of version control in Chapter 5, so we won't discuss them again here. However, one further issue that version-control systems face is the difficulty of merging the separate versions of an asset after two artists have worked on it. The boxout titled "Managing unmergeable files" explores this issue in more detail.

Managing Unmergeable Files

Matt Hoesterey
Design Lead, Microsoft

Many projects, particularly games projects, run into problems where a single file contains information that needs to be updated by multiple team members. Where two team members make changes to a file in parallel, there are two options when it is checked back into the version-control system: to merge both sets of changes, or to discard one of them and force the artist to begin again from the version of the asset the other has updated.

Merging files is a notoriously error-prone process. But making files unmergeable can be worse. My worst experience with unmergeable shared files was with a particularly clunky pipeline for building character abilities. Since the system was designed for use by non-technical artists, the information was stored in Excel spreadsheets we shall call CharacterType_Ability.xls, one for each character class or monster type.

Each time a designer wanted to create a skill, they filled in various attributes, such as casting time and damage, in the spreadsheet. An animator would then assign the correct animations to the skill, and an FX artist would assign the correct FX for casting, being hit by the effect, and so on. Each CharacterType_Ability.xls document could contain up to a hundred skills.

The problem was that often, a designer would be working on multiple skills in the same CharacterType_Ability. xls document, but be unable to check it back into the version-control system half-finished, since that would break the build for everyone else. The animators and FX artists who were trying to test their assets in-game would then be forced to wait their turn with the document. To add to the pain, one team could be iterating on old skills while another was building new ones—both requiring access to the same documents.

The simplest solution to the problem of unmergeable files is not to create them in the first place. This is easier when most of the planning work can be done at the start of a project.

However, even then, avoiding shared files is not always possible. Perhaps you're using a game engine or middleware that introduces them into the pipeline. Or perhaps you're working with a legacy pipeline that has always generated them. In such cases, you need to decide whether it is better to try to remove shared files as they arise, or to live with them.

When making this decision, weigh up the relative costs. How many shared files will be generated? How many person-hours of wasted effort does each one represent? Will this change as the company grows? Conversely, how many person-hours will each one take to remove?

If the cost of removing shared files outweighs that of living with them, you can at least try to minimize their impact. One way to do this is to split each shared file into a hierarchy of smaller, individually editable sub-files: for example to split a shared file containing a list of animations for every character in the game into individual files corresponding to each game character. This reduces the chance that two artists will need to work on the same file at the same time. However, this can quickly become cumbersome: in the example above, it would be necessary to create a corresponding animation list each time a new character was added.

Another, much more situational, avenue to explore is shared editing tools. Let's say that several team members need to tweak values within the same file: for example, the ambient light color and intensity in different game zones. A tool that lets them edit these values simultaneously, each working on a single, central version of the file, could avoid the problems a shared file would normally create. However, such shared editing tools can break the isolation of your sandbox environment, invalidating any tests carried out within it. Shared editing tools can provide a powerful solution to a big problem, but always consider their impact on testing.

A third option is to switch the data into a format in which it is possible to merge data automatically, or at least semi-automatically, using existing tools. For example, if characters' abilities can be set out in a suitable formatted text file, it may be possible to use the text-merging capabilities of the version-control software to merge changes from multiple users.

Access Control

Logistical and security considerations dictate that not every artist should have access to every asset in a production. At the lowest level, such permissions are handled by the file system, but the asset-management system may also need to be aware of users' access rights—for example, to provide an approval process, or a publish

mechanism whereby artists can only see new assets when they have been marked ready to be picked up. A good asset-management system will also enable users to lock checked-out files to prevent other users from beginning work on the same, unmergeable files.

Awareness of Deleted or Archived Files

It is also common for the asset-management system to have some knowledge of the status of each file beyond its location in the network: in particular, whether it has been deleted entirely. If a facility uses offline storage, a good asset-management system should also be able to tell you when an asset has been moved to tape, what the tape number is, and where that tape can currently be found.

Automatability

Any operation that requires an artist to carry out the same tasks over and over again is a prime candidate for automation via the asset-management system. In VFX work, a classic example is animation. Any time an animator releases new animation curves, a geometry cache should be generated. Rather than have the animator create each cache manually, tying up their workstation until the calculation is completed, it is more efficient for the asset-management system to send the job to the render farm automatically whenever a new set of animation curves is checked in. Any slow, CPU-intensive, readily distributable task may be automated in this way.

Games pipelines also make use of automation extensively for testing—for example, reporting crashes, frame rates and memory usage while running automated soak and smoke tests—and for assembling the numerous different builds required during the course of production. These builds correspond to each possible configuration of the code (debug, release, submission, and so on) for each target platform, and for each SKU or "Stock-Keeping Unit"—the different configurations of the game available for sale, including Collector's Editions and territory-specific releases. Old artist workstations are often recycled as "autobuilders": machines dedicated to this task.

Transparency

Many artists perceive asset management as introducing obstacles into their workflow, or forcing them to work in certain ways, so it is desirable to hide the complexities of the system away from them where possible. The ultimate goal for any asset-management system is to become completely transparent to its users, so that people talk only about saving and opening files as if they were using the standard Save and Open dialogs within an application.

To integrate successfully with a host application, the asset-management system must provide a user interface for the artist,

importers, and exporters to load and save files in the appropriate location and format. This raises a question we have touched on in previous chapters: is it better to save a file in an application's own native format, or to convert it into an application-agnostic format such as Alembic? Conversion may result in data being lost—for example, the construction history of a model—but ensures that the asset can be loaded by artists in other departments who use different software. A further option, though a more complex and storage-heavy one, is to do both: to release an asset in the application's native format, but to create an internal data representation of the model for use with other applications on release. In games development, this task is made more difficult by the fact that it is common for data to be stored in formats used only by a particular game engine, or even a particular game—formats that often evolve over the course of a project.

Integration with a host application should be context-sensitive: that is, it should use constructs that are idiomatic to that host. (For example, in visual effects work, the way the asset-management integrates into Maya and Houdini should reflect their respective workflow and UI conventions.) It should also be scriptable, particularly in more complex workflows, so that the artist is not always required to control every part of the process manually.

Asset Management on *Avatar*

Nolan Murtha
Digital Effects Supervisor, Lightstorm Entertainment

During our work on *Avatar*, we learned an incredible amount about tracking the individual components of a shot. When we started, we were just tracking basic takes, then evolving them into shots as they were selected for the edit, but by the end, we could track the location of every tree, cloud, and character. We also began keeping track of animation data for every moving asset, so that we could rebuild scenes with new timings and render them out to visualize variations of a shot. This could all be set up and executed without a human ever opening a 3D software package.

One of the most critical, and powerful, reasons for such minute tracking comes in the form of scene building and real-time visualization. *Avatar*'s "virtual camera", as it came to be known, relied on scenes being rendered in real time. The team at Lightstorm would build immersive environments representing the world of Pandora and populate that world with the movie's characters. We then used motion capture to record the movements of a "camera" object in the real world, mapped that data to the viewport in the 3D package—and presto: a virtual camera through which one could look into the digital environments.

The difficult task for us was that no DCC package is built for a combination of real-time rendering and content creation. Traditionally, artists would have to create data in one package, then move that data into a game engine in order to see it at its best. The artists involved in *Avatar* had to build scenes that ran in real time yet still existed in an editable environment. This was one of the main motivations for such obsessive asset management. By building a high-resolution model and a series of lower-resolution variants, we could automatically select the most appropriate version to use when rebuilding a shot. Our real-time scenes were all just low-resolution proxies for the hero models to be used in the final renders.

The result was that the shooting stage became a giant sandbox for James Cameron, the director. He was able to move pieces of the environment as he shot, change animation timings, and alter lighting and effects. Most importantly, all of these decisions were reflected in the high-resolution files. If he placed a tree on the stage, when we saw the final renders six months later, that tree—or a much higher-resolution version of it—would be in exactly the same position.

This enabled the director, production designers, and other key creative people to iterate on ideas very quickly, making informed decisions they knew would carry though the production. One just has to look at the famous "Hometree Destruction" sequence to understand the power this represents. Under normal circumstances, it would have taken a director months of work with all kinds of VFX, CG, and animation supervisors to plan and execute a sequence like that. On Pandora, we were able to get the timing of every character, explosion, and especially the fall of the great tree correct before even sending the shots to a VFX house. *Avatar* brought about many new methodologies and tools for digital filmmaking, but one of the truly unsung heroes of the production was the asset-management system that allowed us to work in the ways that we did.

Section 9.4 How Asset Management Differs Between Film and Games

Having reviewed the goals of asset-management systems in general, let's examine how the relative importance of these goals differs between film and games. Asset management for film and asset management for games are two very different problems. First, the nature and volume of the data being managed differs enormously, as does the nature of the infrastructure required to support it. Second, the relative importance of version control and dependency tracking varies. We will look at each of these in turn.

As we discussed in Chapter 6, film productions typically generate much more data than games. This is particularly true of visual effects productions, where work must look absolutely photo-realistic, even at very high resolutions, making it necessary to create very detailed assets. Films also generate a lot of large image sequences: both background plates and rendered CG elements ready for compositing. Furthermore, the tight turnaround times common in VFX work mean that many user requests must be processed by the asset-management system simultaneously.

As well as being able to cope with the volume of data and number of user requests, the asset-management system must also be able to interface with the facility's infrastructure. This encompasses a wide range of hardware—workstations, core servers, render farm, storage cluster, and so on—and software. The latter ranges from low-level multithreaded C++ libraries crunching numbers for physical simulations or image processing, through high-frequency message-passing middleware, to high-level scripting languages such as Python.

Structuring Metadata for Film Projects

One of the most important functions of asset management is to monitor the files in the system from many different perspectives. Typically, this is done using metadata attributes that represent aspects of the files that the production needs to track. These attributes can relate directly to the file itself ("What kind of file is this?" and "Where is it stored on disk?") or to organizational considerations ("What shot is the file used in?" and "Who worked on it last?")

A key task of the asset-management system is to declare and store such metadata, and to make it searchable. In its purest form, metadata can be described as key-value pairs. The keys define the structure of the metadata, and the values define the properties of individual assets.

Here are some examples of metadata keys that might be stored with an asset in film work:

- Job, Scene, Shot
- Asset Type
- Name
- Version
- Creator
- Timestamp
- Approved
- Deleted
- Location

Two means for associating metadata with assets are approval and tagging. As we discussed in previous chapters, the asset-approval process varies from facility to facility, although common stages include blocking, primary, secondary, CBB, and final.

In contrast, tags are arbitrary strings that users can assign to assets in order to track them. For example, let's say that your client has decided to work up a sequence in "beats" corresponding to significant points in the action. The next client may not want to use the same approach. Tagging provides a mechanism by which artists can identify the assets that belong to certain beats, enabling you to answer questions like "which shots must we work on for Beat 1?" without having to introduce the notion of beats as a dedicated attribute for each asset.

But beware: it is easy to overuse tagging. Only allow artists to add those you really need. You should also be careful that the tags themselves are not referred to directly within code, as this tends to result in unmanageable code bases consisting of long if/else statements. The asset-management system should not base decisions on whether a particular asset has the "beat1" tag.

In contrast, games typically generate less data, over a longer period of time, and require a less complex hardware infrastructure. However, their software environments are, if anything, even more complex, since content is created not only in large commercial applications but in small bespoke tools written to author highly game-specific data: level editors, animation blend-tree authoring tools, state machine editors, game scripting IDEs, and so on. To modify each of these tools to work with a central asset-management system can be a huge engineering task.

The relative importance of version control also differs between film and games. While the film industry is more comfortable maintaining large numbers of files versioned only by naming convention or location and allowing individuals to "opt in" to the current version, formal version-control software is one of the most critical pieces of infrastructure for any game team.

A game is, ultimately, a complex piece of software, with millions of lines of code and thousands of graphics assets that need to work together. Often, the code and the content change in lockstep: a change in code requires new or updated assets, and vice versa. If the code and assets are out of sync, the game won't look or play right. On a large title, several hundred programmers and artists will be working on those resources during the course of production. Ensuring that the source code and data are very tightly managed is the only way to avoid chaos.

Another difference between film and games is the relative scale of the problem of dependency management. Games are built around a complex web of relationships between assets and code. Changes to any part of that network can have unpredictable ramifications: for example, an artist who changes the length of an animation may unwittingly alter a character's effectiveness in combat. Unfortunately, there are no off-the-shelf tools that can make sense of this intricate spiderweb of dependencies. It is, however, important to understand how assets relate to one other so that the pipeline can be designed in order to minimize such unforeseen consequences.

But what do we mean when we say that one asset is "dependent" on another? We will examine this question—and its consequences for pipeline developers—in the remainder of this chapter.

Section 9.5 Dependency Tracking: What is Asset Dependency?

The classic example of a dependency relationship between assets would be that between a 3D model and its textures. Most dependency relationships are straightforward one-way connections—and in most cases, the dependencies are explicitly recorded in an art file. The model, for example, expects a certain set of textures, and trying to open or render it when those textures are unavailable will generate error messages for the artist.

Because missing dependencies are a source of friction, it's common for the pipeline to provide artists with tools to police these kinds of relationships. This could be as simple as a game engine providing a set of predefined fallback textures that appear in place of the missing assets. Providing the fallbacks are garish enough to attract attention, they should alert team members to missing dependencies without actually crashing the game and bringing development to a stop.

Other teams prefer a more elaborate approach that analyzes art files for dependency relationships to ensure that dependencies are saved along with the core asset: "The model you're trying to check in uses two textures that are not currently in source control. Would you like to add them?"

The real problem with dependency management is that the relationships between assets become more complex as a project grows. Imagine that a games animator notices that something is wrong with the hat of one of the characters in the scene they are working on. The problem is obvious, yet finding its cause may require working backwards through several layers of nested references, either inside an art package or in the game itself, until the offending data is found.

As we have noted, this problem is particularly acute in games, since any asset may potentially be dependent on any other. Even if you ignore many of the less useful dependencies, the complexity of the relationship between files or other data stores is immense.

Section 9.6 Dependency Tracking: Upstream and Downstream Dependency

Dependency tracking is the process by which an asset-management system tracks the relationships between assets: both which other files are used to generate the asset in question (its "upstream" or "incoming" dependencies) and which others use it in their turn (its "downstream" or "outgoing" dependencies).

Tracking may be unidirectional, or bidirectional. Unidirectionally tracking downstream dependencies enables the asset-management system to notify users of those downstream assets that they require an update when a new version of a file is checked into the system, or to make that update for them automatically.

Bidirectional tracking is more complex, but enables users to check how frequently an asset is used, and where. This is valuable if a production is running over schedule, or if a game is running out of memory, and content must be cut: it's much better to drop an asset that appears only once than it is to drop one that shows up on every level.

Opting for bidirectional tracking doesn't mean that it is necessary to record both ends of every asset relationship. There is a fundamental asymmetry in the way assets are used. Most assets exist in order to be placed into something larger: animations inside scenes, props inside levels, and so on. The big "container" assets, like game levels or film shots, gain and lose assets all the time. Tracking these changes within the container is fairly simple, since this only means updating a single list of assets, but updating all of the individual assets as

they are placed or removed is much more complicated, and requires much more work on the part of the tools team.

If your dependency information is externalized—that is, if it is recorded in a database or a separate file, rather than stored within the assets themselves—most of the benefits of upstream tracking can be achieved by data analysis. Databases are great at working out upstream dependencies by walking through the lists of assets in each container and chaining them together to compile the complete dependency list. Although this process may not be real-time, it's usually fast enough to enable a production to run smoothly, and saves a lot of engineering effort.

Section 9.7 Dependency Tracking: Manual Versus Automated Systems

Before we look at how an automated dependency-tracking system is designed, let's consider the alternative: manual tracking. This comes with the obvious drawback that it relies on human input. People can't be trusted to update dependency metadata correctly, particularly when under the pressure of a deadline—exactly the point at which accurate data is most crucial.

But let's not write off humans just yet! To develop an automated solution is expensive and time-consuming; humans are cheap and adaptable. Give a human a spreadsheet and with little or no development effort, you have a dependency-tracking system—not necessarily a consistent or thorough one, but one that can work well if focused on a small subset of dependencies.

For example, in games work, that spreadsheet could list the animations needed to build a character's blend tree, their location, and their status. Typically, this would consist of a few hundred animations—a tiny subset of the animations used in game, and an even tinier subset of all the assets—but perfectly adequate for specific tasks, and small enough to update manually.

Team size is critical here. A small or even medium-sized team with a low staff turnover and an established naming convention will survive quite happily without a dependency-tracking system. Increase the team size or staff turnover and automated dependency-tracking becomes essential to maintain productivity.

Section 9.8 Dependency Tracking: Storing Dependency Data

Next, let's consider some of the issues that affect the design of a dependency-tracking system. The first of these is the form in which to store dependency data.

Tracking dependencies will probably make it necessary to store hierarchies, trees, or even graphs of connections. This is difficult to do effectively in the relational databases traditionally used in asset-management systems, since these are based around flat data, not graph structures. Document or object databases do a better job of this, but there are now newer databases, such Neo4j and AllegroGraph, that are based on graph theory, and store nodes and edges in a more natural format. These are generally faster, more scalable, and more feature-rich than the equivalent models in SQL.

Section 9.9 Dependency Tracking: Visualizing Dependencies

A good pipeline should include tools to visualize the network of dependencies that make up the production. Without them, it can be very hard to get a real understanding of how many resources are really being used at any given time. Game teams, in particular, are always worrying about the amount of memory at their disposal. A good dependency-tracking system makes it possible to spot ways in which memory use can be optimized: for example, a subset of the prop library that shares a lot of textures and which would take up less memory as a unit, or a character that has an expensive animation set, and which should be trimmed down.

Visualizing dependencies is also important when budgeting run-time costs. Placing an extra model in a level may seem like a cheap way to add extra color—but not if that model comes with an enormous texture, or a huge set of animations. The real run-time cost of an asset includes the costs of all its incoming dependencies on other run-time assets not present in the scene. Therefore, in order to control costs effectively, it's critical to be able to visualize the relationships between assets and assess their impact on the game.

Resource cost is less of an issue in film production, but it is still important for a film team to be able to visualize asset dependencies: for example, to see how many of the props in a scene are finished and how many are still being worked on. It is also useful for artists to be able to see what impact their changes will have on the production. If you can give your artists a clear view of how their work is being used downstream, you will minimize unpleasant surprises.

Visualizing dependencies is essentially a problem of graph theory. The dependency graph for a big production can be staggeringly complex, but the basic building blocks are just assets and the links between those assets. Relatively simple scripts can collect this information by analyzing the files created by art tools, in-house software, and the game engine, and assemble it into a node graph.

The real challenge is presentation: getting the information in front of the team in a usable format. It seems natural to present dependency information as a tree or node view, similar to the outliner or graph views in art tools. This works well for small subsections of the project (for example, showing the inputs of a single asset) but breaks down quickly for larger amounts of data.

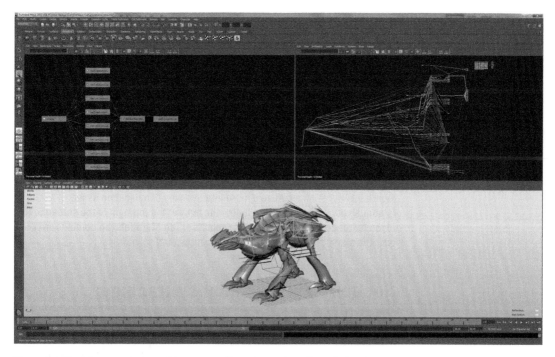

Figure 9.1 Graph structures provide a compelling way to describe relationships between assets, so long as the amount of information being displayed is small, as in the upper left of the image. When there is too much information, the graph can quickly become illegible—as in the upper right.

On the other hand, websites, which are inherently built around links between pages, are a natural way to represent the links between assets. Once you have analyzed the graph, creating HTML or wiki pages that correspond to your assets makes it easy for artists to navigate complex data sets using familiar user interfaces. For example, the asset page for a model would include upstream links to its textures and downstream links to the scenes or game levels that use the model itself. It's also a good idea to include summary pages for tracking big-picture items: total numbers of assets, resource usage, assets grouped by review status, and so on.

Figure 9.2 Hyperlinks can be a more intuitive way of navigating asset relationships. Here, a user can follow the links at the top right of the screen to any of the materials that use the texture selected. The Materials tab contains links to textures and to models that use those textures, and so on.

Section 9.10 Dependency Tracking: Resolving Implicit Dependencies

Another issue to consider is that of implicit dependencies. The most intractable problems arise when the relationship between two files is not discoverable by looking at the assets themselves. In games, a notorious example is the character skeleton. In many games, technical constraints require a character's skeleton to be the same everywhere it appears. This means that if an artist accidentally renames, deletes, or adds a bone to an existing character, the entire pipeline may grind to a halt—despite the fact that the hundreds of files affected by the change are themselves unchanged, and probably still look the same to anyone who opens them up in 3 ds Max or Maya.

Implicit dependencies are *trouble*. They can change existing content without warning, or break it completely. They are also difficult to track, since—unlike our original example of a model and its textures—they don't consist of simple referenced files. Finding and fixing the problems implicit dependencies cause will probably involve a long trawl through recent changes looking for something suspicious: hardly an efficient use of anybody's time.

The only real solution to the problem of implicit dependencies is not to have them. When a dependency relationship exists between

two files, it should somehow be made explicit. For example, the relationship between a master skeleton file and the animations that depend on it could be expressed by using the file-referencing functionality inside the art tool. This would automatically push changes from the master file to the animations. Use of referencing in a case like this turns a nasty, potentially dangerous implicit dependency into a simple explicit dependency—albeit one that, depending on the pipeline, might also make it necessary to reprocess or reexport all of the files in question.

Alternatively, an implicit dependency can be made explicit by recording it in a database or by creating a file (usually called a "sidecar file") whose job is to track the relationship. In the example above, there might be an XML file that lists all of the animations that depend upon the master skeleton file. When the master is changed, the users can be warned about the large number of files that need to be updated. Conversely, when individual animations are opened, the animation file can consult the tracking file to make sure that it is in sync with the master.

Section 9.11 Dependency Tracking: Caching Queries

It isn't always necessary to query the database each time you need to evaluate a dependency relationship. Some queries, such as retrieving a shot list, can be made many times without the result changing. In such cases, it is wasteful to query the database each time. A better model is to query the database once, the first time the information is requested, then store the result in an intermediate cache. Future queries can then use the cache in preference to the database. Once the cached information becomes stale, the result can be obtained from the database again and placed back in the cache.

Databases do this form of caching anyway, but it can also be provided as an external service, such as Memcache or Redis. The cache is normally an in-memory key-value pair store. Each item has a "time to live" value, and when this is reached, it is removed from the cache. If the cache is full, items are removed based on their remaining time to live, or according to a "least recently used" model.

In addition, if a query is slow to process but yields predictable results, you might decide to precompute it. For example, if you know you will always need a list of assets for a shot, whenever a new asset is created, you could add it to a list stored somewhere else. This involves extra maintenance—and you should always be able to recalculate the value from the database should something go wrong—but it is a common optimization technique. Again, the results can be stored in a cache, or added to the database as a separate table.

Section 9.12 Dependency Tracking: Grouping Assets

The asset-management system should also enable users to combine assets into groups. These groups should themselves be version-controllable. For example, a character is made up of multiple assets: the model, skeleton, muscle rigs, shaders, textures, and so on. Rather than dealing with these assets individually, a grouping asset can be defined to store the information. It is much easier to tell artists that they should load version 56 of Character_1 than to present them with a list of versions of each individual asset and expect them to load them all separately.

The assets within a group should also be subject to some kind of approval process. In film work, most of the dependencies between these assets come back to the geometry. The UVs of the model are used by the texture artists to define which regions to paint, but may also be used by the rigging team to paint weight maps. In turn, these rigs are passed on to the animation team, which then exports geometry caches for use by the lighting department.

Let's say that the lighting department requests an update to the geometry of a model, which in turn requires updates to its UVs. In a system without approvals, the model would be immediately available to all downstream disciplines. If lighting were to pick up the new model before rigging and animation, none of the cached animation would work. This problem can be avoided by providing approval tags that prevent one department from picking up an asset before others have completed the work required.

That concludes our exploration of dependency tracking—and of the technological aspects of pipeline design in general. In the next chapter, we shall look at the human aspects of the process: how the pipeline can be used to manage the way in which people work.

An Overview of MPC's Asset-Management System

Hannes Ricklefs
Global Head of Pipeline, MPC

At its core, MPC's asset-management system has a mechanism for uniquely identifying individual assets such as models, rigs, textures, caches, images, config files, color decision lists, look-up tables, and QuickTime movies. These assets are identified by type and given unique names. Changes are tracked by an incremental version number. As a way to define a location for each asset, they are associated with a context based around job, scene, and shot. We can refer to assets using a simple dot notation, in the following format: job.scene.shot.type.name.version.

In many cases, individual assets need to be grouped together to form more complex structures, much as atoms link together to form molecules. One example might be the grouping of a character with its animations. We call these collections of assets "packages" and treat them as version-controlled assets in their own right.

A package provides a structured grouping of multiple types of assets, some of which may be packages in their own right. In the example given, the character being associated with the animation is also a package that defines the relationship between a rig, model, textures, and other similar assets.

We define different types of packages, much as we define different types of assets. As well as defining relationships, the package definitions establish rules for validating the consistency of data and automatically generating other assets. For example, when a new version of a model is released with an updated topology, the system can detect that existing animation caches will no longer work with that model, and can regenerate them.

The packaging system therefore describes a hierarchical network of assets, the dependencies between them, and the rules to govern the regeneration of assets should their upstream or downstream dependencies change. The power to retrieve these relationships and dependencies provides staff with a mechanism to identify the status of related assets within the pipeline.

To streamline the production process even further, the system also supports approvals. A change to an asset will only be propagated to a downstream package if that downstream package is tagged appropriately. For example, lighting artists can only work with animated character packages built from approved character packages and approved caches. This is important as it allows us to verify that an asset is working correctly before propagating it into shots. This system can be thought of as a series of locks and keys. The packages have locks on them, and the assets can only unlock them and go inside if they have the right keys: that is, approvals.

9A

INTERLUDE: DIGITAL ASSET MANAGEMENT AT LAIKA

Jeff Stringer
Director of Production Technology, Laika

Laika's feature films are developed entirely in house from script to final print (or DCP). The characters and sets are designed to be built by hand in our shops and the sequences and shots are digitally captured frame by frame on our stages before being delivered to our VFX team for additional elements and final compositing. We track the assets digitally from the first draft of the script through story, character and set design, onto the stage and into VFX. Our system is filesystem based and relies upon a network of customized publishing tools to ensure names and paths remain consistent, allowing for radically different design and build processes in each department. Once in the filesystem, everyone uses Shotgun to browse, access and link assets, versions, and notes. Almost everything created can be linked back to three main asset types for the production: character, set, and shot.

Some of the challenges we face in developing an asset management system include: importing physical design elements like sculptures, woven costumes, and hand drawn designs into the digital filesystem, tracking thousands of set parts from their original design through the shops where they are built and to the stage where they are shot, tracking facial shapes for approved performances through 3D printing, quality control, delivery to stage as kits for animation, and feeding all the designs into a traditional VFX pipeline for building CG characters and set extensions and developing FX for anything that can't be shot on stage.

Here is a high-level outline of the pipeline, the kinds of data that we are tracking and how we are linking the assets together. All the publishing, parsing and reporting is done with custom software developed by our production technology team.

Early Story Development

Beat boards, concept art, and reference are published from either Photoshop or a stand-alone publishing app that names and locates

the files on our fileserver according to their type, and are linked to official characters, environments, or categories of look development called style guides. The beat boards are the precursor to sequences. All this artwork is viewable in Shotgun where status fields are updated to indicate approved versions of each category. We have added tools in Shotgun for retrieving, and continuing designs that are published as works in progress so that artists do not need to browse the filesystem itself. Reviews with directors and production designers are also facilitated through Shotgun playlists, which works really well for managing notes and updating a version status. Approved design versions are shared with other departments and fabrication teams through Shotgun and printed reports.

Script

Once the script is greenlit we parse it and establish the sequences and scenes that will eventually be boarded and developed into shots. The parsing application can do an initial breakdown, linking sets and speaking characters to the scene assets. All of this is created in Shotgun and can be updated and edited there as the script is versioned up. The scene, set, and character assets become the first units for creating a preliminary shoot schedule. They also create the defined categories for all the design artwork and storyboards that continue to be published from look development and editorial. The preliminary shoot schedule is what connects the asset build schedules for sets, puppets, and face replacement to the animation schedule.

Story to Edit

Storyboards are published to editorial. Each board is tracked with a unique number and artist name in order to facilitate revisions, reuse and assembly in pitch tools. Once edited into a sequence the cut can be published in Shotgun, linking boarded scenes to the original script based scenes and their assets. The cut can also be reviewed in Shotgun and the breakdown of assets updated. The runtime of the editorial published scenes is used to calculate the estimated duration of the shoot task for scheduling animation on the stages. When the scenes are eventually broken up into defined shots, the asset list is further defined, allowing us to project weekly asset delivery requirements for sets, puppets, and face replacements. The sooner the story solidifies the better our projected schedule is, but it never comes together all at once so our system allows for shots and their less specific parent scenes to coexist on the long term schedule.

Set Fabrication

Starting with approved concept design art, art directors breakdown environments into sets and set components based on what

they see in published storyboards. Each component is designed for build, with illustrations, architectural drafts, and reference photos. The designs are published and linked to the set components. In Shotgun, those components have links to the sets, which are linked to the shots and their shoot dates, which informs the set fabrication teams what needs to be built, and when. Every set has a digital Build Bible in Shotgun, which is a collection of all the approved designs for all the components and props that make up a set. Versions of the Bible are delivered as reports to the shops that specialize in different areas, from buildings, architectural details, graphics, greens, and props to soft goods. The data tracked in the Bible includes, among other things, counts for an item, pantone colors for paint, brush stroke details, parent and child assets, and type of approval required. The same details can be delivered to VFX, if the item is part of a set extension shot.

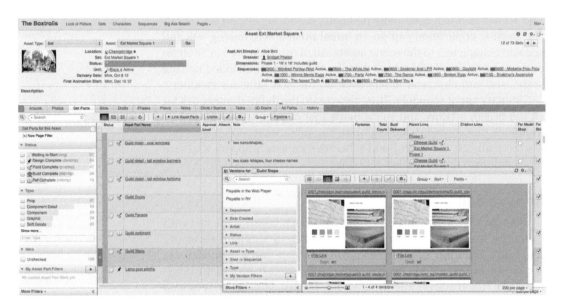

Figure 9.1 Interlude In the Art Dept the creation of sets is tracked from design to fabrication. Details on the paint and construction technique can be accessed by a variety of shops through the Shotgun interface. Photo courtesy of LAIKA, Inc.

Puppet Fabrication

Puppets are built by hand with little use of the digital asset tracking tools. The artists utilize the shot breakdown and scheduling tools to get an accurate puppet count by week so they know how many of each character is needed and by when, since the lead time on a first puppet can be several months. They also publish photographs of each completed phase of design and production so that there are digital records of the final armatures, molds, paint, hair, and costume designs.

Through Shotgun, these high quality design assets are available to the shop leads who build duplicate puppets in VFX as reference for digital doubles and background characters. The Puppet department also uses an armature database to manage inventories of custom machined parts and components that make up each character. As parts are designed, the Autodesk's Inventor files are published and linked to the character so when a puppet needs to be repaired or a duplicate built, the armature parts list for every joint and limb can be found quickly.

Face Replacement

The department that designs and builds the faces of our puppets is called RP, named after the Rapid Prototyping 3D printers they use to mass produce the parts that make up a character head and face. These heads are enormously complex—a typical hero puppet head can have as many as eighty distinct parts.

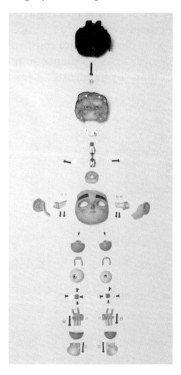

Figure 9.2 Interlude Tracking assets for Laika's hero puppet heads is particularly important. Custom parts are digitally designed and printed on 3D printers for the core assembly, which must fit hundreds of facial shapes. Photo courtesy of LAIKA, Inc.

Most of those parts make up the core which attaches to the puppet neck, and have articulated eyes and lids and registration magnets where the eye and mouth shapes can be snapped into place; these eye

and mouth shapes are replaced by the animators, frame by frame, to create the performance. The design process is all digital, based on an approved clay sculpture, which is scanned and brought into Maya. From there, modelers design the core, the eye rigs and registration system that fit the face. Faces are rigged and animators create facial performances for each character in each shot. Digital assets are tracked throughout this process through publishing tools that link the model and rig to the character and the facial performances to the shot. The range of acceptable shapes are printed and arranged into character based kits in a physical library. Shot based kits, called XSheets, are tracked in Shotgun for all the approved performances. Facial librarians can look up a shot and find the XSheet, which tells them which shapes to assemble for delivery to the stage. We also track data on usage so that we can find opportunities to print fused eye and mouth shapes and avoid VFX cleanup of finished animation. We would like to have more ability to track the physical assets, i.e. the thousands of face shapes in the library. We are in the process of developing a database to track the individual shapes with unique numbers that are printed on the asset and can help the librarians find compatible batches of prints. Color quality changes over time, so shapes printed at different times are not compatible for frame by frame use.

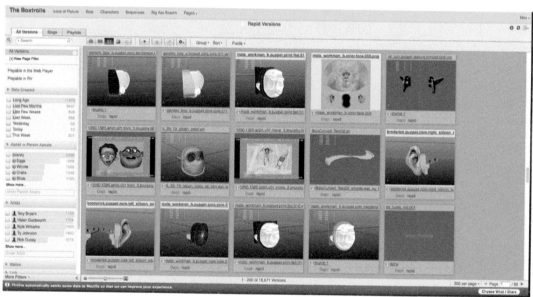

Figure 9.3 Interlude Here are some of the digital assets being tracked for the creation of puppet heads and facial animation. Photo courtesy of LAIKA, Inc.

Stage/Camera/Animation

The primary assets, tracked as part of the stage workflow, are the shots. Frames are published from the stage as lighting tests, character

blocks, rehearsals, hero animation, clean plates, green screen elements, and camera passes of all kinds. They are linked to a shot asset on publishing and, if approved, turned over to VFX. Shotgun holds all these versions, approval statuses, and editorial instructions. Additionally, for the camera team, we track the location of lenses, motion control switches, color accurate displays, and capture systems through an equipment check-in system that shows locations on a map of the stage floor. There can be as many as fifty active units in the peak of production so finding a special lens would be a challenge without this information. Animators and lighting techs also use Shotgun and RV (from Tweak) on the stages to view the cut, current storyboards, surrounding shots, and any previs or layout that may be published for a shot. VFX teams also gather and publish survey information including HDRs, reference camera frames, and photogrammetry source photos from most units.

VFX

Our VFX team uses common third-party tools such as Maya, Nuke, Houdini, Katana, and Renderman to develop CG assets and create final composite shots of all the stage passes. They publish workfiles and versions of every step along the way and we have tools for pulling current and approved versions of elements into the downstream tasks. All the versions are in Shotgun and linked to the asset or shot and the task and artist.

Reviews are managed through auto playlists that gather all daily publishes. Notes are also tracked in Shotgun and linked to shots and artists. Most of this is considered a standard VFX workflow. For asset development, all the exhaustive design work that is done in the puppet and set fabrication departments is used as the basis for digital characters or set elements that need to be created. VFX assets can be linked in Shotgun to a parent asset allowing them to inherit the designs and reference. The use of multiple passes on the stage is also made easier through our Count Sheet tool. The tool parses cut list files from Film Scribe and uploads them to Shotgun. Editorial can work with the directors to assemble plates and set in and out frames, retimes, etc. and then pass this information through Shotgun to Nuke. Our compositors can load a Count Sheet which brings in all the necessary passes from the stage shoot and lines them up to begin work.

10

PRODUCTION MANAGEMENT

Tim Green; Matt Hoesterey; Hannes Ricklefs; Mark Streatfield; Steve Theodore; Rob. Blau: *Head of Pipeline Engineering, Shotgun Software;* **Ryan Mayeda:** *Product Producer, Shotgun Software;* **Manne Ohrstrom:** *Senior Software Engineer, Shotgun Software*

Section 10.1 What You Will Learn From This Chapter

Pipelines aren't simply about tools: they're also about the people who use those tools. In this chapter, we will look at the approaches pipeline developers can take for managing people as well as data.

We will start by looking at the methodologies by which productions are managed, then go on to discuss more specific strategies that teams can adopt to ensure that their pipelines work to maximum efficiency—and ultimately, that projects are completed on schedule, and to budget.

Once we have explored the theoretical issues, we will look at some of the technologies involved in project management, including the tools required to track how close assets are to completion, manage asset reviews and track notes, and to schedule production tasks.

Section 10.2 Production-Management Strategies: Agile Versus Waterfall Development

We will begin by looking at the methodologies by which a production can be managed. Two of the most common are the "agile" and "waterfall" models. The terms originated in the world of software development, but are now widely applied to project management.

In agile development, self-organized cross-disciplinary teams each "own" a piece of the final product, collaborating to evolve it over time. Development proceeds iteratively, in short cycles, and development and testing occur simultaneously, with the feedback guiding future development. As each new feature comes online, it is integrated into

the final product, which expands gradually: a key principle of agile development is that you could, if necessary, cut features that have not yet been implemented and still have a working product.

Agile development is great when the form the final product should take is not well understood. Its key drawback is that the course of that product's development is difficult to predict. An iterative workflow may foster creativity, but it can conflict with the rigid milestones set by backers or publishers.

In contrast, waterfall development is a far more rigid, linear approach, in which a product is built in sequential phases, often defined as requirements analysis, design, implementation, testing, integration, and maintenance. Each phase must be completed before the team moves on to the next.

Waterfall development is very efficient when the final product has been planned in detail, or where development needs to produce predictable results in specific time frames. However, since it is a highly structured process, pure waterfall development does not easily accommodate the kinds of changes in product specification so common on graphics productions.

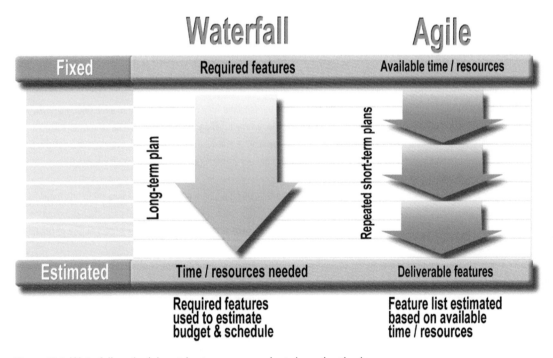

Figure 10.1 Waterfall methodology tries to manage projects by estimating how much work will be needed to meet a given set of requirements: if the estimates are wrong, more time or staff must be assigned to the project. Agile methodology, in contrast, tries to achieve short-term goals within fixed budgets: if the estimates are wrong, features are dropped or redesigned to fit within the available time and staff constraints.

In practice, facilities rarely use either methodology exclusively. Even a studio that leans heavily on waterfall development may move towards a more agile methodology when exploring a new technology. The suitability of each methodology also varies between market sectors. Films, with their rigid briefs and tight deadlines tend towards waterfall development; games are usually more agile.

Implementing an Agile Methodology

Tim Green
Senior Programmer, Supermassive Games

Our agile development process proceeds as follows. We start by placing known high-level goals on a "backlog": a board with cards pinned to it. There is one card per goal. The cards are arranged along the X-axis of the board from left to right so that goals that must be achieved earlier in development appear before those that depend on them. Cards are also grouped by discipline along the Y-axis, where possible.

Cards to the left show detailed goals, but goals grow progressively vaguer as you move to the right. As development proceeds, the board is continually updated, with the team removing cards on the left as tasks are completed and adding detail to those on the right as those goals become clearer.

Points can be assigned to cards to represent goal size and goal risk. In general, the further to the right of the board a card lies, the more unknowns that must be faced in order to meet it, and the larger the risk. However, there are exceptions: writing the manual for a game is a low-risk goal, for example: it just happens to sit far to the right because the gameplay must be locked before it can be completed.

We start by guessing at a conversion factor to convert points to the time required to achieve each goal, using an arbitrary unit that we can adjust later as more data comes in, without having to have awkward conversations like, "You've just taken two weeks to complete what should have been a one-week job." As goals are met, we track the error in the conversion factor and amend it so that it tends to a more accurate value. This provides an increasingly accurate model for predicting future progress.

Once work begins, each goal is broken into tasks, each task being a single piece of work assigned to one individual. These tasks are written on Post-it notes, and are placed on another board alongside their goal card, then removed once done. This more detailed board holds a sprint's worth of work, where a "sprint" is a short, predefined period of time: typically one to two weeks.

The technology that binds this process together is critically important, and boards, cards, and Post-its are only one way to go about it. They have the advantage that people can see the goals without having to open software to do so, and it's obvious when someone makes a change, since you see them walk over to the board in order to make it. In addition, since the "interface" (writing on paper with a marker pen) is so natural, it's much easier to focus on the actual content of the cards.

The disadvantage is that, beyond searching in the waste paper bin for old Post-it notes, there is no way to track a project's development history. In addition, space is a limiting factor: big projects demand big boards, and it can be difficult to accommodate large data sets, such as all of the animation tasks for a project. There are digital solutions available that do much the same thing, and these may be the only option in some cases: particularly where the members of a team don't all work from the same office.

Section 10.3 Production-Management Strategies: Maximizing Efficiency

Next, we will look at more specific strategies for maximizing the efficiency of your pipeline. But before we do so, let's review the reasons why productions don't always run according to schedule.

Client Schedules Change

The most obvious reason that productions don't always run smoothly is that external circumstances change. This is more significant in visual effects work than on games or animated features because of the position VFX occupies in the production process. Live shoots often overrun—because a stage is unavailable, because the actors are tied up on other jobs, or because bad weather affects an outdoor shoot, for example—resulting in plates being delivered late to the vendor. Since the movie's release date is fixed, being dictated by the needs of marketing and distribution, the time available for visual effects work can shrink dramatically.

Goals Change

Creating a game or a film isn't like building a bridge. The end product is intangible, and that makes it easier for the client—the producer or director—to change their mind about the requirements. It's quite possible to be given only feedback like, "Keep showing me things: I'll know what I want when I see it," or to go through weeks of iterations on a shot, only for the director to decide that they preferred version one.

Tools Change

The software and hardware used by the pipeline is fallible, with internally developed tools often being tested on the job. Things have a habit of breaking, often at the most inopportune times. The wait for commercial tools to be patched, or for in-house software to be updated, recompiled, and tested, causes inevitable delays, particularly if an artist doesn't have other tasks to move onto. Down time due to server or network issues also reduces pipeline efficiency.

People Aren't Machines

Even if your tools work all the time, the staff operating them won't. People go out for meals and cigarette breaks; they get ill or find new jobs; and occasionally, they even want to go home in the evenings. Moreover, they make mistakes. When managing a production, it is always necessary to account for delays caused by simple human error.

Facilities have little control over the first two factors. It's hard to predict when a studio will deliver the plates, or what changes a client will ask for in review meetings. But they can control their own infrastructure, and to a lesser extent, their staff. We'll look at infrastructure first.

Over the course of a week, usage of the renderfarm in a visual effects facility—and, to a lesser extent, the build farm in a games studio—will go through peaks and troughs. A high number of jobs will be submitted on weekday evenings, particularly Fridays; Sunday night and early mornings will be quieter.

Neither extreme is desirable: having jobs backlogged on the farm will waste artists' time, but having machines on the farm sitting idle will waste power. The same applies to storage and network bandwidth, both of which are resources with limits. During peak times, storage capacity quickly gets used up, which may result in artists sitting idle when space is allocated to more important shots.

Certain software processes also tie up workstations until they are completed, preventing staff from moving on to other jobs. For developers, compiling software is the usual culprit. For FX artists, it's running simulations. For lighters, it's rendering. And for animators, it's Playblasting. There are several possible strategies here. One is to use brute force, pushing time-consuming jobs onto the farm, or providing artists with two machines so they can switch back and forth when one is busy. Another is to optimize the software so that these tasks can be completed more quickly. Another is simply to provide staff with tasks they can work on in other software until their primary tools come back online: for example, producing documentation or training.

However, from a pipeline developer's point of view, the hardest task is to get staff working efficiently. Unlike machines, people don't assimilate all of the input data, process it, then output a mathematically correct result first time. Instead, they use a far less efficient workflow: given the available inputs, they produce an output, review it, then repeat the task incorporating what they have learned.

We can improve on how we use humans in our pipelines simply by recognizing their weaknesses and playing to their strengths. Humans need to iterate to produce good content, so wherever a human interacts with the pipeline, build in iterative capabilities and make each iteration short. If you have to economize on development effort somewhere, it's usually better to have somewhat outdated technology with a fast iterative workflow than it is to have cutting-edge technology that is slower to iterate.

Section 10.4 Production-Management Strategies: Finishing On Time and On Budget

Of course, maximizing the efficiency of a production is only a means to an end. The ultimate aims of production management are

to ensure that projects are completed on schedule, and to budget. Next, we will look at strategies for planning those schedules—and ensuring that you stick to them.

Build in a Buffer

In previous chapters, we discussed the need to capture data from each project you complete in order to predict more accurately how long future productions will take. But you should also build in extra time to protect you from unforeseen eventualities. A producer who sets a schedule in which overtime is the only margin for error is setting up conditions that are almost certain to result in long working hours and tired, demoralized staff.

Building in extra time also helps to improve the quality of the finished product. People become less creative when under time pressure, and more inclined to cut corners. A programmer who is already working twelve-hour days will be less concerned about whether their code is reusable, for example. Given a passionate team, under-scheduling slightly often yields disproportionately better results, since people will put in extra hours to make the product "even better" rather than just "getting the job done".

However, in visual effects, building in a meaningful buffer is almost impossible—both because of the huge number of external factors that affect a production, and because some directors simply never finalize shots until a deadline requires them to do so. Instead, it is enough to know how many shots are due, and whether it is possible to complete them in the time left. Rather than scheduling buffers, it is better to make sure that the cost budgeted for each shot covers both the artists' time and the studio's overheads. It is all too easy to leave out support costs when pricing up a shot.

Start Small, Then Crew Up

Rather than maintaining a constant team size throughout a production, it may be more cost-effective to run a small, tight crew for 70 percent of the project to give this core team a chance to iron out the kinks. Once the pipeline is tested, the edit is locked, and the key shots or story arcs approved, you can crew up for the final 30 percent of the project. The same applies to hardware resources: it can be better to buy in render nodes or storage space for the final push than to have them sitting idle for the majority of a production.

Of course, those extra staff have to come from somewhere. In a large facility, it may be possible to take them from other projects. In such cases, weekly scheduling meetings are essential to rationalize the competing needs of different project teams. Otherwise, they will need to be recruited externally. This means keeping an eye on the

local talent market—junior staff are easier to recruit around graduation season, for example; while freelancers become available when nearby facilities crew down on productions—and building in adequate lead times, particularly when hiring senior staff, who may have to be recruited internationally.

However, keep in mind adding people late in a project increases the load on the existing team members, since they will have to brief and supervise the newcomers. Being unfamiliar with the facility's tools and processes, new staff will inevitably also introduce more errors, causing a dip in efficiency. Adding extra hardware late in a production can also have catastrophic effects. For example, the extra traffic generated by increasing render capacity can slow down your network or throttle your storage.

Stagger Your Crunch Periods

If you are working on more than one project at a time, it is essential to ensure that the deadlines are well staggered. A delay to one project will tie up staff and hardware resources for longer than expected, causing effects that may then ripple out to other productions.

Plan What to Drop and What Not to Polish

If a project is overrunning and no more resources are available, the solution may be to do less than you originally planned. In film work, this could mean dropping entire shots. This is usually a last resort, since it can leave holes in the plot—or at the very least, force a sequence to be reedited—and must be driven by the client, usually in response to budgetary rather than time pressures. A less drastic alternative is to scale back effects: for example, by reducing the number of characters on screen, or the size of an explosion. Finally, you could just dial back the quality: accepting that you can only get a shot "90 percent there" may be a considerable time saving—and the audience may not actually notice the difference.

In a game, the equivalent is to drop features, or even to drop entire levels. It is important to plan for this from the start of a project: in a story-centric game, dropping a level late in production may have a huge impact on the narrative. It is much better to designate certain levels as "bonus levels" from day one, and produce them only once more critical tasks are complete.

If All Else Fails, Contract Work Out

If even cutting content can't save a project, you may be forced to contract work out. In visual effects, this is described as a "911

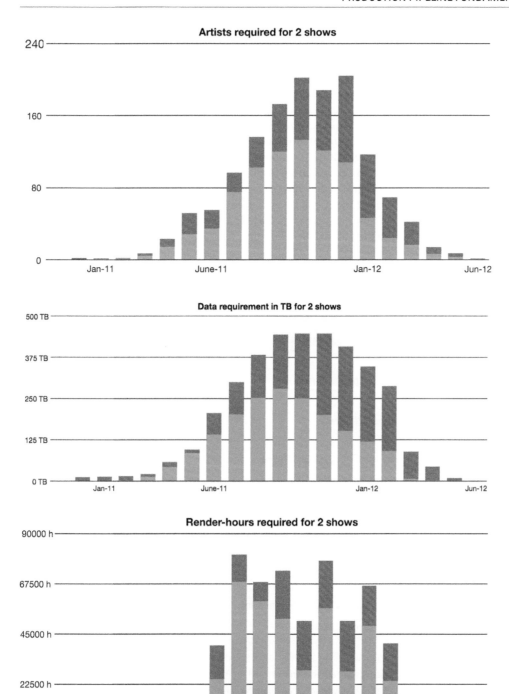

Figure 10.2 Film productions typically start small, expand, then taper off again. These graphs show the course of two productions running simultaneously within a facility: at the top, the number of artists required; in the center, the amount of data generated; and at the bottom, the number of render hours required. The figures are hypothetical, but are based on real-world examples.

project": Facility A realizes late in production that it is unable to complete all of the work on time, so it places a "911 call" to outsource the remainder to Facility B. It goes without saying that this is a last resort: in addition to increasing costs, the quality of the effects on a 911 project often suffers.

So far, this practice is rare in games development: although outsourcing is common, the nature of games work means that it must be planned further in advance. For this reason, many games outsourcing contracts also have support agreements built into them to ensure the contractor will be available should an unforeseen need arise after the initial contract has ended, like a bug or a change in the script that demands an extra pickup line.

Managing a Production

Manne Ohrstrom
Senior Software Engineer, Shotgun Software

Ryan Mayeda
Product Producer, Shotgun Software

Rob Blau
Head of Pipeline Engineering, Shotgun Software

Managing a production is like managing a cruise ship—except that the ship usually has more than one captain, and the destination is almost guaranteed to change after you set sail. Nevertheless, the ship owners expect that you will arrive on time and burning your last drop of fuel. A strong production management team is your best chance of accomplishing this feat.

On the macro scale, the goal of production management (PM) is to bring the project in on time and on budget. On the micro scale, this translates to:

- Making sure people know what to work on and when to work on it
- Making sure people know the context of the work they are doing
- Tracking when things are done and approved

Let's look at these points in more detail. First, you need to let people know what to work on.

To communicate who is working on what is to communicate a schedule. Whatever unit of work you schedule in (tasks, tickets, and so on), and whatever your scheduling methodology (waterfall or agile), a good production team makes sure that everybody also knows how long they have to complete the current task, and what they will be working on next.

In order to do this, you need to know:

- How the project will be broken down into schedulable units (the bidding process)
- How the schedule will be published so people know what to work on
- How updates to the schedule will be communicated
- How to schedule loosely in the long term and in a more granular way in the short term

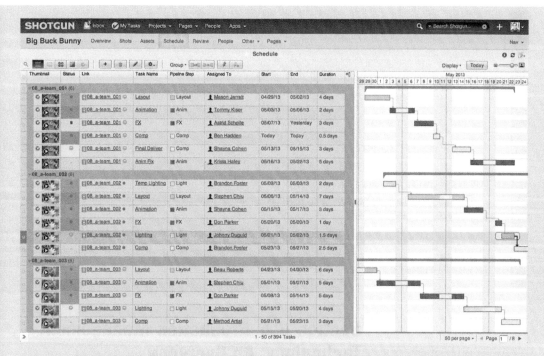

Figure 10.3 Good scheduling is the key to production management. Tools like Shotgun's Project Timeline app help here, enabling users to map out the multiple phases and milestones of a project visually.

Once everybody knows what they should be working on and when, they need more detailed information on how to set about the task. Nobody should be told to "go model a car" and be expected to come back with the exact model that a project needs. Everything in a production has a context that needs to be communicated to an artist for them to do their job properly. This context can be broken down into several categories:

Reference Imagery

Be they downloaded from the internet or created internally, each artist should be supplied with an approved set of reference images, along with notes explaining why each one is significant. (For example, it should be clear whether a particular image has been provided so that the artist can refer to its color palette, or to the content of the image itself.)

Related Work

At most points in production, an artist will be creating content of a similar type to that created previously. The more of this history they can see—from examples of models that have already been approved to an animatic from the editorial team—the better off they are.

Notes

In the world of production tracking, good notes are key. An artist should have access to all of the feedback and requests for changes relating to the jobs they are working on.

After the work has been done, it is part of production management's job to know if it has been approved or if further iterations are needed. Tracking approval implies tracking different iterations of the work and associating a status with each.

The need to collect approvals and notes usually requires some kind of formal review process. Reviews are one of the most useful, but also one of the most expensive, types of meeting in a production. To make the most of them, somebody from production management should be involved, regardless of whether the review in question consists of a supervisor walking the floor, or a more formal meeting in a dedicated screening area.

The more structured the review process is, the easier it is to capture the wealth of information it generates. If possible, the content should be prepped ahead of time, so that everybody knows what is being reviewed, and to make it easier to associate approvals and notes later.

What kind of tools you need for production management depends greatly on the size of the crew and the length of the project. A feature animation created by of hundreds of artists over a period of years has much deeper needs than a commercial created by three people in a matter of weeks.

But as a general rule, when evaluating production-management systems, be careful how much tracking you are signing up for. It can be difficult (if not impossible) to automate large chunks of the workflow, and production managers and coordinators tend to be busy people who will stop entering data unless it is clear that it is to the production's benefit to do so. Being selective about what information makes it into a production-management system and ensuring that it is easy for the data to get there is critical to successful production tracking.

Section 10.5 Production-Management Technology: An Overview

A pipeline is the technological embodiment of a production process. Its key parts correspond to departments within the studio, each of which itself consists of a group of artists. Therefore, it isn't surprising that many studios incorporate tools for managing the work of those artists into the pipeline: since the pipeline is designed around the way the studio works, it should be easy—at least in theory—to add features that will enable studio management to see how the project is progressing, assign tasks to individuals or teams, and to monitor schedules.

In practice, of course, it's rarely possible to provide perfect information using software alone. The answers a manager wants are usually subjective: a computer can provide a list of "finished" scenes or "completed" assets, but only human beings can decide which are actually good enough not to need reworking. Similarly, while a computer can track which files a given artist has opened or changed, it knows nothing about the quality of that artist's work. Moreover, the illusion of good information can be worse for a project than a frank acknowledgment of the "fog of war" that shrouds most productions. For all these reasons, integrated production tracking is a controversial subject among pipeline teams.

Nonetheless, it's worth considering the many different ways the pipeline can assist project managers. Here's a quick overview of the production-management features that are sometimes integrated into pipelines.

Section 10.6 Production-Management Technology: Tracking Assets

Most projects involve so many files that no human being can hope to keep track of them all. Therefore, most asset-management systems provide information about the status of assets for you: which ones are merely prototypes, which ones are completed, or which ones have issues that need to be corrected. Ideally, the system will produce charts and reports that allow managers to see how the project is faring.

Managing status data is fairly simple: in terms of the storage and the visualization tools required, it isn't that different to the many other kinds of metadata in a project. The tricky part is generating good data in the first place, since there is rarely a single, simple way of describing the status of all the assets in a project.

For example, a static environment model would ideally develop in a linear way: from concept, to prototype, to detailed model, to detailed model complete with textures. At this point, it would be "done", in the sense that it is ready for incorporation into a larger environment. In practice, creative feedback breaks this linear flow. Perhaps a building that looked great in the concept art fails as a 3D model; or perhaps the concept itself has to be changed to match an environment's new design. It is often necessary for status-tracking systems to maintain not just the current status of an asset—for example, its file type, or the space it occupies on disk—but also its status history. It may be important to know not only that this asset is at the concept stage, but that Supervisor X sent it back to the concept team because of feedback from a client or project lead.

It's also worth noting that different kinds of assets will pass through different stages of development. The development of an animation from blocking pass to finished work is very different to that for the model described above. When designing an asset-tracking system, it's important to make sure the users have input into the nature and order of the stages in each asset's life cycle. Many commercial systems, like Shotgun and TACTIC, enable users to create their own workflow steps.

Another point to consider is how the status of an asset will be updated, and by whom. This will reflect company culture. A small, tightly knit studio might allow individual artists to set the status of assets on their own, while a larger studio with a less cohesive team might need to create a more formal process in which assets must be forwarded to a supervisor or team lead for review.

Section 10.7 Production-Management Technology: Managing Notes

We've already looked at how the status of an asset is intimately connected to its development history, and how assets are frequently

"demoted" to a less-done state because of technical or creative feedback. Many asset-tracking systems therefore log this development history and this feedback so that artists have some idea of where each asset has been, and where it is supposed to go in future.

The first thing to log is who has worked on an asset during the course of its development. When a file needs to be debugged, it's far more efficient to contact the last artist who worked on it and ask what's going on rather than trying to diagnose this from first principles. What seems like a puzzling artistic choice might be as simple as a piece of reference geometry that ought to have been deleted: something that would be obvious to the original artist, but might not be to somebody who has never seen the file before. Most version-control systems provide this kind of information for free, but it's important to make sure it's easily accessible to the artists and technical people who need it.

The second thing to log is the nature of the feedback given on the asset. The most common system for handling such "notes" is through internal emails, which often suffice in simple cases. However, in a bigger team, it may be necessary to implement a more formalized process. Making sure that the data stored in such a system is complete is difficult: if important aspects of the feedback are in emails rather than in the database, the artist may have false or misleading information, which can be worse than none at all. For this reason some asset-tracking systems try to route all asset-related communications through a central system. While this addresses the theoretical problem of partial information, it only works when there is substantial buy-in from the team as a whole. If a significant portion of the production staff prefers email or other less formal methods of communication, the system becomes hard to trust.

Section 10.8 Production-Management Technology: Reviewing Work

Before notes can be generated, an asset must be reviewed, either by the client, or by a senior artist or supervisor. Next, we will look at the way in which reviews are conducted, and the technology that may be used to do so: first for film, and then for games.

Dailies, reviews of work from the previous day, are the lifeblood of a film production. They dictate the rhythm of a production like a heartbeat. There are two principal types of reviews: those conducted at the artist's desk, usually by a supervisor; and those conducted in a screening room. The latter are usually more formal, and involve more people, often including the clients themselves. However, the fundamental requirements are the same: both types of review rely on the right people and the right assets being present, the means to play back those assets smoothly, and the means to record notes.

For a desk-side review, less specialized software is required. The asset-management system should already enable the artist to locate assets they have worked on, while their workstation should be powerful enough to manipulate models or Playblast animations. However, it may be necessary to provide tools to make it easier to review a shot: for example, by "onion skinning" animations (ghosting in the previous and succeeding frames), or by wiping from one version of a shot to another.

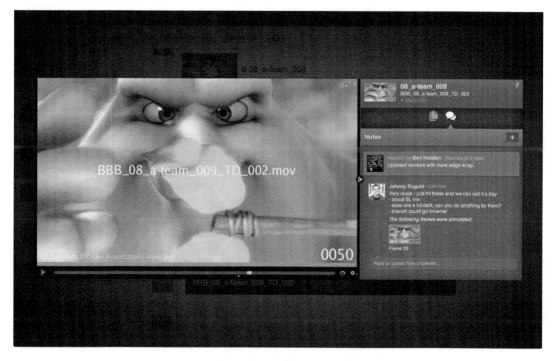

Figure 10.4 Reviews may be conducted remotely, as well as at an artist's desk: Shotgun's Screening Room enables users to play back and review media directly in the browser, or through integration with Tweak Software's RV. The system also provides tools for creating and assigning notes.

Standard workstations are rarely powerful enough to show full-resolution color-correct images at speed, especially in stereo. This is why final approval is always done in a screening room. Such screening-room reviews are more complex, involve more people, and require more preparation.

First, everyone should know when the review is taking place, and who should be there (usually only senior staff from the department whose work is being reviewed). Second, to prevent confusion, every single item being reviewed should have a unique identifier within the pipeline. Third, there should be a standard system for queuing up an item of work for review, including (although not limited to) transcoding it into the correct format and converting it to the correct color

space for the review system, and staging it on the correct disk so that it plays back smoothly at full resolution. Finally, there should be an easy way for everybody present to give and take notes. It isn't uncommon to print out note sheets for every item under review and hand them out to everyone present so that they can jot down their contributions. These sheets should include contextual information, such as the notes on previous iterations of the same shot, thumbnail images, editorial notes, VFX notes, and continuity notes.

The software needed in the screening room depends on what resolution, bit depth, and frame rate you are working at, and whether you are working in stereo. Systems that rely on caching will usually start stuttering when asked to skip quickly from one hero frame to the next, but systems that can play back 5 K 10-bit stereo frames without precaching require a lot of power and very fast I/O.

Another difference to desk-side reviews is that the presentation display (the projector) is separate from the control display (the monitor). To avoid distracting the people trying to review the content, the interface of the software used to control playback is usually visible only on the monitor. While all of the relevant files should be queued up in advance, reviews are a dynamic environment, meaning that people may ask unexpectedly to see an old version of a shot for comparison, or the current version of a different shot. A good review system will make it easy to find this content and queue it up while the current movie keeps playing. Bonus points are awarded if you can wipe between the two, or even overlay them with a custom alpha map such as a checkerboard so that squares from the bottom image show through to the top (useful for catching stereo errors). In addition, it should be easy to see each shot in the context of the edit. This means being able to queue up the previous and succeeding shots quickly, and being able to toggle "edit handles" (extra frames at the start and end of a clip) on and off.

Since listening to, and acting upon, the reviewers' requests ("Can I see that thing we watched last week where character X ran into the shot from the left? That's how he should be moving here!") can require your full attention, it's usually a good idea to have one person whose sole job is to run the review station. In addition, while everybody should be able to take notes, there should be a primary note-taker who will be responsible for collating all of the feedback and sharing it after the review. This note-taker should be able to decipher the often-cryptic shorthand that people use, and be able to make intelligent decisions about who a note was intended for.

Notes should be recorded in the production-tracking system, alongside the date they were made, and the name of the person who made them. It should be possible to mark any request for change as resolved once it has been addressed. If time and technology permit, it's also a great idea to record the dailies session and provide the

video/audio corresponding to each note along with the text. Video is by far the easiest way for an artist to know exactly where the director was pointing his laser pointer when he asked for a particular building to be pulled forward.

In games, it's all about iterations. Unlike in film, game studios tend not to use a process of daily reviews, largely because the art assets and the system through which they are displayed—that is, the game engine—evolve in tandem. During long stages of the development cycle, this display system is either unavailable, or incomplete. Even when it is, it may be hard to evaluate assets meaningfully: it may be difficult to make judgments about animations if the gameplay systems that drive them are still in development, for example.

This is one reason for the growing popularity of interactive editing tools like those provided with commercial engines like Unity, CryENGINE, and the Unreal Engine. These tools let artists to see their work through the same rendering technology used in the game, enabling them to iterate content without the need for a lengthy build process, or a time-consuming play-through of the game. The key challenge for teams that use interactive editors is to make sure that new features are implemented without introducing differences between the editor view and the result in-game. For this reason, many editors include emulation modes that simulate differences between hardware platforms.

Despite these complications, every studio has some process for reviewing assets, levels, and gameplay as they evolve. Many studios schedule regular meetings among artists, not unlike those used in film. Often, however, the real review process is an "all call" or company-wide play-test. Play-tests give the team the opportunity to see how the game is fitting together as a whole, providing a better understanding of the overall state of the project than painstaking reviews of individual assets

However, play-testing is still an imperfect medium for reviews, since few games are stable and fully functional until late in development. It's unnerving to work on an asset for several weeks without feedback from managers, or the ability to see your own work in context.

The need to reduce the time for which artists are working blindly is one of the reasons many game developers have embraced the agile development model. In agile development, game code and content evolve together in short focused bursts: for example, a new kind of visual effect might be developed by a graphics programmer, a gameplay programmer, and a couple of artists working together closely. Each collaborator will check the others' work, with the results not being seen by the company as a whole until the next scheduled test.

Agile methodology tends to favor short deadlines and interdisciplinary teams. This has led many developers to reorganize the layouts of their offices around small groups ("pods" or "strike teams") rather

than larger departments. We rely heavily these days on email and other forms of electronic communications, but nothing beats simply spinning round on your chair and talking to a colleague sitting behind you. The combination of small teams and open seating is particularly popular during the early phases of a project, when there are a lot of unknowns to be explored. As the project matures, or if the pipeline is already well-established—for example, when working on a sequel— the small groups may fade back into larger departmental groups.

It is also common to break the game into larger sections that can be produced in parallel: usually levels. Again, this means dividing staff into multidisciplinary teams, with the management of tasks within each team being handled on a fluid basis. Under such a model, only high-level management and scheduling work is done at the project level.

Section 10.9 Production-Management Technology: Scheduling Tasks

Since an asset-tracking system that records the status and development history of each file already contains so much data, it isn't difficult to see why some teams try to extend this approach to project-management information. For example, the same system that tracks whether Asset Y is ready for lighting can also be used to tell Artist X to set up the lights and have them ready by next Monday. Systems that go down this route typically end up reproducing key elements of traditional project-management software, such as Microsoft's Project: they track who is assigned to do what and when; generate reports showing managers which parts of the project are lagging, and where resources are sitting idle; and make it possible to view and schedule around dependencies.

The success or failure of these kinds of systems depends largely on working culture. A studio with a company-wide devotion to accurate process tracking can get a lot of value out of integrated management. First, integrated systems can automate many common communications processes. Artists might, for example, be able to notify their supervisors that assets are ready for review simply by checking in completed files; while supervisors could kick assets back to the art staff for further work just by entering notes into the system. New work generated in this way could even be logged automatically to accommodate union or vendor accounting requirements.

Second, automated tracking systems can generate vital information when it comes to planning future projects. It's far easier to produce reasonable staffing plans if there is solid, empirical data on the real costs of previous productions. Artists' estimates of how long it will take to tackle a job are notoriously optimistic, and omit the many creative meanderings, technical problems, and random accidents

that delay tasks in the real world. When combined with the power to collect data automatically from the version-control system, good task-tracking tools can provide the people who need to budget future projects with more achievable sets of numbers.

However, end-to-end tracking software is typically associated with a waterfall methodology, in which there is a strong emphasis on planning and prior allocation of resources. Like waterfall development in general, automated systems create the illusion of detailed knowledge—and if the system does not match the way the team really works, this is a dangerous illusion. If artists feel like the system is trying to micromanage them—or worse, that it's spying on them—they will quickly cease to cooperate with it. It's also possible that the nominal beneficiaries of the tracking information will not want to commit to a new system just because it is integrated with the asset database. It can be hard to convince veteran managers who have become comfortable with particular scheduling tools, reporting programs, or spreadsheets to move to an integrated system.

A variant of end-to-end tracking that is common in games is to use systems designed for tracking bugs. Bug-tracking software usually provides the option to assign work to individual team members, and minimal completion-tracking functionality. For example, a bug might come in from a tester who notices a flaw in a particular character's animation. This bug may then be assigned to a lead animator who will review the problem and figure out if it reflects an issue with the game code or with the art itself. In the former case, they will refer it to a lead programmer; otherwise, it will be passed to an animator for a fix. When the bug has been fixed, a notification will be sent to the original tester for verification. However, bug-tracking systems are not usually ideal for time-management: their primary goal is simply to ensure that issues are fixed rather than forgotten, not to schedule them around future deadlines.

Section 10.10 Production-Management: One Final Thought

Given the scale and complexity of modern production projects, it's important for a pipeline team to provide as much support as possible for the management staff who will have to grapple with the tens of thousands of individual tasks and hundreds of artists involved in the project. This is particularly true on big projects where many of the staff are only passing through as contractors or outsourcers: it's hard to rely on "management by walking around" when half of your artists are a continent away.

At the same time, it's vital that the management software you create or deploy adds value to the production, instead of adding a layer of unwelcome bureaucracy. As we've stressed many times in this

book, the creative energy of your team is a vital resource, and you don't want to squander it on mundane clerical tasks.

Perhaps the most important single thing the pipeline team can do in building a reporting system is to get buy-in from both the artists who will be adding information into the system and the managers who will be using it to monitor the project. A glitzy piece of software that nobody actually uses is a far less effective tool than a well-maintained Moleskine notebook. In this regard, process-management tools are like everything else in the pipeline: they are valuable in direct proportion to how well they are embraced by the team.

INTERLUDE: COLOR AND SOUND

Jim Houston
Principal, Starwatcher, Digital and Chair, ACES Project Committee, AMPAS

Color and sound are integral part of any film or game, but many aspects of the process remain an enigma to VFX production. Following is a collection of information provided by various experts in their perspective fields, beginning with color and moving on to sound in film, then games.

Section 10 Interlude 1: Color Management in Workflows

Jim Houston

A sometimes overlooked element in the design of workflows is the need to standardize the display and use of RGB image files wherever the content is going to be shown. A key part of any production today is communication via images, and it is important in a networked, virtualized, production world that all of the people creating, approving, reviewing, and watching a new production are seeing and talking about the same thing.

Sometimes, this is straightforward. If all of the content is being made for a fixed device, say an iPhone, then it is sufficient to work in an sRGB color space and keep everything on that device for viewing. But to make content for a wide variety of different display devices, it is essential to establish a production color management strategy.

Consider how the content will be viewed from the moment of creation until it is delivered to consumers. What types of displays will it be shown on? How many different deliverables will it have? What is the best quality version that can be made? Can the content be delivered from a single master element, or do multiple versions have to be created? What software or hardware is being used to capture and manipulate color? Is the content being viewed up close under daylight conditions, or is it being shown in a darkened theater? All of these will lead to a choice of color space and the output quality that needs to be created.

Games too have special considerations. Given the wide range of capabilities in consumers' monitors, how do you manage visibility of dark scenes? Is there sufficient contrast to see shadow details or grey text over black? Can you take advantage of more colorful LED monitors? How about future color spaces that now exist for UHDTV? If you are aiming for realism, how can you render the most accurate objects, characters, sets, and lighting conditions?

All of these questions lead to consideration of color science questions, for without some understanding of the technology, it is hard to create the art.

Workflow Design for Images

Images are created, whether you are aware of it or not, in a color space. You look at them and manipulate them in a color space to get a desired result. Whether it is photography or computer graphics, the color space determines the range of colors that can be displayed and sets the tonal scale of the luminance that is reproduced on a monitor. For many computer-based applications, a common color space is sRGB. For video applications, ITU Rec BT.709 is common, and UHDTV (Rec BT.2020) will soon appear. For film production, a wide variety of color spaces comes into play: camera RGB, custom monitor setups, DCI-P3 Projection, laser projector primaries, etc.

The design of a workflow needs to consider what image files are being used and what color space the files represent for every step of the workflow. This begins with the color characteristics of the source image. If captured with a digital camera, knowledge of the camera's spectral color sensitivity, or use of a calibrated color space for the camera files can help establish the source reference color for later conversion and manipulation. It is common in various workflows to convert to "working color spaces" for use within a facility or within a particular software package. Improper conversions can inadvertently limit the range and quality of the color space that was available in the source image. This can happen, for example, when a production workflow is designed around how the image looks on a particular monitor. Manipulation of the image specifically for that monitor's color space may limit both the dynamic range and the width of the color gamut making the content less useful on other media with greater capability. This method of working is known as "output-referred" color, and can be limiting if a wide variety of display media such as film, digital projectors, and UHDTV are the targeted medium for the content.

A workflow design also needs to consider the ways in which the "signal" (the image on a wire) is moved from one device (or software package) to another. This requires, in the hardware case, some

knowledge of both the computer output and the input of a display. Is it HDMI, HD-SDI, or Display Port? There are many times when conversion of the signal will be necessary and these must be examined and managed as well. A common situation where this arises is when a LookUp Table (LUT) needs to be applied to transform the appearance of an image in its original captured form to the color-rendered version for display.

Setup and Calibration

Display devices often need to be calibrated for consistency, and in particular, the brightness of the monitor should be set to a known and consistent luminance. For most video applications, this is $100 \, \text{cd/m}^2$. If your workflow design relies upon WYSIWYG "what you see is what you get", then all of the displays need to be made consistent with each other. Test charts or color bars are useful to provide a visual check that a monitor is performing as expected.

Deliveries

Content may be viewed on a wide variety of displays and a complete list of deliveries is essential to determine how best to make and deliver a color correct image across all media. Whether colors are designed up front for rendering, or tweaked afterwards with color grading, calibrated displays and appropriate metadata to identify the working space of each file are essential to maintaining accurate color. Both automatic conversions and manual 'trim passes' to manage color gamut differences need to be planned for and managed in the workflow design. Special considerations apply when the output medium is film because it is a subtractive color space that is quite different from what can be seen on normal viewing monitors. Use of a film preview LUT throughout a film destined workflow is recommended for achieving the best results in this case. The object of a workflow design is to make sure that all of the work steps are properly managed, and the best image quality can be maintained and shown to all users in the production.

Color Management Systems

While most images are shown in some form of an RGB color space, there are many varieties of settings for output displays which can make a big difference in the way an image looks. One of the most significant to understand is the color space encoding: the relationship between the colors to be produced versus the code values in a pixel that represent the color. For every code value in an image, there is a unique color that is supposed to be reproduced based upon the

color primaries. The color encoding also defines the "transfer function", the relationship between the colors in a linear RGB space and the output gamma (or other curve) of a display device. Several different RGB encodings are possible: linear light, video gamma, and log. Each of these has advantages and disadvantages and they are all in common use. Linear light is similar to the way light behaves in the real world and is useful for compositing, CGI rendering, and conversion from imaging sensors. Log is useful to preserve a wide range of values in integer systems. Video gamma is ideal for display RGB on monitors as it reasonably matches the performance of the human visual system. There are many different RGB encodings and they can be converted back and forth with combinations of LUTs and color conversion matrices.

In most desktop systems, there is already a color management system that is well defined and available on most modern operating systems: The International Color Consortium (ICC) profile system. This system allows definition of the colors in an image file by assigning an ICC profile, and also allows automatic conversion and viewing of the image on output devices that have been characterized with their own output profile.

The film industry has been lacking a similar capability for production color spaces that covers high dynamic range and wide-color gamuts. The Academy of Motion Pictures Arts and Sciences has been developing a color management system for these unique requirements, now known as the ACES System (Academy Color Encoding System).

ACES System

ACES is an image- and color-management architecture designed primarily for the production, mastering, and long-term archiving of motion pictures and television. ACES provides a set of digital image encoding specifications, transforms, and recommended practices that enable the creation and processing of high fidelity images for a wide range of output devices.

Working Space

ACES is a working RGB color space which encompasses the entire set of visible colors, provides more than thirty stops of dynamic range, and uses a linear light half-floating-point encoding based upon the OpenEXR file format. Linear light in ACES means that, as much as possible, the original scene colors are captured and preserved in the RGB file—known as scene-referred color. Other images in known color space can be easily converted to ACES thus allowing the mixing of elements from a large number of different sources including CGI, digital cameras, and film.

Input Images

For every medium that might be a source for ACES, it is necessary to have an Input Device Transform (IDT) which provides a color calibrated conversion from the captured image into ACES. For film scanners, there is a densitometric color space called ADX (Academy Density Encoding) which can readily be converted into ACES as well. Images that are created for video output or computer monitors can also be converted into ACES, but this path loses the high dynamic range and wide color gamut capabilities of the system since you are only converting the range and color that was originally seen on the monitor.

Viewing Transform

Like the historical film system's negative and print, the ACES color space is intended to preserve the widest latitude and precision but looks incorrect by itself in the same way that a negative looks wrong. An essential part of viewing ACES files is a Viewing Transform which adds contrast and saturation for a dark-surround theatrical viewing environment. This is called the Reference Rendering Transform (RRT) and it provides a consistent reproducible image wherever it is applied. All ACES images are intended to be viewed through the RRT. Final deliverables can be made from this output to other devices and viewing conditions.

Output Images

The characteristics of calibrated output devices are described in Output Device Transforms (ODTs) which compress the large range of the RRT image into the visible portion that a display can reproduce. In practice, the RRT and the ODT are combined and turned into a LUT for a particular type of output device. Custom gamut mapping strategies can be created in ODTs, and conversions for film recording are also possible. ACES values may be converted to ADX film densities for film recording. If a project has been finished in another output medium ("output referred"), it is possible to convert it to ACES files by use of an inverse transform from an RRT/ODT back to the ACES values that would have created a particular color.

Archive

With a single RGB color space, a single Viewing Transform, and a small set of well-defined transforms, the ACES system allows content to be saved for the future in a well-known state that aids archival users, and preserves all of the original captured dynamic range and colors.

ACES supports flexible image pipeline development for many different processes including film and digital acquisition, CGI and GPU

renderings, digital intermediate, visual effects production, re-mastering, and on-set color management.

Future of Color

For a long time, video and film have relied upon consistent well-defined color standards that have served well for at least fifty years. New technologies, digital cameras, OLED TV's, HEVC "BluRay", laser projectors, 3D TV, UHDTV (4 K and 8 K) are pushing greater realism including resolution, high frame rates, color, and dynamic range.

Creators of new content need to think carefully about the longevity of digital material made today, as tomorrow is looking brighter and more colorful.

Section 10 Interlude 2: A Day in the Life of a Motion Picture Sound File, Circa 2013

Geoffrey G. Rubay, Sound Designer, Sony Pictures Entertainment

Whether Animated or Live Action, sound for motion pictures will begin with a recording of some dialog. That dialog may only be an assistant camera person announcing the scene and take for a scene that will consist of someone walking around or just some room tone, but if the first thing recorded does not include dialog, there will be some dialog recorded soon thereafter. For animated features, the sound is typically recorded in a voice recording room. For live action, it may be on a soundstage or on location. Whether interior or exterior, the dialog will be captured digitally. Whether on a workstation in a studio or a portable recording device, the sound is digitized and stored into a computer file that has a long journey ahead from the moment it is created to playing its part in finished production.

Current Standards

The current standard for motion picture sound recordings is Wave or Broadcast Wave files (WAV or BWF respectively) at a sample rate of 48 Khz. 16 bit recordings are acceptable but 24 bit is the standard. 16 bit files (usually a mistake) are quickly converted to 24 bit. WAV files for motion pictures should contain uncompressed linear PCM audio data. 48 k/24 bit Audio takes approximately 8.24 MB per minute per track.

WAV/BWF files are largely interchangeable with the major difference being additional chunks (the "bext" chunk being the primary one—bext is an acronym for "broadcast extension") of metadata being added for "professional" use. The files are variants of the RIFF file format originally created by Intel and Microsoft. Belying their history, these files have a fatal flaw: they have a practical file size limit

of 4 gigabytes (2 Gig in many circumstances). We will see why this matters next. WAV files are acceptable members of mxf and AAF file groups.

WAV files are often members of a "multichannel" group. In practical terms, this could be a surround audio master that has channels for Left, Center, Right, etc. These can be mono files named "myfilm_v1_6chmaster.L.wav" for the left channel with five more files adding .C, .R, .Ls, .Rs, .Lfe for the various surround channels. The problem is that the files can become separated from each other or if one of them gets renamed on a disk or server, it can be hard to fix. Polyphonic WAV files can contain many channels. The channels could be surround tracks to make an audio master or many tracks from a recorder capturing sound on a film set. In animation or ADR recording, it is common to record more than one channel. The tracks could be a close microphone, or distant and a small lavalier mic very close to the actor to mimic a body mic from the set. Instead of naming the audio tracks .L, .C, .R, etc. the files are simply named .1, .2, .3, etc. The file size limitation can begin to rear its head at this point. It is very convenient to bundle all of the channels together but the math looks like this for an eight channel audio master for a two hour feature:

8.24 MB per minute X 8 channels X 120 Minutes = 7,910.4 MB or approximately 8 gigs.

This is too large for a standard polyphonic WAV file.

While there is a standard for "chaining" files together, the practical issues of files getting separated from each other or renamed remains. There is a new standard file called RF64 (basically a WAVE file with new header data that says "I'm 64 bit") which leverages the ability of 64 bit operating systems. The practical limit on file size is 16 exabytes or 16,000,000,000 gigabytes which will hopefully be large enough for the foreseeable future. Further information regarding the various formats is readily available on the internet from SMPTE, EBU, AES, AMWA, etc.

Dialog Recording

Back to our dialog recording. We record a line or series of lines from a scene or sequence. Now what? The recording will be captured by a workstation or a purpose-built location sound recorder. Location recorders—manufactured by companies like SoundDevices, Zaxcom, Aaton, Nagra to name a few—either generate WAVE files directly or export them when needed. These files may or may not be named something very useful. While this is improving, the files may need to be renamed. These recorders can also embed metadata into the files regarding scene, take, channel IDs, contents of channels, etc. which can be viewed and utilized later. This can be critical as the files may be named on the device Sound0001_001.wav which does not exactly

leap from the screen and scream "I'm track one of Scene 1, Take 1 of some film and I contain a recording of the Boom microphone." Files are usually renamed something like "CL2_0001_001_1.wav" which is "Cloudy 2, Scene 1, Take 1, Track 1". Embedded metadata sounds wonderful and there are many implementations that show promise, but it can be very spotty in practice so filenames—good ones—are the one thing that can be counted on. Recordings made on a workstation are more easily named and can be renamed at the end of a session or quickly thereafter to fix any issues that may arise. Filenames for animation projects may look something like "CP_0600_004_AF_02.wav" which is "Cloudy Principal, Sequence 600, Shot 4, Anna Ferris (which actor is speaking the line in case this changes or if it is a temp line while the production waits for the opportunity to record the actual cast member), take #2".

Filenames can have an untold effect on a production. If done well—and possibly more importantly—done consistently, one can encounter a file and know what it contains. When done poorly, the problems begin quickly and never seem to end. Many people adopt the theory with regard to file naming that you should be able to throw all of the files in one folder or directory on a computer, sort them by name and they should all group by content and sequence or reel.

Where does the recording go next? In a live action production, to a lab where it will be "synced" with images on its way to the cutting room. The files from the set are stored and later passed on to the sound department for use in post-production. Animation sound files proceed directly to the cutting room. If more than one track is being recorded, Polyphonic files are preferred as they are handled as a single item by most NLE's (Non Linear Editing systems) like Adobe, Avid, FCP, etc. This is a critical moment that bears further examination.

In a feature production, the sound and picture (exposed negative or files/tape from a camera) are typically sent to a lab for some sort of "processing". Whether the process is electronic or chemical, the goal is to ready the results of shooting for the long journey ahead. Sound and image are joined and related to each other in the hope that they run in sync with each other. Images photographed at 24 frames per second and sound recorded at 48khz join up nicely. The "sample rate" works out to a nice even 2,000 samples per frame. Using timecode to line up and the common audio visual reference point of the "sticks" on the slate clapping together at the head or tail of the shot to verify, a sync relationship is established. The result can be transferred to files (or tape or both) for review in dailies and also sent to the cutting room to begin the editorial process.

Often the files sent to picture editorial are lower resolution than the master media. The picture files could be an intermediate codec that works well for the NLE. The sound may be a "mix" prepared by the production sound mixer or a mix generated in the telecine suite

or lab. There may be *many* sound channels represented by a single mix track. The mix may be a "split" track where scenes involving multiple characters are assigned to individual tracks. For example, track one could contain the boom microphone and track two contain the wireless or body mics for greater isolation. The mix or split mix tracks may be proxies for many tracks recorded on set. Eight tracks of sound is not uncommon. If the footage is of a concert, for example, there could easily be twenty-four or more tracks. If the picture editor requires more control of the sound than that offered by the mix tracks, the additional tracks can be loaded and used in the NLE.

The NLE keeps a database of the sources to enable tracing back to "master" elements from the set. This database is used throughout the editing process. The master visual elements are constantly being used by the visual effects department to create images required by the production. Likewise, the sound department will use the original master sound elements when creating the final sound track. The quality of the database created and maintained by humans greatly impacts the ease of the processes down the line. Likewise, corners cut at this point never stop creating problems for everyone involved.

The earlier statement regarding "24 fps pix and 48 khz sound lining up nicely" is true. What if the editorial department wants to work at 23.9 FPS? The sound still runs at 48 khz (not 47952 hz as in the past when NTSC video was involved) so what then? Sometimes the production sound mixer will capture the sound at 48,048 hz so that the sound can "slow down" to run in sync with the slower moving images. This sort of arrangement needs to be worked out prior to the commencement of production, hopefully. This difference in "samples per frame" is the most common culprit when things slip "out of sync". 48 k sound meant for 24 fps pictures being played with 23.9 fps pictures will drift or "walk" out of sync. The longer the segment, the further they will drift apart. This can be easy to miss when a segment is just a few seconds long and lacks proper leaders and sync pops.

Too often, sections of picture and track move to and from various facilities, in and out of various platforms lacking a true sync reference. In the past, segments of film and magnetic sound would need to be projected or transferred via telecine. They were physically the same length and would be visually marked to allow them to be synchronized. The sync "pop" (one frame of usually 1 khz tone) that played at the same moment a punch in the film or the "2" of a SMPTE countdown leader assured the viewer that things were in sync. Likewise, at the end of the segment another "pop" would play three feet (two seconds) past the last frame of picture—again visually accompanied by a punch or "2" on the screen. This allowed editors and technicians to verify sync. As we entered the digital age, the "2 pop" fell out of favor. Possibly out of ignorance or to save on space—I don't know why—but sync will often be "assumed". The age old adage regarding "assume" applies. Also, Murphy's Law seems to be strictly

enforced in film making, so beware. Communication, clear markings, standardization, properly maintained equipment combined with testing and verification are required to keep things in sync. Hoping things will turn out ok rarely works.

As the production proceeds, the editor begins creating scenes or sequences from the raw materials. In an animated production, this will involve creating the story from the recordings of voices, still images with sound effects and music added as needed. As the "cut" progresses, the editor may need to send a scene or sequence to sound or visual effects for work to be done. Maybe shots will go to animators for the animation process to begin. The sound department may create sounds that will be used as reference for animation as well. These are typically added to the cut by the picture editor and sent to the animators or VFX artists. More often, animators and VFX artists send images to the picture editor who in turn communicates with the sound department. In either event, eternal vigilance with regard to sync and technical excellence is its own reward.

Our original recording from the set or voice recording booth continues to be used in the NLE. It is included every time the sequence is played or sent out for other work. As the production progresses, there may be a need for a mix. Whether a temp mix or preparing for the final mix, the original master recording continues to be referenced. The picture editor will "turn over" a cut of the picture to the sound department. The turnover usually consists of a video file with an embedded sound mix, an AAF or OMF translation of the timeline edits from the NLE and possibly an EDL that traces back to the original audio files. The original sound file is not usually included in the NLE but is referenced by it. As mentioned before, the NLE may only contain proxy audio and video files, whilst the EDL allows the various departments to use the original master elements whether they be audio or visual items.

The sound department will prepare edited tracks for use making the final version of a project. Utilizing the EDL, they can trace back to the audio masters and use all of the available channels to prepare for the mix, much like the lab or visual effects departments will trace back to the original camera materials when needed. The sound department will often use some of the files turned over from the picture department. These files may have some unique characteristic that is either not easily replicated or it is inefficient to do so. The adage "sounds good— is good" is used regularly at times like this.

When preparing for the final mix, the sound department will create tracks that are often subsequently "premixed". The original recordings are used at this point—possibly for the last time. The process of premixing or "pre-dubbing" allows the sound mixing team to take edited tracks from sound editorial and prepare them for use in the final mix. During premixing, the mixers will adjust level, eq, and

dynamic range as well as possibly choose panning position—what speakers a sound will play from. These premixes are used in place of the original master files. There will be premixes for dialog, ADR, group ADR, sound effects, background effects, Foley, etc. The primary purpose of the premixing process is to make things more manageable in the final mix. Time can be spent taking thirty or forty tracks of Foley that all require various treatments and turn them into something that needs minimal adjustment later.

During a final mix, the premixes are further adjusted to make "stems". The stems contain groups of premixes. Minimally, there will be dialog, music and effects stems. These stems will be formatted to match the widest release format expected. For example, a stem to be used in a 7.1 film would have channels for left, center, right, left surround, right surround, left rear surround, right rear surround and Lfe (Low Frequency Effect) or "boom". When all of the stems play together, they form the basis for the finished mix or "Printmaster". The term Printmaster is really a more historical one as it refers to the soundtrack that will be used on the release "Print". It's a bit simplistic now as a feature will often be released in many formats simultaneously around the world. Many people have begun referring to Printmasters as just "Masters". You can think of the stems as "layers" of sound that all play together to form the final mix, like all of the layers of visual elements that need to be composited to form the final visuals.

The "wide" stems are useful when making masters for subsequent versions of the film. For example, removing the dialog stem of an English language film forms the basis of the "foreign" version of the film. Other examples include using 7.1 stems to make 7.1 Home theater masters or 5.1 mixes or Dolby Stereo compatible masters or Mono DME mixes, etc.

Polyphonic WAVE files of Premixes, Stems and Printmasters are usually named something like:

CL2_01_v12_0411_DX_Premix
CL2_01_v12_0411_DX 7.1 Stem
CL2_01_v12_0411_7.1_Printmaster

These are all files that can be used for Reel 1, version 12 and/or the April 11th version or Cloudy 2. The version number and/or date allow users of the file to expect it to run in sync with the same version of picture. These files can be archived and users in the future will know what to expect from the sound files. These filenames are typical of those used "in production". Studios or distributors will often have specifications regarding final delivery of sound elements and these are rarely the same from studio to studio. The importance of using consistent and clear filenames throughout a production cannot be over-emphasized.

Section 10 Interlude 3: Audio Differences Between Live Action and Animation

Dave Lomino, Operations Managers, NT Picture & Sound, NT Audio

There are notable differences between audio in live action versus animation, from how the sound is captured to when it is applied. Beginning with live action, one of the first questions is how much audio is added beyond what is captured on set. Traditionally, only about 20 percent of the sound recorded on set made it to the final cut of the movie. Today, this probably still holds true for larger budget films. The rest is added as ADR, sound effects, Foley, and backgrounds. The sound design is intended to be a natural representation of the sound for each scene. Effects may be embellished, but the intent is not to shock the movie watcher out of the experience.

At the other end of the spectrum, technology has enabled filmmakers to produce (sellable) movies with smaller budgets. Whether it is a reality TV show or a low budget horror movie, more films are skipping dialog replacement and sound design and only using production sound.

So how are these different audio files, streams and tracks managed? In the film world, sound and picture are separate entities and separate processes until the moment of exhibition. For release on film, the sound is transferred from its magnetic form to an optical form. Now there is a tangible "picture" of what the sound looks like; the pre-digital stereo track looks like the picture of a continuous oscilloscope waveform, the digital soundtracks look like coded black and white dots. The optical sound image gets exposed with the picture image and becomes a composite print. At this point, the sound is married to picture. Projectors read the images and convert it back to electrical impulses to be processed in the sound system. For release in digital cinema, the final sound and the final picture are brought together in a package. At this point, the sound is married to picture.

Much of the work we do at NT Audio is at the very end of the post-production process. Studios must preserve the value of their assets. Final soundtracks are transferred to 35 mm magnetic film or to LTO tape or back-up hard drives, and final picture is transferred to black and white 35 mm film as color separations (called YCMs) or to LTO tapes or back-up hard drives. Why use film as a preservation medium? There are pros and cons. Film is expensive and may be hard to get in the future, but it can last a hundred years and still be easily set-up to be played back into whatever platform exists in the future. Drives are cheap but may not still operate or be compatible in the long term. The same with LTOs, migration is mandatory every five to ten years.

Obviously fully animated films use the digital medium. In my experience, the music track for a fully animated film is more constant

throughout. It often replaces backgrounds. When mixing audio and dialog, it is generally inefficient to finalize sound while the picture editing is still occurring. At some point, either imposed by schedule or the creative process, a shot, a scene, a reel, the movie, must become finished and "locked". The sound crews work on matching the sounds to the final picture cut and mixing these sounds together. Any further changes to picture would now affect many synced sound elements and jeopardize the schedule. The sound work is really to support and/or enhance the visual experience. Traditionally, all the picture work needs to be decided before sound work moves forward.

When dubbing for a foreign language you must keep in mind the animated mouth movements are done to a guide track, then actual dialog used should be similar to the guide. For dubbing in a foreign language, the sync is placed as well as possible, usually lining up the end of a line with the end of the mouth movement.

Section 10 Interlude 4: The Game Audio Pipeline

Kenneth Young, Head of Audio, Media Molecule

Audio takes up a lot of space. Every aspect of a game that the player will encounter has an audio consideration, so there are a lot of files to manage. And the files can be quite big—streaming audio assets such as music, ambience, voice, and cinematics have relatively large file sizes even when shrunk with lossy compression. Not only that, the interactive nature of videogames means the audio needs to change and adapt to the evolving context (e.g. the game state controlling the music's intensity and progression, or a day–night cycle affecting the ambience), which increases the amount of audio required to create a satisfying experience. Even a simple sound effect such as a footstep, whilst relatively small, needs multiple variations to combat repetition as well as a unique set of samples correlating to each surface that a character can walk on. It all adds up to audio having one of the largest footprints of any component of your game—video is the only other real contender for this crown.

Whilst the scale and scope of a game project will affect the complexity of its audio pipeline, the high level workflow remains fundamentally the same:

- Source audio asset creation. Firstly, uncompressed audio files are created by a sound designer or composer.
- Audio asset setup. These files are then configured for in-game use.
- In-game audio asset build process. The compressed in-game assets are then created.
- Implementation of audio assets. Finally, the assets are hooked up to in-game events.

Let's explore these steps in a bit more detail and consider some of the common problems encountered in a typical game audio pipeline.

Source Audio Asset Creation

Whilst splitting up the pipeline and describing it in a linear way makes it easier to grasp, in reality each step is deeply interwoven and affects the other. For example, these source audio assets can't be created without understanding how they will eventually be implemented—this "chicken and egg" scenario means that for much of the project these two aspects will do a merry dance together as they work their way towards the final game experience, workflow, and pipeline.

Similarly, it's tempting to think that there's nothing about this initial aspect of the pipeline for a build engineer, IT manager, or technical director to be concerned about. But not only does the overall pipeline and process affect the resultant content that passes through it, there are nonetheless considerations for all parties at each step along the way:

- These source assets need to be checked in to the game's source control repository. They are a dependency needed by the build process—without these files there's nothing to build.
- For in-house audio staff, i.e. personnel creating assets that you have a responsibility to support, you need a backup solution for all the work that went into creating these source assets. Whilst it's not unheard of for artists to check in their complete source (e.g. Photoshop or 3ds Max projects) that's not a good idea with audio folks' work—an individual audio project (e.g. for a single piece of music) can be several gigabytes in size, which is an awful lot of wasted time and network bandwidth if everyone on the team is synchronizing that data, not to mention incredibly frustrating for those poor people working offsite! So, a separate repository just for audio personnel to back up their work is wise, and it's pretty much essential if there is more than one person on the audio team and they have overlap in their responsibilities. Just keep an eye on your server space—audio has a habit of growing rapidly once it hits its stride.

Audio Asset Setup

This process involves the audio team grouping individual audio assets into complex audio events and setting up their parameters—an audio event is what the game will trigger in order to make some audio happen, but how the audio then behaves (and whether it decides to even play at all) is defined by how that event has been configured here. It might be a group of sounds from which one sound is randomly selected and played back with a random variation in pitch

(as in the aforementioned footsteps example), or it might be a complex dynamic event that changes depending upon two different game states being fed into it (e.g. the rotational velocity and length of a grappling hook rope as it swings through the air and is manipulated by the player).

This work is most commonly done in an interactive audio "design tool", which could be a piece of proprietary tech or it may be a middleware solution—game audio tech generally consists of a runtime audio engine plus a design tool (or software suite) for setting up and configuring the audio and its behavior. There are a couple of things to consider here:

- This audio project metadata needs to be checked in to the game's repository—it's also needed by the build process and gets turned into the equivalent in-game binary assets.
- It's very easy for the design tool's project file to become a workflow bottleneck even with just two audio personnel trying to access it on a daily basis. Whilst the project file might be mergeable (if it's stored in a text-based format such as XML), this is error prone and not user-friendly. If your design tool doesn't have a solution for multiple users then using multiple project files split into sensible categories (music, ambiences, voice, creatures etc., or even just good old-fashioned 'levels' if that suits the game you're making) can vastly improve the situation. There are many ways to skin this cat but, ideally, you want to allow for granularity so that lots of people can work on the audio at the same time, whilst also providing some manner of high-level control that allows entire categories of sound and music to be easily adjusted (both off-line and in real-time by the game).

In-Game Audio Asset Build Process

This is where things get interesting! Whilst a smaller game project may reference and load all of its audio files directly—even foregoing an interactive audio design tool and opting to set up everything painfully by hand in the game's code—for most game projects the audio assets will be built into compressed "soundbanks" (collections of packaged up, compressed sound files). This can range from just one soundbank for the whole game (a memory resident bank composed of all the sound effects, perhaps with streaming files being accessed directly) to one soundbank per audio event (i.e. hundreds of soundbanks) and everywhere in-between, depending on how the audio needs to be divided up for the game to access. Basically, whatever works best for the game at hand is good here, but a smooth workflow which minimizes human error should be the top priority.

Historically, soundbanks were loaded in their entirety, so there was a direct relationship between the content of a soundbank and the requirements of a game's loading scheme. Managing this manually

was difficult and problematic—if you forgot to put sounds into a soundbank, or there wasn't enough memory for a soundbank to load into, the sounds wouldn't be loaded for the game to play. As games grew and large streaming worlds became a possibility, there was an investment in automated build processes to determine what sounds were needed for a given location and package them up for optimized loading. These days, automated bank building, dynamic memory management, and good diagnostic tools have created a powerful playground for audio designers to bring our virtual worlds to life with sound and music.

But on small- to medium-sized projects, manual configuration and management of soundbanks by the audio team is still *de rigueur*. This isn't quite as hairy as it sounds—modern audio engines are able to load sounds by pulling them out of a soundbank which means you can avoid having a large, unmanageable number of them. However, fitting everything into memory is still a restraint which needs consideration, planning, and technical solutions.

As with any build process, turnaround time is one of the most critical factors—the longer it takes for audio content creators and implementers to hear their work in the game, the slower they are able to iterate on it and the less productive they will be. A build process which requires them to wait for a complete deploy of the game (if that's when the audio is packaged up and built) is a broken one and rather behind the times. Ironically, this is more likely on larger projects with a complex build process. Ideally, content creators should be able to build their changes locally so they can preview and test them prior to committing their work—one advantage that a small project has is that by building the soundbanks manually they are able to do precisely this. Generally, a reboot of the game is needed to hear changes to audio content, but real-time update is possible (albeit technically tricky and a bit hacky) and is becoming increasingly common.

Trusting the audio team to always faultlessly commit the latest soundbanks isn't a foolproof solution, so a hybrid approach whereby the game deploy build process will build up-to-date banks based on the latest submitted audio project files may be useful.

Implementation of Audio Assets

There are a multitude of implementation methods for audio in a game:

- Directly calling a sound event in the game's code
- Inserting a call to a sound event into a script
- Creating bespoke solutions for complex audio implementations (e.g. setting up interactive music transitions, though middleware is increasingly useful here)

- Creating data-driven audio systems for common tasks (e.g. setting up and tagging physics audio with ease)
- Implementing sound events and triggers directly into the game's environment or level logic using a level editor
- Implementing sound events into other systems, such as animation, using their editing tools

Any method which enables audio implementation without taking up a coder's time has obvious benefits for all parties and project quality. But perhaps it's worth drawing your attention to those last two methods which are based upon the notion of audio functionality being tacked on to an already existing piece of tech (such as a level editor, or an animation tool). This makes sense when the audio is being driven by another system and is a good way of tying the two together. Access bottlenecks are intrinsic to this kind of solution—if audio event triggers are being added to an asset (be it a level, area of the map, or an animation) then the audio implementer needs sole access to that asset in order to make their changes. Process plays an important part in resolving these kind of workflow conflicts, but it's not unheard of for audio implementation to be segregated into a separate editable layer—this can work but it's not a magic bullet because it means that changes to an asset don't update the audio layer and are done in ignorance of the audio, which may actually end up creating more problems than it solves. The right approach here really depends on the project, the team and the tools.

One of the most radical changes that can happen towards the end of production, once the core of the audio experience has already been implemented, is the delivery and implementation of localized assets. This may affect every asset that contains speech, which just so happen to be some of a game's largest files, and will multiply their footprint by the number of supported languages—sixteen languages is common these days for a console release, and the number is constantly growing as new markets emerge around the world. Tools for analyzing and comparing localized assets to the primary language's master assets are invaluable and help maintain consistency across languages as well as assist in looking for problems such as missing or misnamed assets, or rogue files that are the wrong length. A pipeline which automates the process of adding localized assets to the game (e.g. drop the files in the appropriate folder and off it goes building banks, setting up file substitutions, and tracking changes) is how it should be and makes deploying the game to localization QA relatively fast and painless at a very busy time of the project.

As with every other aspect of game development, audio requires a magical blend of technology, craft, and teamwork, all of which need to be mastered if we are to create compelling interactive entertainment experiences for players to enjoy.

Section 10 Interlude 5: Game Audio: 2D, 3D, Mono and Stereo

Geoff Scott, Composer/Musician/Producer, Altitude Music

3D vs 2D Playback of Mono Sources

Understanding how a sound will be integrated will give you insight into how a particular group of sounds should be mastered. Furthermore, knowing if a sound will be attenuated on the fly could fundamentally change how you design it in the first place. Thinking of these sounds as 2D or 3D could help you in your preparation of assets, and in your evaluation of them, after they have been integrated.

2D audio is any mono sound played without dynamic attenuation or positioning. They are typically routed through the center channel, but in a basic stereo setup the files are played equally through the left and right channel simulating a centered effect. For example: voiceovers and UI sounds. These sounds are relatively high priority in the sonic spectrum and should be heard on top of the mix and in front of you.

3D audio is any sound that is dynamically attenuated or positioned. 3D sounds are positioned in the left right spectrum and are usually attached to in-game objects.

A few examples:

- Static objects, like a waterfall or windmill, where you want them to get louder as you approach them and quieter as you move away, and to be dynamically positioned—this can really add to the emersion of the environment
- In-game animations, like a combat attack or emote from an enemy (often 3D positioning and attenuation can give the player a strategic advantage by locating the direction and distance of an enemy using sound)
- Dynamically generated ambient sounds, such as birds, which can really create a "non-looping", organic environment (this implementation is often paired with other parameters like dynamic pitch shifting, random sound file calling, and frequency of playback).

Note on stereo audio sources: They fall into the 2D category, in the sense that they are not positioned or attenuated. However, stereo files will be perceived as 3D since they will contain content that will be heard to the left and right of center with more dynamics in general.

Mono vs Stereo

In order to decide if a waveform should be stereo or mono, you first need to know how the sound will be used and/or integrated. Different audio engines have different feature sets and should inform

what is allowed. In some cases there won't be an inclusive audio engine, there may be just a few features within the code base that allow, for example, streaming audio or the ability to trigger a sound on an event or animation. It is also important to make the stereo/mono distinction in consideration of performance, where a mono file is half the size of a stereo file that has the same length. As a general rule, if a source file is mono it should never be made stereo. Below are a few general guidelines for preparing your audio assets.

Mono examples:

- Voice overs
- User interface sounds and alerts
- 3D Sounds (sounds that are dynamically played and attenuated across the stereo or 360 degree field)

Stereo examples:

- Music
- Ambience
- Audio prepared for video

Section 10 Interlude 6: Audio Flexibility in the Game Environment

Kevin Patzelt, Audio Director, Undead Labs

One thing that is constant during the game development cycle is change. No matter how "final" a list of assets from art or design appears, there is always going to be refinement, adjustments, and tuning. More often than not, these changes come at the last minute and will most definitely affect the aesthetic of the audio design. One way to prepare the audio design for this situation is to organize and implement assets with flexibility as part of the audio pipeline.

The easiest way to accomplish this is by utilizing middleware such as FMOD. With multi-track editing it is easy to create combinations of sounds using multiple layers instead of committing to a one-event-one-sound implementation. As one example, if you're designing a sound for a car impact that explodes, the sound will likely include moments of metal crunching, glass shattering, tires screeching, pieces of the car impacting the ground, and the vehicle exploding. Thinking as a sound designer, these sounds might be authored into a single sound file. However, if the end of the project nears and the art or design of this vehicle impact changes and the car no longer explodes, the sound editor will have to go back to the original assets to redesign the sound. If instead, each layer of the sound is available as its own file and the sound event is constructed through the functionality of the middleware, it would be easy to remove the explosion layer and have the rest of the sounds continue supporting the new impact visual. These situations have arisen in almost every game system in my latest project, from combat to physics impacts to Foley.

This approach will require more processing power from the game engine as it has to sum several assets together to create a single event. If the overhead is available, you can ship the project with these fragmented events. By doing so you've provided much more audio diversity to your sound design as each layer can have randomizing values set for asset selection, pitch, and volume. No two events will ever sound the same. However, if an optimization pass is required, you've been able to tune each layer as the design is finalized and these assets can be easily summed together using FMOD's internal recording tools to output single files of your complex events (note: projects that utilize Wwise or other middleware can easily rerecord the output of the project into any audio editor to achieve the same goal). The beauty to this is that the summed sound files will be utilizing the pitch and volume variation you've authored into the original events and will be ready to play at the proper volume when reimplemented into the engine to replace the layered event. Having just completed a project using this approach prevented a lot of sound design rework. This was especially crucial since in a department of one, that time was simply unavailable.

Working this way requires a negotiation between flexibility and efficiency. The audio pipeline of your project will help determine this balance. Deciding which sounds are grouped together and where they are located in the project structure will enable the audio designer to respond quickly when changes or optimizations are required. Continue with the example of the car crash from above. All of these layers could be implemented individually, however some could easily be grouped to maximize efficiency. The metal crunching and glass shattering that occur on the initial impact would be a likely candidate for being summed into one sound. The tire screeching, however, will probably continue to stay as a separate layer and is most likely loaded in a different project or work unit if using FMOD or Wwise. Keep in mind that the more your assets are spread out in your middleware structure, the harder it is going to be to sum those events together if an optimization pass is needed.

In game projects there tend to be a set of global sounds that are shared and reused throughout the title. User interface sound effects are usually on this list but so are sound categories like fire, explosions, or even physics impacts. With pitch and volume changes, individual sound assets can be transformed to support a broad range of visuals. The more a sound is used, the less likely it should be summed to simplify a layered event. Summing an event with a commonly used sound could be more efficient but you are losing a great amount of flexibility, especially if that sound sample exists multiple times in the game. This is especially valid if these common sounds are globally loaded in your title.

The key to this approach is realizing that there is no "right" way to implement and manage a layered pipeline. It's about finding the right balance for your project.

11

TYING IT ALL TOGETHER

Tim Green; Matt Hoesterey; Hannes Ricklefs; Mark Streatfield; Steve Theodore

The mantra of design, design, design will help assure the pipeline you create will satisfy the needs of the project as it expands and contracts. If you design your pipeline through guesswork you will most likely fail so don't simply build your pipeline based on random requirements that occur to you as you put things in place. Pipelines are an investment and like many things in business you'll often need to balance your list of essentials between the long and short term.

Section 11.1 What You Will Learn From This Chapter

In this chapter we will offer an overview of what this book has covered, what requirements must be considered and pitfalls to avoid. As always, we will include the similarities and differences between film and games, attempting to highlight the unique requirements of each. We will close the chapter with a short list of educational resources.

Section 11.2 Analyze the Business Requirements

It's best to recognize and document unmovable constraints early in the project where even a simple thing such as knowing if you have to support Linux and Windows can affect your design. Take time to think about how your pipeline needs to work, get key stakeholders involved, discuss the requirements, actually draw it out on paper. How much time do you have to build it? Every project has deadlines and a common pitfall is spending too much time on the "plumbing" and not enough building the project. Having the best pipeline in the world won't do you any good if you miss your deadline and the company goes out of business.

Consider what makes your facility unique: is there a particular culture or ideology that makes your company stand out? What methodology do you want to promote in your pipeline? Is your pipeline

task, asset, or story driven? Thoroughly reviewing the pipeline's needs will influence how data is structured and flows through the pipeline, and act as a rationale for some decisions.

What are the core values of the production the pipeline needs to support? You need to be able to prioritize features and make investments that support the unique challenges and needs of your production—it doesn't make sense to create a complex, innovative motion capture pipeline for a production focused on giant spaceships, or to create a custom fluid renderer for a show where all the water shots are off in the distance, or building a sophisticated fluid simulator that becomes useless when the amount of detail sent to be rendered takes months to compute. Conversely, you should consider ambitious plans when they support the ambitions of the project: the ultimate job of the pipeline is to let the artists find the creative heart of the project, so identify and tackle the hardest challenges.

The skills that make up the company culture are important factors that should drive the style of pipeline. What people do you have available already and what people do you still need? If you don't have the people you need it may take many months to find the right person and many more months before they get up to speed.

As a general rule, the longer your project's pipeline needs to be maintained the more time you should put into building it. Does your company have plans to transition to entirely new technology in a year or are you making a massively multiplayer online game that will need to be maintained for ten years? What elements of your pipeline will you be able to use on future projects? Some elements of your pipeline may be project specific while others may be used again and again over the years. Are you creating a one-off product for a unique platform? If an element of your pipeline is project specific, a general rule is that it should save you time on that project. Spending a week building an automated import system to save your artists from having to manually import thousands of assets could be worth it, but spending a week building a tool to automate a tedious one day project specific task is not a wise use of your time. However, if an element of your pipeline will be used on future projects then it may be worth spending more time building the pipeline then it will return in savings over the course of a single project.

In film where multiple projects are often worked on in tandem with various teams ramping up and winding down, it is important to understand what the long-term vision/ambitions of the studio are. Will there be the need to support multiple project types: animated features, VFX productions, TVC, digital installations, etc.? What is the expected global shot count? Are there are any potential acquisitions or mergers? Will the workload be shared with other companies or will they run in complete isolation? Studios tend to fall into certain specialties; studio A might be perfect for characters and crowds, studio B is fantastic for FX, studio C is known to deal with large volumes. Each one of these

examples has different requirements, software as well as hardware, for supporting the different workflows, so be sure to understand where the emphasis should be placed.

It is equally important to understand the overall approach for how the work is to be completed, and it's crucial to know at what stages in the pipeline will work be presented to the client and in what format; do you need to do animation approval on fully composited shots or are you going to show animation as simple playblasts?

You need to recite this to yourself constantly: the purpose of a pipeline is to assist artists and production staff to accomplish the visual goals of the project. Therefore, building an efficient pipeline is often an "outside in" approach. First, you must understand who your customers are, and next you decide what you need in order to get started.

Section 11.3 Process Decisions From Workflow to Mapping the Organization

Understanding what needs to be achieved at any stage of the pipeline not only makes it clear what the overall work entails but also helps define the priorities, such as which components to build first because they are essential, and which requests are simply nice to have. To properly handle this, begin by considering the following constraints:

- What is the schedule and resource plan for both human and machine resources?
- How is custom software going to be built, source controlled, configured, and deployed?
- What software languages will custom software be written in?
- What system is going to be used to track bugs with custom software (Track, RT, Bugzilla, Mantis) and what support contracts with the "internal" clients (the other departments) will be put in place?
- What's the workflow, and how do you want data to flow through the company? For example, should the compositor be able to publish a new camera version, or should that always go back to the camera department? What are the pre-requisites for lighting to start?

Understanding the data flow will help design an effective workflow. Pay particular attention to blockers; you don't want to block people from working because they don't have access to the data they need.

What are your reviewables? At each stage of the pipeline you need to define what is the reviewable content and decide how you look at the asset being produced, provide constructive feedback and integrate that back into the system for the next step; you don't want to make a closed box, you should be able to view every asset made at any stage.

What individual or group will be accountable for the pipeline? The accountable person or group should at all times know how the pipeline works and what the pipeline is capable of. They should approve and be responsible for any changes to the pipeline to ensure they are consistent with the overall design.

Evaluate your options in render farm software, renderer, etc. Don't just push for the one that sounds the sexiest or comes with a nice fancy logo. Evaluate the different products, decide which fits the problem you are trying to solve, which you can afford etc., etc. Make it an objective decision, the best, most informed decisions you can, but above all, make a decision.

When evaluating interactive tools, consider how they would work in a large team environment. Consider if the file being edited by the tool needs to be shared and merged, and the ease of inserting the tool into a pipeline. How will data flow into this tool from an upstream source, how will data flow out of the tool to a downstream target? Even if the tool offered the best UI for the job it is of no use if the data it authors can't be accessed and used downstream. This is especially important in games when considering interactive tools such as level editors, animation blend tree authoring, or particle systems editors that are demoed in a meeting room environment by a sales team.

The only thing that is consistent is change, an adage that holds true from film directors reconstructing entire sequences or large game projects replacing the target platform to commercial tools integral to your established pipeline that are no longer available. Change to the pipeline is inevitable, and when it occurs it is important to evaluate carefully and announce those changes to all relevant parties. This ensures the upcoming changes are understood, that the team knows when they will be implemented, and how those changes will affect the workflow. However, it will be almost impossible to plan for all scenarios at the outset. You can't always predict what shifts will occur, but you can predict that change will happen no matter what, and preparing for the inevitable mutation allows for a much better success rate. Building such provisions into a pipeline can be costly, but it's far more expensive when a change is required and your pipelines are too rigid to accommodate it.

Section 11.4 Technical and Infrastructure Decisions

It is equally important to look at the basics required to build a pipeline as well as deciding what to buy and what to build. You need to consider the foundation, the core technologies that will form the spine of your pipeline. At the very least this will include the asset management system, production tracking, a naming convention/directory structure and a file interchange format. Identify what these are and make sure everything else revolves around them.

As you are defining the criteria you must do so while resolving the following:

- What operating systems will be used?
- What software will manage the render farm and what processes will run on it (Qube, Alfred, Tractor, Opensource options such as SunGridEngine)?
- What are the requirements for the asset management system? Will you use Shotgun/Tank, Tactic, or Build a Custom solution? Are you going to keep track of hours and burn down rate in a program like Excel or are you planning on integrating a full-blown product tracking solution? How are assets being organized? Have you thought about access time? How are work files separated from build files? Have you reduced unnecessary redundancies?
- What network infrastructure is being built—star based, subnet? What hardware is going to be available for switches, etc.?
- What middleware solutions will you need? Have you done your due diligence to understand all the potential pitfalls and risks involved with using a specific middleware? Do you know how long it will take to integrate?
- How big is your team? How many people will need access to a particular file? Have you designed your pipeline to avoid shared and unmergeable files?
- How will user accounts be authenticated and how will account permissions be implemented and managed?
- How will you review the material, both internally and with the client?
- What storage vendor, amount, and archive options should be catered for? Is there a requirement to archive all production data and to what required time periods?
- What are your hero applications? For any CG work: Maya or Houdini? For rendering: PRMan or Arnold? For managing the render farm: Tractor or Rush? What Software will be use for each of the disciplines? Will you need to purchase/run more than one?

3D packages such as Maya, SoftImage, 3DStudioMax, and Houdini have capabilities that often overlap, raising the question if a studio should buy one, two, or if all should be used.

What hardware vendor will be used for the renderfarm and workstations? What renderer will you use and how will you use it? While a pipeline should be able to support multiple renderers, integrating a particular renderer well takes a significant amount of time. You should try to work through a layer of abstraction whenever you interact with the renderer, but it is more important to spend the time making sure that you are able to exploit the advanced functionality in your renderer. No lighter would give up a clean workflow around progressive rerendering so that a renderer that their project isn't using could be supported.

Another primary concern is how to build scalability into your pipeline—at the very least you have to acknowledge its existence and

identify areas that will obviously need to scale, will easily scale, and will need serious investment to scale. If you bolt it on as an added extra you'll never get the full benefit your pipeline can offer.

As you make these decisions make sure you avoid pitfalls caused by trying reinvent the wheel; with a little research you may discover someone else has done it before, and they've done it better than you. What technology can you use that is open source (Alembic, OpenEXR etc.), and what do you need to buy? Can you contribute back to these projects if you need to make changes? And consider what breaks the rules. Exceptions to the rule are ok, but only if there is a good reason. If you make a decision that doesn't fit with the rest of the pipeline, understand why you are making that decision, identify the consequences, and document the information and reasons for the decision.

But wait, there's more! A good pipeline needs to provide debugging tools that help you find and diagnose platform specific problems you may run into. You will want to provide a common infrastructure for all your tools to manage debugging and diagnostic information. This can range from the very simple, such as a standardized location for log files, to a more complex system where errors are logged to a database and problem notifications are sent to the pipeline team when problems arise. If your studio already uses an issue tracking system, the easiest way is to leverage it but however you decide to proceed, encourage all pipeline developers to use the same standards and tools for handling error reports. Debugging problems with the pipeline is tough enough, and it's a lot tougher if no two parts of the pipeline report problems the same way.

You will need a strategy for distributing tools to your users, making sure that users are kept up to date and bug fixes are easily distributed to the team while balancing immediacy with safety, deciding on an approach that ensures evolution of the pipeline tools doesn't disrupt the production.

- How much of your tools development will be exposed to the users?
- Will they see everything you create as soon as it's ready, or will you send tools through a formal QA process?
- Will you release tools when they are done or on a pre-planned schedule?

Once you've worked out the format you'll also need to consider the physical method for distributing tools. A simple system such as keeping the latest version of the tools on a shared network drive is simple to implement but requires discipline on the part of the users. Using a version control system leverages the version management tools you already have, as long as your users are already accustomed to working with them and keeping themselves up to date. However, a version control system won't automatically run any update procedures, such as file format conversions or refactoring of old data, it just makes sure that users have the same bits on their disks.

Another option is web-based toolkits, like Microsoft's ClickOnce or Java Web Start, which allow tools to "phone home" to a web server and automatically update themselves as needed. However, they also require a server and the IT resources needed to maintain it. Web-only tools that run in a browser are always up to date by definition and can be shared with teams all over the world without extra effort, but keep in mind web-based tools don't natively have the ability to interact with the users' local file systems and are best used for things like working with databases or submitting files to remote servers.

Section 11.5 The Unique Considerations of Film and Games

While many pipeline requirements for film and game pipelines overlap, each has distinctive requirements. For example, with multiple studios (a common situation in film and a growing one with games), when passing data between facilities you need to consider bandwidth requirements, if you require a dedicated network link, how the work will be shared, and what means of communication you need to provide.

In film or in game cinematics, you must consider what is the approach to rendering, if it will it be physically based, raytracing or scanline. For example, the decision to use a raytracer such as Arnold might reduce the need for storage but the need for render capacity will increase. On the other hand, using Pixar's Renderman increases the requirements for more storage but might require less render time.

In games, always bear in mind what type of game are you making and what platform you are building for. Building for PC has unique considerations, as does building for multiple consoles, and each of the platforms requires specific steps for testing. The more game platforms you are building for, the more complex your pipeline will need to be, with each platform requiring different export processes. Different platforms can have different performance capabilities and often different assets will need to be created for each platform. A game shipping on the PC ported to Xbox, for example, may need lower resolution textures created for characters and environments. Depending on the platform, a good pipeline can make this process easy by allowing assets to reference multiple textures. You need to set up your pipeline to accommodate these variations.

Each pipeline that provides data for the various game systems must be built and tested before production, and there are many different types of data required by the game. The art data sources, though byte for byte the largest quantity of data, are only a few types amid many, such as the physics simulation world, AI data, or gameplay logic. Many of these data sources are co-dependent and it is not uncommon for art data and gameplay data to be so tightly coupled that the

artist authoring one will also (under direction from the game play team or coders) author the other, such as the physics mesh that is similar to the visible mesh, but less detailed. This is often a culture shock for modelers and animators moving from the film industry to the games industry.

Does your pipeline setup support branching? In games development it's often necessary to branch. If your product will be required to branch it's important that your source control solution support that requirement.

If you are distributing the project online you must make sure you have all the necessary online infrastructure to distribute your product. You may need to optimize download times, and if you do, you must decide how your pipeline supports these future optimizations.

Section 11.6 Building and Proving Pipelines

The race to finish the pipeline before the first day of full production is frequently complicated by unexpected discoveries or changes of direction during prototyping. Planned features get cut, and new ones added, while the first day of production draws inexorably closer. It is, alas, far from unheard of for production to start while key areas of the pipeline are still on the drawing board. Careful coordination with the people in charge of the production schedule can minimize the inconveniences to the project, but starting full production with a half-finished toolset is still a significant risk.

One way to minimize the risk is to design the pipeline for graceful evolution. Much like a website or online service, a pipeline is really an ongoing service rather than a simple set of software tools—it will never be "finished". Instead, the pipeline and the individual tools that comprise it should be built with modular pieces that can be expanded and refined as the project matures. Baseline functionality needs to be ready on day one so that the art staff can begin work; this means that key decisions such as how to move data through the pipeline or how to track assets are made early. However, refinements to the user interface and productivity enhancing tools for artists can come online gradually—not only does this lessen the danger of racing too heedlessly to meet the production deadline, it also means that user-facing decisions can be made with feedback from a larger, more informed pool of users.

Fortunately for pipeline developers, the agile programming movement provides an excellent set of practices for working in precisely this kind of service-oriented, fluid environment. The agile philosophy stresses fast delivery, ongoing improvement, and quick responses to emergent problems over massive centralized planning. Agile encourages coders to work closely with their "customers" to define needs clearly and then serve those needs iteratively. Agile teams typically work in "sprints"—short, tightly focused bouts of work (often as short

as a week or two), each of which delivers only a single feature or system. The next sprint is then planned based on the priorities of the moment, helping to keep the team focused on the problems which are actually currently important to the project rather than things that seemed important in a planning meeting eighteen months ago. Since pipeline work is all about dealing with the emergent chaos of production, it's easy to see why the agile approach, which stresses adaptation to change and willingness to shift direction as circumstances dictate, has come to dominate the way pipeline teams look at their work.

An important complement to the agile methodology is the heavy use of automated software testing, usually referred to as "Test-Driven Development" or TDD. In TDD, coders create simple testing programs in order to ensure that the behavior of their code doesn't change in unexpected ways. Suppose, for example, that a team uses a piece of software to generate predictably structured file names for their pipeline. The tests for that bit of code would feed in a known set of parameters and guarantee that the expected results were produced. This adds a very valuable level of safety and stability to the constant churn of an ever-evolving pipeline.

Section 11.7 Development Methodologies

The primary goal for building a pipeline is to constantly ensure work is safely and efficiently passed through all the artists from start to finish, but how you achieve that is a primary concern.

It is important to define user interface guidelines including style guides for UI elements, how command line tools should behave, coding standards, and error handling. To encourage an intuitive working experience, avoid inconsistent UIs and application behaviors, and instead seek to reuse UI libraries to help to keep the look, feel, and user experience consistent. Building a modular structure and providing APIs that reuse the custom software is a way to achieve this. Storage management such as creating, deleting, moving, and renaming of directories and files is one example. Another would be database connectivity, image sequences (renaming and renumbering), access to the asset management, and production scheduling. Be sure to include detailed documentation, since often people under pressure will lean towards writing their own code rather than spend time understanding someone else's.

Be sure the APIs don't tie to particular software vendors or open-source projects as there is no guarantee that the software will be available, supported, and maintained in the future. The same applies to hardware; it's common for vendors to ship custom APIs meant to open up features specific to their own hardware. If these features become an essential part of your overall system it could be quite time-consuming to move over to a different vendor at a later date.

While building any pipeline, it's important to keep the aspect of security in mind. Both authentication (confirming the person is who they claim to be, a step normally achieved through username and password) and authorization (does the user have the permission to execute this operation) are essential. The VFX industry is subject to very strong security audits, controlling how people enter the building, what websites can be accessed, how staff log on to the machines, what restrictions allow uploading data to the internet, and the ability to mount external storage devices, burn DVDs or CDs, or check if the network is partitioned. It's not uncommon for these audits to happen multiple times throughout the year, from both the MPAA and from the client studios. Acknowledging the security requirements while building your pipeline is highly recommended, as having to retrofit them at a later date can be very costly.

One concern is how you create accountability. It's important that people are held responsible for maintaining a pipeline. Often the best way to ensure that your pipeline doesn't degrade over the course of a product is to assign a sole owner who is responsible for monitoring and maintaining the pipeline. That way should someone break a naming convention, create a duplicate folder structure, or invent their own coding standard a responsible entity will be set in place to alert the transgressor of their mistake and ensure that the problem is fixed.

Without logging there is no record of what happened and what went wrong. Logging should be a base service and should, in some form, be present in each and every tool in your pipeline. Logs are not perfect, they do have their problems if they are improperly designed. No log at all is nearly as bad as one that offers no way of easily extracting information from a mountain of data.

When logging data, consider that someone will need to trawl through to extract information about a fail-condition, a task that often is needed under stressful circumstances. Providing a consistent set of searchable keywords and sentence structure that plays nice with regular expressions could spare many minutes if not hours of time that it takes to identify the cause of a problem. In some circumstances a better approach is to ditch linear logs altogether and store structured logging information in a database, providing a mechanism for the user to drill down to the required information. Take time to consider what could go wrong and build in provision that will reduce the time you spend fixing problems at someone else's desk. Make the diagnostic tools good and the user will fix their own problems, leaving you time to write more tools.

You might go as far as to say that a pipeline almost becomes unnecessary if everybody works to clearly defined processes. If everything is laid out, documented, understood, and people don't make naming errors it should—in theory—be possible to run a production without the need of any software that provides version control and dependency tracking. But seriously, who believes that will happen?!

Section 11.8 Further Education

There are multiple options/resources to learn more about VFX as a whole or pipelines in particular, ranging from online blogs to user-groups, from mailing lists to educational courses. While still too few, there is an ever-increasing and ever-changing number of additional educational sources available. It is impossible to list them all, but here are a few to get you started:

Credited and Non Credited Courses

Further education in the form of bricks and mortar university courses and online tuition provide a more formal and structured approach to learning the art of VFX and game production, often in collaboration with a number of industry partners.

- Entertainment Technology Center, Carnegie Mellon: www.etc.cmu. edu/site/. Located in Pittsburgh, Pennsylvania, USA, a two-year program focusing on interdisciplinary collaboration of artists with computer scientists and engineers, working together on common projects.
- MIT Open Courseware, Massachusetts Institute of Technology: http://ocw.mit.edu/courses/find-by-topic/. Under the catagory of engineering, this school offers a wide range of undegraduate to graduate computer science classes. Located in Cambridge, Massachusetts, USA.
- Full Sail University: www.fullsail.edu/degrees/campus/software-development-bachelors. Located in Winter Park, Florida, USA, the Software Development bachelor's program offers instruction on software-based solutions from design to implimentation.
- University of California: www.universityofcalifornia.edu/academics/engcs.html. With many locations throughout California, UC offers a substantial selection of computer science and engineering courses.
- Autodesk University: http://au.autodesk.com/?nd=au_las_vegas. Both on-line and on-site training on all things Autodesk.
- DigiPen Institute of Technology: www.digipen.edu/. Offers degree programs and continuing education is areas ranging from computer science to animation. Located in Redmond, Washington, USA.
- Bournemouth University: http://courses.bournemouth.ac.uk/courses/undergraduate-degree/software-systems/175/. Offering courses ranging from IT management to forensic computing and security to software development for animation, games, and effects. Located in the UK.
- Birmingham City University, Computer Games Technology: www.bcu.ac.uk/courses/computer-games-technology. Also in the UK, the study program covers the fundamentals of computer science, user interfaces and AI (Artificial Intelligence).

- Abertay University: www.abertay.ac.uk/studying/schools/amg/computergamescourses/. Dundee, Scotland based offering game courses ranging from applications developement to games technology.
- University of Bedfordshire: www.beds.ac.uk/howtoapply/courses/undergraduate/computer-games-development. Covering skills such as writing game code from scratch to integrating various game technologies. Located in Bedfordshire, UK.
- Creative Skillset: www.creativeskillset.org/games/. A UK-based information source for education and training in games.

Online Sources

There is a seemingly endless number of online resources for information covering aspects of the industry from new releases to news to forums. Some are updated daily, others archive papers that remain valuable for a long time. Many VFX professionals have launched their own websites covering everything from creating plug-ins for software applications to how-to guides. As with all information found on the Internet, you must be mindful of how reliable the information is, but the internet can be a great source for community websites. It would take a second book to list all the sources available, a book that would never be up to date or all-encompassing, but below is a fraction of the more popular sites to get you started.

- fxguide: www.fxguide.com/. A very popular news site that is updated daily.
- Slashdot: http://slashdot.org/. Another popular news site "powered by your submissions."
- Gizmodo: http://gizmodo.com/. A news site that covers a broad range of topics.
- Game Studies: http://gamestudies.org/1102. Focusing on games, a collection of thought-provoking articles discussing "ideas and theories."
- Center for Computer Game Research: http://game.itu.dk/index.php/About. A collection of articles and papers from some of the best sources, including IEEE and AMC SIGGRAPH.
- Digital-Tutors: www.digitaltutors.com/11/index.php. A membership site offering a wide range of courses from basic modeling to scripting.
- fxphd: www.fxphd.com/fxphd/courseInfo.php. This site offers a range of courses with a special section just for pipelines (see checkbox menu near the top of the page).
- CGTalk Development and Hardware forums: http://forums.cgsociety.org/forumdisplay.php?f=108. A subsection of CGTalk focusing on development and hardware discussions, news, and opinions.
- Studio Sys Admins: www.studiosysadmins.com/. An active forum of developers, engineers, system administrators, hardware/software

vendors, and CTOs etc. who discuss problems related to the more technical side of building a studio.

- Scriptspot: www.scriptspot.com/
- Tech-Artists.Org: http://tech-artists.org/
- The Toolsmiths: http://thetoolsmiths.org/. The blog of the IGDA special interest group on tools. It has been a forum for discussing pipeline programming since 2009.

Conferences and Organizations

There are a number of conferences held throughout the year whose focus is digital media production, although the level of pipeline-related content does vary from year to year. Most of these conferences publish their proceedings online which can be accessed, sometimes for a fee, as reference. This might include videos of a talk, technical papers, or links off to other sites. If you can't make the conference in person, use of these proceedings gives you access to a wealth of information which is usually of research/university standard.

- FMX: http://www.fmx.de/. One of the primary European conferences covering animation, effects, games, and transmedia.
- AMC SIGGRAPH: www.siggraph.org/. Two conferences a year, one in USA/Canada and one in Asia. The biggest conference within the VFX industry covering a wide variety of topics.
- NAB: www.nabshow.com/. Held in the USA looking at content creation, delivery, and management.
- VIEW Conference: www.viewconference.it/. An Italian-based conference on computer graphics, interactive techniques, VFX, and computer games. While it focuses mainly on the graphic side of production it does offer the occasional course on topics related to the pipeline.
- GDC Conference: www.gdconf.com/. The Game Developers Conference, held every spring in the US, is the global gathering of the games industry. In addition to a full program of case studies and lecture courses on all aspects of game development, the show hosts several events of special interest to pipeline developers. The Tech Artists Bootcamp is an all-day series of lectures for technical artists where many key aspects of the pipeline, including both general tools programming practice and special problems in graphics are covered. The Technical Art, Technical Animation, and Tools Programming roundtables are open forums for specialists to discuss technical problems and share experience.
- E3 Conference: www.e3expo.com/. For the latest in games and electronic entertainment held in the USA.
- IBC Conference: www.ibc.org/. European conference similar in nature to NAB.
- Createasphere Digital Asset Management conference: http://createasphere.com/. Annual conference in New York City.

- DAM NY: http://henrystewartconferences.com/dam/damny2012/. Conference covering the "art and practice of managing digital media".
- Eurographics: www.eg.org/. A European professional computer graphics association.
- IEEE Computer Society: www.computer.org/portal/web/guest/home.
- The IGDA (International Game Developers Association): www.igda.org. The largest professional forum for game developers. Local IGDA chapters around the world host regular meetings, usually in association with local development studios or educational institutions.

User Groups and Mailing Lists

Almost all open source software projects have some form of community associated with them, usually in the form of a mailing list or group. If you use or are even simply interested in a particular piece of open source software, you should consider joining the discussions and becoming active in the community. By subscribing to the mailing list you'll be exposed to other users and uses of the software which might create new opportunities for the way you work, ensure the project continues to thrive and grow, and be able to more appropriately contribute feedback and ideas for future development. In particular, for those projects maintained specifically for the VFX community, you'll gain an insight into some of the inner workings of a studio that become apparent in the day-to-day discussion. You can also go one step further and become a contributor to the project.

- Global VFX Pipeline Google group: https://groups.google.com/forum/#!forum/global-vfx-pipelines. One of the more popular pipeline groups that is frequented by many of this book's own contributors.
- Python Programming for Autodesk Maya https://groups.google.com/forum/?fromgroups#!forum/python_inside_maya. The group tracks the development of Maya's Python integration and is of particular interest to pipeline developers.

Occasionally these groups meet in person, either as part of a larger conference such as SIGGRAPH or a more local meet-up in one of the primary urban VFX hubs. Becoming involved in these groups is a good way to reach out to the larger community and put yourself in contact with other expert minds tackling the same problems on a daily basis.

INTERLUDE: VIRTUAL PRODUCTION IN FILM AND GAMES

Gary Roberts
Virtual Production Supervisor, Digital Domain

Section 11 Interlude 1: What is Virtual Production in Film?

Virtual Production is the process of making films, video game cinematics, TV shows, commercials, music videos, and more, in the digital world in real time. Virtual production works in the traditional filmmaking world, brings new techniques and workflows to offer creative freedom and efficiency for filmmakers, commercial directors, and game developers alike. Virtual production bridges a wide range of disciplines often merging deeply into pre-visualization, performance motion capture, live action (on set integration with CG elements), post visualization, and much more. Virtual production therefore has its own set of challenges when it comes to handling assets and associated tasking.

It is worth noting that virtual production "is" production. We are making the film, the TV show, the video game cinematic within this process. This frames the topic of assets, asset management, and tasking.

One of the interesting challenges in virtual production is that it is a live interactive process for everyone on set and in production. Shooting in the virtual world (or partially, when it comes to live action integration) is generally done in real time which allows creative storytellers, filmmakers, and the entire technical team behind the production to make quick iterative changes to the physical worlds on set to compose a shot or define a character's performance. This real time approach allows traditional filmmaking techniques, terminology, and disciplines to be used within virtual production. Everyone within the team has to react quickly to requests and changes to assets (physical and digital) and more importantly, track these changes and asset modifications so they can be passed downstream into other departments during and after virtual production has ceased. No one waits long for these changes, so we

need tools and workflows that are quick to use, adaptable, and allow for such changes. Those changes can include physical actors' performances being relayed onto their digital characters as well as performances being altered, digital and physical changes to environments, sets, props, set pieces, vehicles, set decor, lighting (digital), atmospherics, etc.

At all times throughout the production process, we try to react to creative and technical requests in a way that allows us to migrate the requests and digital as well as the less common physical changes downstream in a "legal" and defined manner so they can be used correctly. Often this is difficult, given the quick time frame, as we need to react to the director in a timely manner. When this happens, it's important to make note of anything that crossed out of the legal range and then legalize it before handing it off to downstream processes and departments. It's all part of being in production.

Section 11 Interlude 2: Naming Conventions

One of the earliest considerations is what to name things, so much of what we do boils down to correctly naming assets, and making these asset names human as well as script-readable. A great deal of effort is put into naming assets, and in particular, stage takes that are captured during virtual production. This is to facilitate tracking of all elements within stage takes through production, since they will eventually comprise a desired scene and, more importantly, shots within a sequence. The naming of a stage take is important as it is tracked through editorial, camera work and on through a director's cut and into final VFX shot production. Naming the stage is one of the single most important things to get right.

Virtual production often begins not in shot world, but in scene world. A scene covers several shots and may often include two things. One could be several "setups", defined as a unique change or configuration to the physical and/or digital set. It can also include a change in the performance within a scene due to the scene not fitting in the physical capture volume, or when the scene needs to be broken up for performance reasons and tiled together. The second requirement might be "passes", where different actors or the same actors play different characters within the same scene. As we migrate through production we are adding elements to this naming convention, such as master scenes, camera shots and versions. We need to be able to track a shot back to a sequence, to a scene, to a slice of a stage take, and in turn then pull out sets, props, characters, actors, reference material notes, etc. The stage take name is important, since it gets noted in multiple places; on the slate, burn-ins, video assist, sound, motion capture, script supervisor, digital script supervisor, editorial, video witness cameras, art department, etc.

Section 11 Interlude 3: The Standard Phases

Virtual production covers a wide range of workflows depending on the production, but for simplicity's sake we will break it down into pre-production, production, post production and final delivery. Throughout these phases, asset management and associate tasking is an obvious necessity and one that should not be underestimated. Often we have to adapt to different workflows and interfaces that a production may choose to use. Generally an asset database and tasking management are achieved through unique but highly integrated software and interfaces.

Pre-Production

Pre-production typically involves receiving and/or developing key assets. Often these assets come in from third parties and may or may not be consistent or legal for the scene world. Typically, digital environments and props need to be created that can be used in virtual production within both a scene world and a shot world. Elements for the construction of these often come from the previs or storyboard team, the art department, and on-set surveys from principal photography (LIDAR, scans, photogrammetry, photo reference, etc.). If we are really lucky we can utilize digital assets from the previs team. Often they need to be decreased in complexity and polygonal resolution (along with textures) so they can be run in real time. They also need to be constructed in a way that allows for easy asset change on set in real time (i.e. moving a chair, re-positioning a tree, removing a wall, opening a door, etc.). As we do so, all these assets are assigned an asset code and tagged. At the same time, we are cheating lighting and atmospheric effects so we can give the feel for the scene and shot in real time on set. (It is worth noting that recent productions have found great success in planning and specifying these digital assets so they can be built, used, and handed off from the previs team and directly used in virtual production. The cost savings and economies of scale are valuable when this happens.)

Digital motion capture puppets (characters) are constructed to spec for virtual production. These often change at the last minute due to the creative process and virtual production has to react and accept these changes throughout production. Characters are assigned an asset code, and version; this information is important since asset generation based on actors playing the characters also has to be considered. Often characters are based on the look, movement, and physicality of the actor playing them. Virtual production is involved in the scanning, facial survey, measurement, and reference photography of the actors. From this information, physical assets are created (3D prints of heads, faces, hands, teeth, etc.) as well as digital versions. From here,

characters are conceptualized and motion capture puppets created for virtual production.

It is worth noting that any facial capture required from an actor to drive a character's face generally requires a detailed survey of the actor's face prior to production. This is often achieved via an array of video cameras filming a directed and technical performance of the actor where they are taken through a number of facial expressions (poses) and performances that will be used downstream to produce the animation of the character.

On top of this, props, set decor, lighting set-ups, and atmospheric assets are all created and managed in a similar manner leading up to the shoot.

These types of key items are also assigned to scenes and sequences, then handed to the virtual art department, art department, and ultimately construction and prop makers to build the physical versions of the digital assets. These need to be associated (asset name and version) and tracked throughout production.

At this stage it is important to introduce the term "global scale". Often actors can play characters that are larger or smaller than themselves. In these cases the physical world has to be scaled appropriately and tracked against the stage take that contains this performance.

Other "flat" assets—plate assemblies, camera tracks, storyboards, etc. are also gathered and made legal for virtual production, and tracked through the pipeline. Often these are in shot world and need to be placed and associated into the scene world.

Preparation also includes assigning asset names to actors, stunt actors, animals, and anyone/anything that is present on set as part of the performance. These will be tracked all the way through production as most physical elements have a digital counterpart. Metadata is used throughout. Everything is tracked back from the physical stage to the digital stage and through to the now infamous stage take.

Other items often treated as assets include video witness cameras that will be used on set, and face mounted cameras and head gear that actors will wear for performance capture. All of these are part of the pipeline and have asset names assigned and entered into the database, and all are associated back to the stage take.

During pre-production the production team (with the aid of the virtual production team) has to break down the previs, storyboards, and editorial reference that may exist into sequences, scenes, and then setup, and passes that can be captured on set. This is the top level node in the hierarchy of the asset management tree.

All of the above are critical for success in production, especially as we have to react quickly, make (and track) changes, and deal with time as our fourth dimension. Flexibility is the keyword here and all tools and scripts that support the generation of the above in pre-production and the changes required during production (below) must be modular, well understood by the artists using them, and flexible. This allows for

quick changes and for an artist on set to break the rules if needed in order to react to a director's request. It is essential for an artist in virtual production to understand what each tool and script does and the workflow around them, so they can adapt to change quickly and in an organized manner.

Production

On set during production, if everything is well prepared according to the processes described above, the virtual production team should be able to react quickly to the requests of the director, DP, editor, VFX supervisors, and virtual production supervisors (as well as actors and stunt coordinators). During the shoot itself we are not only using and creating digital and physical assets, we are also generating new assets—and large amounts of them.

Witness video cameras are used to obtain as much video reference of the performance on set as possible, given budget and logistic constraints. These operated cameras are striped with the same stage time code as all other devices and they record onboard to memory cards for full HD media as well as passing a live video feed to video assist for playback purposes on set. Video HD material per camera is downloaded on a daily basis and delivered to editorial and virtual production.

TSound is on-set recording audio which is striped with the same timecode and stage take name as all other devices. The motion capture team is recording the body movements of all actors and props and face mounted cameras record actors' facial performances—all of which are striped with the same time code and stage take name. Real time 3D visualization is rendering out the virtual version of the scene, striped with time code and given to video assist for record and playback purposes. Digital script supervisors are taking down all notes corresponding to the digital and virtual production world and the script supervisor is present and performing their tasks.

If the virtual production team has done their job in pre-production, all of this media is generated on set with the correct time code, metadata, and naming conventions and entered into the asset and tasking databases ready for use by all departments downstream.

During the shoot, favored performances are noted (ideally) and made ready for the next phase in virtual post production.

At this stage changes are being made to assets. Simple position changes (like moving a chair) are easy to record and note during the shoot. Often new props are created on the fly. These all have to be generated quickly and if time permits, created legally within the pipeline (naming conventions, rigging, etc.). Often they cannot be, so they are rigged quickly with notes to legalize post-shoot. Sets can change due to performance considerations and the same process is engaged. Physical changes and digital changes alike must be considered and tracked.

Scenes are generally captured on set and given the nomenclature as described. On top of this, with the use of a virtual camera, coverage within the scene can be shot and specific moments in shot world can also be captured. This is where the strict naming convention and asset tagging to the stage take is critically important.

Post-Production

Editorial has the task of ingesting all of the flat media from production, including all witness camera footage, real time render from the virtual production team, sound, and the playback rushes from video assist.

Figure 11.1 Interlude EA MOH Warfighter images. This is a frame from the performance assembly turn over that is provided by editorial as part of the virtual production pipeline. This video is the master layout for the performance assembly and shows witness camera footage from the shoot, Face Camera footage for each actor and a real time render through the virtual camera. This performance assembly layout is the chosen performance from stage and informs all downstream teams of what is needed along with confirmation that all assets are in sync and correct. *Copyright © 2012, Electronic Arts. EA MOH Warfighter images.*

Editorial then cuts together a performance assembly. This is the best performance(s) for a given sequence and it is delivered to virtual production in the form of several assets, QuickTime renders from the stage media detailing the performance and some form of an Edit Decision List (EDL) which details stage take name, stage time code in and out, destination scene or shot time code, and the characters required.

This performance assembly turnover from editorial becomes a task order for virtual production to produce a polished real time version of the performance selected. More often than not this process is done on set as the shoot commences and is also executed once the performance capture shoot is completed.

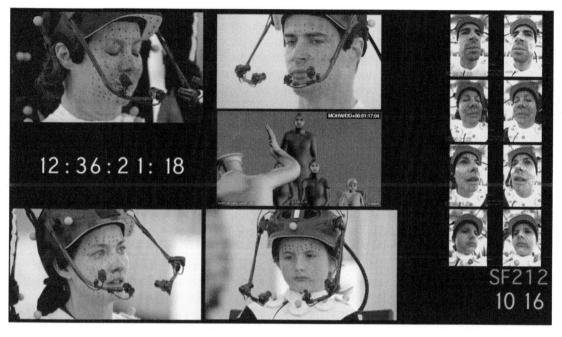

Figure 11.2 Interlude EA MOH Warfighter images. This is the final rendered image after VFX shot production of the very same image as seen in the performance assembly example (above). *Copyright © 2012, Electronic Arts. EA MOH Warfighter images.*

Virtual production then associates the EDLs back to all 3D assets captured during the production shoot and creates real time 3D performance of the assembly requested that can then be turned into shots to support the director's cut. We collate all 3D and 2D assets from the shoot, producing new final assets that match the requested assembly. Much of this process is automated with scripts that parse readable EDL files and can dive into the respective databases.

Motion capture data from a stage take request is cleaned up and made final for the body animation of the character and props. This ensures the character will appear in camera in final VFX shot production as they will during shot production in virtual production. This process can include stitching multiple performances from different actors and takes for the same character within the assembly.

Facial capture video data from stage is taken and a projected "Kabuki" is created that can be displayed (projected) onto the digital character's face for the creative team to view facial performance.

Digital environments are created for the assembly that combine all of the changes that happen on set, along with lighting and atmospherics. If the production is live action with CG elements, plates are tracked, with temp roto and comp work to integrate the CG elements (often characters and set extensions) into the plates.

What gets created out of all this work ultimately is a master scene assembly which matches the editorial performance assembly. This is typically a Maya or MotionBuilder file that contains all assets and is often referenced. This can be in scene world, sequence world, or even shot world. Master scenes are initially named by editorial and derived from the master stage take that was generated for the scene. Metadata is passed through on all digital assets where possible. Often animation adjustments and additions are required on top of the character's performance (derived from the actor's performance). These are implemented in layers within Maya/MotionBuilder and tracked, along with notes for turnover back to VFX shot production.

Once the master scene assembly is created, sync-checked and approved by editorial, then virtual production can enter shot world (unless we are already in shot world due to the nature of the production).

Shots can be created out of the master scene assembly in many ways, but ultimately camera and shot composition is being created for the director, DP, and editor. During this process, shots are created out of the master scene, and the digital assets adjusted accordingly for shot composition. Digital props, characters, and set decor are moved for composition purposes, and rough lighting is set—all this is done in real time as much as possible.

Once a shot is completed (typically after several revisions), renders are produced and delivered back to editorial to support the director's cut. A 3D master shot file is generated which contains all the assets and animation for the shot length. This is typically converted directly into a layout file which is delivered as part of the VFX turnover for final VFX shot production.

As soon as a sequence is approved for final turnover so the VFX work can begin, editorial turns the shot sequence over to virtual production as well as VFX shot production. Virtual production now is tasked with creating final assets from the production shoot, based on the shot turnover from editorial and the 3D master shot file that was used to create the render for the shots.

Editorial's turnover package is similar to that for the performance assembly. Now in shot world, editorial delivers a QuickTime and image sequence for the shot(s), along with count sheets, and EDLs describing the performance edits in stage timecode space and destined for shot frame space. Reference QuickTimes (from the witness video cameras) for each actor's performance, both body and facial, are also turned over.

Virtual production ingests the EDLs (ideally via tools and scripts) along with the reference QuickTimes. New assets are generated from the stage takes acquired in production. Background characters and

props that were not ordered during the performance assembly process are generated as described above. Final face delivery is then generated. This is a 3D asset that is generated from the face mounted cameras and is essentially the 3D surface and eye tracks of the actor as seen by the face cameras. This animating surface is then used along with any facial survey assets captured during pre-production to "solve" the actor's performance onto the character prior to animation taking over to fine-tune the performance.

All final 3D assets are then trimmed and delivered in shot space to match the count sheets. Often target assets have changed from pre-production to now. Character, environment, and prop design may have changed for creative reasons, so all existing 3D data is retargeted or modified to be used on these new asset versions. These 3D assets are then turned over along with the 3D master shot file for VFX shot production to begin.

The sheer amount of data and processes that are part of virtual production can seem complicated, complex, frightening, and overwhelming, especially if this description is an introduction to the topic. But an experienced virtual production team is able to lead filmmakers through the process, which is actually very logical, so that they experience the numerous benefits and avoid the complexities. The above process, when organized and executed well, is economical and very efficient. It allows filmmakers and story tellers to find a cut very quickly and iteratively before final VFX production begins.

If you get lost and confused within virtual production, you can do what we did for our team. Create a task category called "the praw". This is where something gets lost in the process and needs to be figured out. Weekly praw meetings on big productions are essential. Meet to discuss what is stuck in the praw and allow it to gain exit from being stuck. Why "the praw"? It's "warp" spelled backwards and reflects the complex nature of virtual production—it always involves four dimensions and often a fifth.

Section 11 Interlude 4: What is Virtual Production in Games?

Whilst we are not directly in game development, we are often indirectly involved with game development via virtual production for cinematic sequences and via motion creation for in game motion blend trees and motion transitions.

Section 11 Interlude 5: Virtual Production and Asset Creation/Capture

Generating movements from actors for motion blend trees and motion transitions to support character movements at run time

within the game engine is highly relatable to crowd simulation for feature films.

For both crowd simulation and blend/transition trees for games we are given the task of generating specific animations with metadata tagged to aid in describing the action(s) from performances directed and captured from actors on the motion capture stage.

Typically, the large degree of thought, planning, and effort is driven by the game/crowd team as they naturally have the creative eye and mind behind the game and the development of the AI system(s) along with player control system(s). These systems determine the individual action units which are required for all game characters. These action units are basically a single animation for a given character that is required to support the blend tree and transition tree that is required.

For both crowd simulation for feature film and motion blend/transition tree development there are usually several motion capture shoots as the process is often complex and needs iteration to gather and perfect all of the desired action units (animations) for the project throughout the development cycle.

Pre-Production

The virtual production team is typically involved once the major action units are defined and the animation list is defined. This is usually turned over in a table format (Excel or database). Often this list is large with hundreds and often thousands of motions, and lists each action unit by:

- Name and category (combat, locomotion, etc.)
- Type (terrain, airborne, vehicle pilot, etc.)
- Prop associations (which props this is affected by)
- And often body mask/filter (the area of the body to which the desired motion is required)

Our first task is to see if we can consolidate multiple action unit animations into single performance takes. This gives continuity and consistency for performance and directorial's sake, and also allows some economies on set with regard to the time it takes to capture all these motions.

We then add a review phase to determine a set of common body poses that need to be defined to allow motion consistency between the actions units. This is defined by the blend tree itself and between motion transitions—all standing ambient action units should start and end in a relaxed common pose. These common poses are usually named and associated to within each stage take that covers multiple action units and/or transitions. Our task and asset creation has already turned into a hierarchy and association management. This is a true theme for pretty much this entire process.

Next we review motion categories, types, and prop associations and ensure the consolidation of having multiple action units in a stage take

is still valid and makes sense technically as well as creatively. We then assign a meaningful stage take name or ID to each consolidated performance take. This simply allows easier management on set for calling out which take and action we will be capturing, so all departments on set are clear and communication is smooth.

Often when props are used, common hand positions on the prop are desired for motion consistency. These poses are labeled and physically marked on the props. These are also associated within the newly forming animation shot list which is derived from the action unit list.

The desired common poses often have key foot positions, especially during the standing, seated, and static ambient movements. These are generally low in number but often have a physical asset created to help determine foot position on set as each take is captured. This physical asset is usually cut outs or tape markers so actors can at least start a movement in the correct pose (foot position really can help center of mass positioning for the pose) and photographs for reference. We will also often create a digital form of the pose during the capture session and use this as reference via real time visualization on set.

At the end of this pre-production task, we have a few assets:

- A newly formed shot list, which refers stage takes and associations directly to action units
- Common Pose assets (definition, label, description, physical asset)
- Physical Prop assets
- Hand position poses on props (definition, label, description, and marking on props)

Production

Now we are ready for the production shoot itself. At this stage, it is worth noting that everything we capture on set is not going to be ideal in a technical sense because it is hard for actors to repeat movements with the same common poses or transition poses. We do our best during preparation of the shot list by consolidating multiple action units into a single stage take, to assure we get the most of the actor's performance, both creatively and technically, knowing we will be adding some animation artistry after the fact to make each action unit work well technically.

Preparation is key for these types of shoots. Budgets dictate a low number of shoot days with a high number of action units and movement transitions being captured.

The shoot is pretty straightforward in terms of tasking and asset generation. We have our shot list, we have a clear idea of what is contained in a stage take and motion capture is acquired of the desired performance. Assets generated from these shoot days include:

- 2D and 3D Motion Capture Data, striped with studio time code
- Video witness camera material, striped with studio time code
- Shoot notes based on the shot list

Often during these sessions, new stage takes are generated with a new action unit or movement transitions because a different way of achieving the desired actions is discovered. Often you can only do so much planning and you need to work through things. A rehearsal session before hand always helps in pre-production!

During the production shoot, preferred takes are chased and circled and noted in the shot notes. These are used in post-production to aid in refining the selection list and generating desired motion captured animation for each action unit and motion transition.

Post-Production

After the shoot, a refined selection process with the game/crowd team is then performed. For every desired individual action unit and motion transition (along with common poses) a select is made. This is literally frame specific from the stage take that contains it. These frame range selections are usually defined by frame in and out, or time code in and out from the stage take itself.

Once these selects are made, the virtual production team processes and finalizes the motion capture data onto the game rig as animation. The virtual production team then tags the action unit or movement transition with defined metadata tags that relate to the name of action unit, the category, type, prop associations, and body mask/filter. This process is often automated with a script/tool that pulls from the original action list generated during pre-production.

The action unit or motion transition is then named as the preferred name and delivered to the game/crowd team for implementation and also to the animation team for modification to take the actor's performance and technically make it work with the chosen motion transitions, blend tree, and common poses (including body masking/filtering).

The whole process in terms of asset management and tasking is a relatively simple one (basically hierarchical associations and metadata tagging) but one that is often overwhelming due to the sheer size of the action list.

Section 11 Interlude 6: Future

As you can imagine, the above process sounds archaic these days and is definitely a slow process that requires a lot of planning, multiple shoots to aid in iteration, and a deft experienced hand in developing these blend trees and motion transitions. Large databases of compressed motions (action units) are often needed and can consume valuable memory and CPU cycles to decompress when needed.

The future is certainly brighter with modeling and simulating characters' movements in real time in the game engine and thus being less

reliant on large volumes of motion captured animations. Up until a few years ago, these modeling and simulation techniques did not look particularly good visually when compared to a set of motion captured animations that were masterfully blended together and transitioned in-between. Newer techniques and added CPU horsepower (both on GPU and CPU) is now allowing some very exciting techniques in procedural modeling, dynamic and physical modeling, along with run time character rigs allowing IK/FK blends in real time to adapt to the environment and a multitude of situations. A lot of research and techniques are being generated into statistical analysis of specific human (actor) movements that can be used to generate training models (statistically) that can then be used to drive physical and procedural character animations in real time. They look good and they are interactive in a manner that immerses the player and enriches the landscape for gaming. The interesting thing is they still often require motion capture to aid in the training of these behaviors and simulations along with specific animations for key events that are triggered when needed. It's an ever changing technical landscape.

12

UPCOMING TRENDS AND TECHNOLOGIES

Tim Green; Matt Hoesterey; Hannes Ricklefs; Mark Streatfield; Steve Theodore; Rob. Blau: *Head of Pipeline Engineering, Shotgun Software;* **Scott Houston:** *CEO, GreenButton;* **Kathleen Maher:** *Vice President and Senior Analyst, Jon Peddie Research;* **Jon Peddie:** *President, Jon Peddie Research*

Section 12.1 What You Will Learn From This Chapter

In previous chapters, we looked at how today's production pipelines are structured. In this chapter, we will look at how and why those structures may change in future. We will explore how new data-interchange formats and methods of virtual computing are enabling companies to collaborate more effectively; how new workflows like virtual production are linking pre-visualization and post-production more closely together; and how new media like high-frame-rate cinema and games as a service affect the studios tasked with creating them.

We will look first at trends that primarily affect visual effects and animation, then those affecting game development, although there is some overlap between the two categories. Throughout the chapter, you will also see references to the growth of cloud-based tools and services: an important trend in its own right, and one we will discuss in more detail later in the book.

Section 12.2 Open Standards and Open-Source Tools

Over the past few years, open standards have made great headway in the worlds of animation and visual effects. Those that become widely adopted are a boon to the industry, as they make it much easier to exchange data between applications, and even between studios.

One of the first to see widespread use was OpenEXR, a file format for storing the High Dynamic Range (HDR) data used to record

real-world lighting conditions and recreate them within digital environments. Originally developed by Industrial Light & Magic and made open-source in 2003, OpenEXR has been adopted near-universally in DCC tools and pipelines. The format continues to be expanded by contributors including ILM, Weta Digital, Pixar Animation Studios, and Autodesk, with version 2.0 being released in April 2013.

More recently, Alembic, the geometry interchange format originally developed by Sony Pictures Imageworks and Lucasfilm and released as open-source in 2011, has begun to be adopted as an alternative to proprietary formats like FBX.

As the scope of production work expands, the number of interchange standards needed increases. Most visual effects productions now split the work between multiple effects vendors. Often this means assigning the foreground elements of a shot to one vendor, and the background elements to another. In the past, this was relatively straightforward, but now action sequences in which multiple characters interact with the environment are becoming commonplace. In future, there will be a need for an open meta description language to make it easier for a facility to ingest data created by the other vendors on a project, and hand it back to them in a format that can be analyzed through code rather than solely through custom scripts.

Some aspects of studio infrastructure also now have viable-open source implementations. Many tools now support OpenColorIO, also actively sponsored by Sony Pictures Imageworks, and fast emerging as a standard for color management.

There are now even good open-source options for tasks like managing software deployment over a network, in the form of Walt Disney Animation Studios' Munki, or Rez, which was originally developed by Allan Johns of Dr. D Studios.

This is only a selection of the open standards and open-source tools currently available. It is definitely worth seeing what can be found online before beginning a development project, as modifying an existing open-source solution is usually easier than writing your own.

Section 12.3 WebGL and Associated Technologies

WebGL is a reasonably new technology for rendering interactive 3D and 2D graphics within a web browser without the use of plugins. It is based around the OpenGL ES 2.0 graphics programming API, exposed through the HTML5 Canvas element, and supports the GLSL shader programming language. WebGL enables developers to access the computer's graphics card to speed up image processing and physics simulations, and is compatible with mobile devices, making it increasingly popular for games and for visualizing large data sets.

Technologies such as WebGL suggest that desktop DCC applications could soon be available online as hosted, cloud-based services, permitting simultaneous collaboration between many artists. This opens up many new possibilities within a visual effects pipeline: artists in a studio could collaborate with those on set; a client with some artistic ability could provide feedback that goes beyond written notes; remove reviews could become interactive, instead of a supervisor simply viewing an image sequence or QuickTime movie; and artists could work from anywhere in the world, instead of being confined to an office.

Although data security is also a potential issue, the challenges posed by such a pipeline are primarily related to asset management: getting the data being created remotely into and out of an application such as Maya so that it can work with the rest of the pipeline, and joining it up with a production-tracking system such as Shotgun.

As a result, technologies like WebGL have led to research into version control for 3D assets. In some pipelines, assets are versioned linearly, and rely on two people editing the same asset stream at the same time. However, as workflow becomes more collaborative, concurrent edits are becoming more common, with nonlinear versioning resulting in the need to merge multiple change sets. Usually, this requires human assistance to manage conflicts, so research is now being done into providing an effective framework for versioning and tracking assets at an object level as opposed to a file level in order to resolve the problem.

Section 12.4 GPU Computing

At the start of the 2010s, there was a lot of hype surrounding GPU computing. Using the GPU for computationally intensive tasks was seen as one of the "Holy Grails" of visual effects: something that would provide a much-needed performance boost in many areas of CG, notably rendering and simulation. However, at the time of writing, much of this enthusiasm has died down. While large facilities do make use of GPU computing—particularly for specialized tasks such as rendering hair or FX—the required shift in development logic, the still-evolving technical standards of GPUs and APIs such as OpenCL and Nvidia's CUDA, and the limited debugging resources have made companies realize that there is a significant overhead in developing for the GPU.

Instead, companies are looking more to multicore CPUs and multithreaded CPU computing techniques to improve their workflows. Many facilities are now looking into developing multithreaded algorithms using template libraries such as Intel's TBB (Threading Building Blocks) or OpenMP to provide highly parallel and performant algorithms over native implementations on the GPU.

In games, the situation is a little different. When rendering in real time, both CPU and GPU are important: most modern AAA titles can't even run without dedicated high-end dedicated GPUs. Rather than whether to use the CPU or the GPU, the key question facing game developers is how to make best use of both.

Section 12.5 Big Data

Organizations of every sort produce a lot of data—and a VFX organization is no exception. Although the data it generates may be of a different type to that produced in health care, transport, or defense, being able to collate and mine that data enables a facility to run productions more effectively. Just parsing all the log files generated would probably lead to useful insights as to how the pipeline is actually being used and where common problems lie. However, since the volume of data generated is too large for a human to handle, this process must be automated.

In recent years, a lot of effort has gone into collecting such organizational data in a rational, centralized way, mining the data for business intelligence and visualizing the results in a form that humans can comprehend. Let's look at two examples of how this might work for VFX.

The first is rendering. A common approach to scheduling renders is "first come, first served", with some form of prioritization laid over the top based on criteria such as the relative urgency of a project or shot. But perhaps we can be more intelligent. By analyzing previous renders (for the same artist, the same project, the same shot, the same asset, or the same software) we might be able to make better decisions about how to queue and distribute jobs to make the best use of the computing resources available. With sophisticated enough analytics, we might be able to make decisions such as, "All the other jobs for this shot have either failed before frame ten or completed successfully, so we'll just run the first ten frames. If they pass, we'll start to run the rest concurrently," or, "These shots are I/O bound and don't benefit from being put on more powerful hardware, so we'll run them on the older hardware that is less frequently used."

The second is scheduling. We rely on artists (or more likely, supervisors and producers) to predict the time it will take to complete a given task. This might take into account whether an artist is at a junior, mid, or senior level of experience, but nothing more specific about them; and may only use an estimate of how complex the work is to complete. By analyzing task data, we can assess performance in more detail, tracking how long individual artists have actually taken to complete similar jobs in the past. This information can then be used to build a more accurate schedule.

Section 12.6 Virtual Production

The term "virtual production" means different things to different people: an issue that led to the formation of the Virtual Production Committee, a joint effort between the American Society of Cinematographers, the Art Directors Guild, the Visual Effects Society, the Previsualization Society, and the Producers Guild of America, intended to define standards within this emerging field. However, one key component of virtual production is the adoption of real-time graphics techniques on movie projects. The virtual production process enables directors to view live footage of the actors on set integrated with placeholder versions of the CG elements of a shot.

Virtual production is now becoming the norm for any movie requiring large-scale visual effects. When creating characters, creatures, and environments, everything is done digitally, from building costumes to lighting, animation, and camera work. One aim of virtual production is to involve the director in this process from the start. Traditionally, directors could only see half of a movie on set: instead of digital environments, they saw green screens; instead of digital characters, they saw live actors in motion-capture suits—or worse, inanimate props used as stand-ins. As a result, mistakes were often made, and since the live shoot is still one of the most expensive parts of a film—typical estimates range from $1,000 to $2,000 per minute—those mistakes could be costly.

One huge benefit of virtual production is that questions about the CG work can be answered much earlier in production. Rather than handing VFX companies a written description of the action, blocking animations can now be approved before the director even reaches the set. For example, on *Real Steel*, all of the fight sequences were animated during the pre-visualization phase of the movie, meaning that the live shoot itself could be completed in record time.

With more data being created during pre-visualization, the issue of how to integrate the phases of production has become increasingly important. Currently, it is often impossible for visual effects facilities to use any of the previs assets, beyond viewing QuickTimes of the animations as reference material. As a result, directors often complain that they see a drop in the quality of the CG as they move from pre-visualization to VFX, as the effects vendors need time to work up assets to the quality of those used in previs before they can improve on them. There is a great need for better standardization of the format in which material is passed between facilities—or to involve the visual effects companies from the very start of a project.

Another big challenge for effects companies is how to capture all of the relevant material on set. In a virtual production process, the director may approve anything from the virtual camera moves to the placement of the digital environments during the live shoot. This data must be recorded in a format that can later be ingested into a VFX

facility's pipeline, regardless of whether the shoot is taking place in a controlled studio environment with high-speed internal connections, or a remote location in the desert.

Some of the main technical challenges relate to lighting and capturing facial performance. Cinematographers use lighting to tell a story, so effects houses need to be able to reproduce in real time all of the techniques available through the use of physical live sources on set. With facial capture, the challenge is to make the hardware required more portable and to reduce the number of people required to set it up, enabling directors to record actors in a much less obstructive way.

Through its reliance on real-time graphics, virtual production is bringing the worlds of visual effects and games closer together. Games already have the ability to generate very realistic-looking environments, FX, and character performances in real time, and there are already efforts—for example, with Crytek's CryEngine—to enable animators to work in a more traditional CG environment, then export the results to a game engine to visualize them via a virtual camera.

Section 12.7 High-Frame-Rate Cinema

High-frame-rate cinema looks likely to become one of the next challenges for visual effects facilities. Although the medium is currently in its infancy, influential directors such as Peter Jackson and James Cameron seem determined to make high frame rates the "next big thing" after stereoscopic movies. The two are connected: higher frame rates are becoming a necessity on stereo movies to remove the strobing caused by fast-moving cameras, and to increase the clarity of the image.

The reason that high-frame-rate cinema looks likely to succeed is that it requires no change to existing delivery mechanisms. Unlike stereoscopic movies, which required cinemas to buy completely new equipment, modern digital projectors can already handle higher frame rates. In addition, the problem of converting movies created at high frame rates back to a traditional 24 fps (Frames Per Second) seems already to have been solved.

The challenge for visual effects facilities is the sheer number of frames that must be produced. An average VFX shot is around five seconds long. At 24 fps, this requires 120 frames. At the 48 fps used on movies such as *The Hobbit* trilogy, it requires 240. And if frame rates rise to 120 fps, as now seems possible, it would require 600. All of these figures are for a movie shot in mono: for a stereoscopic project, they would be doubled.

It is also important to note that this does not simply represent an increase in render times: many other departments are affected, including match-moving, roto, simulations, lighting, and compositing. One

interesting suggestion for reducing the load is to shoot at variable frame rates, with shots that don't feature fast action being shot at lower rates.

Section 12.8 Virtual Machines

Virtual machines offer a flexible, cost-effective alternative to buying lots of dedicated hardware. In the past, if a facility wanted a desktop workstation, it would buy an actual computer. If it wanted a server, it would buy another computer and install web service software on it. When that web service was not in use, the hardware would sit idle.

Virtual machines—software systems that execute programs as if they were physical machines—permit much more flexible use of that hardware. Rather than requiring separate computers on which to install old versions of Windows in order to run legacy software, for example, a company can set up a virtual machine on its existing hardware and install the legacy operating system on that virtual machine. The virtual machine can then be moved to other hardware without the need to rebuild, reinstall, or reconfigure its software. In addition, unlike its physical counterpart, a virtual machine can be cloned. It is not difficult to see that being able to virtualize machines is a huge benefit when setting up render farms on film projects, and when setting up autobuilder farms and soak/smoke test environments in games development.

Another advantage of virtual machines is that the hardware on which they run does not need to be stored in the facility itself. Desktop machines, particularly those for visual effects work, need top-of-the-range processors, graphics cards, and memory. These components use a lot of power, and generate a lot of heat and noise. Being able to store the hardware in a more manageable environment with cooling, uninterruptable power supplies, failover, and so on, is not only a huge logistical benefit but makes the artists' working environment more pleasant.

Virtual machines also make it possible for artists to work on a shared virtual desktop: for example, to provide training or to review work. In many studios, staff are separated across several floors, or even several separate facilities. Virtual systems make it possible for one artist to log into another artist's workstation without having to be physically close to them—or even in the same time zone.

However, there are still practical problems to be solved. Both games and visual effects work require processor-intensive applications that are difficult to share via older methods such as VNC (Virtual Network Computing). Hardware vendors are now developing technologies through which they can provide truly real-time experiences to users sharing the same virtual desktop. Examples include Nvidia's GRID VGX platform or Hewlett-Packard's HP Remote Graphics Software.

Why Visual Effects Needs Cloud Computing

Scott Houston
CEO, GreenButton

Another current trend in visual effects is the rise of cloud computing. We will look at this in more detail at the end of this chapter. But for now, here's an anecdote from the days before cloud computing that may help to illustrate why it is necessary.

I was the CTO for Peter Jackson at Weta Digital during its work on *The Lord of the Rings* trilogy. It was 2003 and there were two months to go until *The Return of the King* was due to launch. Peter Jackson had called a special meeting to review some of the latest scenes. He pulled up some low-res drafts of the battle of Pelennor fields showing the riders of Rohan charging down the hill to meet the orcs in front of the city of Minas Tirith. In total, there were around a hundred thousand orcs and tens of thousands of riders of Rohan. Each of these characters was individually generated and placed on the battlefield by software called Massive.

My jaw hit the floor. Just rendering a single frame of one of these crowd scenes was estimated to take several hundred hours, and our data centers were already running at full capacity. There was no way we could take on these shots and get the film completed on time.

We did a few calculations on the back of a ciggie packet, then went to Barry Osborne, the producer of the trilogy, and told him: "You've got two options. One is to build a brand-new data center with a thousand processors to get everything completed in time." "Yeah, right," he replied. "What's option two?" "You can tell Peter Jackson that he can't have his shots!"

Apparently, that's not a smart thing to do. So he wrote the check and we built a brand-new data center. As Weta was its biggest customer at the time, IBM had the new blade servers rushed to New Zealand on a private jet. There were helicopters dropping kit to the site daily. The data center was built in ten days—an extraordinary feat—and the film was completed on time, but the additional cost and effort for less than two months of usage was immense.

If the cloud was around back then, Weta could have rented the extra server capacity remotely, and all of that stress, cost and effort could have been avoided. Not to mention the gray hairs!

Section 12.9 Games as a Service

As consumers' expectations continue to rise—and with them, the cost of developing new AAA titles—the days of traditional standalone games may be coming to an end. Many games are now being built with longevity in mind, with downloadable content, monthly updates to MMOs, and constantly updated "freemium" games all gaining in popularity. As the content that makes up a game begins to migrate from the player's computer to the developer's servers, the process of building "games as a service"—games that are delivered partly or wholly over the internet—is introducing new tasks for pipeline developers.

First, freemium titles need custom billing servers that let users buy the optional content from which the game's revenue is generated. Developers may also need complex data-mining systems to track players' progress and adjust aspects of gameplay to ensure that they

stay engaged, thereby maximizing profits. Since any interruptions to play may be costly, pipelines for such games also need to provide mechanisms for pushing out "hotfixes" without taking a server down. Any fixes that do require servers to be taken offline must be made as quickly as possible.

In addition, pipelines for games as a service need to be built to last for years after a title's initial release. A lot more work needs to be put into the development and management of the pipeline to ensure that it does not fall apart over time, creating workflow issues and introducing bugs.

Section 12.10 Pipelines as a Service

And if a game can be provided as a service, why shouldn't the same be true of the pipeline used to create it? The pipeline as a service (or "studio in a box") is a concept in which a facility would buy in or lease its entire pipeline in much the same way as it would any other software product. This has a particular appeal for studios that are created to work on a single project, then disbanded; or on projects with a very short lead time where pipeline development is not possible.

When faced with this idea, many developers' first reaction is that pipelines are just too complex ever to be offered as an out-of-house service. This may be true, but it is surprising how many individual parts of the pipeline are already being outsourced. Most large developers currently outsource motion-capture, localization and voice recording, and QA to specialist companies; and at least part of the modeling work to outfits in countries where manpower is cheaper.

Even leasing services in this limited way poses challenges to pipeline developers. As we have already discussed, it is essential for artists to be able to see the content they are creating in-game before sharing it with the rest of the team. Outsource content providers don't fit well with this model, since it is unusual for developers to trust them enough to give them the game engine and all the tools required to test their work in-game before submitting it.

It is also common for an outsource content provider to deliver data in a lump. But throwing a huge lump of data at a games pipeline is rarely a good idea. Modern pipelines are highly iterative, and are designed to work best with a constant stream of data, enabling developers to evaluate each small change in-game and make any fixes necessary before the next one arrives. The more data that is introduced at a time, the greater the likelihood of causing a serious crash. When working with outsource providers, it is often necessary to dedicate in-house staff to processing the content they generate, introducing it into the system a bit at a time. The further downstream the task being outsourced lies—QA is an obvious case in point—the more in-house staff that need to be assigned to this task.

Overview: An Industry in Transition

Jon Peddie
President, Jon Peddie Research

Kathleen Maher
Vice President and Senior Analyst, Jon Peddie Research

The digital content creation market is changing dramatically. Some of the causes are economic and others are technological, but their cumulative effect is a rate of change that is unprecedented in the industry's history.

In the realm of movies and TV, the digitization of content and distribution has reached a tipping point. In the years from 2008 to 2013, there has been an upheaval in the industry that is difficult to communicate through numbers alone. Content is still being created and tools are still being purchased, but the people who are creating content are not the same people who were creating content ten years ago, and the tools being used back then are not the same as the ones being used today, or the ones that will be used in future.

The most obvious changes are that high-profile companies have gone out of business, and new companies have been started. Studios are divesting their in-house post facilities and increasing their use of contract houses worldwide. The trend has followed the course of digitization, which has all but swallowed up the production pipeline. Fujifilm has announced that it will no longer ship film for production. Process houses Deluxe and Technicolor are planning for an all-digital future. It is estimated that 75 percent of all movie production in 2013 is being done using digital methods.

Digitization means that film is no longer used in the production of movies, eliminating expensive equipment and more complex analog workflows. Even while digital cameras were coming into use, the practice of using film in part of the production process persisted as long as content was ultimately distributed on film. But the end of film as a distribution medium is coming more rapidly than anyone expected. It is clearly on the horizon in the US, and while film will continue to be used in many other countries, the studios and their distributors have signaled their plans to move to all-digital production and distribution.

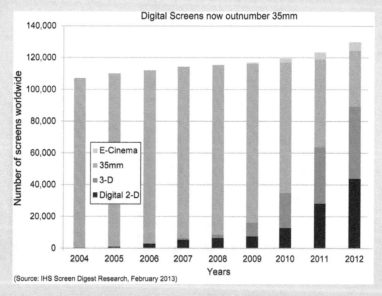

(Source: IHS Screen Digest Research, February 2013)

Figure 12.1 The transition to digital formats is picking up speed worldwide. As the graph above shows, digital 2D and 3D screens now outnumber 35mm. In addition, e-cinema, used primarily in India and China as a secure, low-cost digital projection format, is growing rapidly. Source: HIS.

Everything Changes

The transition to digital has already changed the landscape of vendors providing tools and services to the film and video industries. Those companies that depended on "turnkey systems" consisting of both hardware and software have been challenged by the move to software. Victims include famous names such as Autodesk, Avid, Grass Valley, Quantel, and Thomson (now known as Technicolor), all of which have lost a significant portion of their revenue due to the switch to digital, while many smaller players have disappeared completely.

Although the ways in which people work do not always change as rapidly as does technology, the process of capturing images is becoming more streamlined. It's amazing to think that the usefulness of digital cameras was in question as late as 2006 and 2007, yet now they are used in the majority of US movie productions. Low-cost cameras and software tools are replacing the expensive systems that barred the gates of professional content creation to smaller facilities.

The Crisis in Post

The ripples from this change are spreading out through the entire process of creating and distributing content. Profit margins in effects and post-production have always been low because companies are constantly trying to do things that have never been attempted before. As work is done and redone to get the perfect effect, those margins go down, until some companies actually lose money on projects. The transition to digital has reduced margins still further because there are now so many more people capable of taking on those projects. As Debra Kaufman of Creative COW has written in an excellent piece on the subject: "VFX facilities have operated for years without standardized contracts and viable bidding practices. They have been, and continue to be, vulnerable to changes in technology and studio policy."

Although demand for post work is not going down, jobs are disappearing, particularly in the US. Right now, blame is being placed on international providers willing to do the work for less, regions that offer subsidies US companies can't match, and the willingness of companies worldwide to exploit idealistic young workers.

It is very likely the cause of the problem—the big movie studios, which try to keep prices low by putting difficult jobs out to tender—will have to become the solution as well. Studios will have to work with more realistic estimates of what work will cost and develop a more collaborative relationship with their effects vendors.

However, those doing the work will also have to become more efficient. Many in the industry believe this means working with standard tools and off-the-shelf packages and plug-ins, along with much more efficient content and asset management.

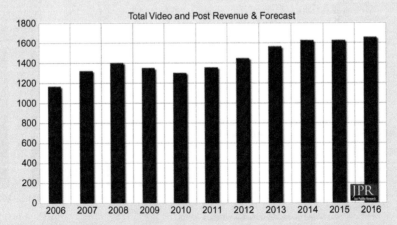

Figure 12.2 Companies selling video and post tools are expecting to see a period of growth as professionals and consumers work with digital video footage for a variety of outlets. Source: JPR.

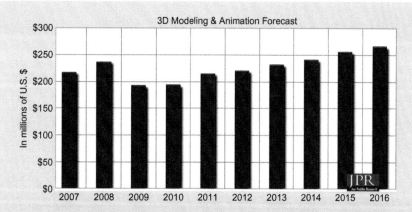

Figure 12.3 The 3D modeling and animation business is key to game development, television, movies, and special effects. Ironically, as can be seen by comparing the graph above to Figure 12.2, it is a relatively small business segment with modest growth. Source: JPR.

Standards Come to the Fore

With more and more companies now working on individual projects, there is a clear need for better methods of collaboration and sharing data: a difficult challenge in an industry that thrives on originality and the big reveal.

In the past, tools vendors have preferred to protect their systems with proprietary formats: formats that may make it difficult to exchange data with other similar tools. Autodesk's FBX file format is still commonly used for some workflows, but the company struggles to maintain its usefulness. Professionals are united in their demands for tools that make collaboration easier. Walt Disney Animation Studios has developed Ptex, a more efficient, easier-to-use texture-mapping system, and made it available open-source, while Sony Pictures Imageworks has done the same thing for its Alembic data-interchange format. The rapid adoption of both technologies suggests that we will see more such cooperative efforts in future.

Now that workflow is becoming entirely digital, new tools offering new ways to create content will come to the fore. A good example from the past decade is the rise of digital sculpting tools such as ZBrush and Mudbox. In future, there will be more use of reality-capture tools, including photogrammetry applications, scanners, and point-cloud tools.

Another growth market is that for cloud-based tools for collaborative work. The problems with working with large files in the cloud are being addressed aggressively by hardware companies such as Nvidia, AMD, and Intel, which are accelerating the necessary algorithms; and storage companies such as Fusion-io, which uses Flash memory to enable huge local caches and fast server performance.

Semiconductors Change the World

Over the past decade, two things have happened to change the content-development industry: processors have reached the physical limits of performance, and processor developers have leveraged the power of parallelism.

As Figure 12.4 shows, the performance of CPUs and GPUs has increased in tandem. In the past, both CPU and GPU manufacturers increased the performance of their processors by increasing their clock speed. At a certain point, however, CPU clock speed could no longer be increased; and while more individual processors can be added to increase performance, CPU processing does not scale linearly.

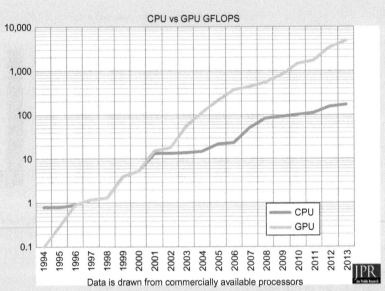

Figure 12.4 When GPUs moved to massive parallel processing, the rate of increase in their performance exceeded those of CPUs by up to 270 percent. Source: JPR.

GPU makers, because the tasks of graphics processing and rendering are inherently parallel, recognized the need to increase overall performance by adding more processors and developing an architecture that enabled them to work in parallel. As a result, GPUs have increased in performance dramatically faster than CPUs—by as much as 270 percent. This has had a huge influence on the industry, particularly in game development, where the GPU is being used to run physics algorithms and handle all the lighting and shading of a scene.

Finally, new types of hardware are being developed. At the time of writing, Caustic Professional, a division of Imagination Technologies, has just introduced a dedicated ray tracing hardware accelerator that will take hours off the rendering times of ray traced images.

INTERLUDE: CLOUD COMPUTING FOR VFX

**Tim Green; Hannes Ricklefs; Mark Streatfield;
Matt Hoesterey; Steve Theodore; Fran Zandonella;** *International Senior Pipeline TD, Rhythm & Hues;* **Dave Fellows:** *CTO, GreenButton;*
Todd Prives: *CMO, Zync*

Historically, owning infrastructure has been the dominant (if not only) model for VFX. Each studio buys and maintains its own hardware in a dedicated (often on-site) data center. This private cloud forms the hub of the company containing the renderfarm, storage, and other essential services such as license management, email, intranet hosting, etc.

However, as cloud computing has become ubiquitous in the world of web applications and mobile technology, so too has it had an impact on film production. Studios are beginning to adopt cloud paradigms for managing their infrastructure whilst software and hardware vendors are offering new products that leverage this business model. Unfortunately, take up has been slow due in part to concerns such as bandwidth capacity, security, and pipeline integration.

It is now possible for a studio to hand some of these components off to an external service provider using a public cloud, reducing the management overhead and operating cost. It has been of particular benefit to studios that have offices around the globe and those that find themselves in a continual flux of scaling up and down between projects. In reality, a hybrid approach is often employed with a combination of private and public cloud solutions being used, depending on the service in question.

Whilst the business models of the popular offerings may be structured more closely around the needs of the web, they can (and are) still very relevant to creative media production (as can be seen with the growth of commercial toolsets like Adobe Creative Cloud). Film certainly has extreme data and processing requirements, but there are increasingly specialist cloud and service providers offering adjusted models that suit it better.

Cloud computing allows access to on-demand computing resources, typically at per minute or per hour pricing. Instead of having to buy a fixed number of in-house machines upfront for heavy computing as VFX facilities traditionally have done, they can instead treat cloud computing

as a utility, paying for what they use when it's running, and paying nothing when it's not. From a budgetary standpoint the spend for computing resources goes from an Op-ex spend to Cap-ex and is more easily and clearly able to be billed to the specific job.

Section 12 Interlude 1: Cloud Services

The cloud is a somewhat ambiguous term describing technology and solutions that are hosted and managed by a provider and delivered as a service over the internet or private network. The name "cloud" came about due to system design diagrams typically depicting the internet as a cloud shape. Cloud computing shares similarities with older approaches such as grid and utility computing, where resources are pooled and shared amongst a number of users or tenants. However, cloud computing has matured in a number of areas in both technology and business models which have led to wider adoption and popularity. Three key characteristics of cloud computing are defined as:

- On-demand self-service: Consumers can gain access to the service without involvement from the provider.
- Resource pooling: Computing resources are dynamically allocated to consumers as per demand.
- Measured service: The underlying system meters consumption of computing resources for each consumer allowing them to only pay for what they consume.

The idea of cloud computing could refer to any number of different setups. It could be as simple as someone running ten identical servers in an office 30 miles away where they offer remote access for a specific type of job, or the more commonly accepted massive Amazon or Google data centers housing hundreds of thousands of different machine types with any number of different uses available to anyone with a credit card.

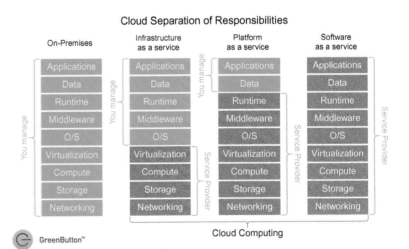

Figure 12.1 Interlude The above graph represents the separation of responsibilities between the service provider and the VFX facility.

The primary types of cloud computing, referred to as service models, are Infrastructure as a Service (IaaS), Platform as a Service (PaaS), and Software as a Service (SaaS).

Infrastructure as a Service

In this model for cloud computing, raw compute power (CPU and/or GPU) and/or virtual machines are made available to a consumer for general purpose computing. This "bare metal" approach requires the end user to install and configure each aspect of their environment from the operating system up. This offers the most flexibility for a studio as they are free to run and utilize the resource as they please, but requires more management on their part. In addition to computing power, data storage also belongs to this category. In VFX, this model can be used for rendering, simulation, media transcoding, and other general purpose operations that are data or processor intensive.

Platform as a Service

The platform as a service model provides computing power with a basic layer of abstractions, software, and development tools (such as a database, web server) that allow the developer to focus on building an application then use the provided tools to package and deploy the application to the platform. The end-user is only responsible for providing their application, however it must be compatible with the platform provided (i.e. there is less flexibility over base components such as an operating system when compared to the infrastructure as a service model). This model is typically only appropriate for developing new applications, as certain constraints are imposed by the platform that can make it difficult to port legacy applications. This model is commonly used to provide cloud based rendering services, where the service comes with the renderer of choice already installed and configured.

Software as a Service

This model exposes complete software applications through the cloud for the end-user and is perhaps the model people are most familiar with. The end-user has no control over the underlying infrastructure or platform, and interacts only with the software (application) being provided. Typically this is done via a web browser and is particularly suited to collaboration and productivity applications.

GPU and Specialized Clouds

Some renderers can take advantage of GPU computing power and in many cases can significantly increase performance. The availability of GPUs in public clouds is somewhat limited today. Amazon

Web Services have a limited number of GPGPUs (General Purpose Graphics Processing Unit) available. However, it's likely that you will see GPGPUs in greater abundance in the next couple of years. There isn't anything specific you need to do to take advantage of these other than select the appropriate instance type when provisioning (and of course be using a renderer that supports GPUs). Note that in Amazon Web Service, GPUs are only available in certain regions.

Specialized clouds are also growing in popularity. These are clouds focused on the needs of a particular vertical market. As an example, for Digital Media they would have GPU capability, perhaps iSCSI (Internet Small Computer Systems Interface) storage interfaces available, ability to easily setup virtual desktops for running software like Maya remotely, and higher speed CPUs (most public clouds have fairly low-spec commodity CPUs).

Section 12 Interlude 2: Using the Cloud

There are a number of important ways in which the cloud is going to reshape production in the coming years. This section describes some of the challenges and considerations that need to be taken into account when looking to leverage the cloud for film production. These challenges will be more, or less, significant depending on the scope of the project in question, that is its complexity and the commercial nature.

Pricing

When looking at cloud computing options, it's important to have a good understanding of your budgetary constraints as well as your existing infrastructure. The benefits of cloud computing revolve around the ability to dynamically and easily gain access to computing resources when they're required. Rather than needing to invest in expensive hardware with a big upfront cost, the cloud allows you to pay only for what you use, when you need it.

Another issue, in particular for larger facilities with constant work, is pricing. Utilizing a pay-as-you-go model makes financial sense for medium to smaller facilities and freelancers, particularly when maintaining hardware, and an inconsistent flow of jobs occasionally requiring heavy computing power can benefit from cloud services. Smaller studios and start-ups may find the flexibility and low upfront costs of cloud services makes them a very attractive alternative to building out a large traditional IT system. Larger studios, particularly if they already have significant investments in hardware and personnel, will need to look very carefully at the costs and benefits of supplementing or replacing existing functionality with hosted solutions and software services. However, larger facilities delivering jobs on a regular schedule often find that buying and building their own

infrastructure, when it comes to heavy resources such as rendering and storage, is still more cost effective than if they were to pay per hour on a 24/7 scale.

Scalability

The cloud has an obvious appeal to the visual effects industry since there are always periods of extreme business followed by low periods. During the last weeks of a project it is not uncommon for the needs of the production to completely outbalance the available resources within the facility. It wouldn't be cost-effective to build out a studio to completely fulfill these needs, as the expense of such a build out would be too costly. During such crunch times it is more important to have good scheduling and planning to ensure the project's delivery. The cloud offers the potential to provide this additional infrastructure when needed without the necessity (and the delay) of physically installing, testing, configuring and maintaining boxes on-site.

The cloud allows you to cost effectively scale horizontally, but could limit how far you can scale vertically as you have a more restricted server choice, unless you run a private cloud. Ideally, you want to build a pipeline that can scale in both directions. Horizontal scaling (also known as scaling out) is to add more servers; or better yet, scale elastically, growing and shrinking dynamically based on demand. Vertical scaling (scaling up) is to change the resources of the server by changing RAM, CPU, GPU, etc. In a private cloud, you pick the servers; in commercial cloud you can only use what the service provides.

Connectivity and File Transfer Speeds

As the cloud requires data to be sent over large distances to a remote data center, connectivity can be a concern for some studios. With many gigabytes of source data needed to create the rendered frame, large quantities of data must be efficiently transferred between the studio and cloud. As a result, the latency and bandwidth of the connection can become a limiting factor for adopting cloud-based solutions. In some cases data transfers take place over the open-internet; for private clouds this can be overcome by a dedicated private network. A perceived bottleneck with using cloud services is the massive data sets from CG renders and high resolution live action plates, and how to get those to and from cloud locations. There is no set bandwidth that guarantees performance and trying to predict when this will occur isn't really useful. Maybe by the time we can all upload HD.exr frames to the cloud in real time, we'll all be needing to deliver 8 K stereo work!

One important potential pitfall is the wide divergence in internet speed and reliability. Outsource providers in China, for example, so far are rarely able to take high-speed, uninterrupted access for

granted—many game studios which use web-based distribution for custom tools have difficulty working with Chinese partners who can't count on "always on" access to the global net, and whose workers often don't have internet connections directly from their desktops.

When it comes to moving large amounts of data around, the internet can't match the bandwidth of an in-house network. Consequently cloud processing of large files has a long built-in startup time. As artists must fine-tune an image through many iterations, they'll continue to prefer fast local resources to slower machines in the cloud for the foreseeable future. When crunch time comes, however, anything that can help will be more than welcome. For small and midsize studios in particular, the ability to rapidly scale up to hundreds of extra processors will be vital.

If the cloud is to be used as an integral part of a rendering pipeline then a solution for exclusively transferring the differences in assets could be worth the investment. The common utility application rsync is an example of a solution that only sends deltas between file versions. However, advancements in software development of file management increasingly allows for direct access to cloud resources for both rendering and storage with no manual intervention.

This direct access integration and storage not only supports 3D renders, but 2D compositing to be rendered in the cloud on applications such as The Foundry's Nuke, previously considered as cloud unfriendly due to the size of the elements needed (both live action and CG) for a composite.

Instead of trying to tackle the bandwidth upload issue head on, a more practical approach is moving many of the tasks involved in content creation to the cloud from inception. If any CG elements are rendered on a cloud platform, they can remain there to be used throughout the content creation process, into compositing, and encoding and distribution. Using this process, live action plates can be uploaded immediately upon acquisition on set so by the time they are needed for rendering or encoding or color, they are available. The VFX process results in so much data duplication it's often best to upload from the beginning so, as data sets grow larger, future upload times are minimized.

Regardless of how you tackle data transfer, having backup network routing, a great relationship with the ISP, and a backup ISP reduces the risks of catastrophe impacting your schedule. When rendering in the cloud or storing data offsite, external factors such as construction cutting through the fiber optic backbone, an explosion at the ISP providers substation, or some other natural catastrophe (earthquakes somewhere along the data route), can make a system seem slow. Even rain can be a disaster if data is being transmitted over a microwave dish or if the infrastructure is flooded due to the highest rainfall on record. Any of these catastrophes can happened despite a "reliable" internet,

and always come at the worst time—during crunch and right before a delivery.

Asset Management

One of the primary challenges in enabling a rendering pipeline to function in the cloud is the accurate detection of required assets for a particular scene. If these dependencies can't be identified programmatically then the scene isn't going to render correctly and any compute time consumed will have been wasted.

Many renderers such as Maya, V-Ray, and Blender support single scene files that encapsulate everything required to render that scene. However, for more complex projects, typically there are a number of external assets involved. RenderMan Studio in Maya will generate tens of thousands of files for a single scene, including RIBs describing the scene and geometry along with textures, shaders, and other external plugins. The directory structure, referred to as the RIB tree, is sacred and needs to be preserved in the cloud when rendering RenderMan scenes. One option is to run Maya in the cloud on each render node and initiate the render with Maya. This eliminates the need to export RIBs and reduces complexity.

Section 12 Interlude 3: Collaboration

Cloud services offer easy distribution of information with low management overheads and good security, all without requiring you to expose your own internal network to the internet. Hosted software, such as Shotgun or Tactic, is specifically designed for managing film and game production making it easier to collaborate remotely.

In addition, having this on-demand power and flexibility makes a great deal of sense for a distributed workforce. It's much easier to commission a CG artist to work remotely on a three-month project when you know they'll be able to render on fifty machines in the cloud and turn work around faster and cheaper than spending the same amount of money on ten dedicated render nodes that they would have to set up and manage.

Once the decision has been made to leverage the cloud as either a standalone capability or to supplement an onsite renderfarm, there are other potential benefits that can result. One of these is collaboration with other studios and digital artists with the cloud acting as a central storage hub for a distributed workforce. With digital assets already stored in the cloud it makes it easy to share these with other artists, with clients for feedback, have others contribute to your projects, and contribute to other projects. Having all assets in a single accessible location for multiple workers means not having to buy expensive

in-house storage accessible only by local staff. Instead you have an infinitely scalable solution that your employees around the world can access. A cloud-based digital marketplace could facilitate sharing and monetization of assets. These concepts are somewhat underdeveloped today but it is inevitable that this will evolve over the next few years.

Backup and Redundancy

Very few companies can afford the large-scale investments in data safety that big cloud providers enjoy. Manually creating and storing tape-based backups of a local server is the current standard, but with the rise of archive-oriented cloud services like Amazon Glacier, studios may prefer to handle backups remotely over the web to multiple data centers in secure locations instead of letting them go home in the IT supervisor's packsack. Smaller studios will especially benefit from access to secure backups.

Security

One of the obvious considerations with the cloud lies with the fact it is hosted publicly and accessed over the internet or private network. This can be a concern for some studios, particularly for commercial projects. One of VFX's main hesitations of working in the cloud is the concern their data will be transported off-site; many film studios strictly forbid this in their contracts with these facilities. Despite the fact that many of the larger cloud providers offer a stringent set of security guidelines and take steps to assure unauthorized access to data is much more difficult than accessing locally at their facility, the concerns of moving protected data "offsite" scares away many artists and studios from using the cloud.

Data needs to be uploaded to the cloud platform's storage and reside in the cloud at least while the scene is rendering. The rendered outputs then need to be downloaded back on site. This means you have data being transferred and data being stored. This is referred to as "data in transit" and "data at rest". To protect the data you need to address both:

- Data in transit is easily protected by using transport encryption. HTTPS is the standard for encrypting data being transmitted over the internet. All of the major cloud providers support transferring data into their storage using HTTPS.
- Data at rest is protected by the cloud provider but not encrypted.

Providers have made significant investments to secure their platforms. Some provide two-factor authentication into their storage services, making it extremely difficult for any would-be hacker to compromise your data. If this still isn't sufficient, then the data can be encrypted prior to upload to the cloud. This adds significant complexity and isn't typically warranted for most use cases.

Further complicating this is the lack of a true certification from the MPAA to say that a cloud is "authorized" by their standards. The closest a cloud provider can come to such certification is to have a security audit done by a third party that evaluates according to MPAA standards and awards a "best practices" outcome. This standard has been achieved by some cloud providers. Now it becomes the responsibility of the VFX facility to close the deal by convincing the film studio the cloud service is secure enough to incorporate into the production. Atomic Fiction in Emeryville, CA became an example of one such success of cloud computing with Paramount Pictures' approval to render over four hundred VFX shots for the Robert Zemeckis/Denzel Washington film *Flight*. Until the MPAA awards an actual security certification, and the major motion picture studios feel confident in cloud services and security from the top down, selling cloud services to the studios will largely be an individual per-project crusade for the VFX facilities.

Reliability

When using a cloud computing environment the reliability of the service must be considered. Reliability (often referred to as uptime) is measured as a percentage of time within a year that the service is available. Cloud providers offer over and above 99.9999 percent (known as the six nines) of uptime which allows the service to be down for just 31.5 seconds a year.

Managing Licenses

Licensing is an important consideration. Many companies producing software for the VFX industry are still built on a traditional model, selling expensive licenses upfront that include restrictive policies concerning usage of their software in the cloud. The key value of the cloud is the ability to scale up thousands of nodes within minutes to handle burst demand. However, the cost of purchasing additional annual licenses to run on each of these nodes can be a limiting factor when implementing a rendering pipeline in the cloud, and, in their EULA (end-user license agreement), vendors can explicitly forbid their licenses to be run in the "cloud" unless express permission has been granted.

As more users move their workflow to the cloud, companies will no doubt adapt their policies to accommodate such considerations. Vendors, such as Adobe's Creative Suite and Shotgun Software's cloud-based project and asset management tools, have already begun to take steps in this direction.

There are solutions in the market where key software vendors such as Pixar or Autodesk manage their licenses in the cloud and meter consumption of the end users, who in turn enjoy the advantage of paying a

single fee, in some cases metered by the millisecond, monitoring consumption of computing power, storage, and the software license. This means thousands of cores can be provisioned for a render job without expensive licensing implications.

Becoming Locked In

One of the downsides to cloud services and to the whole "software as service" model is that it puts your company into a peculiar kind of thrall to the service provider. If you own the DVDs and the hardware keys that your 3D software runs on, you can stick with a version that meets your needs and continue to use tools and equipment geared around the version you like. If you're a subscriber to a service, you don't necessarily have the choice of when and how to upgrade. The flexibility and low in-house footprint of a cloud service have much to offer, but when it's your own hardware and run by your own staff, you are the only one who gets to decide when and how your pipeline changes. In some ways it's similar to the difference between buying movies on DVD and subscribing to cable: it's nice not to have to manage a cabinet full of discs, but you control the schedule and don't have to worry about your favorite show being canceled without warning.

Cluster Management

Configuring a rendering environment in the cloud can involve quite a bit of effort, particularly if this is to be an automated capability. The topics that need to be taken into account include:

- Automatically provisioning render nodes as required
- Ability to queue up render jobs
- A mechanism to break the job up into individual frames and have these distributed across the available render nodes
- Downloading required assets for a particular frame from cloud storage to the local disk on each render node
- Uploading rendered outputs back into cloud storage
- Saving and making available any log files and standard output from the renderer so diagnostics can easily be carried out when jobs fail or outputs are incorrect
- Ability to monitor available memory on each render node
- Automatically shutting down instances when they are no longer required

There are also considerations around how you communicate with the system remotely. Using a web/REST API is one example. Of course, some of the above can be manually initiated and configured as required, which may be more appropriate for occasional use instead of building a fully automated cloud rendering system.

Application and Pipeline Integration

Once a cloud capability is in place you need to consider how to interface with this system while avoiding introducing friction to the pipeline. The two main use cases that require support are digital artists rendering test scenes and renders with all final assets contributed. The first use case calls for the ability to easily offload renders to the cloud from within the artist's environment, such as Maya integrated by using Python. A workflow would include:

- Identifying if the scene has any external file dependencies
- Uploading the scene and dependencies to cloud storage, i.e. S3 in Amazon Web Services or Blob storage in Windows Azure
- Sending an instruction to the cloud rendering system specifying any additional rendering settings

Memory

It is important to know how much memory processes are going to require and ensure virtual machines in the cloud are sufficiently specified. Performance will drop off drastically—or worse, the renders will fail, if memory limits are reached. Higher memory instances typically cost considerably more so it pays to keep a close eye on memory requirements when creating scenes.

GLOSSARY

2D (film, games) Acronym for two-dimensional. When used in image creation, often refers to a flat hand-drawn style. When used in image output, refers to the final steps (compositing and DI stages of film production) to output the image as two-dimensional media. In games, also often refers to the case where a game's presentation and gameplay is restricted to a single plane.

2.5D (film, games) A way of projecting paintings onto simplified geometry to give the sense of depth and parallax to an environment. This technique of projection mapping is typically used for matte painting and set extension, basically taking a single image and projecting it on a simple 3D geometry. In games, 2.5D refers to the case where a visual element or gameplay has full freedom of motion in two dimensions, and limited freedom in a third (for example, a character who can walk freely on an undulating landscape, but cannot jump or otherwise move vertically away from the surface of it).

3D (film, games) Acronym for three-dimensional. Can refer to the stereoscopic component of a film, or computer graphics employing three-dimensional geometry, or the computer graphics process as a whole. Some refer to 3D to mean stereoscopic content, other use 3D to mean 3-dimensional imaging.

3D Conversion (film) See Dimensionalization.

3D Studio See 3DS Max.

3DS Max (film, games) 3D modeling and animation package from Autodesk. Originally "3D Studio Max", and often referred to as "3D Studio" or simply as "Max".

911 (film) A project that is behind schedule and is sent to another studio for some emergency work to get it delivered on time.

A

ACES (film) Academy Color Encoding Specification. A new color space defined by the Academy of Motion Picture Arts & Science Technology Committee to provide a more accurate color pipeline.

After Effects (film, games) Basic compositing software from Adobe often used for previs or simple animations. After Effects can be used for quite complex VFX in certain situations (e.g. *Iron Man*).

Agile (film, games) A development methodology (primarily used for software development but also production) that emphasizes short iterative cycles and rapid response to change over detailed long-term planning.

Alembic (film) Open source file format for geometry caching developed by ILM and Sony Imageworks. Quickly becoming a standard for geometry caching.

Alfred Commercially available renderfarm management software by Pixar Animation Studios.

anaglyph (film) Anaglyph glasses are used in stereoscopic production. They are among the simplistic methods of visualizing depth using glasses with colored lenses, typically with one eye blue and the other red.

animatic (film, games) A rough, blocking version of a shot (perhaps rendered gray scale, with only key pose animation) used for establishing the action. "Animatics" is still more commonly used to refer to hand-drawn story board artwork edited together with some limited animation. (Previs almost always refers to CG created materials.) This is used in games as well, where it generally refers to a rough version of a gameplay or cut-scene sequence put together using still images or very simple

models, animated to give an idea of the pacing and flow. In games this is generally distinct from previs in that animatics are always just video sequences, whereas a "previs" may actually be something running in a game engine with rough artwork and test game code.

animation (film, games) The discipline responsible for generating the animation of any creature, character, objects, vehicles, cameras, etc. Methods used to generate animation include keyframes, motion capture, and procedural/algorithmic animation methods.

AOV (film) Arbitrary Output Variables, originally used in Renderman to output data (surface normals, lighting passes, etc.) as an image. Used in lighting and shading.

API (film, games) Acronym for Application Programming Interface. A library (or libraries) that act as the publicly exposed entry point for a piece of software that allows other developers to interact with that library in a deterministic fashion. Calling a method in the API allows the developer to execute a particular function or process and obtain a result which can then be incorporated into a larger piece of software or process.

Application Programming Interface See API.

approval (film, games) Description of the completeness state of an Asset or Shot.

Arsenal (film) Open source render management software originally created by Blur Studios.

artist A creator of a specific piece of content.

Aspera (film) Commercial software that allows companies to collaborate using private, high speed data transfer.

asset (film, games) The term asset is used in two related ways. Generically, an asset is an identifiable piece of content in a production, such as a character, an environment, or a prop. However, the entire collection of stored files used to present the visible content to the audience is also referred to as assets: for example, a character is informally referred to as "an asset", but in fact the visible character reflects many different assets: models, animations, textures, and so on. Different files might be presented under different circumstances (a low-resolution version of a model for distant shots, a more detailed one for close-ups)—but they all comprise the same asset in the generic sense.

asset management (film, games) The process of tracking, managing, and versioning the assets of a shot. This is usually a system with a database backend, storing metadata for physical assets on the file system. The asset management system will track simple information such as creation date and user, but also more complex data such as up/downstream dependencies.

Avid (film, games) The company that created the commercial editing package AVID DS and Alienbrain Asset Management. Avid is widely known for the Media Composer editing software used by professional film editors.

B

beat board (film) Sketches used by story artists to communicate the timing of the character's action.

bid (film) The process of costing the work—defining the budget, deliverables and timeline for a project. This is then submitted to the production studio to win the work. If awarded, the bid will form the basis of the work you do.

blendshape (film, games) A method to generate deformation based on underlying modeled shapes. Often used to generate facial animation. Numerous key deformations' shapes can be easily combined to create animation. The typical methodology is to create shapes for each facial extreme pose, muscle expansion, or muscle contraction. Blendshape animation is common to most 3D software packages. Blendshapes are called morph targets in 3 ds max and Shapes Animation in Softimage.

blend tree (film, games) In film this technique is used in Massive for blending between character animations. A technique for blending a hierarchy of character

states that combine multiple individual animations to create the desired action being performed at runtime, according to parameters which may be varied by game logic as needed. For example, interpolating from a walk animation into a run.

Blender (film, games) 3D open source software used for modeling, texturing, animation, lighting, compositing, etc.

blockbuster (film, games) Describes a hugely successful movie or game.

block stage (block animation, block lighting) (film) The initial process in many departments starts with "blocking", a rough draft to determine where to place characters and their rough motion (in animation) or where to place lights and reflections (in lighting).

block read The act of reading a single fixed-size block of data from storage. Individual files on the filesystem are split up and stored in a number of these blocks, which may or may not be laid out in a contiguous manner on the physical disk. If the blocks required for an operation are scattered, the time to read them increases as the drive must seek each one individually to retrieve it.

bridge file See Intermediate File.

Bugzilla Open source bug (defect) tracking system used by developers to keep track of software problems that need to be fixed.

bug tracking The process of recording and responding to reports of problems with a piece of software.

burst capabilities (film) Rapid scaling up of resources (processors, memory, file storage, network bandwidth) for crunch periods and scaling down when no longer needed. Provided by hardware in the cloud.

C

C programming language (film, games) A compiled programming language mostly used in older programs such as the Linux and Unix operating systems. Some older pipeline software or pieces of software have been written in C.

C++ (film, games) A compiled, object-oriented programming language that is a superset of the C programming language. Often used for programming plugins for packages such as Maya. One of the most popular languages for building large applications, due to its ubiquitous nature, performance, and object-orientated structure.

cache (film, games) In general computing terms, a temporary store of data that can be referenced to avoid either repeating an expensive computation, or accessing a slower storage device ("to cache" meaning to place data in such storage). Common examples include CPU cache RAM (RAM directly attached to a processor that stores data being worked on to reduce accesses to the slower main RAM) and disk caches (standard RAM used to reduce accesses to slow hard drives). In film and game production, software commonly stores the results of expensive simulations (such as physics systems or character animation) in "cache files", allowing the results to be used without repeating the calculations, thus massively improving performance. If, however, the input parameters to the simulation change, the cache file must be regenerated by re-running the calculations.

caching See cache.

Capex Acronym for Capital Expenditure. Money spent by a company to buy or improve a physical asset (such as a building) that will generate a future benefit. For example, a growing company will have a capex when they buy a bigger building for their staff. Applies to non-physical assets as well (for example, buying or upgrading software).

casing The capitalization of letters; the difference between "a" and "A".

case-sensitive A comparison between sets of letters that takes capitalization into account (see casing). Some computer operating systems, such as Unix or Linux, see the capitalization of file names as significant. In these case-sensitive OSs, file names containing the same letters but different capitalization are regarded as separate entities.

case-insensitive A comparison between sets of letters that does not take capitalization into account (the reverse of "case-sensitive", above). In case-insensitive operating

systems such as Windows, file names containing the same letters but different capitalization are regarded as equivalent.

CBB (film) Acronym for Could Be Better. Typically used when a shot has been nearly approved. CBB acknowledges that the shot may need to be worked on more, but it is fine for now.

CDDB Centralized database of (audio) compact disc information.

CDL (film) Acronym for Color Decision List. A file format used to exchange primary grading information between different software.

change order/request (film, games) In film, when the work requested for a shot has changed significantly from the bid such that the original budget or schedule submitted in the bid is no longer reasonable, a VFX studio will submit a change request to acquire a change in budget or schedule. It can be a very challenging phase for many studios as generally the budget is not controlled by the same person who is actually requesting the changes. In games, the term is often used to mean exactly what it says—usually when finaling a game and someone wants something changed, they will raise a "change request" that gets evaluated against the schedule/risk/etc. and is then either approved (and assigned to someone to do) or denied. This is all part of the "change control" process.

changelist A changelist represents a grouping of modifications to files that are submitted to a version control system such as Subversion (SVN) or Perforce. In most systems, changelists are treated as atomic units—a changelist submission or retrieval may either succeed (updating all the affected files) or fail (updating no files), but not partially succeed (updating some files). Changelists often also carry additional metadata, such as a description of their changes, the name of the submitting user, and similar. Changelists are also commonly used as a way to refer to a particular version of files, and may be tagged with further metadata to identify them as belonging to a given release or workflow step.

checkin The process of putting a new version of something (asset or code) into a system such as an asset database or code versioning system like SVN or Git. Adding a file to a version control system or asset management system.

checkout The process of requesting access to the latest version of a file in a version control system or asset management system. Checkouts make the file available and/or writable on a user's local computer, and may optionally mark it as unavailable to other users.

Chef Open source infrastructure configuration management used to centralize and automate deployment of changes. Similar to Puppet.

CHM Compiled HTML files, most commonly used by Windows applications as a format for distributing help files and documentation.

ClearCase Proprietary source version control system used for software development.

client (film, games) In business terms, the studio, publisher, or production company that commissioned the work. Also, in software terminology refers to a machine which is not performing a calculation or accessing data locally, but instead sending requests to a "server" machine which handles them and returns an appropriate response for the client to act on (for example, by presenting it to the user). See Server.

Collada A file interchange format used to exchange digital assets between graphics packages, specifically 3D models.

color space (film, games) The color model used to represent color: different image formats store color differently, for example DPX file is traditionally logarithmic, EXR is linear. Color space includes both the numeric encoding of the color data and also, critically, the /bounds/ of that encoding.

compiler A compiler converts human readable program code into the binary format executed by a computer.

compositing (film) The discipline at the end of the pipeline which combines all rendered elements into the final image.

Concurrent Versions System See CVS.

conditional files Files whose presence or absence on disk is used as a way of controlling an automated process. For example, a script might search for directories containing a file called "render" and automatically render all the files contained in those folders.

conform (film) The process of matching/inserting shots into the master edit. You receive an offline from the client, then as liveaction plates or VFX shots are turned over, they are conformed to this offline to ensure correct start/end frames, shot number, shot order, etc.

content (games) Anything in the game that is in some way represented in the final product to be consumed by the player. This could be art, a game level, sound FX, music, character equipment, etc. Content does not generally include the program code for the engine, gameplay, or tools, although in some cases scripting information (which may act like program code) may be considered as content.

copyleft A form of license agreement for copyrightable material intended to foster sharing by requiring that anyone modifying the material make those changes freely available under the same terms as the original. Copyleft is a play on the word copyright.

CryEngine (games) Licensable 3D game engine that is free for non-commercial users.

Crytek (games) Game company that created the game engine, CryEngine.

culling In 3D graphics, the process of removing objects or surfaces that are hidden from view. Objects can be geometry structures that are not in camera frame, or that are facing away from the camera, or that are so far from the camera that it doesn't matter that they are not seen. This process increases rendering speed by removing unseen elements.

cut (film, games) Describes the current order and in and out points (which sometimes include handles) for shots. Normally described through the format of an EDL by the client. In games, it means removing content from the game, either to save runtime resources or production time.

cutscene (games) The short story moments between action play in a game. These include short movies or animations that advance the game story or introduce or develop characters. The gamer has little or no control over the game during the cutscene.

CVS/cvs Acronym for Concurrent Versions System, an older open source version control software used for managing software revisions. It is a method to keep track of the change history of a file. CVS is a precursor to Subversion (SVN). "cvs" is the command name.

D

data mining The process of using software to automatically sift through data in order to pull out actionable and useful information. For example, software logs can be data mined to analyze how frequently the software is used, how often it crashes, how long particular tasks within the software take, etc.

data wrangling (film, games) The activity to move data around within the facility to keep the individual storage disks under a specified threshold.

daily (film) A proxy (usually QuickTime) version of a shot that is used for review.

dailies (film) The daily task of reviewing work for feedback.

DCC Digital Content Creation is an acronym applied to any software used to create assets such as textures, models, or animations.

deformation The process of reshaping a mesh (see Mesh); most commonly deformation is used to simulate the movement of muscles or cloth.

deliverables (film, games) Agreed upon items given to the client. Deliverables may include final images, videos, models, textures, animation, playable builds, and shaders. In games deliverables also include playable versions of the game.

delivery (film) The "package" of data that is sent to the client. Generally this is a QuickTime and high resolution image sequence, but might be styleframes or even asset files.

dependency (film, games) A relationship between two assets in which changes to one asset can affect the appearance or behavior of another. For example, changes to the skeleton of an animated character may cause changes in the animations which depend on that skeleton. The nature of the relationship may be ambiguous, but can be defined based on context. For example, version one of the rig might depend on version one of the model, but if a new version of the model is published, we might need a new rig.

depth of field (film, games) Also referred to as DOF, the distance between the nearest and farthest objects in a scene where the elements are in focus. Elements outside of the DOF (foreground and background) are blurry. The DOF is used in cinematography to focus the viewer's attention upon what the director deems important.

dev management Development management.

DI or Digital Intermediate (film) Process of color grading and final mastering.

digi-double See digital double.

digital double Also referred to as digi-double, a full high resolution digital representation of a character in the film. Term can vary between facilities. For example, at one studio a digital double can refer to lower resolution stand-ins that can be swapped for an actor but only at a distance, while a CG character that withstands close scrutiny is referred to as a "hero" character and is considered distinct from a digi-double.

dimensionalization (film) Also referred to as DM, the process of adding depth to single view sequences to make it stereoscopic. Numerous techniques exist that generally involve 2.5D mapping and rotoscoping. An alternate perspective must be created for every frame of every shot. Traditionally shot sequences or 2D movies can be converted to 3D Stereoscopic using Dimensionalization techniques.

DLL See Dynamic-Link Library.

DM See dimensionalization.

DOF See depth of field.

Drawing Exchange Format See Drawing Interchange Format.

Drawing Interchange Format Also known as Drawing Exchange Format or DXF, a data file format created by Autodesk used for interchanging AutoCAD drawings with other CAD systems.

drive imaging See ghosting.

DXF See Drawing Interchange Format.

Dynamic-Link Library (DLL) Microsoft's shared library format for C++. Shared libraries contain functions that can be called by software as needed, thus reducing the footprint of the software. Since multiple applications can use the same functions, this allows them to share functionality.

E

EDL (film) An Edit Decision List is a file describing the cut or edit of a film in a machine readable format.

Edit Decision List See EDL.

editorial (film) The department responsible for updating the cut/edit with the latest version of the client.

element (film) A (normally) live action image sequence that forms part of a shot. This could be the principal action, individual green screen elements as different layers, etc.

endian See endianess.

endianness In computing, the order in which binary data is encoded for storage. Different computing platforms use different orderings, and data or programs encoded for one endianness can't be correctly read on a system which expects another. This is frequently a problem for games which ship the same assets onto different hardware platforms, since the files need to be rewritten with the appropriate endianness for each target platform. An encoding is said to be "little endian" if the

least significant bytes of data are encoded from lower memory addresses to higher, and "big endian" if they are encoded from higher addresses to lower.

engine (games) The core software which provides rendering, handles player input, and manages the progress of time in a game. Engines are abstracted from the actual content of the game, and are reusable across projects.

entity (games) The software representation of an object in a game. Entities typically have special properties or game functions, such as reacting to player actions or changing as the game progresses.

environments (film, games) The physical setting in which the action takes place. In games the term is frequently used interchangeably with "levels". Also, the department responsible for generating 3D environments, 2.5D environments, or traditional digital matte paintings.

EULA Acronym for End-User License Agreement.

event authoring The process of creating event data (see event data).

event data (games) Gameplay information associated with an animation, used to tell the game to begin an action when the animation reaches a particular point in time. This allows the game engine to synchronize visual effects or sounds, for example, with the animation.

exporter (games) A piece of software that writes an asset out from a DCC package into an intermediate file format.

extensions See Plugins.

F

face See polygon.

FAT (hardware) Acronym for File Allocation Table. Refers specifically to the "FAT" filesystem (and FAT32 and other variants) developed for MS-DOS and still in use today on Windows systems for certain purposes (external drives, mainly).

feature set The set of functions or affordances offered by a software package.

Fifth Kind Software package that helps manage the production to client relationship. Similar to Shotgun, but aimed more at the relationship between one client and multiple VFX vendors rather than an internal workflow for a studio.

File Allocation Table See FAT.

filmout (film) The process of sending the digital image sequence to the lab for printing onto physical film and later projection/review. As a filmout is costly, it is usually done last, as a final review for quality.

Final Cut Pro (film) Editing package.

Flame (film) Software used in film and commercials for visual effects, compositing, and color management, from Autodesk.

flipbook (film, games) Used to quickly preview animation, compositing, or stereoscopy, at full playback speed by playing each frame using either hardware accelerated rendering or cached pre-rendered data. Often the images are of a lower quality or a smaller size than the final image.

floating license (film, games) Software license method used in larger production studios for maximum sharing of licenses among a team. All purchased licenses can be accessed by any team member independently of the computer they use, as the licenses are not locked to any computer.

FMV (games) Acronym for Full Motion Video. Compressed video stored for playback—for example, a cutscene.

forking (games) Programmer slang for "splitting into two separate paths". For example, you might have started a fork of an existing toolset to support a new game on the understanding that the early needs will be similar to known stuff, but eventually the project will diverge from our existing tools.

frame (film, games) A description of a single image which forms part of a shot or game video output.

framecycler (film) Playback package. See flipbook.

Full Motion Video See FMV.

G

Gameware (games) Game creation software development and middleware tools from Autodesk.

GB Gigabyte, a unit for data storage. 1 gigabyte (GB) = 1024 megabytes. This is currently the subject of debate, as a number of people (hard disk manufacturers being one) want to redefine computing measures to match other SI units, and use 1000 instead of 1024 as the base.

GCC Compiler A collection of open source compilers from the Free Software Foundation. Supported languages include C, C++, and Java. See compiler.

geometry Overarching term to define geometric representation of surfaces in both 3D and 2D space. Some of the more common forms are polygons, subdivisions or NURBS.

ghosting Copies the configuration, applications, and contents of a hard disk and converts them into an image that can be placed on another hard disk. Used to quickly install the same operating system and software configuration on multiple machines. Also called disk cloning, system cloning, or drive imaging.

GIMP Acronym for GNU Image Manipulation Program. Open source 2D image manipulation/paint program.

GIT A modern, decentralized version control software originally created for Linux kernel development.

Gnu Public License Also known as the GPL. A copyleft-style open source software license. See copyleft.

GPL See Gnu Public License.

gray box level (games) A prototype environment, containing rough or unfinished geometry and textures. Used for rapid iteration and gameplay experimentation. Sometimes referred to as "whitebox" or "massout" levels.

greenfield project A project created with no preexisting infrastructure or pipeline.

grooming (film) The process of adjusting the appearance of fur or particle-based growth. The department responsible for generating fur grooms for any character/creature that requires fur as part of their appearance.

H

handle (film) Additional frames (usually 8 or 16) added to the start and end of a shot during production. Used for processes that require some pre/post roll steps (such as simulation) or in situations where the cut is unconfirmed, providing additional space in which to work. It is common for animation to animate and tracking to track into the handles so that if the edit changes you don't have to go back and redo the whole animation/track.

HDRI Acronym for High Dynamic Range Image, an image that has a wider range between the lightest and darkest areas of the picture than standard digital imaging techniques allow. Stores the intensity levels more accurately than other image formats. High Dynamic Range images support multiple exposures that are stored in one image file allowing more information to be available than in standard images. This is extremely useful for controlling the image's quality as well as facilitating the integration of CG elements with live action elements.

HFS+ Acronym for Hierarchical File System created by Apple for the Macintosh OS.

Heads-Up Display (games) Also known as HUD. User interface elements which are overlaid directly on top of the player's view of the game world. Some 3D graphics applications also use the same technique to provide user feedback.

heavy iron Programmer slang for "extremely powerful hardware" or "highly optimized software".

Hiero Software package for conform, shot management and review from The Foundry.

High Dynamic Range Image See HDRI.

high level Simple, broad overview without any deep detail.

hooks (software) Conditional triggers exposed by one software package which can invoke another piece of software before, during, or in the midst of a particular operation.

Houdini (film, games) 3D package created by Side Effects Software.

HUD See Heads-Up Display.

Hudson An open-sourced, web-based build service which can be used to schedule a variety of tasks such as code compilation or data packaging.

I

image layer (film) The description of a particular part, or layer, of the image. Image layers are important for compositing to have ultimate control of all the individual pieces that make up the final image. Each image layer can be adjusted separately to allow for greater flexibility for creative input without the need to re-render the whole image.

instance In programming, a concrete example of a particular data structure is said to be an "instance" of that structure. In rendering, a single object which is duplicated exactly in many different locations. Instances are typically faster to render than ordinary copies, because they are known to be exact clones and can be represented only with reference to their position, rotation, and scale.

inter-axial (film) When creating stereoscopic content, the inter-axial defines the distance between the two cameras which actually mimics the distance between the two eyes of the viewer.

interpreter Software component that runs programming code without prior compilation. Often the scripting systems included in 3D art packages, such as MaxScript or MEL.

J

JavaScript A scripting language originally used for adding interactivity to web pages but now seeing increasing use as a lightweight language for scripting in other applications or developing small standalone tools.

Jenkins An open-sourced, web-based build service derived from Hudson which is now independently developed by Jenkins CI.

JIRA Proprietary bug (issue) tracking software used by programmers to keep track of software problems.

JPG Compressed image file format created by the Joint Photographic Experts Group.

JPEG See JPG.

K

Katana (film) Look-development/lighting/scene assembly application originally developed by Sony Imageworks and now supported commercially by The Foundry.

L

layout (film) The department responsible for setting up the contents of a shot, sequence, and movie. The key is to visualize the content of a shot with basic animation from an early stage to enable the director to understand how the shot will work in context of the movie. See **animatic**.

legacy software Old software that may still be in use or may be retired and still have files that need to be converted into a current format.

level (games) A playable game environment. The level may or may not correspond to a single physical location.

level designer (games) An artist or game designer who specializes in building game levels, typically using a dedicated level editor.

level editor (games) Software used for designing game environments.

level integrator See level designer.

Level of Detail Also known as LOD. An optimization strategy which tries to minimize memory or rendering costs by switching to less detailed versions of assets as on-screen objects move farther from the camera.

LIDAR Acronym for Light Detection And Ranging.

lighting (film) The department responsible for taking 3D scenes and rendering 2D image layers to be handed to compositing. The process of lighting the shots, a creative process.

lightmaps (film, games) Pre-computed lighting data applied as a texture to static 3D objects in order to quickly simulate complex lighting efficiently at runtime.

lightprobes (film, games) Stored samples of incident light at a point in space which can be used to quickly approximate complex lighting on moving objects. Compare with lightmaps, which are applied to static objects.

live action (film, games) Real actors being filmed on set delivered to the VFX or game studio to work on.

localization data (games) Data used to produce language- or region- specific versions of game data, such as subtitles or user interface text.

LOD See level of detail.

logging The process of recording actions as they are performed in software to a file or database for later inspection.

logging spam Overuse of logging, resulting in information overload.

look development (film) The department responsible for setting up the "look" of any asset. In general this is the final stage of the asset development where all pieces get assembled together and the shader attributes get tweaks to convey the look requested from the client.

Look Up Table See LUT.

low level Delves into the deep technical aspects.

LUA A lightweight programming language, popular for in-game scripting but also used in some 3D art tools.

LUT Acronym for Look Up Table. A software technique that pairs keys and values to store the mapping between two devices. For example, LUTs are frequently used to map the color spaces between devices such as the artist's monitor and the digital projector.

M

Maquette (film, games) A physical model created to evaluate a concept. A maquette can be used as an artist's reference or scanned to create a 3D model.

Mari (film) 3D painting and texturing application originally developed by Weta Digital and now supported commercially by The Foundry.

matchmove (film) The department responsible for reconstruction of the physical camera that was used to shoot the plate in 3D space.

Maya (film, games) Commercial 3D package available from Autodesk used for modeling, animation, effects, and lighting.

Maxscript The native scripting language for 3 ds Max.

MEL Maya Embedded Language, the original scripting language for Maya.

Mercurial Source control system.

metadata Data about other data—for example, the name or creator of a document (as opposed to the actual content of the document, which is the "data"). Metadata can be stored as part of the file itself, in associated file system structures, or externally (for example, in a database). Metadata such as the studio name, shot name, version number, and suchlike are commonly used to provide information to users, whilst internally the asset pipeline may track other metadata to generate statistics (for example on memory usage or dependencies).

milestone (games) Major events during game development used to track a game's progress.

MoCap Acronym for motion capture, including both the process for capturing the motion data but also the process for authoring and preparing the captured data.

modeling The department responsible for generating geometry. The process of creating the model.

MongoDB Open source NoSQL document database.

MotionBuilder Software to capture and edit motion capture data from Autodesk.

motion transition (games) The transition between two subsequent animations. As a character completes one animation and begins another, it is often necessary to adjust the character's position or movement to disguise the transition from one motion to another.

MPAA Acronym for Motion Picture Association of America, the trade association of six major studios in the United States (Disney, Fox, Paramount, Sony, Universal, and Warner Bros.) that monitors copyright protections and sets the film ratings (R, PG, G, etc.) for the US release.

Mudbox (film, games) Digital sculpting and painting software from Autodesk. Used in modeling and texture painting.

MXS The file extension for MaxScript files.

MySQL Open source relational database.

N

nearline (film) Some film studios classify their data storage hardware into multiple tiers. There will be storage that is immediately available to the productions and the renderfarm. This storage will most likely be limited in size. Nearline provides the ability for productions to "park" certain data on these nearline disks (or other media such as tapes accessed via tape robot) to make room for the current work. The main benefit for using nearline is that data can be made available much quicker than data that has been archived. A separate bit of storage not available for production but which provides extra storage where people can shift files in and out based on the age of the data and the last time it was accessed.

NPC (games) Non-player character. A character which is controlled by the game rather than by a human player.

NTFS Acronym for New Technology File System, a Microsoft Windows proprietary file system that is a successor to the FAT file system. It provides built-in security and encryption.

Nuke (film, games) Commercial 2D compositing and visual effects package originally created by Digital Domain and available from The Foundry.

O

occluders (film, games) Elements that sit in front of other elements from the camera's point of view. Commonly used to increase performance by obviating the need to render distant objects. Sometimes used for casting shadows.

offsite Literally, "off site", meaning "not at this location". Often used in reference to data stored somewhere else, "offsite", for example, data backups are stored offsite in case there is an emergency (fire, earthquake) at the original location. Also refers to work done somewhere other than the central location.

off the shelf software Software that is not a bespoke creation built to order, but purchased as a pre-existing package.

OneFS Isilon's proprietary file system used in distributed networks.

one-off (film) Often refers to a shot that has singular requirements not present in other shots. Has the connotation of being more expensive because the setup or development work cannot be amortized.

onsite The opposite of "offsite". Used in reference to data storage location or to work done at the local location.

openEXR (film) HDR-based file format developed by ILM and made available for free.

open source A licensing arrangement which allows users to copy and redistribute the source code for a particular piece of software. The license may impose conditions of use, for example, requiring that the redistributed software also be open source (see

copyleft) or used for non-commercial purposes. Many open source softwares are available free of charge, but not all of them.

operating expense Also known as opex. The ordinary on-going cost of running a business, as distinct from capital expenditures on new hardware or facilities on an ongoing (daily) basis. The operating expenses exclude all capital expenditures and include things that are consumed on an ongoing basis, such as power, maintenance, rent, utilities, and salaries. See also Capex.

Opex See operating expense.

outsource (film, games) To send work to an external company for completion. Outsourcing can occur at numerous stage of the production, sometimes just for portions like modeling, or sometimes for the complete sequences or complete projects.

overtime Also referred to as OT. During production peak times, team members are asked to work extra hours in order to deliver the production shots on time.

owner The person who is responsible for a particular asset or piece of content.

P

package (film, games) A high level grouping concept for assets. A package describes a combination of assets which belong (are used) together. For example, a character package would include the model, rig, and texture assets.

paint-prep (film) Paint preparation. The department responsible for removing and cleaning up the original received plates of any unwanted elements. In addition the preparation of these shot plates to remove unwanted artifacts. Examples are vignetting and any lens distortions.

petabyte 1,024 terabyte.

pipeline The process that is followed to take an asset all the way from the point of creation through to the finished version in the film or game.

pipeline supervisor A role in the film, VFX, or game studio that oversees the pipeline and its development. Can apply to studio wide or per project.

pipeline technical director (film) A role in the film or VFX studio (can be studio wide or per project) who works closely with R&D and artists in implementing and developing the pipeline. The Pipeline TD bridges the gap between artists who need tools quickly and the software department who produces tools on a longer schedule.

plate (film) The original film scanned in before any visual effects have been added to it. See also element.

playblast A Maya-specific term for flipbook.

plugins An extension module that plugs in to add functionality to the base program. Many software products allow customization to the base package via plugins.

practical (film) An effect achieved with real-world objects and physical effects such as liquids or pyrotechnics and lighting or wind machines, rather than being rendered exclusively by a computer.

pre-comp (film) The equivalent of a "cache" or "bake" in the compositing workflow. After a particularly heavy compositing operation, the resulting image sequences will be rendered (cached) for use in further compositing operations to avoid the unnecessary (and time consuming) recomputation of data.

production tracking (film) Project management. Tasking work and managing the production process based on the work - > review - > feedback - > work cycle.

proxy (film) A low resolution version of an asset. It is typical for rendered sequence to be rendered initially at quarter size, so a full HD sequence would be rendered in SD for instance. Rendering at smaller resolution and quality allows the team to focus on the essential elements of a given shot. Once it is approved, it is much easier to tweak the elements to make the rendering works fine at higher resolution. The number of hours that can be saved is very high. A proxy generally applies to an image sequence, whereas Level of Detail is the more common term for the same idea applied to 3D assets (LOD).

publish The process of creating a new version of an asset for use by other departments or team members. Involves exporting the data to disk and creating an entry in the asset management system.

Puppet Open source infrastructure configuration management. Similar to Chef.

Python Interpreted (scripting) programming language used by many film studios and 3rd party packages to create tools for artists. The language makes it easy and quick to make changes to the program.

Q

QA Acronym for quality assurance. See quality assurance.

QC Acronym for quality control. See quality assurance.

quality assurance Also known as QA. The publish time process through which you technically check assets to ensure their integrity and suitability for further progression through the pipeline. In games, the department responsible for testing the game and identifying software bugs or design flaws. Also the process of testing the game.

quality control Also known as QC. See quality assurance.

QuickTime A video container format (.MOV), compressors and playback tools developed by Apple Computer.

R

R&D/RnD/rnd See research and development.

RAM Acronym for Random Access Memory.

redraw In realtime rendering, the process of re-rendering the screen frame buffer to display a new frame.

renderfarm (film) High performance compute cluster set up specifically to render images.

renderer The software used to create an image from a collection of model, texture, lighting, and animation data.

rendering The process of creating an image sequence by interpreting model, texture, lighting, and animation data algorithmically. Rendering may simulate physical processes, such as the reflection and refraction of light, or it may use a completely arbitrary set of rules to create the final image by evaluating the scene data.

render pass (film) A render pass is a specification about the data to be rendered. For example, the most standard render pass is the so-called beauty pass. The shadow pass only captures the shadow information, whereas a holdout pass renders a mask for each of the assets within a scene.

render wranglers (film) The staff tasked with watching the renders and making sure that the renders complete. If things get stuck on the renderfarm, the wrangler will figure out what is going on and notify the appropriate person (artist, systems) if they cannot push the render through.

reporting dashboard A user interface that aggregates data and displays it in a useful way to the user. The term is inspired by the dashboard of a car, where the driver can see the status of everything relevant to the car's operation (fuel, miles driven, tire pressure, etc.).

Request Tracker System for tracking bugs and other production requests.

research and development The department which discovers and creates technical solutions to artists' and productions' problems. Solutions may be in the software and/or hardware domains.

restore To retrieve data that had been previously stored using a backup system.

re-topologize To create a new mesh or subdivision surface from an existing one, preserving the overall visual appearance of the original but with a new arrangement of polygons. It is often necessary to re-topologize models in order to facilitate better animations or deformations.

review (film, games) The critical appraisal of work, either creative or technical, internal or client driven.

revisions The sequential versions of a file stored in a version control system. Also means revising the artistic work as it moves through the stages towards completion.

rig To bind 3D geometry to a virtual skeleton and its animation controls, which will be used to deform the 3D geometry as the skeleton animates. See deformation.

rigging The department responsible for generating rigs, rigBounds and rigPuppets.

rotoscope (film) The department responsible for generation of mattes within a shot plate. Often refers to selecting a moving object or character and cutting them from the background (often a greenscreen), following the movement frame by frame, so the rotoscoped object can be placed over a new background.

runtime (games) The game software which will be shipped with the game and run on the target hardware.

Rush (film) Commercially available renderfarm management software.

rushes (film) see Dailies.

RV (film) Playback package.

S

SaaS Software as a service, software and its associated data that is hosted remotely (in the cloud) and accessed via a web browser or thin API (which wraps lower level communication protocols such as HTTP).

sandbox (games) A scratch area where programmers or artists can do their work without affecting others. Used in conjunction with a source control system where a user "checks out" their work, works in the sandbox, and then "checks in" their changes into a repository from which others can then retrieve it.

scene graph A hierarchical data structure which represents the logical structure of a 3D graphics scene. The scene graph provides data to a renderer which can be processed to create a final image.

scheduler Component of the renderfarm management software that allocates tasks to the renderfarm based on a configurable scheduling algorithm.

SCM See Software Configuration Management.

scripting programming language A programming language hosted inside another application which allows users to quickly create new tools and workflows by utilizing functions of the program and linking them together with new logic or interfaces to external programs. Popular scripting languages include JavaScript, Python, MEL, and MaxScript.

SDK Acronym for Software Development Kit. Provides structure for coding and application interfaces (APIs) to leverage functionality of a software package in order to create customized solutions.

seek time The time taken by the read head of a disk drive to move to a particular location in order to read or write data.

sequence (film) A collection of scenes or another term for scene.

set dressing The process of populating an environment with props.

scan (film) Can be used to describe a plate or element, or the data retrieved from a 3D environment acquisition technique such as LIDAR.

shading A piece of code used to combine resources and data and produce a final pixel on the screen, incorporating any necessary effects such as texturing and lighting. Also, the department responsible for the setup and development of custom shaders.

shader (film, games) A piece of code used to combine resources and data and produce a pixel on the screen, incorporating any necessary effects such as texturing and lighting.

Shader constant (games) A named, typed variable used as data to feed to a shader. Known as a "constant" because whilst the value can change on a per-material or per-model basis, it is constant for any given batch of polygons.

shot (film) A set of continuous frames that depicts the movie action between two cuts (edits) that form a basic story-telling block, or the file the artist is working with. In some studios, shot and scene are used interchangeably.

shot assembly (film) Building a shot from its constituent parts, usually in preparation for lighting and rendering.

Shotgun (film) Production tracking package.

shrink wrap software See off the shelf software.

simulation/sim (film, games) The processing of data to generate results that mimic a real-world (or imaginary) system, such as the behavior of crowds, fluids, hair, or the destruction of a building. Can be performed both as part of the asset pipeline, or, in the case of games, in realtime during gameplay.

SLA Acronym for Service Level Agreement. Software/hardware, the agreement between a facility (film or game studio) and a vendor (usually hardware or software). This agreement explicitly spells out the measurable level of service and response the customer will receive from the vendor, and it is usually based on the price the customer pays.

snapshot A read-only copy of data from a particular moment in time. Some facilities have a backup or rollover filesystem that will copy the data at a particular time (often multiple times per day). If a file goes missing, that version or a previous version can easily be recovered, usually by the artists themselves.

Software Configuration Management Also known as SCM. The process of managing software changes. This includes controlling changes by creating a baseline and managing versions of the software so that it is possible to return to previous points in a project. Version control systems such as Perforce, GIT, SVN, and CVS are all examples of SCM systems.

software stack The collective term for the top to bottom set of software used in a pipeline.

SourceSafe Version control software from Microsoft. Discontinued in 2010.

spike capabilities See burst capabilities.

SQL Acronym for Structured Query Language. The standard language for communicating with relational databases.

stereoscopy Also known as stereoscopics or 3D imaging, it is the process of creating a perception of depth through the use of binocular images. Two offset versions of the image are presented separately to the left eye and right eye.

stale policies Defines how long a piece of data needs to be stale (not accessed) until it can be deleted from the system.

string A sequence of characters forming a piece of text.

source control Also called version control or software configuration management (SCM), which are essentially interchangeable. Both refer to keeping a historical record of multiple files with the ability to get the "latest" version of all of them or to selectively go back in time to an earlier state. The process of using software to track changes to a set of project files (typically a programming project, but often a game) over time. Examples of source control tools are Perforce, Git, Subversion, and CVS.

subdivision surface Technique for producing surfaces which appear to be smooth by repeatedly subdividing a polygonal 3D mesh.

Subversion Open source version control software used for managing software revisions. It is a method to keep track of the change history of a file. See source control.

SVN/svn SubVersioN version control software, "svn" is the command name. See Subversion.

T

tags Metadata used for categorizing files.

takes (film) A variation of a particular shot, normally applying to live action plates.

TDD See test driven development.

tentpole (film) Refers to a movie production, usually big-budget, where the expected profit is suppose to cover the loss of making the production by the movie studio.

There is a close relation between tentpole movies and blockbusters as any movie studio hopes for the tentpole movies to turn into blockbusters.

Test Driven Development Also called TDD. A process of coding where automated tests are written first.

texture A piece of structured image data over the surface of some geometry which is mapped or projected onto the geometry. For example, a simple cube might be textured with an image of bricks, creating the appearance of a brick wall when rendered.

texture map See texture.

technical artist Also called a TA. An artist specializing in aspects of production which require scripting, automation, or advanced graphics knowledge. The term is commonly used in games.

technical director (film, games) Also called a TD. The definition of this term varies greatly between facilities. Generally, a person (artist or technologist) who creates art or software using programming as part of their suite of tools. In games, a TD is the top-level technical person in a studio and in many cases is analogous to the term "CTO".

third party extensions See plugins.

toolset The collection of programs, scripts, and techniques which make up a graphics pipeline.

topology The arrangement and interconnection of the triangles or polygons comprising a mesh (see Mesh).

total stations An instrument used in surveying for measuring angles/distances.

tracking (film) See Matchmove.

Tractor (film) Commercially available renderfarm management software by Pixar Animation Studios.

Triangle In graphics, a 3-sided collection of points in 3D space. Many rendering and physics calculations use triangles because they are guaranteed to be both convex and planar which gives them useful mathematical properties. Most 3D graphics are rendered from collections of triangles (see "Mesh").

TDD See Test Driven Development.

TVC Acronym for TeleVision Commercial.

U

UI Acronym for User Interface. The interface between the user (artist, programmer, etc.,) and the technology (computer, cell phone). This term is often used interchangeably with Graphical User Interface (GUI). Examples of GUIs are the windowing systems that sit on top of Macs and PCs. UIs include and extend beyond GUIs into anything that connects the user to the technology, e.g., voice activation, touch screens, etc.

Unity (games) Cross platform game engine from Unity Technologies.

Unreal (games) Cross platform game engine from Epic Games.

V

vendor (film, games) In film each VFX facility is a vendor to the client for the film being made. In games, vendor refers to the company that made a piece of software/library/engine that you're using.

version (film, games) Verb: To create a new version of something (software, asset, artwork). Noun: A piece of artwork, asset or software that has changed from its original form and may continue to change. A particular piece in a series of the same thing.

version control Source control and version control are essentially interchangeable. Both refer to keeping a historical record of multiple files with the ability to get the "latest" version of all of them or to selectively go back in time to an earlier state. If there is a difference in emphasis, it would be that "source control" is more commonly applied to version control of programming source files, whereas "version

control" is the more general term that includes any kind of files, and less commonly used is the phrase "revision control". In all cases, the idea is the same: a database that covers many files that can be asked to update local hard drives to match the most recent state of the database, but, if necessary, it can also show what things looked like in earlier versions, for comparison purposes or to undo a change.

versioning up (film, games) The act of creating a new version of the software, asset, artwork, etc. being worked on.

VFX Acronym for Visual Effects

VFX supervisor (film) Manages the creative and technical staff to create all the visual effects of a film. The VFX Supervisor works closely with the project's director(s) and producer(s) to best realize the director's vision within the producer's budget.

view With stereoscopic films, refers to the left, right or mono eye.

visibility group (film, games) A collection of graphic objects which can be rendered or ignored as a unit. For example, the contents of a building might form a visibility group, which could be turned off to save rendering time until the player enters the building.

Visual Studio A proprietary developer environment from Microsoft, often used when developing applications on Microsoft Windows platforms.

W

Wiretap (film) API to access the internal structure and file storage of Flame projects.

witness camera (film) Also refered to as witnessCam. The additional cameras used alongside the main camera during the filming process to capture information used for motion capture reference.

X

XML Acronym for eXtensible Markup Language. A text-based generic file format which can be used to store arbitrary data in a human-readable format.

Z

ZBrush 3D modeling and texturing software which uses subdivision surfaces to create very high resolution models commercially available from Pixologic.

INDEX

Printed and bound by CPI Group (UK) Ltd, Croydon, CR0 4YY

22/10/2024

01777635-0009